Wealth, Poverty, and Human Destiny

Wealth, Poverty, and Human Destiny

Doug Bandow and David L. Schindler, editors

Wilmington, Delaware

2003

This monograph was supported by a grant from the John Templeton Foundation. The Intercollegiate Studies Institute gratefully acknowledges its support.

Cataloging-in-Publication Data:

Wealth, Poverty, and Human Destiny / edited by Doug Bandow and David L.
    Schindler. —Wilmington, Del : ISI Books, 2002.

    p. ; cm.

ISBN 1-882926-83-8 (cloth)

    1. Wealth. 2. Poor–Social conditions. 3. Economics–Sociological aspects. 4. Essays. I. Bandow, Doug. II. Schindler, David L.

HC79.W4 W43 2002   2002107928
330.16–dc21   CIP

Interior book design by Holly L. Feldheim

Published in the United States by:

    ISI Books
    Intercollegiate Studies Institute
    Post Office Box 4431
    Wilmington, DE 19807-0431
    www.isibooks.org

Manufactured in the United States

Table of Contents

Preface

The volume in your hands is the fruit of a joint project undertaken by the John Templeton Foundation and the Intercollegiate Studies Institute (ISI) to investigate whether and to what extent the market economy helps the poor. To be sure, this is a broad question and an old one, exhaustively debated for well over a century now. But the Templeton Foundation and ISI were particularly interested in what the answers and approaches to that question look like now, at a time when the collapse of old political barriers and the advent of new economic, technological, and information-sharing structures have ushered in an age of globalization. And both Templeton and ISI believed that the matter was worthy of receiving more examination within a theological context—for upon reflection, it is clear that the meanings of such fundamental concepts as "wealth," "poverty," and "freedom" shift when looked at through the lens of the Western religious tradition.

Furthermore, in the post–Cold War world, the political preoccupations that necessarily overshadowed questions of the relationship between capitalism, freedom, and wealth for a half-century or more no longer threaten to overwhelm their open consideration. Real communists are now almost impossible to find; committed socialists—especially of the orthodox Marxist variety—are almost as rare. But on both the political Left and the political Right, one now finds both pro-globalists and anti-globalists, partisans of the international hegemony of the dynamic and mobile capitalist society and critics of the same. Such political confusion is a good thing, insofar as it leads to a more searching consideration of the matter at hand by all sides.

For religious believers, the moral import of these economic questions would seem to make their careful consideration something of an obligation. But it is not always realized that even among those who subscribe to traditional doctrinal Christianity, there are different schools of thought as to how men and women of faith should regard the global capitalist order, especially as it affects the poorest among us.

The essays presented here by editors Doug Bandow and David L. Schindler present, in essence, two very different points of view: the first, represented by Bandow's contributors (Hill, Novak, Gregg, Morse, Griswold, and Neuhaus), tends to construe free-market economics as the real-world option that most benefits the poor, even while it emphasizes the moral and social context in which this sort of economic system must be embedded. These contributors also argue for the essential compatibility of the liberal (that is to say, free-market) economic order with Christian teaching and belief. Schindler's essayists (Walker, Long, Cavanaugh, Crawford, Lewis, and Davis) are not as sanguine about the new capitalist order; they regard it as depending on a philosophical liberalism that is not neutral but fundamentally opposed to Christian theology and social thought. Furthermore, they view this liberalism as subtly undermining the possibilities of achieving individual virtue and genuine community.

These chapters have not been written in a point-counterpoint fashion, but the differences of opinion and interpretation that emerge are as obvious as they are instructive. Editors Bandow and Schindler consider all twelve chapters in their responses and attempt to highlight for readers the most important points of convergence and divergence within the arguments of the book's contributors. Two pieces, one by Wendell Berry and another by Max Stackhouse and Lawrence

Stratton, are included here as appendices. They serve as additional background to this important debate over the moral status and religious implications of twenty-first-century capitalism. It is our hope that readers will find this book a useful aid to reflection as they consider their own posture towards the economic order in which, increasingly, we all find ourselves entangled.

— JEREMY BEER
Senior Editor, ISI Books
January 9, 2003

1

Creating and Distributing Wealth: Whose Responsibility?

Peter J. Hill

The issue of material inequality among people and the appropriate policy response to this reality is one of the most contentious in modern democratic societies. The debate focuses on government's role in reducing that inequality. One of the primary attractions of Marxist socialism was its promise of a more egalitarian society. Now that centrally planned, socialist economies have been found to be both inefficient and exploitative of their citizens, the debate has turned to inequality in market societies. An oft-expressed sentiment is that though markets are efficient, they are unjust, since market processes create significant economic inequality. Therefore, modern egalitarians argue, a legitimate role for government is to equalize the distribution of wealth or income in society.

In this chapter, I shall argue that the opposite is the case: government should not attempt, as an explicit policy, to redistribute income or wealth.[1] My argument has three components. First, the concern for material inequality represents a harmful distortion of an appropriate and laudable human motive, a desire to help the infirm, the suffering, and the unfortunate. Second, efforts to achieve justice through redistribution of income foster far greater injustices because of the inequality of political power that such redistribution requires. Third, redistribution as a policy goal involves structuring the rules of the game in such a manner as to inhibit the most important means of poverty amelioration available: wealth creation.

What should we care about?

Most religious and ethical systems, Christianity not least among them, express a level of concern for the poor in society. These belief systems outline a clear responsibility for those with material wealth to alleviate the suffering of the poor and even take as a measure of religious commitment the degree to which one helps the poor.[2] For instance, Proverbs 19:17 says, "He who is kind to the poor lends to the Lord" (NIV); in contrast, one "who oppresses the poor shows contempt for their maker" (Prov. 14:31). However, as legitimate and widespread as is this concern for the poor, addressing poverty by attempting to reduce inequality has serious shortcomings.

Discussions of inequality focus on the relative size of the economic pie held by particular groups. The percentage of income received by each quintile of the population is a common measure of inequality. For instance in the United States in 1997, the lowest 20 percent received 5.2 percent of the national income, the next 20 percent received 10.5 percent, the middle quintile 15.6 percent, the fourth 22.4 percent, and the highest 20 percent received 46.4 percent.[3] Income distribution in the United States is clearly not equal. Focusing on the relative size of the shares, however, tells us nothing about the well-being of the poor. All that we know from this data is the relative share each group receives from the total pie. We know nothing about the size of the pie, whether the bottom quintile is malnourished or not, what types of housing they have access to, what their life span is, whether they drink clean water or not, and what level of health care they can purchase.

Another measure that has a strong relationship to the quintile groupings is the Gini index, which varies between zero and one. An economy that has an index of zero is one with complete equality, while an index of one would represent complete inequality. The most recent World Development Indicators from the World Bank list Gini indices that range from .231 (Austria) to .629 (Sierra Leone).[4] The Gini index is useful because it summarizes the income distribution data into a single number. As an indicator of economic well-being, however, it faces the same problem that the quintile shares measure does, in that it simply provides no information.

Egalitarians often quote the income distribution data and deplore any rise in inequality because of their inference that greater inequality means greater hardship for those in the bottom portion of the distribution. The fallacy driving this perception is the belief that world wealth is a zero-sum game. If there is a fixed amount of income or wealth in a society, then increases in inequality must indeed represent increases in hardship for some. But total wealth is not fixed. For instance, India has a Gini index score of .378, while the Gini for the United States is .408. The share of national income received by the lowest 10 percent in India is almost twice the share received by the lowest 10 percent in the United States (3.5 percent compared to 1.8 percent).[5] If one accepts the egalitarian assumption that greater income equality means a better world, one would assume that the poor in India are better off than the poor in the United States. But the fact that GDP per head in India is $460 compared to $34,260 in the U.S. indicates that the larger share of the pie received by the poor in India tells us little about their economic status relative to the poor in the United States.[6]

Even when income distribution becomes more unequal (the usual term used is "worsens," nomenclature that presupposes that an increase in income inequality is bad and that a decrease is good) within a particular economy, this change still provides no information on the well-being of those we ought to be concerned about, namely, the poorest sector of the population. Suppose that the income of the top 20 percent increased by 4 percent over a given period and the bottom 20 percent increased their income by 2 percent. Now contrast this situation with a situation in which the top 20 percent found their income decreasing by 4 percent and the bottom 20 percent experienced no change in their income level. By egalitarian standards, the second situation represents an improvement in the position of the poor relative to the first, for in the first case, income inequality would be increased. And yet in the first situation, unlike the second, the poor would now have access to better health care, higher nutritional levels, and better housing, surely things we ought to care about if we really are concerned about the well-being of the poor.

But, an egalitarian may respond, the poor measure their well-being with respect to other people, and if a society's income distribution becomes more equal, the poor feel they have improved their lot, even if their economic status in absolute terms has declined. It is true that individuals often measure their economic status with regard to the status of others, but that does not mean we should allow such comparisons to drive public policy. To do so capitulates to the base human tendency to envy what others possess. Policies that focus upon income equality legitimate envy. Rather than encourage people to rejoice when their fellow citizens do well, such policies encourage people to focus on resenting the achievements of others instead of celebrating their own achievements.[7] If some in a society find ways to create wealth, and if that wealth creation does not harm the well-being of others, why should those who have not shared fully in that wealth creation be resentful?[8] Envy and resentment will never be eliminated, but building public policy upon these most base of human motivations is a bad idea.

Focusing on material inequality creates several other problems. Most discussions of inequality have implicit assumptions about legitimate and illegitimate reasons for differences in income. Differences in effort and ability are often deemed to be valid reasons for the generation of differences in wealth, whereas luck, discrimination, and inheritance are seen as unfair or unjust reasons for the generation of such differences. However, two experiments indicate that substantial differences in income can be generated simply through differences in people's willingness to work, in conjunction with minimal ability differences.[9] In Canada, an experiment gave men and women the opportunity to participate in something called the Cannabis Economy. (This experiment was designed to determine the effects of marijuana smoking on productivity.)[10] All of the participants were twenty to twenty-eight years old and all had twelve years of education or more. Subjects were not allowed to leave the experimental facilities, and they were provided with housing for the ninety-eight days of the experiment. They had the opportunity to weave woolen belts on small portable handlooms if they so desired, for which they received $2.50 per belt. The material was supplied free of charge, and they could work as many or as few hours as they wished. The subjects used their earnings to purchase food from the hospital cafeteria and the canteen. They could also take home any savings at the end of the experiment.

A second experiment occurred in the Central Islip State Hospital in New York. Chronic psychotics were given tokens for their performance of janitorial chores. The jobs were optional: the patients' basic needs of food, housing, and medical care were provided, so the tokens were only used to purchase additional consumption items. All participants had the requisite skills to perform the tasks.

In both economies the earnings of the highest group were over ten times those at the bottom. The Gini indices generated in these experimental "societies" were very similar to the indices of most Western economies. The conclusion of the researchers was that differences in abilities and willingness to work are sufficient to generate the income differences seen in the United States and other Western countries. When the effects of luck, original wealth position, and natural disasters were removed, there were still large variations in earnings. Although this does not answer the question of whether existing income distributions are legitimate or not, it does raise the issue of whether or not intervention to rectify existing distributions is actually an attempt to alter what could be called a "natural distribution," a distribution reflecting people's innate abilities and their desire for leisure or work.

What type of inequality?

Most advocates of government as an agency for the redistribution of income assume that this task can be carried out with few or no costs. Such is not the case. The achievement of greater economic equality can only come with the creation of great political inequality. Only when the coercive power of government is extended into numerous private spheres of action can substantial gains in material equality be realized.[11] In addition, the use of the term "redistribution of income" implies an original distributor. But such is not the case, either. In a free society, incomes result from the uncoerced interactions of individuals pursuing their own goals. They buy and sell products, transfer resources by gift, work for wages and salaries, and control most of their own lives. Since there is no original distributor of income, it is not possible to have redistribution unless some social agency becomes that distributor. Therefore, setting out to "redistribute" income requires a substantial alteration of institutional structures, an alteration that concentrates enough power in the hands of the coercive agency of government that choices are restricted. Robert Nozick has pointed out that to suggest income be redistributed is akin to arguing for the redistribution of marriage mates.[12] Since there is no one distributing marriage mates, it is difficult to see how one could redistribute them unless one replaced voluntary interaction with coercive, top-down direction. The same applies to income.

It is clear that all societies at all times generate substantial differences in income. The 2001 World Bank data quoted earlier indicate that some societies are more equal than others, but all societies have a degree of inequality. Even in Austria—the most egalitarian among the large number of countries for which data are reported— the bottom 20 percent of the income distribution receives only 10.4 percent of total national income, while the top 20 percent receives

33.3 percent. The experimental economies reported earlier show that in societies where fortune, inheritance, and access to means of production are equalized, the simple willingness to work will still generate quite unequal incomes. In other words, the diversity of humankind naturally reflects itself in material inequality, and thus efforts to reduce inequality require the use of substantial coercive power.

If individual rights are recognized and protected by government under the rule of law, economic inequality will result. Therefore, reducing inequality means moving away from the rule of law and stable property rights. Equality before the law, defined as the equal treatment of people in equal circumstances, is one of the great attainments of the modern liberal order. Reducing that equality to reduce material inequality is a costly project.

In the twentieth century, between 80 and 100 million people lost their lives at the hands of communist governments.[13] These deaths came not from defending borders against external aggression, but from attempts at social engineering in which the primary motivating force was radical egalitarianism. Stalin's elimination of the kulaks, Mao's Great Leap Forward and Cultural Revolution, and the killing fields of Cambodia represent the most egregious cases of attempts to achieve a socially sanctified objective through the coercive power of government. Equality before the law and recognition of individual rights were sacrificed to a higher goal: remaking society to meet a stated objective. While modern democracies do not use coercion in the brutal manner of these communist societies, it is important to remember that the desire to create greater equality has been a motive force behind some of the greatest tragedies of the twentieth century.

Some of the same problems that plagued the attempts of communist regimes to remake their societies according to a social ideal plague modern democracies in their attempts to redistribute income. A sufficient concentration of power to perform the "good" of redistribution can be captured and used for evil ends. Most egalitarians do not want *complete* equality, believing that some inequality occurs because of meritorious behavior or meritorious differences in individuals. But the information problems in determining merit are enormous. Much of what we call merit depends upon motive, and motive is difficult to ascertain. Is the physician earning $200,000 a year motivated by the desire to relieve suffering or is she concerned with her own well-being? What about food production? How much of it is carried out for laudable reasons and how much for selfish? It is beyond the capacity of government to obtain adequate information about meritorious behavior, and even if such information could be obtained, reaching any sort of consensus about the trade-offs between different forms of behavior and individual rights would be even more difficult.[14] Therefore, attempts to rectify material inequality will be arbitrary in nature and will seem quite unprincipled. Once the redistribution project is embarked upon, it is unlikely that the citizens of the redistributing society will find that the results meet even minimal standards of justice.

This is not to say that societal judgments about merit are inappropriate. The only question is, who should make them and how should rewards and punishments be meted out? Numerous institutions, ranging from families to churches to communities, need to make judgments about moral worthiness. Moral considerations are of crucial importance for a well-functioning society and moral judgments need to be enforced by societal pressure. But these numerous decentralized groups find it far easier to generate appropriate information about merit than does centralized government. Due to their different functions, they can measure merit along many different dimensions. And it is perhaps most important that these institutions do not have the power to use coercion to enforce their judgments, a limitation that prevents many injustices.

The use of government to enforce property rights and to protect against force and fraud does involve morality. Judgments must be made about what immoral behavior is and how it will be restricted. The information needed to keep people from invading other people's lives, however, is far different than the information and social agreement required to determine the meritorious and nonmeritorious behavior that generates income differences. Government is not the appropriate repository for judgments about merit beyond the rule of law, which involves stable, predictable rules that apply to all citizens and include the enforcement of voluntary contracts and protection against aggression.[15]

Another important consideration is that equality before the law is an attainable objective. While not perfectly realized in modern societies, there are numerous historical cases of constitutional democracies that have done a good job of respecting the rights of individuals and maintaining equality before the law.[16] As I will detail in the next section, efforts to achieve greater material equality not only reduce equality before the law but also may be fundamentally unattainable. Therefore, it is tragic when government gives up a function that it can perform to try to achieve goals that are either impossible or come at great cost.

I have argued that rectifying material inequality can only be done through massive amounts of government power exercised unequally with regard to the members of a society. It is also the case that this exercise must be an ongoing phenomenon.[17] Assume that government intervention creates a desirable distribution of income at one point in time. If people are allowed to engage in voluntary transactions, there will be an immediate move away from this desirable distribution. People will pay premiums for the opportunity to watch certain athletic or artistic performances, they will seek to purchase scarce items in the marketplace, and even the satisfaction of nonmaterial human preferences will cause subsequent income differences. Therefore, state intervention to achieve a particular distribution must be a perpetual activity. The government must continually restrict human freedom and take resources from one group and transfer them to another group if the distribution is to meet the social objective of equality. Advocates of income redistribution through government must recognize that they are advocating a permanent and large presence of that government in the lives of its citizens.

It is not just restrictions on individual freedom and the reduction of equality before the law that result from efforts to achieve greater material equality. Other important social structures would suffer through attempts to achieve material equality. Choices within the family are a major cause of economic inequality. People pass wealth to family members. They teach and reinforce certain behavioral patterns and moral principles that, when worked out in the marketplace, have a substantial impact on incomes. They invest in the formation of human capital among family members through expenditures on education. Any attempts to alter the income distribution of a society must reduce the role of the family and lessen the ability of families to control their own resources. Between 75 and 80 percent of all income generated in the United States comes from human capital,[18] and a substantial portion of that capital reflects family teaching about work habits, job choice, and higher education. Only if the state assumes responsibility for many of these choices can economic inequality be lessened.

Caring for the poor

The general concern about material inequality is a perverted form of an important and justifiable moral concern: the material suffering of the poor.[19] Many of the problems of the poor come from unequal access to courts of law and an unwillingness on the part of the state to defend their rights to themselves and their physical property. When one looks at the gross injustices that have occurred throughout history, almost all of them would not have occurred had government performed its limited functions of maintaining equality before the law and protecting individual rights. Nevertheless, Christian doctrine, along with the teachings of many other religions, supports the premise that the better off have significant responsibilities to alleviate the suffering of the less fortunate. Since this moral obligation is clear, the only question is what is the best way to carry out this obligation.

Wealth creation is the most effective anti-poverty measure available. Starting around 1750, several Western societies sustained increases in income over time.[20] This increase in per-capita income represents a sharp break from historical trends and, in the context of those trends, is truly amazing. Real per-capita income has, on average, doubled every generation in the growing economies.[21] Thus, over the last 200 or more years, the process of wealth creation in Western economies has reduced the material impoverishment of millions of people.

By 1950, this trend of growth had reached one-third of the world's population, and since then it has reached many other parts of the world, especially Japan and East Asia, which have experienced sustained increases in per-capita income.[22] No conceivable amount of wealth redistribution could have reduced material suffering to the degree that economic growth and wealth creation have. Millions of people around the world have more to eat, better housing, more access to clean water, and better health care because of economic growth. A simple measure of the increase in economic well-being is captured in life expectancy statistics. It is important to note, therefore, that worldwide life expectancy has increased from twenty-seven years in 1600[23] to sixty-six now. Citizens of some of the more developed economies even have life expectancies that exceed seventy-five years.[24]

Economists have long sought to understand the reasons for economic growth and to explain the sharp differentials in economic well-being across different economies. Although numerous explanations have been tried and found wanting, recent work supports the hypothesis that institutional framework is the most important determinant of the degree of wealth creation within any given economy. One of the measures of the institutional environment has been provided by James Gwartney and Robert Lawson.[25] Their Economic Freedom Index measures the extent to which government operates under the rule of law (greater protection of property rights and access to a nondiscriminatory judiciary increases the freedom index) and the degree to which government intervenes in market transactions (a larger government, more regulation, higher tax rates, and restrictions on international trade lower the index).

The latest data available for the Economic Freedom Index are for 2000. In that year, the countries in the bottom quintile of economic freedom had a per-capita GDP of $2,256, while for the top quintile it was $23,450. Differences in growth rates are even more startling, with the bottom quintile showing an actual decrease in GDP per capita of 0.85 percent for the years 1990–2000, while the freest economies (the top quintile) grew at 2.56 percent annually during the same period. Other indices show similar results.[26] Thus there is strong evidence that increasing the well-being of the poor depends upon a structure of well-defined and enforced property rights, and a government that enforces the rule of law.

Some have criticized the use of this aggregate data as a measure of the well-being of the poor, since it does not provide direct evidence as to whether the poor have improved their situation or not. It is possible that the well-being of the rich has increased and thus raised national averages, even though the lot of the poor has not improved. The work of Seth W. Norton sheds light on this issue.[27] Norton tests the influence of institutional variables upon actual measures of the well-being of the poor. His primary measure is the Human Poverty Index (HPI), a measure developed by the United Nations that concentrates upon the most deprived people in a community. Rather than measure per-capita income, the HPI measures the degree of deprivation along several dimensions, including the number of people in the population not expected to survive to age forty, the proportion who are illiterate, the percentage without access to health services, the percentage without access to safe water, and the percentage of malnourished or underweight children under the age of five.

This measure has several advantages when one is determining the well-being of the poor. First, it does not depend on calculations of gross domestic product or gross domestic product per capita, data that may not capture fully the status of the least well off. Second, it focuses on actual measures of human deprivation, which is the appropriate concern if one cares about the suffering of the poor. Norton examines the influence of different institutional measures of secure property rights and their influence upon the Human Poverty Index. His results are striking. The data concentrate just on the poor countries in the world, and in those countries, a move from weak property to strong property rights lowers the proportion of people not expected to live to forty from 25 percent to between 6 and 9 percent. Illiteracy drops from 43 percent to 13 percent and those without access to safe water from 35 percent to 6.5 percent when the measure of property rights moves from weak to strong. Similar data are reported for access to health services and the percentage of children under five who are malnourished.

The work reported above is only a small portion of the numerous research projects carried out in the last decade on the influence of institutions on well-being.[28] The overall conclusion is strong; if one wants to reduce poverty, it is necessary to have a strong but limited government that enforces the rule of law, freedom of contract, and private property rights. But this raises the important issue of the effect of efforts to achieve a more egalitarian society. Since such efforts require the substantial attenuation of property rights and the concentration of large amounts of coercive power in the hands of government, it is clear that these redistributive measures will result in lower levels of economic growth. Thus the misplaced focus on alleviating material inequality hampers the most effective means of poverty amelioration: the creation of wealth.

Other research supports this conclusion. James Gwartney, Randall Holcombe, and Robert Lawson examine the effect of government expenditures on the growth rates of the twenty-three OECD countries from 1960 to 1996.[29] Total government outlays as a percentage of GDP averaged 48 percent in 1996, an increase from 27 percent in 1960. Larger government, however, has meant slower growth. The authors estimate that economic growth is maximized when government outlays equal 15 percent of GDP. This means that efforts to redistribute income (and most of the expenditures above 15 percent have a redistribution rationale) have been expensive in terms of their reduction of income growth. The United States has had a more modest increase in the size of government than any of the other countries, going from 28.4 percent of GDP in 1960 to 34.6 percent in 1996. But even this increase has had a substantial negative impact on per-capita income. Had the U.S. maintained the size of government at its 1960 level rather than increasing it, real per-capita income would have been $5,860 higher by 1996. In other words, for an average household of four, family income would have been $23,440 higher.

Further evidence of government inappropriately using its power for purposes other than maintaining the rule of law comes from the work of Hernando de Soto[30] and the literature on rent seeking. The term "rent seeking" refers to efforts to achieve special favors through government, and the concept has been developed widely in the economic literature during the last several decades.[31] Rent seeking means that property rights are not secure from government expropriation since it is the transfer of property rights that rent seekers are asking the government to effect. There is much evidence that rent-seeking societies are both unfair and inefficient.[32]

De Soto has expanded the rent-seeking literature by looking at the property rights held by the poor. In his first book, *The Other Path* (1989), he argued that the informal economy, which dominates so much economic activity in poor countries, exists because of the substantial barriers to legal activity in these economies. As an experiment he and members of his research institute attempted to establish and register a small business in Peru. It took 289 days and $1,231 (thirty-one times the monthly minimum wage in Peru) to secure formal legal approval of their business. More recently, in *The Mystery of Capital* (2000), de Soto examined the legal barriers to establishing ownership rights to a home or land. In Egypt it takes six to eleven years to establish property rights to land, in the Philippines thirteen to twenty-five years, and in Haiti nineteen years.

De Soto argues that the biggest barrier for the poor to participation in economic growth and capturing the benefits therefrom is the lack of access to secure and stable property rights. He estimates that there is adequate capital (9.3 trillion dollars) for the poor in the form of their homes and land, but that this property is not available as collateral for loans since formal title is almost impossible to obtain. The exclusion from the formal sector imposes large costs on the poor because they cannot take advantage of many economies of scale in production, cannot benefit from specialization, and do not have access to modern technology and knowledge. Informality of enterprise and a lack of well-defined, enforced, and transferable rights mean the elite and politically astute have greater control over resources and capture most of the gains from rent seeking.

All of the above evidence leads to the conclusion that if one wants to help poor people, one needs to create the conditions that are conducive to wealth creation. Efforts to redistribute income change institutions in ways that hinder this wealth creation process.

A final important issue is the question of how redistributive programs work. As one thinks about democracy and the use of majority rule to determine political outcomes, it would seem that, once redistribution is a potential activity, some fraction of the top portion of the income distribution can form an effective coalition with those in the middle to prevent distribution to those at the bottom. They can do this by paying those in the middle some portion of what the redistributive take would have been from those at the top. It is unclear what the percentages and coalitions would be and the size of the transfer, but a rather straightforward prediction is that, once redistributive programs are put into place, they are likely to result in transfers from the well off to those in the middle rather than a transfer of resources from the rich to the poor.[33] The empirical evidence provides strong evidence for this argument.[34] Most programs that transfer resources in the United States are not means tested and result in massive movements of income from the rich to the middle class.

Another problem of using government to redistribute income comes from the difficulty of changing material well-being through coercive transfers. Transfers alter the incentives that individuals face and therefore alter the returns from engaging or not engaging in certain activities or behavior. Economics provides powerful evidence that people tend to equalize returns over time, which limits the ability of government to bestow benefits upon desired recipients. In the words of Gwartney, Stroup, and Sobel:

> In a world of scarce resources, government must establish a criterion for the receipt of transfers. If it did not do so, the transfer would outrun the government budget. Governments typically require transfer recipients to (a) own something (for example, land with an acreage allotment), (b) to do something (for example, fill out complicated forms, pass an exam, or make political contributions), or (c) be something (for example, unemployed or poor). Once the qualification criteria are established, people will incur costs seeking to meet it until the marginal costs of qualifying increase to the level of the marginal benefits of the transfer. Therefore, the beneficiary's *net* gain will nearly always be substantially less than the cost of supplying the transfers.[35]

Thus the use of government to redistribute income is unfortunate on several counts. Redistribution will slow down the process of wealth creation and slow down the increase in the material well-being of the poor. And wealth intended for redistribution to the poor will often be wasted through rent-seeking activities or will be usurped by other groups.

Conclusion

Using government as a vehicle for income redistribution is an idea that is flawed on several counts. First, it focuses on an inappropriate measure of human well-being, namely, the relative size of shares of the economic pie rather than on the economic well-being of particular people or groups. Second, greater income equality can only be achieved by creating greater inequality in other areas, particularly in status before the law. Unfortunately, the poor and disadvantaged are the most likely to suffer when equality before the law is compromised. Finally, the most effective means of reducing poverty is through wealth creation, and most attempts at income redistribution hinder the wealth creation process. In short, government ought not to be engaged in redistributing income.

2

The Poverty of Liberal Economics

Adrian Walker

The poor, Jesus famously said, will always be with us. Jesus' followers have often been accused of misusing these words of their
Master as an excuse to ignore the systemic causes of poverty. Christians, the charge runs, have preached private benevolence as a substitute for the more arduous, and more courageous, task of fighting to
change the unjust economic structures that are responsible for poverty in the first place. Among the many Christian responses to this
oft-heard accusation, two more recent ones are particularly notewor-
thy. The first, represented by certain schools of Latin American liberation theology, attempts to enlist the Church in a socialist-inspired
struggle for a more just society. The principal enemy in the struggle is
capitalism, the supposedly exploitative nature of which this stream
of liberation theology attacks as the root cause of poverty.

Towards an economics of gift

Rejecting the anti-capitalism of the liberation theologians, exponents
of the second response point out socialism's dismal record of economic ruin and repression of individual freedom. This second response,
best known through the writings of "neoconservatives" like Michael
Novak, is no less concerned with attacking the systemic roots of
poverty than is liberation theology. But unlike the liberationists, the
neoconservatives insist that the capitalist free market, not the socialist centrally planned economy, holds the key to eradicating pov-

erty without violating individual freedom. Only the free market, the neoconservatives argue, has demonstrated the ability to raise society to unprecedented heights of material prosperity while at the same time creating unprecedented guarantees of, and opportunities for, the expression of individual freedom.

We do not have to look beyond our own shores to see that the neoconservative proposal highlights important truths. Our own welfare system, for instance, has turned out to be a colossal failure. Significantly, a major reason for this failure has been the policy of redistributing the wealth of responsible economic agents without expecting and enabling the beneficiaries of this redistribution to become responsible economic agents in their own right. Such a policy is unfair, not only to those who are already responsible economic agents, but also, and even more so, to those whom the redistributionist ethic, for all its much-touted "compassion," essentially treats as objects of beneficence rather than as (potential) subjects of responsible economic agency themselves. That is, the welfare system has failed because it has not treated the poor as human persons having an innate dignity to be developed and expressed also in the economic sphere.[1]

The neoconservatives are therefore right to insist that a sound economy must give ample scope to the self-expression of human dignity through economic creativity. They are also right to affirm that economic freedom is a sine qua non of such creativity. No less an authority than John Paul II has said so in his social encyclical *Centesimus Annus* (1991). Nevertheless, the neoconservatives go wrong by assuming that what I will call "liberal economics" is the best context for understanding what economic freedom is. By "liberal economics," I mean the theory, going back in all essential respects to Adam Smith, according to which the market alone organizes the economic life of society, not by marshaling the coercive power of the state, but by maximizing individuals' freedom to enter into informed, mutually beneficial contractual exchanges for specific economic purposes decided by "self-interest." Milton Friedman gives eloquent expression to this claim:

> The basic problem of social organization is how to co-
> ordinate the economic activities of large numbers of people.
> . . . In advanced societies, the scale on which co-ordination
> is needed, to take full advantage of the opportunities offered
> by modern science and technology, is enormously greater.
> Literally millions of people are involved in providing one
> another with their daily bread, let alone with their yearly
> automobiles. The challenge to the believer in liberty is to
> reconcile this widespread interdependence with individual
> freedom. Fundamentally, there are only two ways of co-
> ordinating the economic activities of millions. One is
> central direction involving the use of coercion—the
> technique of the army and of the modern totalitarian state.
> The other is voluntary co-operation of individuals—the
> technique of the market-place. The possibility of co-
> ordination through voluntary co-operation rests on the
> elementary—yet frequently denied—proposition that both
> parties to an economic transaction benefit from it,
> *provided the transaction is bi-laterally voluntary and
> informed.*"[2] (emphasis in original)

Now, my purpose in critiquing the liberal notion of what economic historian Karl Polanyi calls the "self-regulating market"[3] is not at all to argue for the imposition of a state-planned economy in its place.[4] Nor is it to deny in any way that free economic exchange is a necessary (albeit not a sufficient) condition of a healthy, workable economy. It is rather to suggest that liberal economics puts forth a bad model of what free economic exchange itself is. This assertion may come as a surprise to some, especially to liberal economists, who are accustomed to seeing themselves as providing an unbiased "scientific" description of how the economy actually works, rather than as dispensing an ideology about human freedom. Yet ideology is just what is at stake here.[5]

We see a central expression of it in the claim—laid out forcefully by Milton Friedman in the passage cited above—that economic freedom consists primarily in the liberty of individuals to enter into mutually beneficial contractual exchanges. This claim, which may appear innocent enough at first, turns out, on closer inspection, to entail that the economic freedom (supposedly) provided by the market is indifferent towards the objective good of the person. But, as I will argue below, a freedom indifferent to the objective good of the person is actually an unfreedom that leads to a coercive social order. That this is so does not mean that we ought to do away with contractual exchange, but rather that, notwithstanding liberalism's insistence to the contrary, contractual exchange cannot be the primary paradigm of economic freedom without *ipso facto* undermining the very economic freedom of which liberalism (wrongly) prides itself on being the sole guarantee among economic systems.[6]

Instead of delivering economic freedom *tout court*, liberal economics delivers a certain, liberal form of economic freedom—one that, as we will see below, is actually an *un*freedom. One of the stratagems by which liberalism conceals this fact is its hallmark claim that the market is neutral, by which it means that it impartially leaves open the question of the objective good of the person in order thereby to allow people with different worldviews to cooperate without first having to harmonize their respective convictions about that good. Notice, however, that this so-called "neutrality" is nothing more than a repackaging of the claim that voluntary contractual exchanges are essentially indifferent towards the objective good of the person, and that such indifferent contractual exchanges constitute the paradigm of economic freedom. Of course, liberal economists would no doubt counter that the market must be "neutral" in this sense in order to protect individual economic actors from coercion by the state. Unfortunately, this reply begs precisely the question that is at issue: is freedom truly best served by an agnosticism about the objective good of the person (masquerading as the impersonal laws of the market)? The answer, I will argue, must be a decisive No.[7]

The claim that the market is neutral with respect to the question of the objective good of the person is nothing more than a cover for liberalism's imposition of a definite, decidedly liberal paradigm of economic freedom. It is important to see, however, that rejection of this paradigm does not necessarily entail an absolute rejection of the idea of the free market. If, in fact, by "free market" we mean simply "free economic exchanges," then we must acknowledge that a free market is both desirable and, indeed, practically necessary. Any economic system, such as that of the former Soviet Union, that tries to orchestrate economic exchanges from the outside using the coercive power of the state is doomed to sin against both the dignity of the human person and the requirements of good economics. It is in this sense, it seems to me, that John Paul II has given his qualified blessing to the notion of the free market in *Centesimus Annus*. The problem, however, is that liberalism means something much different from, and much more dubious than, just "free economic exchange" when it speaks of the "free market." When liberalism uses the words "free market," what it is actually saying is that contractual exchange among self-interested individuals, seen as indifferent in its structure to the objective good of the person, is the primary, if not exclusive, paradigm of economic life. It is this understanding of the free market, not the idea of "free economic exchange," that I will set out to critique. At the same time, I will be arguing that the best, most central paradigm for understanding free economic exchange is not contract among self-interested strangers, but gift-giving among neighbors. Since current market economies are largely liberal, the paradigm shift that I am recommending would entail a profound rethinking of many familiar economic practices and structures that we commonly take for granted. Although this rethinking would call into question many comfortable certainties, it is not necessarily violent or utopian. On the contrary, the gift-giving paradigm can contain all that is of value in the liberal understanding of the market, even while reconfiguring the latter's logic in a profound way within a nonliberal context. This reconfiguration is necessary both to protect human freedom and to secure economic good sense—a double desideratum that liberal economics, if consistently applied, cannot fulfill.

Back to the neoconservatives

Before going on to show why liberal economics cannot fulfill the double desideratum of securing human freedom and putting into practice sound economic rationality, I must deal briefly with a possible objection that it is unfair to the neoconservatives to accuse them of relying too heavily on liberal economics. This objection is a significant one. If, in fact, I am wrong about the neoconservatives, then the necessity of a paradigm shift to an economics of gift will seem less compelling. What, then, of the neoconservatives? Have they, perhaps, worked out a viable rethinking of liberal economics that already does what I want to argue an economics of gift would do?

The first thing that must be said is that, to the extent that they are Christians, the neoconservatives can hardly embrace without qualification liberal economics' insistence on the market's agnosticism about the objective good of the person. Or so it would seem. For instance, Michael Novak—in what follows I will limit myself to Novak, perhaps the most influential spokesman of the neoconservative position—distinguishes sharply between the institution of the market and the liberal ideology that some would bring to it. In Novak's view, the market, as an institution, carries no objectionable ideological baggage, for the simple reason that as an institution it is just a forum for free economic exchange—nothing more, nothing less. At the same time, Novak insists that the institution of the market does not exist in abstraction, but is always embedded in a larger moral-cultural framework that sustains it.[8] Looked at from this point of view, Novak argues, the market is a highly moral enterprise that requires a distinctive ethos—an ethos that can flourish ultimately only in the context of what Novak calls "Judeo-Christianity." Novak even claims, especially in his later writings, that "Judeo-Christianity" not only (uniquely) fosters the capitalist ethos, but actually helped to create it in the first place.[9]

Novak thus appears to limit the scope of the public agnosticism about the objective good of the person that some liberals would claim for the market. He seems to be no advocate of what fellow neoconservative Richard John Neuhaus famously castigated as the contemporary secular establishment's "naked public square." In the end, however, Novak's distinction between liberal institutions—in this case the market—and liberal ideology is just another version of the liberal neutrality claim. When Novak distinguishes the free market from liberal ideology, he trades on the same ambiguity in the term "free market" analyzed above. He is confusing free economic exchange *tout court* with free economic exchange as liberal economics understands the notion. His very distinction between the institution of the market and liberal ideology thus turns out to be a form of liberal ideology itself. By the same token, Novak unfairly awards the liberal paradigm of economic freedom a hegemony that excludes, without argument, any alternative paradigm—such as that of gift-giving among neighbors—that might reasonably challenge the exclusive rights he accords to the liberal one.

The primary paradigm of free economic exchange remains, for Novak as for liberal economics, contractual exchange among self-interested strangers, seen as formally or structurally indifferent with respect to the objective good of the person. It is this that Novak means by the institution of the market. Thus, when he distinguishes the market as an institution from "liberal ideology," he is obscuring the fact that what he means by the market as an institution is already charged with a liberal ideology that favors contractual exchange among self-interested strangers, contractual exchange formally indifferent to the objective good of the person, as the primary paradigm of economic freedom. Obviously, Novak differs from many classical liberals in that he insists that economic freedom, so understood, ought to be tempered by a moral ethos shaped within (ideally) "Judeo-Christian" religious concerns. But what this insistence really amounts to is that Novak thinks that Christians ought to have objections to liberal economics only when and insofar as individual economic agents misuse the economic freedom the market supposedly provides. Novak's solution? Leave intact the liberal understanding of economic freedom and add a moral discipline from the outside. Unfortunately, Novak thereby begs the question of whether or not liberalism's understanding of economic freedom is actually able to receive, without distortion, the requirements of "Judeo-Christian" morality. And this question-begging reflects an even deeper problem with Novak's proposal: his failure to acknowledge sufficiently that the problem with liberal economics is not first and foremost the ethical lapses of individual participants in the (liberal) market but, more fundamentally, the paradigm of economic freedom as essentially involving contractual exchange among self-interested individuals.[10]

Despite Novak's own intentions, then, the logic of his proposal ultimately remains too liberal in too many crucial places to allow the Gospel to enter the economic sphere in its integrity. By the same token, it fails to convince as an argument that the market as Novak understands it is the best vehicle for the Christian mission to address poverty on a social level. Let us understand this failure properly. Novak's argument is unconvincing, not simply because he has not succeeded in giving an adequate account of the free market. No, it is unconvincing chiefly because it assumes that what the "free market" means concretely in the liberal tradition— what it means concretely in current capitalist economies—is essentially unproblematic for Christians, rather than something whose logic needs to be fundamentally rethought in the light of the Gospel and in the direction of an economics of gift. Novak turns the "good news" that Christ came to preach to the poor into a tributary of liberal economics.

Now, Novak's unwitting domestication of the Gospel in the service of the liberal economic ethos does not simply violate the rights of Christianity. When Novak renders the Gospel publicly harmless, he reinforces a logic—a liberal logic—of economic organization that is inhumane and, indeed, ultimately unworkable even on its own terms. Needless to say, an inhumane, dysfunctional economy is not at all the "good news" for the poor that Novak claims democratic capitalism to be. This is because the economy is not the domain of neutral technique, but an extension of basic human community—and because ultimately we cannot understand man apart from Jesus Christ, who alone fully reveals the mystery of man "to himself" (*Gaudium et Spes*, section 22) and so unlocks the deepest meaning of man's worldly activity (including economic activity) precisely as worldly.

The failure of neoconservatism to baptize liberal economics— indeed, its "liberalization" of the Gospel—indirectly confirms my initial thesis that the primary paradigm of economic freedom, if it is to reflect the exigencies of the objective good of the person as this is disclosed in Jesus Christ's revelation of man to himself, cannot be that of contractual exchange among self-interested strangers, but must be that of gift-giving among neighbors—and that only such a paradigm enables us to get to the systemic causes of poverty. Such, at any rate, is the claim of the present essay. Obviously, this claim must reckon with two objections that appear to call into question the very desirability and possibility of an economics of gift: Doesn't such an economics imply the suppression of economic freedom? And isn't it in any case economically impracticable, not to say downright utopian? The essay will then attempt to turn these objections on their head by showing that, strange as it may seem, it is actually liberal economics that, if consistently applied, leads to coercion and economic dysfunction. This argument will give us the key to responding, in the penultimate section of the essay, to the charge that the proposal of an economics of gift is "unrealistic." Finally, the conclusion enumerates two basic conditions for the development of an economics of gift. In this context, I will argue that the "poverty of spirit" of the Gospels—the radicalization of the attitude of grateful receiving that is at the heart of the economics of gift—is the only adequate context for the Christian mission to bring the good news to the poor, and, indeed, for the discovery of the principles of a truly humane, truly practical economy that must be at the heart of that mission.

Liberalism's illiberal order

Much of the excitement that the neoconservatives have generated among Christians is due to their promise to overcome the split between the Gospel and culture that has bedeviled modern Christianity, especially since the Enlightenment. The neoconservatives reassure Christians that the dominant form of modernity, Anglo-American democratic capitalism, while not simply an extension of Christianity, is, or at least can be, consistent with Christianity. In particular, the neoconservatives argue that the market need not, indeed cannot, be the domain of *homo economicus*, the profit-and-loss calculator of liberal ideology, but must be understood as the home of the person whom God has created in his own image. They even go so far as to say that the market is the best expression, in the specifically economic sphere, of the dignity of the human person as revealed by God in Jesus Christ. Unfortunately, this claim cannot stand up under scrutiny. For, as we have seen, what the neoconservatives mean by the "market" is, in essence, what liberalism means by the "market": a structure of contractual exchange indifferent to the objective good of the person. Although this indifference goes under the name of "neutrality" (in the sense of impartiality), it is not really neutral at all, but rather implies, under the guise of "neutrality," that voluntary contractual exchange indifferent to the objective good of the person is the paradigm of economic freedom. Let us now consider how this notion of economic freedom actually replaces the authentic good of the person with an ersatz that is profoundly restrictive of human freedom.

In order to understand this replacement, we first need to have a sense of what the objective good of the person is. In terms of content, the objective good of the person is nothing other than the person himself. Nonetheless, the objective good of the person adds a distinct formality, a special point of view. This special point of view is constituted by the fact that the person is a gift to himself given by a loving Creator.[11] The objective good of the person is identical with the person—as a gift to himself. It is this gift-character that justifies our talking about an objectivity in the person's relation to himself as his own good. Because he is a gift to himself, the person finds inscribed in his being an objective ordination—an ordination to give himself as gift within the movement of God's giving. This ordination spells out the fundamental direction of a person's freedom. It includes his subjectivity, but is not simply reducible to it. It is crucial to see, however, that the irreducible objectivity of the ordination to gift does not thereby diminish freedom, but, on the contrary, makes freedom possible in the first place. If, in fact, there were no objective dimension to his personhood, the person wouldn't be able to transcend himself. This incapacity for transcendence would in turn deprive him of his very subjectivity and therefore of his freedom. True subjectivity, in fact, does not consist in a self-enclosed, private interiority, but in the capacity for communion.[12] It is in communion, as a network of mutual giving and receiving, that the person fulfills his ordination to gift-giving and so lays hold of his freedom as what it is, namely, as gift.[13]

We said just now that liberal economics replaces the objective good of the person with an ersatz that restricts the full amplitude of authentic human freedom. We can now add that this replacement begins when the communion just described gives way to contract among self-interested strangers as the primary instance of (economic) freedom. As liberalism conceives it, the contract is not ordered as such to the objective good of the human person. Of course, liberal economics claims that this non-ordination is not a negation of the good, but simply a mechanism for leaving freedom open to embrace the good. Notice, however, that the contract, while not ordered to the objective good as such, does have a finality of its own: the mutual satisfaction of self-interest in the form of financial gain. Thus, while claiming to leave freedom open to the objective good of the person, liberal economics surreptitiously weights it in the direction of self-interest understood as financial gain. The shift from communion to contract effectively puts financial gain in the place of the objective good of the person as the immanent finality of economic exchange.

Admittedly, some liberal economists claim that the term "self-interest" is simply a catch-all for whatever it is that one values.[14] Notice, however, that, when it comes to market exchange, the decisive criterion for determining whether or not to enter into a given contract is not simply one's "values," but a reasonable expectation of financial profit. This suggests that, for the specifically economic purposes of the market as liberal economics understands it, the finally relevant value-content of any individual's judgment about what is best for himself must be the profit-motive. Thus, while liberalism claims that self-interest means whatever one values or chooses, it really means only one kind of value and choice: a financial gain to which any other value is in the end irrelevant or subordinate.[15]

Even on the most benign reading, then, liberal economics imposes a certain ideal of freedom—an ideal chained to the imperative to seek financial gain above all else. In a word, the inner logic of liberal economics inevitably generates the *homo economicus*, the man unable to act for any motive other than financial gain—at least in the market.[16] But what about the other domains of society? Do they remain untouched? What about my initial claim that liberal economics imposes the unfreedom of economic man on society as a whole?

Well, the *homo economicus* is a voracious creature. Like Dr. Jekyll in Stevenson's famous story, he tends to claim more and more of his host, who thus increasingly thinks of himself spontaneously as a "rational" profit-and-loss calculator even outside the marketplace. Fortunately, the pure *homo economicus* is an impossibility. Living, breathing human beings are always better—usually very much better—than economic man. The neoconservatives, like many liberal economists before them, rely on this ampler, "spontaneous" goodness of human beings to neutralize the market's solvent effect on morality and religion. What the neoconservatives miss, unfortunately, is that the anthropology entailed in the neutrality they claim for the market—an anthropology of *homo economicus*—cannibalizes the sources from which this goodness flows. So long as they remain liberals on the point of the neutrality of the market, the neoconservatives leave society defenseless before the relentless spread of *homo economicus*. Why? Because so-called neutrality really means that a contractual exchange indifferent to the objective good of the person has been enshrined as the paradigm of economic freedom. But if freedom can dispense with the objective good in one domain, then, in principle, it can dispense with it in all domains. Wherever the market is "neutral," there *homo economicus* is busily at work remaking society in his own image.

Because it is designed only for economic man, but does not acknowledge this to be the case, the liberal market is already coercive just by being what it is: an unconfessed preference for an ideal economic actor who can seek nothing other than profit as the highest good. Nevertheless, it does not coerce only in this way. Because liberal economics is saturated by ideology, it is too artificial to triumph and retain its predominance without the support of a powerful institution to throw its weight behind the liberal program. The one institution best fitted for the role is, of course, the modern nation-state, which indeed is itself a facet of the liberal order. The liberal state and liberal economics go hand in hand. What liberal economics means by a "free market," in fact, is a unified, translocal national market, the creation and maintenance of which is impossible without the support of the state.[17] In *The Great Transformation*, Karl Polanyi brilliantly documents this fact in many ways, including via an instructive discussion of the original triumph of the market economy in nineteenth-century England,[18] which, Polanyi shows, was the result of massive state intervention. Once again, then, the neoconservatives are in a sense right: the liberal market is part of a tripartite structure that also includes the state and the culture. The problem, however, is that this threefold framework is ultimately a liberal one, in which the state throws its power behind the expansion of a liberal culture through the market. Ironically, then, the very liberal economists who routinely raise the specter of the centrally planned economy in order to fend off systemic critiques turn out (if we attend to the logic of their position) to be advocating the mobilization of the coercive power of the state behind the creation of a certain type of economy—one in which only a certain type of freedom, which is in reality an unfreedom, can flourish.

The poverty of liberal economics

The upshot of our discussion so far is that liberal economics is an ideologically charged construction of an ideal economy—ideal, that is, for a certain type of freedom that, in the end, could belong only to an unfree *homo economicus*. The task before us now is to show how the same mechanism that leads to unfreedom also leads to economic dysfunction, or to the poverty of liberal economics.

The objective good of the person, we have seen, is nothing other than the person himself, seen as a gift to himself given by a loving Creator. We can now add that this objective good connotes a value or, if you will, a wealth. Affirmed into being by God's generous creative gift, the person has, or rather is, a wealth—not a wealth of external riches, but a wealth that is internal to him just insofar as he is in the first place. Because the person's very being is a wealth, prior to any productive action on his part, we can call it an "ontological wealth." "Ontological," in this context, simply means "pertaining to the being of the person," so that "ontological wealth" means, once again, the inner wealth that characterizes the very being or existence of the person as a gift to himself. Moreover, just as the person lays hold of his objective good as a person within communion, here too he enters into the possession, and enjoyment, of his ontological wealth within a communion consisting in mutual giving and receiving in love. It is only in such a communion that he is able to experience the objective good of his own person as an "ontological" wealth inhering in his own person from its very creation. To possess ontological wealth is to rest in the joy of being that is loved into being by a generous Creator—a resting that can occur only in the context of a communion of love among persons all loved into being at once by their Creator. This restful enjoyment is not opposed to productivity, but distinguishes truly fruitful productivity from the frenetic activity of a culture obsessed with quantifiable results.[19]

If we take this "ontological" understanding of wealth seriously, then we have to say that "poverty," as a chronic condition, does not consist primarily in a lack of material goods, but rather first and foremost in a lack of meaningful participation in just the sort of communion mentioned above. Think of the ghetto dwellers who have plenty of "stuff"—cars, televisions, stereos—but who nonetheless continue to live in squalor. This squalor reflects the lack of meaningful participation in the kind of communion of giving and receiving that alone can unlock for the individual the wealth of his being as a person. But—and this is the core contention of the present section—an economy that privileges self-interested contractual exchange as its primary paradigm of economic activity just so far relegates communion to the margins of the marketplace. Such an economy, in other words, actively undermines the conditions necessary for the realization of the ontological wealth of the person. By the same token, the poverty that occurs in a liberal economy is not simply, or even primarily, a failure to produce on its (instrumentalist) terms. It is, even more fundamentally, a conception of oneself as having to produce on just those terms.

Insofar as liberal economies embody the substitution of communion with contract, they tend to produce ontological poverty. They are generators of a *homo economicus* who is deficient in ontological wealth, of persons who are "ontologically poor." Ironically, this ontological poverty is due to the very thing that appears to make economic man rich: his restless profit-seeking. This restlessness translates, in fact, into an inability to repose in the fullness that characterizes his being as gift. To be sure, economic man's compulsive profit-seeking need not simply be an expression of base greed. Often it reflects an unspoken search for self-justification through work, a search that stems, in turn, from a failure to experience being as gift within communion. Understood in this way, the psychology of economic man turns out to be pervasive in our results-oriented culture.

Lest readers think I am attacking a mere straw man, consider the so-called "stress" that haunts not only businessmen, but also lawyers, doctors, accountants, and even academics—to mention just a few professions—in the United States today. "Stress," of course, is just another name for the uncomfortable anxiety one feels when one is under pressure. Under pressure to do what, though? To produce. So unrelenting is this pressure that many professionals find their lives passing them by as they slave away to meet a never-ending, ever-expanding schedule of production. Here we see how *homo economicus* is increasingly informing the ethos of professions and institutions that, at first sight, seem to have little to do with "business" in the strict sense.[20]

This raises, however, a further question: Even supposing that liberal economics does in fact cause an ontological impoverishment of the human person, what could ontological poverty possibly have to do with the hard facts of economic reality? Don't liberal economies at least work in purely economic terms, regardless of their supposedly deleterious consequences for the human person? Clearly, the answer to this question depends, in large part, on what is meant by "purely economic." In fact, we should not be too quick to concede the economic high ground to liberal economics. We saw above that contractual exchange among self-interested strangers cannot be the primary paradigm of economic freedom without denaturing freedom. We will now see that it cannot be the primary paradigm of economic freedom without denaturing the economy itself.

The first step must be to dispel the illusion of invincibility that liberal economics creates by enfolding itself within the techniques of quantitative analysis. This will require showing that the liberal notion of profit, supposedly perfectly quantitative, is in fact a masked qualitative standard—one, moreover, that can be described as a caricatural reduction of ontological wealth. I will then go on to discuss the disastrous economic consequences that follow from this reduction.

I characterized the possession of ontological wealth just now in terms of the enjoyment of one's existence. It is important to see that this enjoyment is not just another name for what liberal economics means by self-interest. Indeed, the converse is actually the case: what liberal economics means by self-interest is a drastically reduced form of the enjoyment of one's existence that characterizes ontological wealth. To be sure, ontological wealth includes something like an "interest" in ourselves. After all, we can't enjoy our own existence unless we are glad that we exist. What liberal economics misses, however, is that the real self, the only self that actually exists, is one that is always already a gift to itself. It misses the fact that we can be "interested" in ourselves as we ought only by acknowledging to the core of our being that we are gift, which is to say, by letting ourselves be loved into being by God. This recognition, the highest act of freedom, is the core of what I mean by the enjoyment of existence.

Now, the enjoyment of existence in this sense is eminently fruitful: it never exhausts itself in ourselves alone, but always overflows itself, or, better, is caught up in God's self-overflowing, which is why it occurs paradigmatically within communion. This fruitful overflow should be the core of an authentic notion of profit.

Profit, rightly understood, is not primarily a quantitatively measurable gain lying outside the person, but a qualitative enhancement
of the enjoyment of his existence as gift. My point, I hasten to add, is
not that profit is irrelevant to economic calculation. Nor am I denying that profit has a quantitative dimension. I am simply saying that
the qualitative dimension is prior to, and determines the shape and
significance of, the quantitative. After all, why would anyone pursue
a greater quantity of money unless he thought it were better—from a
qualitative point of view—to have more of it? In other words, although liberal economics appears to effect a clean replacement of
ontological wealth with a purely quantitative sense of profit, it is
actually doing something quite different. The act of privileging the
quantitative aspect does not get rid of the primacy of ontological
wealth, but simply shifts the burden of ontological wealth onto its
quantitative aspects. The result, then, is not really a non-ontologi-
cal, purely quantitative sense of wealth at all, but rather a reduced
form of ontological wealth masquerading as pure quantity.[21]

Ironically, then, liberal economics does not get even the notion
of profit right. A profit that is just truncated ontological wealth masquerading as "pure quantity" is not even real profit—and so cannot
be an adequate standard for measuring economic value. Consideration of the baleful economic consequences of this inadequacy will
help us see how liberalism's ontological impoverishment of the human person is directly tied to an economic dysfunction—to a "poverty of liberal economics" that expresses its ontological poverty in
the materiality of economics.

Liberal economics' conception of profit as "purely quantitative"
goes hand in hand with what we could call the "growth formula" of
liberal economies: sell more more cheaply. After all, if profit is purely
quantifiable, and if the units of measurement are dollars, then the
most obvious way to increase profit (without gouging the consumer)
is just that, to sell more more cheaply. Notice, however, that it is
impossible to sell more more cheaply without degrading the quality of

the items sold. High quality means expensive production, and expensive production means the practical impossibility of making more to sell more cheaply.[22] Liberal economies thus display a fundamental paradox. On the one hand, the value of, say, an economic enterprise (as expressed, for example, in the price of stock shares) is based on its capacity to make a profit within a specified time frame. On the other hand, this profitability need be only loosely related, if at all, to the quality of the goods or services the enterprise offers. In other words: the basis of the enterprise's profitability is not the objective, qualitative value of what it offers society in terms of goods and services, but the subjective desires of consumers, desires that have to be fanned into flame through advertising. Furthermore, these desires are usually laden with expectations that cannot be fulfilled precisely because so often their object is cheap junk (the result of producers' imperative to sell more more cheaply). Obviously, there are still many firms that operate with a genuine concern for the quality of their products, products that these firms wish to offer as a real service to society. My point is certainly not to make a blanket generalization about entrepreneurs, but rather to identify the logic underlying the way in which liberal economics quantifies profit as a substitute for the fruitfulness of ontological wealth. Relying on its conception of purely quantitative profit as its yardstick, liberal economics systematically mismeasures economic value, focusing on quantifiable pinpoint gains to the exclusion of all other factors relevant to the determination of that value. Value, in liberal economics, is the capacity to make money, regardless of whether or not making money is predicated on *economic* folly in other respects.[23]

To be sure, the quantification of profit, coupled with the imperative to sell more more cheaply, does enable the mass production and consumption of goods and services and, therefore, a certain kind of wealth. Nevertheless, this wealth—the volume of goods and services produced and consumed—is not necessarily a reliable index of economic health because it is imposes a cost whose existence is often ignored, or explained away, but which, in any objective accounting, greatly offsets its actual value: systemic wastefulness. Not only does the fabrication of more cheaper items involve the discarding of great quantities of raw material, but the items that are produced drop out of the cycle of production at the moment of consumption; they cannot (with rare exceptions) be economically recycled. In consequence, producers are obliged to waste resources, sometimes to the point of exhaustion, in order to make more economically non-recyclable items. Take the example of plastics. True, many plastic items are now routinely recycled. Nonetheless, not all plastic items can be recycled, and, in any case, the practice of recycling plastics is a fairly recent one. Vast numbers of plastic products have already dropped irretrievably out of the cycle of production. Is it too much to think that this has put a corresponding pressure on fossil fuel reserves? Without wanting to argue that the loss of millions of tons of plastics to the productive cycle is solely responsible for the problem, can we not at least say that it has contributed significantly to the depletion of oil reserves in the United States (and thus also to the unfortunate dependence of America on certain Middle Eastern countries with whom it has uneasy relations on other fronts, e.g., Iraq)? Of course, it is often argued that the depletion of resources is ultimately illusory; it is always possible, it is said, to find substitute resources, especially since demand shifts with new technological possibilities. Even if this response were true, it misses the point: what I am critiquing is a pattern of productivity—whether or not its consequences are ultimately containable—that is inherently wasteful because it is geared to products that cannot be reintroduced into the productive cycle. An inherently wasteful economy, whatever else it may be, cannot be a healthy economy, especially if the achievements supposed to constitute its health are necessarily built upon the very wastefulness that is a sure symptom, not of health, but of dysfunction.

I am not denying, of course, that liberal economies produce an abundance of cheap goods. My point is rather that this achievement is not a reliable index of economic health. The reason for this unreliability, I am arguing, is that the cheap goods in question are cheap only for the individual consumer at the moment of purchase, not for society as a whole. The very process of creating an abundance of goods that are cheap for individual consumers at the moment of purchase—mass production fueled by the imperative to sell more more cheaply—inevitably causes negative side-effects. Think, for example, of the pollution caused by the (once routine) dumping of toxic chemicals into waterways: the cost of cleanup procedures can run into the multiple millions. Now, someone somewhere—usually the taxpayers—eventually has to shoulder the cost of dealing with such side effects. And the cost is not a metaphorical one, but a real one, calculable in real dollars and cents. Goods whose production involves such costs appear to be "cheap," then, only because these costs are not reflected in what consumers pay for these goods in stores. The question we must ask is whether an economy that buys tiny gains at the cost of net losses can be pronounced sound, if by "sound" we mean "conformable to the exigencies of economic good sense," and not merely "good at increasing the volume of exchanges between producers and consumers," or, what is the same, "good at increasing profits by inducing more people to buy more so-called cheap goods."[24]

If, as the foregoing analysis suggests, the value of the wealth liberal economies generate is significantly offset by the systemic wastefulness upon which this kind of wealth is predicated, then we cannot uncritically accept the ability to produce such wealth as the sole, or even as the primary, index of economic health. To do so is to leave out too much that, in any objective accounting, would have to be considered before we could pronounce an economy healthy. Yet this is just what liberal economics does: it redefines economic health in an abstract, simplistically reductive way that allows it to ignore every criterion of economic health other than the few it deems relevant. This brings us back to the question, don't liberal economies *work* in purely economic terms? Liberal economies can be said to "work" only if we accept their own standards of efficiency. Given the unreliability of these standards, however, we should be very hesitant to concede to liberalism the high ground of economic good sense. If the argument so far has been correct, then we cannot trust liberal economists to judge even economic efficiency properly.

After all, it literally makes no sense, no economic sense, to say that an economy built on the maxim "sell more more cheaply" is a "sound" one just because its massive, systemic wastefulness helps to deliver the pinpoint gains that we have chosen to regard, with the greatest abstractness, as the sole criteria of economic success. The problem with liberal economics, in fact, is not just an ethical failure in the narrow sense, but a failure of economic rationality, of economic man precisely as a "rational" profit-and-loss calculator. Economic man is not only immoral, he is also too stupid to see what is really in his best "interests." And he is both for the same reason: liberal economics' construction of economic freedom as indifferent to the objective good of the person as gift that flourishes in communion. Among contemporary critics of the liberal economy, none has understood and articulated the purely economic folly of that economy's methods of reckoning value with more realism, hard-headed clarity, and eloquence than Wendell Berry, with whose words about the Great Economy, which integrates economic rationality into a stewardship born of the awareness of existence as gift, I would like to conclude the present section:

> [A] human economy cannot prescribe the terms of its own success. In a time when we wish to believe that humans are the sole authors of truth, that truth is relative, and that all value judgments are subjective, it is hard to say that a human economy can be wrong, and yet we have good, sound, practical reasons for saying so. It is indeed possible for a human economy to be wrong—not relatively

wrong, in the sense of being "out of adjustment," or unfair according to some definition of fairness—but wrong absolutely and according to practical measures. Of course, if we see the human economy as the *only* economy, we will see its errors as political failures, and we will continue to talk about "recovery." It is only when we think of the little human economy in relation to the Great Economy that we begin to understand our errors for what they are and to see the qualitative meanings of our quantitative measures. If we see the industrial economy in terms of the Great Economy, then we begin to see industrial wastes and losses, not as "trade-offs" or "necessary risks" but as costs that, like all costs, are chargeable to somebody, sometime.[25]

Unrealism?

The present essay has argued that Christians should be wary of accepting liberal economics as a vehicle for evangelizing or assisting the poor. Defenders of liberal economics such as Michael Novak would no doubt retort that I have exaggerated the incompatibility between Christianity and the liberal economic tradition. Surely, such defenders will say, we can detach the institution of the market from the ideology of "economic man"? I acknowledge, of course, that there is no such thing as *homo economicus* in the pure sense. No one individual person is, or could be, what *homo economicus* is supposed to be, and most individuals are in fact much better than economic man. The point I am making is simply that liberal economics, by installing contractual exchange indifferent to the objective good of the person as the paradigmatic instance of economic freedom (and all this under the guise of "neutrality"), in effect designs the economy for economic man. To repeat: pure *homo economicus* is an impossibility in the real world. This does not mean, however, that liberal economies are unproblematic, but rather just the opposite. Such economies are built to embody an unworkable anthropology that leads to dysfunction even and also in the practical order.

In a certain sense, the neoconservatives make just this point: a liberal economy, they say, depends on a goodness that it does not itself generate. What they miss, however, is that the liberal economy, though it does indeed rely on this "spontaneous" goodness, has no right to do so, since its inner logic tends to poison the sources from which this goodness comes. Indeed, they fail to see that their distinction between institution and ideology turns the market by its inner logic into a habitat for *homo economicus*. Because they do not deeply enough challenge the principles of the liberal order, the neoconservatives can do no more than try to prevent economic man from absorbing the entirety of social life. They are held back from such a radical challenge out of their fear, understandable from a certain point of view, of yoking the economy to the ruinous control of central planners. But if liberal economics guarantees neither real freedom nor real prosperity, might it not be time to begin, at last, the laborious but necessary task of developing an economics of gift that duly recognizes and respects the primacy of ontological wealth?

If, as I have suggested, liberal economics cannot be trusted to tell us what economic health really is, then what reason can there be, besides obstinate attachment to the status quo, to leave our prevailing economic commitments unexamined? Might it not be time to reconsider, among other things, the primacy we have accorded the well-being of the global market over the well-being of local economies? The local economy is, after all, more obviously an extension of the local community held together by the bonds of neighborliness. Needless to say, whatever changes in policy and practice such a reprioritization would involve would have to be accompanied by a great deal of prudence and intelligence operating within a profound awareness of, and respect for, the dignity of persons, the weight of history, and the limits of human nature.

Even with such qualifiers in place, my critique of liberal economics is bound to draw the charge that it is unrealistic. There is no practicable alternative to the present system, it will be said, and any radical challenge to it reflects a utopianism that blithely ignores the hard practicalities of economic reality. Let us be frank: the charge of "unrealism" is often a thinly veiled unwillingness or inability to imagine an economy driven by a set of priorities other than the one already in place. I am not advocating that the government take over the production and distribution of goods and services. But today the specter of a centrally planned economy is a red herring. Not only does the liberal economy have a symbiotic relationship with the state; it also unduly favors the concentration of economic power in big corporations (who else can maintain economies of scale?) that, allied with technology, have a massively disproportionate influence on many aspects of daily life, from the average citizen's access to the news to the scientist's research in his university laboratory. What I am arguing for is precisely that we turn our efforts towards a decentralization of economic power in favor of the locality, the scale of which allows for genuine political deliberation about the most efficient use of resources without the coercion involved in central planning. Of course there must still be a national and international market, but these higher levels must be structured so that the input of subsidiary political units, for example the city, are allowed to protect the individual from the encroachments of big government, big business, and, for that matter, big media. The objective good of the human person requires the sort of economic arrangements that protect genuine contributions to social order "from below" in a way that, we now see, liberal economics cannot. To foreclose debate about such an alternative by dismissing it *a priori* as a pipedream says more about one's attachment to the ultimately illiberal priorities that shape the economy today than about the actual realities of economic life.

The currently dominant set of economic priorities is characterized by the alliance of the profit-motive and technology in the form of economies of scale. This alliance has resulted in the market dominance of easily packageable, easily transportable items that can be accumulated in points of sale and need have no organic connection with the places where they happen to be located. The result is an economy of the shopping mall and of the rest-stop Burger King. It is important to stress that this economy of the shopping mall and the rest-stop Burger King is not objectionable only because it is ugly. Its ugliness is the index of a systemic inefficiency that can be criticized on strictly economic grounds. The root of this inefficiency lies in the kind of ideal economic actor that the alliance between the profit-motive and technology presupposes: *homo economicus* in the guise of the technician. It is the technician who drives the expansion of the present economy, and the technician is one who restlessly seeks to invent processes that deliver a single result quickly and conveniently. But if we assume that efficiency consists in the ability to obtain the greatest possible benefit with the least possible outlay of time, energy, and resources, then the technician's efficiency turns out to be economical only in a highly abstract sense: it may achieve the one desired result quickly and conveniently, but in order to do so it has to ignore the very real costs that are entailed by the very "efficiency" that the technician prizes.

It would, then, be question-begging and highly misleading to dismiss systemic critiques of liberal economics on the grounds that liberal economics "works"—on the grounds, that is, that there is no practical alternative to liberal economics. To the extent that modern Western economies have in fact "worked" and continue to "work," they have not done so for the reasons claimed by liberal economics, but rather because they unconfessedly rely on an integration of economic activity with a fuller sense of person and community that liberal economic theory nonetheless logically undermines. This suggests both the need for, and the possibility of, an alternative account of economic activity that conceives it from the beginning as a direct, albeit specifically differentiated, participation in the pursuit of the objective good of the person, rather than as simply juxtaposed to, and externally influenced by, that good. This account would retain values such as limited government, constitutionally safeguarded freedom of conscience, and the market, but would interpret those values from within a nonliberal framework in the conviction that their liberal interpretation, far from being their only safeguard, actually undermines them.

Finally, let me observe that the proposal of an economics of gift does not entail a maximalism that would require nothing short of perfection from economic actors. It would indeed be utopian in the extreme to imagine that we could create an economic system that would automatically ensure virtue. Any realistic economy must take account of the fallen human propensity to selfishness. Precisely because the objective good of the person includes his subjectivity, it implies full recognition of freedom, even of the freedom to make mistakes, which any prudent legislator must take account of. On the other hand, we must not forget that communion remains the deepest truth of freedom, not only as a yet-to-be-attained ideal *for* freedom (it is that too, of course), but also as the reality *of* freedom, even in the midst of its fallen condition. To talk of an economics of gift, then, is not to indulge in a utopian maximalism, but to tell the truth about man. The question then becomes whether or not freedom flourishes best when this truth is acknowledged or when, as in the case of liberalism, it is effectively replaced by an account of freedom that diminishes and restricts it.

Conclusion: Poverty is not a problem

The burden of the present essay has been that liberal economics, even in its most benign ("neoconservative") form, is inadequate to the Church's task of evangelizing the poor and addressing the systemic cause of poverty. I have also argued for the necessity of developing an alternative economics of gift that can assimilate whatever might be of value in the liberal paradigm without taking over its governing assumptions. Needless to say, it exceeds the scope of the present essay to detail a fully developed economics of gift. Let me conclude, instead, by suggesting two fundamental conditions that any proposal of an economics of gift would have to meet. This will enable us, in synthesis, to capture what is distinctive about such an economics in its approach to the "problem" of poverty.

The first condition is that we understand the task of working out an economics of gift as a primarily theological task, not merely as an exercise in conventional economics. It is not that economics doesn't matter, but rather that conventional economics, deeply shaped by the liberal tradition, gets economics itself wrong by separating it from theological considerations. The historical development of economics as a science occurred in the shadow of the split between Christian life and worldly life. The neutrality liberalism claims for the market is, in fact, a kind of codification of this split, the essence of which is that the goal of worldly activity—in this case, economic activity—is not a form of relation to God, which can only be added to that goal from the outside. This notion is not entirely false, of course. The goal of economic activity does have a certain independence, a "legitimate autonomy," to use the terminology of the Second Vatican Council (*Gaudium et Spes*, section 36). What liberalism misses, however, is that the market's legitimate autonomy, like that of everything else in creation, is itself constituted by relation to God, not in separation from him. The neoconservatives' acceptance of the idea that there can be a neutral, independent liberal economic rationality is thus insufficient. What the neoconservatives overlook is the need for a new model of economic reason. Indeed, the only hope for a sound, humane economy is a new anthropological ideal that takes into full account the gift-character of existence as this is fully disclosed in Jesus Christ, who, in the words of *Gaudium et Spes* (section 22) reveals man to himself. Only such an economic actor, in fact, can properly understand the goal of an economy and how to achieve it, because only he consistently sees that goal, and the means leading up to it, as a specific form of relation to the God, indeed, to the incarnate *Logos*, in whom all things, even the most "worldly," hold together and make sense.

The second *sine qua non* of the new economics of gift is one that the failure of liberalism to deliver on its promises makes so necessary: in order to re-think the economy from the position of the ideal economic actor at the center of this new economics, we must become him ourselves. We need to be transformed into the new paradigm of economic rationality as part of the dynamic of an ongoing conversion to Christ through "renewal of the mind" (Rom 12:2). But we cannot undergo this transformation unless we allow our economic rationality to be formed in a lived experience of Jesus' first Beatitude, "blessed are the poor in spirit." Poverty of spirit, in fact, is the core of the new economics of gift. It is nothing other than the radicalization the Gospel brings to the reception of the gift of being within communion, a reception that is rooted in the very creaturely constitution of the person.

This suggestion may unsettle some who, on account of the split between Christianity and culture mentioned above, are accustomed to understanding poverty of spirit (along with the rest of the Beatitudes) simply as a mode of world-denying asceticism. In reality, poverty of spirit does not remove us from the heart of the world, but plunges us into it so that from there we can become open to what is beyond this world. Poverty of spirit can thus accompany and inform our thinking about, and practical engagement with, the ever-changing realities of economic life. It accompanies us, however, not in a merely general way, but in a specific way directly pertinent to the economy. Poverty of spirit is the opposite of the restless activism of the workaholic. It is characterized by the playfulness born of an awareness that not everything depends on me—an awareness that, paradoxically, allows me to act as if everything did depend on me, albeit now in a spirit of playfulness. But this playfulness is the enjoyment of existence as gift that, as I argued above, is the key to ontological wealth. Poverty of spirit, then, is itself the exercise of ontological wealth. To be poor in spirit is to be ontologically rich, because ontological wealth is nothing other than the fruitful act of letting oneself be loved into existence as the gift of God within communion, the act of being dispossessed in order to be given back to oneself as (infinitely) more than one could be on one's own.

It is crucial to see that poverty of spirit is not a sort of pious addition to the economic sense of wealth; it is the main ingredient in the economic sense of wealth itself. This claim becomes clearer when we consider that economic efficiency is best understood in terms of the craftsman rather than of the technician. The craftsman is no less technically competent than the technician, just as he is no less concerned with practical efficiency than is the technician. What distinguishes the craftsman from the technician is rather the craftsman's openness to experiencing his work as a form of participation in "ontological wealth." This openness to ontological wealth is not, however, an optional extra, a moral icing on the cake. Ontological wealth is what enables the craftsman to achieve a better economic efficiency than the technician—and so to generate a real economic wealth that is not predicated on the concealment of the economic disvalue tied up with the technician's brand of "efficiency."

Ontological wealth is what allows the craftsman to avoid the technician's penchant for identifying efficiency with abstract, pinpoint gains while excluding from his calculations the real economic costs of such an abstract sense of efficiency. Now, because of his participation in ontological wealth, the craftsman is also (potentially) one of the "poor in spirit" whom Jesus praises in the Gospels. This gives us the key to the affirmation suggested above: poverty of spirit, far from being a kind of supererogatory adornment, is the ethos of economic rationality, whose presence or absence makes all the difference between economic sanity and economic folly. Conversely, any purported "solution" to the "problem" of material poverty that, like liberal economics, overlooks the poverty of spirit of which Christ speaks will not only put in its place a reductive anthropology—the anthropology of the technician—that not only blocks a real solution to the problem of material poverty, but actually tends to deepen it through the promotion of a systemic inefficiency woefully inadequate to the true practicalities of the economic sphere in the real world. To be poor in spirit is to overcome the divorce between practical rationality, ethos, and religion that, masquerading as "neutrality," is the source of our economic dysfunction. As Wendell Berry writes:

> If we credit the Bible's description of the relationship between Creator and Creation, then we cannot deny the spiritual importance of our economic life. Then we must see how religious issues lead to issues of economy and how issues of economy lead to issues of art. By "art" I mean all the ways in which humans make the things they need. If we understand that no artist—no maker—can work except by reworking the works of Creation, then we see that by our work we reveal what we think of the works of God. How we take our lives from this world, how we work, what work we do, how well we use the materials we use, and what we do with them after we have used them—all these are questions of the highest and gravest religious significance. In answering them, we practice, or do not practice, our religion.[26]

In a certain sense, then, the liberation theologians are right. The task of Christians is to foment revolution. Only the "revolution" they must work for is not a violent attack on existing institutions from the outside, but a revolution of meaning that allows them to be changed—organically, patiently, and with full respect for the dignity of persons—from the inside. In pursuing this revolution of meaning, Christians must use the spaces of freedom left within the current system (left in spite of its founding principles) to show, in their own being, acting, and thinking, that the radical following of Christ is the "light of the world" whose rays extend even to the practicalities of economic life. Part of Christian responsibility, then, is to re-think the founding presuppositions of liberal economics in light of the primacy of ontological wealth as reception of the gift of existence, which is to say, in light of "poverty of spirit" as the key to the meaning even of economic wealth.

Poverty is not a problem. Or to be more specific, we cannot hope to solve the problem of poverty until we learn to stop looking at it as a problem to be solved with the techniques of liberal economic rationality. Liberal economic rationality does not work. And it does not work because it is not formed in Christ's poverty of spirit. Conversely, if poverty in liberal societies is a problem of meaning, or rather of meaninglessness, rooted in liberal economics' own failure to allow poverty of spirit to shape the heart of economic rationality, then the only workable approach to poverty, even so-called "material poverty," is to become "poor in spirit" ourselves—and in that poverty to re-think, with intelligence renewed by Christ, the meaning of wealth and poverty in the light of human destiny. "The West has decided that Christianity is calling us to fight against poverty, or to replace it with relative riches, or at least economic equality, etc.," wrote Alexander Schmemann. "The Christian appeal is quite different: poverty as freedom, poverty as a sign that the heart has accepted the impossible (hence tragic) call to the Kingdom of God. I don't know. It's so difficult to express it, but I clearly feel that here is a different perception of life, and the bourgeois state (religious, theological, spiritual, pious, culture, etc.) is blind to something essential in Christianity."[27]

3

Catholic Social Teaching, Markets, and the Poor

Michael Novak

"*Be not afraid!*" is the favorite injunction of John Paul II to the peoples of the world. Under his leadership, the Catholic Church has made a remarkable new judgment about the institutions of democracy, such as the rule of law, the protection of rights, the separation of powers, and the principle of limited government. It has also reaffirmed the guarded approval of the free economy that has long been traditional in Catholic social thought—respect for the right of private property, the right of free association, and even the right of economic initiative. But John Paul II has also gone farther than that. He has communicated a more penetrating insight into the role of human capital, especially the roles of knowledge, know-how, and practical creativity in creating the wealth of nations. Neither democracy nor capitalism is to be identified as the highest earthly good in his thought. Both democracy and capitalism must conform to the rule of law and subject themselves to sound moral criteria. If they do so, the Church approves of them, and looks upon them with hope and expectation, not with fear.[1]

When we recall the murders, executions, and exiles the Church endured under the French Revolution of 1789 and the Mexican Revolution of 1920, and from many other encounters with "liberal" governments in between, it is not hard to understand why the Church was for several decades hostile to tyrannies that called themselves "liberal." Much that went by that name was in fact illiberal.[2] Yet John Paul II, like his namesake John XXIII before him, has from

the beginning of his pontificate chosen to regard the world of history—the world of our time—with hope and expectation. "Be not
afraid!" He used those very words on his first visit to Poland in 1979,
some six months after he became pope, when the Berlin Wall still
seemed very high and solid. He uses them still. He used them with
regard to "globalization" in September 1999.

I would like, in what follows, to proceed in the spirit of John Paul II,
who has been called by his biographer "a witness to hope."[3] There is no
doubt that if by "liberalism" we mean a philosophy that is materialist,
persecutory, anti-Christian, closed to or perhaps even opposed to belief
in God, then such a philosophy runs counter to Christian thought. But if
by "liberalism" one means a commitment to the best institutions worthy
of human dignity, such as limited government, the protection of political
and civil rights, and respect for religious liberty and the free exercise of
religion, as well as the institutions of a free economy powered by knowledge, know-how, invention, and enterprise, then in that case Catholic
social thought sees much reason for hopeful cooperation with liberalism.
Those are the commitments of "all men of good will," to whom the angels
sang "Peace on earth!" in welcoming the Christ.

Catholic social thought has established critical grounds for both
a profound appreciation of the humanism that infuses the institutions
of democracy and capitalism at their best, and for a vision in whose
light their existing practice (and incomplete development) may be
justly criticized and incited to further progress.

I want to unpack this thesis under five headings: *materialism,*
or the primacy of the spirit; *solidarity*; the *subjectivity of society*
(that is, the liberty, initiative, and creativity of the human subject);
subsidiarity; and *breaking the chains of poverty.*

Foundations of the Catholic understanding of democratic capitalism

Materialism. In 1997, the Synod of America, which brought together
the bishops of North and South America, disparaged those it called

"neoliberals." There is a long tradition in Latin America, as there is in Spain, describing "liberals" as materialists, concerned solely with market processes, profits, and efficiency, to the neglect of the human spirit, human values, and human rights.[4]

In the new economy of today, however, it is very difficult to be a materialist, strictly understood. Consider your last purchase of a new disk or program for your computer. How much *material* do you actually have in your hand? About eighty cents worth of plastic. What you actually paid for is almost entirely composed of *mind,* the fruit of the human spirit, information in a design created by human intelligence. All around us, *matter* matters less and less, and *intelligence* (or spirit) matters more.

Second, as John Paul II explains, the cause of wealth *used* to be explained in largely material terms: At one time, the major form of wealth in most places was *land*. At a later time, especially for Marxist thought, it was *capital,* conceived of as large inert investments in factories and huge machines. In our time, however, economists affirm that the chief cause of the wealth of nations is not material at all, but *knowledge, skill, know-how*—in short, those acts and habits of discovery, invention, organization, and forethought that economists now describe as "human capital," located in the human spirit and produced by the spiritual activities of education and training and mentoring.[5] Human capital also includes moral habits, such as hard work, cooperativeness, social trust, alertness, honesty, and social habits, such as respect for the rule of law.

The one factor, more than any other, that makes the rich countries rich is their investment in and development of human capital. A nation's greatest single resource, economists say, is its people.[6] Put another way, it is not material resources that make a nation rich. Some of the countries richest in natural resources are among the world's poorest nations. Some of the nations with virtually no natural resources are among the world's richest nations. The cause of wealth can no longer be said to be material.

It is true, of course, that there are today, as there were in biblical times, many who confine their horizons to this earth as we sense it, who eat, drink, and make merry until they die. Not a few among the baptized are included in that number. In this sense, materialists there will always be. But in the world of theory, materialist doctrines have run aground. Marxist "dialectical materialism," for example, failed miserably in understanding economics and in generating humane societies. All the evidence of physics and the other sciences now point beyond the reaches of materialism.

On the other hand, no principle is as basic to Catholic social thought as the primacy of spirit. Everywhere today that principle seems to be vindicated: in care for the physically and the mentally ill, in overcoming drug abuse and alcoholism, in turning from a life of crime, in moral formation, in economic development, in nourishing among a people the rule of law and civic commitment, in encouraging people to act with unimpeachable honesty even when no one is looking, and in engendering confidence in the future even in the face of great obstacles. Empirical research seems to confirm the primacy of spirit, and to disconfirm merely materialistic accounts of human behavior.[7]

Solidarity. When Leo XIII described in *Rerum Novarum* (1891) the tumultuous changes then churning through the formerly agrarian and feudal world of premodern Europe, he saw the need for a new sort of virtue (a reliable habit of soul) among Christian peoples, lay people especially, and he wavered between calling it *justice* or *charity*, *social justice* or *social charity*.[8] By the time of *Centesimus Annus* (1991), John Paul II had brought that nascent intuition into focus in the one term *solidarity*. By this term, he did not mean the great Polish labor union which contributed so much to the fall of communism—although no doubt the worldwide fame of the term *Solidarnosc* added helpful connotations to what he intended—but rather the special virtue of social charity that makes each individual aware of belonging to the whole human race, of being brother or sister to all others, of living in *communio* with all other humans in God.

Solidarity is another way of saying globalization, but in the dimension of communal interiority and personal responsibility. Solidarity is not an impersonal habit of losing oneself in groupthink, disappearing into a collectivity. Solidarity is exactly the reverse of what socialists meant by collectivization, for it points simultaneously to the personal responsibility and initiative of the human subject and to communion with others. Solidarity awakens the individual conscience. Solidarity evokes responsibility, enlarges personal vision, and connects the self to all others.[9]

In these days of "globalization," even when that "new thing" is described in merely economic terms, it is almost impossible for any intelligent human being to imagine the self as an unencumbered, detached, solitary individual unlinked to others. Globalization involves a dramatic drop in transportation and communication costs, instantaneous communications, a single global market, Internet and satellite and cellular phone and television, and a geometric increase in foreign direct investment and cross-border trade. Globalization also has an interior dimension. External, economic globalization has changed the way individuals *experience* themselves and the way they *think*.

People find it increasingly hard to think only about local conditions. Is this not a major step in the direction of the realities of solidarity? Are human beings not planetary creatures, one another's brothers and sisters, members of one same body, every part serving every other part?[10]

These are the best of times for those committed to solidarity, and pinching, painful times for those committed to a view of themselves as solitary individuals—pinching like shoes that do not fit.

If a Catholic cannot feel confident in a time of globalization, what is the point in bearing the name "Catholic," which is another name for global? (The imperative for globalization began with the commission "Go preach the gospels to all nations," which turned Christianity away from being the religion of one tribe or one people only, and commanded it to see the whole human race as one people of God.) Globalization is the natural ecology of the Catholic faith.

It is on this ground that Pope John Paul II welcomes the "new thing" of globalization. All the streams that contribute to the definition of globalization, as mentioned above, point to good effects as well as bad, and there is every sign that, for the poor of the world, being included within the circle of exchange and development is better than being marginalized. There is at least a possibility that global procedures will heighten the transparency of local transactions and reduce local corruption. The pope urges international institutions and citizens everywhere to open their arms to the world's poor, and to help bring about a springtime of worldwide development, excluding no one, embracing all. His call to solidarity offers a vision of genuine globalization, and works as a vantage point of criticism for those times when globalization falls short of its potential for human well-being.

The subjectivity of society. The theme of subjectivity in Pope John Paul II has been much overlooked in popular expositions of Catholic social thought. To state the matter briefly, anyone who has a pet in the house knows that animals *behave;* they cannot do other than follow the laws of their own nature. One's own children, however, do not always "behave." They imagine new futures for themselves, invent new projects and new trajectories for their personal development. In part they invent themselves. In the long run, they must become provident over their own identity, responsible for choosing who they will become. In short, children must learn to reflect, deliberate, choose, take initiative, and accrue responsibility for their own actions. Unlike the other animals, they *can* choose against the laws of their own nature, or they can choose to walk in those laws.

To summarize, whereas the other animals *behave,* the human person *acts*. The human person is *the acting person*.[11] Action flows from the interior life of insight, reflection, and decision—acts that only persons can perform, acts that humans have in common (analogously) with angels and with God, but with no other known creatures.

By the time he wrote *Centesimus Annus,* the pope had come to distinguish between "the subjectivity of society" and "the subjectivity of the individual," though both were held to be antipathetic to "real socialism."[12] He then pushed his earlier thought to the new insight that the capacities of the human being for creative action are the cause of the wealth of nations, and from an economic point of view the most important form of capital.[13]

This concept enabled the Holy Father to talk about solidarity in terms of personal responsibility and initiative. Simultaneously, the concept of solidarity enabled him to talk about the individual subject in terms of universal *communio,* the communion of all human beings in the love and being of God.

Without the integrity of the human subject, there is no genuine *communio*. Without *communio,* there is no whole human subject. Without solidarity, subjectivity degenerates into unencumbered individualism. Without subjectivity, solidarity degenerates into mushy and mindless collectivism.

We can grasp the complementarity of these two conceptual tools because we have experienced the excesses of both collectivism and individualism. We have lived through the failures of both socialist and liberal materialism.

Subsidiarity. Simultaneously with the great rushing power of economic and legal globalization there has also arisen a powerful set of demands for greater local autonomy and a stronger role for intermediate institutions and mediating associations. In other words, from outside and from within, the nation-state is under great pressures. These pressures are all the more acute since, at least since the time of

Hegel, the nation-state has been thought to be the mythical embodiment of the *Geist* of a whole people. One can read the history of the last two centuries as an enactment of the myth of the benevolent nation-state, caring for its people as the nanny for her children, rendering them secure and happy. From Lenin to Hitler, Mussolini to Perón, Mao Zedong to Castro, Kim Il Sung to Qaddafi, dictators have loved this myth. They have portrayed themselves as personifications of Popular Will.

Various forms of socialism, social democracy, and the liberal welfare state have all embraced other versions of the same mythic impulse. The twentieth century has predominately been the story of the nation-state, at the expense of every other social structure—family, church, mediating institution. The nation-state has proved inadequate, however, to its own boasts. It has over-promised and under-achieved. Great pressures from outside and from within are bursting through its governing myths.

Catholic social thought itself has invested a great deal of its conceptual weight in a theory of the state, especially the welfare state, which has not met the tests of reality. A massive rethinking is needed, and quickly.

The need for doing so is obvious in the international dimension. The pope often calls for new international institutions to "guide" the new energies of globalization.[14] But much of the rethinking must attend to the intra-national dimension, the vitality of the smaller institutions *within* states that the hyperactive national governments of the last one hundred years have repressed and suppressed. Whole regions, ethnic groups, cities, townships, villages have been neglected. Yet today many diverse local forces are stirring and coming again to life.

The defense of the civic association by the church is at least as old as Innocent IV's vindication of such "corporations" as cities, cathedral chapters, and guilds, independent of the state,[15] and Thomas Aquinas's apologia for the human rights of the members of mendicant orders, such as the new Franciscans and Dominicans.[16] But the Catholic doctrine of "subsidiarity" appears to have been given a great boost by the Swiss and the American experiments in confederation and federalism, respectively. Lord Acton identified federalism—that is, one form of subsidiarity—as one of the great achievements in the history of liberty.[17]

The basic justification for subsidiarity is epistemic. Decisions taken closer to the concrete texture of reality and the immediate interests of the decision makers are likely to evince a higher degree of practical intelligence, not to say wisdom, than decisions taken at a higher, more abstract remove. Practical wisdom tends to demand hands-on, experimental knowledge, the sort of knowledge Jacques Maritain identified as "knowledge by connaturality," a kind of knowledge by "second nature."[18]

Breaking the chains of poverty

Still, with all this discussion of doctrine, it is well to remind ourselves of our main task in this new century. That task is to arrange our institutions so that all the poor of the world may exit from poverty. In the last 150 years we have made tremendous strides in that direction, but much work remains.

Although about three-quarters of the population in the hemisphere of the Americas, for instance, has escaped from dire poverty, still about 78 million persons in that hemisphere live on an income of less than one dollar per day, and 182 million live on less than two dollars per day.[19] The life expectancy of these poor peoples may have been substantially extended, but their living conditions are still unnecessarily harsh. Enough is known about how to create new wealth on a systematic basis that the poverty of these 182 million is unnecessary, even scandalous. It makes us ashamed. It fires our determination to alter their circumstances.

Our goal must be to eliminate the last large pockets of poverty in this world during the next two generations—by, say, 2040. We know that human capital is the most important form of capital. Therefore, education is the most crucial form of economic development, the sine qua non of all others. The good news is that adult literacy around the world has jumped from about 48 percent in 1970 to about 72 percent in 1997.[20] That is a good gain in less than thirty years. In the next fifteen years, we ought to push this number above 90 percent. Nothing would better reduce poverty than this increase in human capital.

But to education must be added job creation.[21] There cannot be new employees if there are not new employers, that is to say, new businesses. The creation of an atmosphere, a legal system, and a banking system favorable to the creation of many new small businesses is an urgent matter for the liberation of the poor. Business formation depends on the exercise of the creativity and the desire for serving others with honest goods and useful services that the Creator has instilled in every person. As it happens, in Latin America and in Africa in particular, women excel in launching new small businesses.

Until now, theologians and bishops have not had to extend a great deal of thought to economic and business matters. If they must do so today, it is for the sake of the poor. Better than to give the poor bread is to help them launch bakeries and other firms, through which they might serve others, as a way of providing for their own families, in an independent, honorable, and prideful way.[22] In no other systemic and practical way can the poor be brought "into the circle of exchange."[23] Such progress will occur only within a market economy. Yet capitalism may be the most besieged liberal institution within Christian circles. The challenge to the morality of markets deserves to be addressed systematically.

Defenses of capitalism

"The driving power of capitalism," writes the distinguished English Christian missionary to India, Leslie Newbigin, "is the desire of the individual to better his material condition. . . . The name that the New Testament gives to the force in question is covetousness. The capitalist system is powered by the unremitting stimulation of covetousness."[24]

This is one justification (condemnation, rather) of capitalism. If it were accepted by a poor nation, such a theory would be its own punishment. Note, too, its image of wealth. Desiring to improve one's material condition is covetousness because whatever one needs for self-improvement already belongs to others—it is theirs and one covets it. But this is to imagine wealth as a fixed sum, all of it previously assigned, and to overlook the dimension of invention, discovery, and the creation of new wealth. It is to imagine all gaining of wealth as "taking."

Leslie Newbigin's view of capitalism as covetousness is one example of a Christian interpretation of capitalism. Bishop Richard Harries of Oxford offers a view far more sympathetic and nuanced one. His title asks, *Is there a Gospel for the Rich?* and his answer is his "conviction that God's liberation is for everyone. The rich need to be liberated no less than the poor. . . ."[25] Intelligently and with discrimination, the bishop discerns Christian potential in the social device of the free market, in private property, in innovation, in the business firm, in profit, and even in the transnational corporation. The bête noire and polemical foil for his book is the "New Right," to which he wishes to supply a sophisticated alternative. He describes Britain as a "post-socialist" society. His aim is to present a more humane and evangelical form of capitalism than any (he thinks) yet dreamed of on the "New Right." He is rather bigger on "affirmative government" than is the "New Right," for example.

In offering his argument on behalf of a market economy, Bishop Harries begins with a leader from *The Guardian* in 1981 which accepted the market as an inescapable fact of life and an important source of much-needed knowledge: "It is the market which acts as an essential signal from consumers to firms telling them how much to produce, when to produce it, and what sort of quality to make." Besides this information, "the profit of corporations (or cooperatives) is also the market's way of signaling success: it is an essential guide to, and source of, investment." In brief, Harris summarizes, to all except a very small percentage of the Labour Party, the free market is "essential, inescapable and, for all its flaws, to be valued."[26] This approval for markets, Harries notes, is "as robust as could come from any 'Thatcherite' economist." John Gray called such a defense of the market the epistemic argument for markets; he offers a brief and elegant statement of it in *The Moral Foundations of Market Institutions*.[27]

But Gray also offers another fundamental and at least partly original defense—the defense from autonomy. More than any other system, he argues, a market system enhances the individual's scope for and frequency of acts of choice. Gray does not see this argument as necessarily universal. It may mean less to East Asian societies, for example, whose social and psychological structure is more communitarian and less individualist than those of the West. Nor does he think an emphasis on choice to be an unmixed blessing. On this as on other things, individuals and societies can go too far. *What* is chosen can matter greatly. Nonetheless, the argument from autonomy is difficult for any Western intellectual to dismiss, since Westerners value choice highly. The best rejoinder from the Left is to suggest that too few people actually possess autonomy in sufficient degree, so that much social (and governmental) effort must be expended in "equalising people" through redistribution.[28]

To his credit, Gray resists redistributionist policies. These are in practice doomed to failure and in principle unjust. But he does argue that any society which favors autonomy must, because of that very commitment, empower all its citizens to reach some basic level thereof. Gray thinks that he has found a way to define this basic desired level through a concept of "satiable needs."[29] Yet since poverty is normally taken as a relative measure—by American standards, for example, more than a third of Western Europeans would be living in poverty[30]— I doubt that Gray's efforts in this direction are sustainable. The human spirit is in principle insatiable.

"If only I could have that," we have often told ourselves, "I would be satisfied," only to find that we never are. Autonomy is always like that. We can never get enough of it. Whatever of it we have always runs into limits, often quickly, and we wish that we had no such limits; we wish to be like God. Even kings and princes rail against their too-narrow autonomy. Such is the stuff of a great deal of the best English drama.

A fourth argument in defense of the market is based upon the growing immateriality of what people are actually willing to buy. Markets depend on people's choices. Kenneth Adams thinks that he has discerned an impending switch in consumers' preferences: "Suppose that our increasing demand is for entertainment, sport, music, theatre, literature and all other areas of human growth: in relationships, in intellectual and aesthetic delight—these will place much smaller demands on materials and energy. Furthermore, as desire grows in those wider, richer, higher areas of human need, it is likely that desire for increase in the material areas will stabilize or decline."[31] This preference switch is represented by the information age. That is to say, an increasing proportion of production today lies in its "spiritual" rather than its "material" components. Industries are becoming cleaner; through miniaturization, physical products are becoming smaller, more powerful, and (usually) cheaper. The full implications of the term "information age" have barely begun to be absorbed by and articulated in theological thought.

The fifth argument for the market—admittedly an odd one— is that the economic plenty produced by market societies has proved conclusively that "man does not live by bread alone." The traditional Jewish and Christian predictions about the discontents inherent in materialism have been confirmed. The textual evidence for this lies in university bookstores in the sections—usually larger than those for traditional philosophy and theology—devoted to astrology, witchcraft, and the occult. "When humans stop believing in God, Chesterton once wrote, "they don't believe in nothing; they believe anything." All around us we see signs of boredom, restlessness, and discontent.

None of these five arguments (except perhaps the first) is alien to pope John Paul II, who, as the hundredth anniversary of *Rerum Novarum* approached, was asked again and again by bishops from Sri Lanka to Sao Paulo to Kiev, "What direction do you now recommend to us, after the collapse of socialism?" The pope was certain to issue an encyclical commemorating Leo XIII's 1891 encyclical *Rerum Novarum;* moreover, after the events of 1989, he had to provide an answer. He recommended "the free economy, the market economy," the economy of creativity and enterprise. He was even willing, although reluctant, to use the word "capitalism," so long as the system intended by that word included a worthy juridical system protecting human rights and a moral-religious system imposing ethical limits.[32] Yet his arguments for this decision are rather different from the five preceding arguments.

Pope John Paul II's argument from creativity flows from his concept of "the acting person," worked out in his book by that title written before he became pope,[33] though at the time, he had not seen its relevance for economics. What makes humans distinctive among the other animals, he held, is their capacity to initiate new projects (especially life projects); that is, to imagine, to create, and to *act,* as distinct from merely behaving. Throughout his pontificate, the pope has focused on this "creative subjectivity" of the human person.[34] In this he saw the *imago Dei:* humans are made in the image of the Creator in such a way that to be creative is the essential human vocation. In this, too, he saw the endowment of a fundamental human right to personal economic initiative.

This argument, it will be noted, offers a different grounding for concepts such as "natural rights" from that offered by Hobbes, Locke, or other Enlightenment figures. The pope's argument is substantially philosophical, and could perhaps be supported by philosophical analysis like that offered by Gabriel Marcel in *The Mystery of Being* and *Creative Fidelity*.[35] The emphasis of certain phenomenologists and existentialists on human "becoming," on "creating oneself," and the like, are other indications of what might be done. This argument also has much to commend it from the viewpoint of commonsense. It is far harder to predict the future of one's children, for example, than that of the household cat. The latter does not have to think about choosing a career at all, let alone to choose among self-invented possibilities. The exact way in which the pope deploys the argument, of course, depends on the doctrine of creation and a long-standing Christian interpretive tradition associated with the Book of Genesis. Thus, the pope's argument is more properly theological than philosophical. Still, it is quite striking.

The pope sees that for much of Christian history the most important form of wealth was land, just as the term "capital" derived from counting the heads (*capita*) of sheep, oxen, cows, goats, horses, and other livestock that marked a farm's productivity, along with fruits, vegetables, and grains.[36] Wealth in land belonged chiefly to the nobility, although in some places smaller freeholds were also conspicuous, especially in Britain and for unusually long and uninterrupted family tenure.

At a later period, the pope notes, wealth (like the term *Das Kapital*) came to be associated with ownership of the means of production—with machinery, factories, and other impersonal aspects. Indeed, in his first social encyclical, Pope John Paul himself used "capital" only for impersonal objects, reserving his use of "labor" to refer to human persons as factors in production, whatever their economic role.[37] In *Sollicitudo Rei Socialis,* he had already seen clearly enough that even common ownership of the means of production, and certainly state ownership, could not guarantee the humanity of an economic system—neither its capacity to produce wealth nor its capacity to respect "the fundamental right to personal economic initiative.[38] *That* right, he saw then, was grounded in the *imago Dei* imprinted on man's soul.

In *Centesimus Annus,* the pope carries this line of thought further. The new, deeper, and more telling referent for the word "capital" is neither land nor the impersonal means of production but, rather, "the possession of know-how, technology and skill." The chief cause of the wealth of nations is human wit—discovery, invention, the habit of enterprise, foresight, skill in organization. "The wealth of the industrialized nations is based much more on this kind of ownership than on natural resources."[39] "Indeed, besides the earth, man's principal resource is *man himself*." And again, "today the decisive factor is increasingly *man himself,* that is, his knowledge, especially his scientific knowledge, his capacity for interrelated and compact organization, as well as his ability to perceive the needs of others and to satisfy them."[40]

It seems to me, after countless re-readings, that the pope might be thinking in these passages of Japan—that tiny land with hardly any natural resources that is almost totally dependent on overseas sources of energy. The cause of Japan's wealth cannot be an abundance of natural resources nor even proximity to its major markets. Instead, the Japanese have highly developed, and make exquisite use of, their human capital. Without even recognizing the Creator for whom Pope John Paul II speaks, the Japanese have shown remarkable capacities for creative action in world manufacturing markets. If John Paul II's theory about the *universal* human capacity for creativity is true, then this is as it should be. Creativity by any other name causes wealth, as natural resources alone do not.

But the very powerful communitarian and centripetal structure of Japanese society brings to light the other argument for markets made by Pope John Paul II: that where human creativity is at play, a new and highly interesting form of community is also at play. In the largest sense, the market of today is a world market; it interknits every part of the world within a single, complex web of contracts, transactions, and networks of supply and demand. Many of these transactions are instantaneous. World markets, for stocks and for commodities, and above all for information (the newest, most vital form of capital), are open for simultaneous viewing of television and computer screens linked to one another around the world in "real time."

Dostoevsky once described charity as an invisible filament linking the world in a network of impulses, along which a simple human smile or an aspiration of love could circle the globe in minutes to bring cheer to someone, even a stranger, faraway. A person who receives a smile, he noted, often feels impelled to pass it along by smiling to someone else in the next chance encounter, and so with the speed of light the smile circles the globe. The new television and computer images, like impulses bounced off cold and silent satellites in space to touch and vivify every part of earth, may only be metaphors for the nerves and tissues that have always tied together the Mystical Body spoken of by St. Paul, but such ligatures seem more visible now. Even in the fifth century A.D., a great Father of the Church, St. Gregory of Nyssa, observed that human trade, exchanging the wool of one place for the wine of another, the clay pots of one culture for the grain of another, is an image of the bonds uniting the one family of God. *Commercium et Pax* was once the motto of Amsterdam, whose scenes of commerce and shipping were painted often by Turner.

Even in the supposedly more individualistic West, the pope sees that the market is, above all, a social instrument. It has a centripetal force. It obliges sellers to find buyers (sometimes at great distances and across significant spans of time). It calls for sequences of action that involve many different hands coordinated by remarkable capacities for foresight and organization. Indeed, most economic activities in the modern environment are too complex to be executed by one person alone; nearly all of them require the creation of a new type of community, not organic but artifactual, not natural (as the family is natural) but contractual, not coercive (as was "real existing socialism") but free and voluntary, not total like a monastery but task-oriented and open to cooperators, even ones of different belief systems and ultimate commitments. In short, the distinctive invention of capitalist societies is the business firm, independent of the state.

About the business firm, the pope is surprisingly eloquent. There has been a tendency in Roman Catholic thought—the document of Vatican II on "The Church in the World," Oswald von Nell-Breuning, S.J., has pointed out, is one example[41]—to notice only four economic roles: the owner, the manager, the employer, and the employee. The creative source of the firm, the practitioner of the virtue of enterprise, is entirely neglected. Pope John Paul II does not fall into this trap. Here is what he writes in *Centesimus Annus:*

> It is [man's] disciplined work in close collaboration with others that makes possible the creation of ever more extensive *working communities* which can be relied upon to transform man's natural human environment. Important virtues are involved in this process, such as diligence, industriousness, prudence in undertaking reasonable risks, reliability and fidelity in interpersonal relationships, as well as courage in carrying out decisions which are difficult and painful but necessary, both for the overall working of a business and in meeting possible set-backs.[42]

Contemplating this modern economic process—this historically unique way of drawing upon the creative individual working within voluntary, cooperative community—the pope writes this quite stunning sentence: "This process, *which throws practical light on a truth about the human person which Christianity has constantly affirmed,* should be viewed carefully and favorably."[43] The modern business process—*business,* of all things!—"throws practical light on [Christian] truth." And then note: The pope urges theologians and other Christians to view this business process "carefully and favorably." The pope is only exercising here the classic Catholic habit of seeing in all things the signs of Providence at work, the hidden presence of that Logos "by whom and with whom and in whom were made all things that are made" (John 1:1–3). Sometimes referred to as the Catholic "sacramental sense" or "way of analogy," this mode of perception lies behind the tradition of blessing the fishing fleets, the fields to be sown, and the harvests. If humans are made in the image of God, then their actions (especially their creative actions) also reflect that image.

It is remarkable, of course, that something so scorned in the theological literature as the business firm and the modern corporation should be set before us by the Roman Pontiff to "be viewed carefully and favorably" for the "practical light" it sheds on Christian truth (I personally know writers who, if I had written that line, would have described it as excessive). Yet such praise fits quite comfortably within an old tradition, in whose light grace was seen to be working even in rather tyrannical and amoral kings; in the thief who died beside Jesus on the cross; and in every neighbor a man meets. To see grace at work is not to see only beauty and light, but real things as they are in this messy, fleshly, and imperfect world. For the Creator looked on this world and proclaimed it "good," and for its redemption he gave his only Son. A Roman Catholic is taught to see grace in flawed and all-too-human popes, in the poor of Calcutta, and (hardest of all sometimes) in himself.

In summary, the pope has advanced two new arguments in support of his proposal that market systems shed practical light on Christian truth and advance human welfare. The first is that markets give expression to the creative subjectivity of the human person, who has been created in the image of the Creator of all things, and called to help complete the work of creation through sustained historical effort. His second argument is that markets generate new and important kinds of community, while expressing the social nature of human beings in rich and complex ways.

There is another reason for proposing markets as a strategy for a Christian theology of liberation of the poor, a proposition for which the evidence of immigration patterns around the world offers prima facie support: market systems better allow the poor to rise out of poverty than any other known social system. Economic opportunity

on this planet is as scarce as oil. Immigrants stream toward it by
the millions.

Great Britain, Canada, Germany, Italy—most of the market systems on this planet receive steady streams of immigrants. The United
States alone between 1970 and 1990 accepted some 16 million *legal*
immigrants (nobody knows in addition the number of illegal ones).
This is as if we had accepted during that time a new population four
times larger than Switzerland's.

Most of these new citizens arrived in America poor. America is
quite good at helping immigrants find opportunities, provided only
that they are willing to seize them, as the vast majority are. Most of
those new citizens were also non-white. Indeed, in America's largest
state, California, English is now the *second* language of a plurality of
households. This is why Americans rank "opportunity" quite high in
evaluating economic systems. Bishop Harries does not quite get this
point; he dismisses "the American dream," which is in fact more
universal than he allows, in peremptory fashion: "It is not an ignoble
[dream] but it is certainly limited. By its nature some fail to make it
and are left behind, and when their numbers run into many million
questions must be asked."[44] Questions must always be asked, yes,
but it is good to have some perspective. Although virtually 100 percent of Americans arrived in America poor, today 87 percent are not
poor. Only about 8 million of America's 30 million officially desig-
nated "poor" persons are able-bodied persons between the ages of
18 and 64; the rest are either 65 or older, 17 or younger, or sick or
disabled. For the 8 million able-bodied, the work of the "opportunity society" is not yet complete.

America is also good at helping most of the American-born poor—
the elderly, those under 18, the sick or disabled—for whom economic
opportunity is not a saving option. Where private family-care is not
available to them, where the many programs of civil society let them
down, government medical aid, food stamps, housing assistance, and
other programs have been supplied to fill the gap.

But for younger adults in good health, the "war on poverty" has actually done much damage.[45] Our government programs have failed our young. The fastest growing group among the poor has been single female householders with young children. This was not a relatively large group before, when people were far poorer than at present, and when current government programs barely existed. Never before have so many males deserted females, with little or no sense of paternal responsibility. The results have been deplorable for children, young mothers, and the young males themselves.

Thus, the great moral and social problem facing the United States today is to devise new ways to help this group of able-bodied poor adults, mostly young, in ways that do not reduce them to a kind of serfdom or further depress their morals. Concerning various ways to correct recent practices, I have elsewhere written (with a team of others) at much greater length.[46]

Here one should stress, rather, the crucial importance of dynamic market systems for raising up the poor of Central and Eastern Europe, Latin America, and throughout the "Third World" (which is actually several quite different worlds). For what these poor have in common is not only a lack of opportunity but a sustained, systematic repression of their right to personal economic initiative. Most of them find in their homelands no institutions that might nourish and support that right: constitutionally protected private property, open markets, cheap and easy legal incorporation of businesses, access to legal and low-cost credit, technical assistance, training, and the like. To gain access to such institutions, many millions must seek freedom of opportunity far from home.

The fact that market systems open opportunity for the poor is one of the most important arguments in their favor. This means, of course, the type of market economy that is not protective of the rich but gives the able-bodied poor many opportunities. Such markets, regularly revolutionized by new inventions and new technologies, bring down many of the formerly rich (as old technologies and ossified firms become obsolete). But their greatest strength lies in the openness and dynamism of the small-business sector, through which so many millions rise out of poverty.

Open markets liberate the poor better than any known alternative. Open markets favor creativity and dynamism. They also narrow the perceived distance between personal action and personal fate. To narrow the gap is to strengthen human dignity. Nonetheless, like all things human, market systems are not without their ambiguities.

One of my favorite writers on social ethics is Ronald Preston of Scotland, a follower of the great American theologian of the last generation, Reinhold Niebuhr. While fussing about its residual problems, Preston concedes much of the historical argument to capitalism, including its stress on the importance of innovation, incentives, private ownership, flexibility (rather than central planning) with respect to the future, and the many utilities of markets. Preston writes rather more complacently: "I propose to argue that the issue is not between the free market and the central, planned economy, but how we can get the best of what the social market and democratic socialist models propose."[47]

Now, this proposal is remarkable in two ways. First, it turns out that Preston's discussion of the social market model and the democratic socialist model stresses the virtues of markets to a surprising degree. Second, Preston's own ideological commitments prevent him from even considering what many take to be a more humane, dynamic, progressive, and Christian alternative to social market and democratic socialist economies—the democratic capitalist model. He simply leaves it out of account.

More admirably, Preston qualifies his own "social Christianity" by taking on board some of the insights offered by writers to his right, such as Friedrich von Hayek and James Buchanan. Moreover, although he seems not to recognize it, many of the arguments that he makes concerning the "ambiguity" of markets are also consistent with the philosophy of democratic capitalism. There are, for example, some things that should never be bought or sold; in some domains, markets are illegitimate; neither democracy nor the market is a device suited for all purposes. On such matters, Preston and I are in agreement.

Yet there is one point on which Preston seems clearly to be incorrect, at least by omission: this is his treatment of inequalities of income. First, he praises markets for what they do well: "[O]ther things being equal, markets are a highly efficient way of getting economic decisions made in accordance with the freedom of choice expressed by consumers: that is, by dispersed exercise of political and economic power. They are incentive to thrift and innovation, so tending to maximize the productivity of relatively scarce economic resources." But then Preston adds a sentiment in need of vigorous challenge: "On the other hand, left to themselves market economics produce cumulative inequalities of income which distort the market by drawing the relatively scarce resources to what the wealthy want and away from the necessities of the poor."[48]

The assumption here seems to be that non-capitalist systems produce less income inequality. But this is clearly not true of the precapitalist Third World regimes of present-day Latin America, Africa, and Asia, in which inequalities of income are of enormous proportions, while for the poor opportunity scarcely exists. Nor was it true of communist societies, whose poor are now known to have lived in squalor and whose elites lived in closed circles of high privilege.

Furthermore, Preston omits another salient contrast. Neither precapitalist societies nor socialist societies have done much to lift large majorities of their populations out of poverty, as democratic capitalist nations have done. The degree of upward mobility in capitalist societies has no precedent in history, and the array of opportunities that capitalist societies offer to the poor for advancement by way of talent and effort has had no equal. Moreover, it does not seem to be true that market economies produce "cumulative" inequalities of income, or that they draw "relatively scarce resources" away from "the necessities of the poor."

To begin with the last assertion, the condition of the poor today is far improved over what it was, say, in 1892 (or 1932), so that the very word "necessities" now entails far higher standards than in centuries past—often we are not talking about mere survival or subsistence. The phrase "relatively scarce resources" is similarly problematic.

Moreover, Preston's accusation of "cumulative" inequalities of income seems doubly dubious. For one thing, during the life cycle of individuals, incomes tend to rise and then fall; for another, there is immense churning among individuals moving up and down within income brackets from one decade to another. Fortunes are often quickly dissipated. Technologies on which a fortune may be based become speedily obsolete; heirs are seldom as talented or as highly motivated as the creators of the family fortune. Downward mobility is frequent. Elites circulate with rapidity. Preston seems to take the unilateral cumulative growth of wealth as a given; but the staggering fragility and the changeability of fortunes would seem far more prevalent.

Possibly, this difference in perception is due to the unique fluidity of American social structure, as contrasted with that of Europe. To a remarkable degree, European societies still consist within aristocratic, feudal institutions; the United States is far more committed to universal opportunity and, in that respect, is a more "purely capitalist" society. Quite often in Europe today, dominant firms are run by the descendants of old aristocratic families.[49] There really is a perception that wealth and power are stable and cumulative. In America, by contrast, the great families of the 1700s have nearly all died out or lost their prominence. With few exceptions, such as the Rockefellers, the same is true of the great families of the 1800s. Many of the great fortunes of today have been acquired by the living; a significant number, especially among the nouveaux riches of film and entertainment, have also been lost by the living. Great inequalities there may well be, but these are remarkably ephemeral. They are also lacking in moral seriousness: it is not position that counts but quality of performance.

Besides, the good Lord himself forbade covetousness five times in the Ten Commandments: envy is to be resisted. Equality of income is an ideal appropriate only to the unfree and the uniform. What matters far more than inequality is universal opportunity. As an ideal, universal opportunity is far better suited to creatures made in the image of God who by God's providence are set in dissimilar circumstances. On this fundamental moral issue, Preston should face more squarely the ambiguities of socialism. He might in that confrontation begin to detect its moral and anthropological errors.

Democracy, capitalism, and pluralism (the three social systems whose combination constitutes democratic capitalism) are, each of them, ambiguous—all things human are. The relevant social question is not, "Is this utopia?" but rather, "Compared to what?" In comparing which system is more likely to bring about universal opportunity, prosperity from the bottom up, the *embourgeoisement* of the proletariat, and the raising up of the poor, the historical answer is clear: for the poor, market systems provide far better chances of improving income, conditions, and status. That is one reason so many of the world's poor migrate toward democratic and capitalist systems.

In a word, market systems combined with democratic political systems offer better hope to the poor of the world than do socialist or traditionalist systems. Despite their inevitable ambiguities, that is one of their strongest claims to moral recognition—a recognition now clearly accorded by Catholic social teaching.

4

Catholic Social Teaching and the Global Market

D. Stephen Long

Must the Church decide which global economic system it should support? Does it have a stake in the question, shall we be socialists or capitalists? To continue to ask these questions at the beginning of the twenty-first century can only appear antiquated, for despite the attention theologians gave to these questions in the nineteenth and twentieth centuries, they now appear settled. Whether we lament or celebrate events that transpired since 1989, Michael Novak seems descriptively accurate when he tells us, "We are all capitalists now, even the pope. Both traditionalist and socialist methods have failed; for the whole world there is now only one form of economics."[1] Some celebrate this as the "end of history" and the "triumph of the VCR," while others lament it as the "end of modernity," which does not designate a completed state, but a state that can never be completed, only endlessly repeated. The "new and improved" becomes our fate, for the critical frame of mind capitalism requires sets itself against all things traditional, even those that were transmitted only a short time ago.[2] Everything must be new; everything must be freed. Whether someone celebrates the triumph of capitalism as the end of history or laments it as the endless end of modernity, the questions with which this essay began can only appear—at this moment in history—as anachronistic. The question is already answered. "We are all capitalists now," if not in theory then at least in practice.

And yet the fact that many contemporary theologians continue to proclaim capitalism's triumph betrays theologians' lingering preoccupation with this question, a preoccupation that is dangerous for two related reasons. First, to announce the triumph of a specific global economic system tacitly assumes and affirms the competence of theologians to make determinations about which global system of exchange should rule over us. But this is both a competence and a form of rule that theologians cannot possess as theologians. Such a claim requires theologians to present themselves as expert social scientists or at least to subordinate theological dogma to the expertise of the social sciences in order to occupy a space where this question can be asked and answered. Second, by seeking to make theology relevant by occupying this space, theologians contribute to their own irrelevance and to the increasing marginalization of theology, particularly dogma. For theology's irrelevance is part and parcel of the end of history and the end of modernity. At either end, theology does not matter. No legitimation for any global economic system is needed from the church, its theologians, or its philosophers. As Jean-François Lyotard has persuasively argued, the state of modern knowledge, with its technological preoccupation and its rigid focus on efficiency, does not need any legitimating discourse; it is self-legitimating solely on the pragmatic grounds that "it works." Both philosophy and theology become at best like works of art in a museum to be gazed at by intellectual connoisseurs. In such a time as this the question, "Which global economic system should the Church, its theologians, and its philosophers support?" would be like asking, How can we reconstruct the medieval guild system? The question makes no sense; answering it can have no meaning. Yet seriously asking the question and providing an answer can only increase theology's irrelevance, for it assumes that what is "real," the standard of measurement against which theology is to be assessed, is a global economic system that is self-legitimating.

In fact, the present historical moment presents an opportunity for theology to recover its specific task. No longer must theologians be obsessed with modernist accommodations, asking ourselves how we can make theology relevant to those disciplines—in particular the social sciences—that seek to present and sell themselves as offering the expertise necessary to navigate the pragmatic corridors of meaning that rule the present age. Theology, especially moral theology, has for too long been a pale imitation of social science. By recognizing that these disciplines need no legitimation—philosophically or theologically—theologians become free to do what theology does—speak well about God. We are freed at the end of modernity to pursue the dogmatic task that is theology.

Theology cannot be theology without this dogmatic task being its center. That task is to explain in each generation how irreversible decisions by those who came before us give us the language that allows us to speak well of God. Theology's sole task is to show how dogmas—which are rooted in Scripture, elucidated in conciliar decisions, and further clarified by the faithful, pastors, and theologians—train us in speaking about God such that God's name—and thus how we are to live—will not be forgotten. For theologians to begin by claiming competence in those disciplines that claim responsibility for global economic systems is already to begin at the wrong point. We must begin with God; that is what makes us "theologians." And all knowledge of God comes as a gift mediated to us from the witnesses who preceded us. If we are to be theologians, then, our first task is the dogmatic task. But related to that dogmatic task is the doctrinal task of envisioning the world, including the world of economic exchange, in terms of the Church's teachings. In this essay I will claim the only competence I know—that of being a theologian. I will perform the theologian's task by telling a tale of two corporations and then discerning how theologians can respond to them by the dogmas and teachings they use or fail to use. I hope this approach will ask the proper theological question, How are we to be faithful in these times, which we must discern by the gift of dogma and doctrine handed down to us?

A tale of two corporations

To read economics theologically is within the proper competence of the theologian. To read theology through the lens of an economist is not. To do the first limits the kinds of questions that can be meaningfully asked, but it does not limit the kinds of activities to which theology must be mediated. As Scripture and tradition unmistakably demonstrate, nothing is more theological than everyday economic exchanges. They must be read theologically. Before pursuing the dogmatic task, which is to assess critically the dogma and doctrines theologians use to help us read economic exchanges theologically, some concrete examples of economic exchanges within modern corporations will be presented. I will begin by narrating the story of two corporations. The first corporation is so unjust that it is a rather easy case—none of the theologians who I use below to assess the dogmatic task would defend the obviously corrupt practices of such a corporation. I only present it to ask if theologians have given us adequate tools to understand it. The second corporation is a much more difficult case. It is not obviously exploitative and in fact does tremendous good in the local community in which its plant has been located since the corporation's inception.

By narrating the story of these two corporations I hope to help think through the differences theology might make for understanding economic exchanges. These descriptions are not intended to be social-scientific analyses; they are at best biographical narrations that I hope readers will find persuasive as reasonable accounts of economic exchange in the modern corporation. The first corporation is an arm of a multinational corporation that prepares shrimp and lobster from the waters off the coast of Honduras for fast-food consumption in the United States. The second is a local, family-owned corporation that makes water meters that are sold internationally, although the production of those water meters is confined to one small city in the Midwest.

I first came across the lobster and shrimp plant while working as a local preacher with the Caribbean Council of the Methodist Churches in the 1980s. I had no interest in economics at the time; I was intent on being a preacher and theologian. The church I attended was on a little island across from the plant. The women who worked in the plant processing lobster and shrimp were primarily Guarifuna—an African people brought to Latin America during the Middle Passage who had rebelled against their slave owners, established a village off the north coast of Honduras, and maintained their traditional African customs for five hundred years. The Guarifuna lived in a village several miles from the plant. The men would do the lobstering; they were often at sea for weeks and months at a time. The women would process the lobster and shrimp. They were paid seventy-five cents per hour for their work, and they worked as long as work was available—anywhere from six to twelve hours a day once the lobster and shrimp arrived. There were no unions, no labor contracts, no health care, and no enforceable laws pertaining to working conditions. The transportation of the lobster and shrimp to the (primarily American) market was a lucrative business for the few Hondurans who owned the processing plant and the shipping vessels. The disparity in living conditions between these ship owners and the workers was obvious. No social science was necessary to see it. All one had to do was open one's eyes, walk through the two villages in which the Guarifuna and the owners lived, and compare them. The Guarifuna village had no running water, no electricity, no paved roads, and most homes were mud constructions with thatched roofs. The owners of the plant and ships had running water and electricity, and their homes were modern constructions capable of withstanding the gale-force winds that often hit the island. Many of them also had second homes in the United States.

The wages paid to the men who secured the lobster and shrimp (often by diving without gear to dangerous ocean depths) and the women who processed them were insufficient to purchase the product they themselves produced. At seventy-five cents per hour, assuming a fifty-hour work week, the weekly pay would be $37.50. A five-pound box of lobster would be sold for nearly half that amount. In other words, the very men and women that risked securing and processing this food, the men and women whose hands were the conditions for making lobster and shrimp available as consumable food items for others, were then excluded from consuming the produce they made available.

This was (and is) clearly an unjust situation. No theologian (I hope) would intentionally defend these kinds of exploitative practices; for, insofar as God and Scripture still matter, these practices cannot be justified. Every theologian who is not simply an ideologue must recognize that such unjust practices occur and object to them because they are sinful and God is against sin. But have theologians given us the language to explain why these practices are objectionable? What difference does their theology make? How do dogmas and doctrines help us name these practices? This is the dogmatic task appropriate to theologians.

Before pursuing more fully that dogmatic task I need to accomplish two things. First I want to avoid any suggestion that I have offered a neutral social analysis of "reality." Second, I will present a more positive modern corporation—a water meter plant—so that I do not gain an unfair rhetorical advantage by taking this lobster and shrimp plant as the typical form of capitalist exchange. Both of these corporations function within the present global economic system. Which of them fits most easily within that system, and which is an aberration, remains an open question.

My description of the shrimp and lobster corporation as "corrupt" is not based on the secure deliverances of some "abstract" universal reason, be it a "natural" law or an objective analysis of "social" reality qua "social" disembodied from a particular tradition. It is grounded in a confessional claim about who God is. That is what makes it theological. This confessional claim is also unavoidable. Moral theologians' efforts to avoid such confessions lead to ironic claims about what they are doing, claims that neglect the conditions that make their work possible. My own conclusion will be that the true social descriptions I have given depend upon Christology, ecclesiology, and the doctrine of the Trinity. Moral theologians on both the political Left and Right object to this dogmatic approach, apparently because it hampers their ability to speak publicly. Thus "natural law," the doctrine of creation, an "incarnational" (as opposed to the Incarnation) or a "sacramental" (as opposed to the sacraments) approach seems to be the order of the day. But why Christology and ecclesiology are too confessional, but something like creation is not, mystifies me. For to speak of "creation" is already to make a confession standing within a particular tradition, and if that tradition is Christian, then one cannot speak of creation without its Christological and Trinitarian resonances.

The example of the shrimp and lobster plant is much too easy. For those of us who stand within the Christian tradition, it is obviously wicked. Using it as the only example of economic exchange would be uncharitable, for not every form of economic exchange in the modern corporation functions in this way. *Abusus non tollit usum*. A much less wicked tale of a corporation concerns a water meter factory that, like many such corporations, plays an integral function within the life of a small Midwestern town. This corporation is not publicly traded; the stock is held by one family—all of whose members live in the community where the plant operates. It is a non-union plant, yet many decisions are made collectively. Profits are shared based on annual productivity and, in an economic downturn, the workers and owners together decide if a reduction in wages or layoffs are necessary. The family who owns the plant is well known for its frugality as well as its members' contribution to the common good of the local community. The family lives in and among the persons who work for the plant. It has used the profits it has accrued from owning the plant to establish a number of endowments that support local young people in their college education or in their pursuit of the arts. Local workers have long sought the coveted jobs at the factory precisely because the family can be trusted. Key to this trust is the family's commitment to their local church, which is reflected in how they operate the plant.

This is not to say that this corporation is beyond reproach. The family gives large sums to charities, yet a worker once questioned whose money it was that was so prodigally distributed. It seems inconceivable for this factory to move from its location in the small Midwestern town where it is located, but it remains a possibility in that the excellent relationship between workers and owners depends on the family's commitments to church and place. Ownership is transferred biologically. What happens if the next generation does not share these commitments? What happens if the moral and legal imperative to maximize profits becomes more decisive than the family's traditional commitments? Given the legal and moral nature of the modern corporation, is it inevitable that in order to survive this corporation will eventually be forced to forgo these commitments if it is to compete?[3]

Which of these two corporations is more normative in the current context within which modern corporations operate? If the primary task of the corporation is to maximize profits within the legal protections afforded by limited liability, then surely it is the lobster/shrimp plant. If the primary task of the corporation is to be understood in theological terms, then perhaps it is the water meter plant.

How should we assess corporations theologically? The descriptions I have offered are, and should be, contested. No single satisfying explanation of the reality of the exchanges that take place in these corporations is possible. Thus I think it unreasonable to assume that a "rational analysis of social reality" qua reason alone will be able to adjudicate the contending descriptions. But neither do I think we must finally resolve the issue politically, where politics is understood primarily in terms of power. As theologians we must be ruled by our inheritance, by how we have learned to speak well of God. Truth must be more basic to our work than the will to power. We must have the kind of conversation within our competence as theologians and people of faith that could, in fact, provide a reasonable basis on which to answer the question of what our theological tradition has to say about these two corporations and the kinds of practices they embody. Which dogmas matter, and why?

The dogmatic task

Every theologian should recognize that participation in the modern corporation is not a priori evil; it can be a faithful form of discipleship. In fact, economic exchanges are necessary for everyday life; we must have them and corporations make them possible. The dogmatic question is what constitutes faithful participation in these forms of exchange. Some theologians find the modern corporation central not only to everyday exchange but also to God's economy itself. Michael Novak finds the modern corporation to be an "incarnation" of God's presence, and an institution that has something like a sacramental mission. Dennis McCann and Max Stackhouse speak of it as a "worldly ecclesia." Gustavo Gutiérrez, like most liberation theologians, does not attribute this kind of incarnational presence to the modern corporation, but like Novak, McCann, and Stackhouse he finds God working in an autonomous political realm without ecclesial mediation. Gutiérrez finds "the frontiers between the life of faith and temporal works, between Church and world," to be "fluid" such that participation in a more secular process of liberation would be participation in "a salvific work."[4] The corporation is neither an incarnation nor a worldly ecclesia for Gutiérrez, but the "process of liberation" is. If corporations participated in that process, then they would have the status afforded them by Novak, McCann, and Stackhouse. John Milbank and Alasdair MacInytre offer a different theological (and philosophical) approach to thinking about the corporation. They do not accept the secularization thesis implicitly and explicitly present in the above theologians. Instead, they narrate the history within which the modern corporation has emerged and suggest that this history is itself already a theological distortion, even a heretical inheritance. Thus the modern corporation is a danger to faith that needs the guidance of the Church's teaching office (at least for MacIntyre) if we are not to lose our souls to it.

The heretical status of capitalist exchanges

Gustavo Gutiérrez associates the process of liberation with socialism. "Faith and political action will not enter into a correct and fruitful relationship except through the effort to create a new type of person in a different society." That "different society," he states, must be socialist. Only a socialist society would allow for the flourishing of the human person consistent with Christian principles. Yet he does not reach this conclusion (one with which John Milbank agrees) through the dogmatic task of the theologian. For Gutiérrez this "different society" is not primarily an ecclesial work. It is to be accomplished, rather, by "respecting the autonomy of the political arena," and thus Gutiérrez's affirmation of socialism is not primarily theological, but arises out of an "effective . . . rational analysis of reality."[5] It does not finally grant sufficient place for what theologians do; instead it allows for an autonomous political realm known primarily through the mediation of the social sciences. The socialist vision is not dependent on Church teaching. In fact, Gutiérrez finds liberation theology preferable to much that is in Catholic social thought because liberation theology takes more seriously the kind of careful social analysis that does not shy away from speaking of the class conflict endemic to capitalism, a conflict that is a "social fact."[6]

John Milbank agrees with Gutiérrez that Christian faith requires socialist forms of economic exchange and the abolition of capitalism. However, he refutes Gutiérrez's claim that this conclusion can be reached by way of a "rational analysis of reality," for no such analysis exists. No "social fact" exists because the social is not subject to explanation but only narration. There is no neutral and universal explanatory mechanism grounded in laws governing natural causality within social systems. Every account of the social is always historically mediated. Milbank finds that the very universal and neutral reading of social reality found in the social sciences already has within it heretical dogmatic commitments.

> If theology accepts modern liberal economics at their own evaluation, then it has, in reality, already made decisions within theology itself, and has endorsed a whole series of buried infinities between the modern scientific approach to politics and economics and the fideist-nominalist-voluntarist current in theology which is inherited, through seventeenth-century writers like Hobbes and Grotius, from the late Middle Ages. The shortest route to unraveling the problem of theology and economics is to become aware of this history. It is within voluntarist theology that the key philosophy of "possessive individualism" has is origins. Jus (right) is first thought of as dominium or as power over property within a perspective which understood God's creative activity and relation to the world in terms of an arbitrary exercise of power.[7]

The abolition of capitalism has a quasi-dogmatic status in Milbank's work only because its emergence had such a status. To be for capitalism is already to side with certain "heretical" theological options against the orthodox, dogmatic tradition.

For Milbank, the Christian opposition to capitalism arises solely for theological reasons. The gift God exchanges with creation through Christ must be the basis of all exchanges. Christianity opposes capitalism because the gift can never be reduced to a contract with nicely calculated profit/loss ratios where individuals enter into exchanges without being fundamentally changed by those exchanges. The Christian life requires a gift economy in which a return is always expected—as it should be when one gives gifts—but never one that can be calculated such that the contract terminates and the relationship dissolves. Instead of freeing us from each other (as is the case with contracts in capitalist exchanges, in which everyone's fate—including that of the corporation—is to be a free autonomous individual), our exchanges should take us ever more deeply into a "mutual but asymmetrical reciprocity." For this reason, Milbank states, "we must have a socialist market. We must strive still to abolish capitalism, albeit this must now be undertaken on a global scale and must often work within businesses, seeking to turn them into primarily socially responsible and not profit seeking organizations."[8] To say we must work within businesses recognizes their legitimacy. But how do we transform them from within? Milbank invites Christians to see their work, exchanges, and ownership within the context of what it means to be Church. The corporation does not replace the Church as a form of the body of Christ; instead it gains its intelligibility within the life of the Church, especially the Church's liturgical performance.

According to Milbank, capitalism not only emerges out of a reaction against the orthodox, dogmatic tradition; it is sustained by a "Weberian resigned acceptance of the fatalities of power."[9] Milbank critiques liberation theologians for thinking they have moved beyond Catholic social teaching through their analysis of social realities via the social sciences. In reality, he argues, liberation theologians perpetuate belief in a kind of "economic providence" as a "purely immanent process" much like Adam Smith's stoic doctrine of unintended consequences. In such a providential reading of social realities, liberation need not be mediated via a particular set of historical events; it can be found already immanent in the social forces working in history without ecclesial mediation. Milbank critiques Catholic social teaching as being too indebted to a "modern natural law framework," but liberation theology does not escape that framework either. In Milbank's account, the social sciences represent a modern version of the idea of a natural law known solely on the basis of a doctrine of pure nature.

The Catholic philosopher Alasdair MacIntyre also argues that Christianity requires capitalism's abolition, but not on the same theological grounds as Milbank. MacIntyre finds grounds in Catholic social teaching for a moral philosophy, rooted in biblical teaching, that refuses "coercive imposition by an external authority."[10] Power and manipulation do not trump truth and goodness. Catholic social teaching (at least as articulated in *Veritatis Splendor*) turns human nature toward the good through a grace that always corrects, completes, and perfects that nature. Such turning toward the good requires "exceptionless negative precepts of the natural law." Without such rules, human nature cannot be turned toward the fullness of goodness; in fact, the "erosion of such rules . . . surrenders human relationship to competing interests and political interests."[11] Modern philosophical notions that reject such teaching have produced "distorted conceptions of freedom" and have turned all "practical situations" into "cost/benefit analyses." Errors in moral teaching—the rejection of rules, a distorted notion of freedom, and the reduction of all relationships to manipulative exchanges of power—produce deformities in political and economic life.

Law directs human action to virtuous ends. Without virtuous ends, law becomes arbitrary and manipulative. MacIntyre finds capitalism to be a consequence of the loss of ends. Thus, because of the logic of the theological virtues, he calls Christians to work for capitalism's abolition. Reflecting in 1995 on his 1953 publication, *Marxism and Christianity,* he states:

> What, on a Christian understanding of human and social relationships, does God require of us in those relationships? That we love our neighbours and that we recognize that charity towards them goes beyond, but always includes justice. An adequate regard for justice always involves not only a concern that justice be done and injustice prevented or remedied on any particular occasion, but also resistance to and, where possible, the abolition of institutions that systematically generate injustice.[12]

One such institution MacIntyre identifies is "the systematic injustices generated by nascent and developed commercial and industrial capitalism."[13] These injustices are both individual and systemic: individual, because capitalism rewards not virtue but vice, allowing vicious persons to benefit at the expense of virtue itself; systemic, because at the origin of all accumulation in capitalism are "gross inequalities in the initial appropriation of capital." Capitalism also pits workers against owners, and it refuses to acknowledge legitimate moral teachings on just wages and just prices.[14]

In sum, Gutiérrez's opposition to capitalism rests on a social-scientific analysis of reality. Milbank anathematizes capitalist exchanges because of the heretical positions that gave rise to them and that they perpetuate. MacIntyre opposes capitalism because of its historical performance when measured against the norms of faithful practice. Drawing upon orthodox Christian teaching and practice and, in the case of MacIntyre at least, Catholic social teaching, two influential theologians and one philosopher find capitalism to be sinful at best, heretical at worst. This does not illegitimate the necessary exchanges of the modern corporation, but it means that workers and owners must recognize the heretical assumptions present in these forms of exchange and look for ways, through the Church's teaching, to achieve their true end. But the story does not end here. Other theologians and philosophers, drawing upon the same teachings and tradition, have come to a starkly different conclusion about capitalism.

The sinfulness of the socialist vision

Some theologians who themselves formerly adhered to a socialist vision now urge theologians to recognize their error in advocating this vision. They now put forth the modern corporation as a quasi-salvific institution. Two such theologians are Max Stackhouse and Dennis McCann, who state, "The Protestant Social Gospel, early Christian realism, much neo-orthodoxy, many forms of Catholic modernism, the modern ecumenical drive for racial and social inclusiveness, and contemporary liberation theories all held that democracy, human rights and socialism were the marks of the coming kingdom. For all their prophetic witness in many areas, they were wrong about socialism. The future will not bring what contemporary theology said it would and should."[15] Stackhouse and McCann not only suggest that theologians' commitment to a socialist vision was based on erroneous social analyses; they also charge that commitment with being downright sinful. They write, "The failure of the socialist vision . . . demands repentance." Why? It falsely portrayed capitalism as "greedy, individualistic, exploitative and failing" and socialism as "generous, community-affirming, equitable and coming." Beginning with this false characterization, theologians naïvely taught that the inevitable transition from the former to the latter was what God was "doing in the world." They were wrong.

Inasmuch as Stackhouse and McCann recognize the false immanent economic providence that Protestant and Catholic liberation theology adopted, they are surely correct to call us to repentance. But why should this settle the issue of socialism or capitalism? Have they really challenged the false idea of economic providence embodied in liberation theology, or do they perhaps themselves still cling to a version of that same false doctrine, such that with the collapse of the Soviet Union they think it now possible to make a definitive declaration about the matter—to issue a "post-communist manifesto"? Why, precisely, are they convinced that Christians must repent for their previous socialist vision and turn toward a reformed capitalism?

McCann and Stackhouse's central argument seems to be that socialism's historical performance has inevitably led to "class consciousness," "revolutionary cadres," and "bureaucratized control mechanisms," whereas capitalism has historically been grounded in the "context-transcending principles of truth, justice and love," which "protect the moral and spiritual rights of persons and groups and dis-

close purposes for living that are not of this world."[16] Theology "shapes
social destiny" by offering a vision that protects the individual and
the universal, the "personal" and the "cosmopolitan," the "material"
and the "spiritual." Christian theology contributes to economic life a
"universal" or "cosmopolitan social ethics" in which voluntary associations can form the basis for social exchanges based on these "context-transcending principles."

McCann and Stackhouse do not defend a "libertarian
neoconservative" capitalism. Instead they call for a "reformed capitalism," one that concedes the propriety of the "profit motive" while
calling for restraint. "Creating wealth is the whole point of economic
activity," they argue, but the profit motive must be pursued only
through "honorable means."[17] Thus, even these defenders of capitalism recognize it cannot stand as is; it needs reform. McCann and
Stackhouse do not draw extensively on Catholic social teaching to
make their case against socialism or for a reformed capitalism. However, they could do so, in so far as it is true that Catholic social
teaching embodies precisely what Milbank critiques: a form of natural law teaching that does not interject any confessional particularity into a cosmopolitan social ethic.

Michael Novak has defended capitalism against its theological
detractors (particularly on the Catholic Left) since 1979, when he
gave a lecture at the University of Notre Dame on the work of the
laity in the world. Like McCann and Stackhouse, Novak's turn toward
democratic capitalism entailed a turn away from his former socialist
vision. He "welcomed the attempts of the Catholic church to 'modernize' itself," realizing that his former socialism was "formed by a
large component of nostalgia for the medieval village."[18] Novak does
not seem to embrace capitalism as uniquely suitable for Christian or
Catholic societies. Many different ethics and cultures can feed it and
are compatible with it. Nevertheless, Novak does argue that Christianity created capitalism. Here he agrees with Milbank, but unlike
Milbank, he does not see capitalism as the result of distortions in

Christian teaching—of heresy. For Novak, capitalism emerges from Christianity because of the latter's rationalization of economic life. Christianity provided the necessary conditions for capitalism because it was congenial to ideas such as "the rule of law and a bureaucracy for resolving disputes rationally; a specialized and mobile labor force; the institutional permanence that allows for transgenerational investment and sustained intellectual and physical efforts, together with the accumulation of long-term capital; and a zest for discovery, enterprise, wealth creation and new undertakings."[19] Novak's defense of capitalism seeks to both draw on and correct Weber's thesis that the rationalization of economic life developed in Protestant cities through the Protestant notion of vocation.[20] Novak locates the origin of capitalism in the Catholic monasteries and rural areas of the Middle Ages. Thus, Novak's argument is much more sociological than theological. Unlike Milbank, he does not first position these developments within a heretical or orthodox reading of the Christian tradition. They are presented, rather, as social facts that are then given theological evaluation. For Novak, the Church's role in the creation of capitalism can primarily be defined in sociological terms. What is significant is the administration of the Church's holdings through certain bureaucratic structures administered by an entrepreneurial, celibate priesthood, which for Novak was the first "highly motivated, literate, specialized and mobile labor force."

Novak diverges from other sociological accounts in that he offers theological reasons for why these purely sociological developments were not aberrations from, but rather faithful developments of, Christian doctrine: "Just as Jacques Maritain had recognized in American political institutions the yeast of the Gospels working in history, so also Max Weber had dimly seen that the original impulses of capitalism spring from Christianity, too."[21] What Weber saw "dimly" was the relationship between Christianity and capitalism; what he failed to see was how this relationship could not be accounted for in sociological terms alone. Theological terms are also necessary, because, according to Novak, capitalism has an "incarnational" dimension. Novak sets his incarnational theology against an eschatological one. The latter is represented by persons like Dorothy Day and positions itself against the world, whereas the former understands the goodness of the created order.[22]

What does it mean to have an "incarnational" view of political economy? As Novak explains it,

> it is important that there be Christians who go out into this city (the earthly city), whatever its stage of moral and religious development, and try to incarnate the Gospels in it as Jesus incarnated God in history. . . . In my earlier years, I thought the best model for this reconstruction lay in a blend of democracy with some form of socialism. Later, I came to believe that socialism in any of its forms would be futile and destructive. I saw greater hope in a more realistic effort to reform and reconstruct society through the unique combination of capitalism and democracy that we have been lucky enough to inherit in America. But my point is that my own strategic vision, which is incarnational rather than eschatological, has been constant throughout my life.[23]

The incarnational notion of the corporation can perhaps best be seen in Novak's essay "Toward a Theology of the Corporation." Here he notes that "when we speak of the body of Christ, we ordinarily mean the church," but the term "incarnation" can also be properly applied to "the modern business corporation." Exactly what he means here is difficult to assess. I am sure this likeness is intended metaphorically, similar to the way ecofeminists refer to the earth as "God's body"; both Novak and the ecofeminists draw on a conception of "incarnational" theology that expands the incarnation beyond the threefold form of the body of Christ—the historical body of Jesus, the Sacrament, and the Church. But, just as I find the claim of ecofeminism to be such a strange use of theological language that I do not know how to make sense of it, I likewise find the term "incarnation" used with reference to the business corporation so odd that I am not sure how it is to be received in theology. If I have read him correctly, Novak seems to be expanding the traditional notion of Christ's threefold body to include a fourth "incarnation"— the modern business corporation.

The theological difference

What difference does theology make for how we can speak well of God and the modern corporation? Novak would seem to find both the shrimp and lobster plant as well as the water meter corporation to be an incarnation of God's presence. But in presenting a fourth form of the body of Christ, and without explaining how it is related to the other three forms, his work loses the capacity to speak well about God and thus cannot speak well about the corporation either.

McCann and Stackhouse's notion of the modern corporation as a potential "worldly ecclesia" is less objectionable than Novak's. But they too do not explain to us how this worldly ecclesia and the ecclesia itself relate. In fact, their desire to avoid confessional particularity in theology in favor of a cosmopolitan social ethic leads them to lose any sense of both the particularity of the Church and the locality of the corporation. The global nature of the corporation requires it to break through cultural and social boundaries and set up universal forms of community beyond biological, cultural, and social ties. This is why the corporation is a worldly ecclesia. Indeed, one sign of the goodness of the modern corporation is that it "has found a home in societies far from its roots." In fact, McCann and Stackhouse go so far as to argue, "Businesses increasingly operate in a context of global competition. Comparative advantage can make selling out, closing down or moving to other lands imperative. The failure to move is in some cases a manifestation of a misplaced patriotism, and may fail to aid underdeveloped regions."[24] They do note that the pressure to move is a "temptation" that could be resisted, but in their thought a commitment to locale and place can also be a refusal to engage in the missionary work that the Christian doctrine of vocation entails, a work that the corporation, as a social body, is also called to carry out.[25]

For Stackhouse and McCann, the modern corporation, as a "worldly ecclesia," is a "secular form of covenantal community." It has a legitimate, if limited, function. But they do not portray the corporation as an incarnation of Christ, as does Novak. Novak is clear that when he speaks of the corporation as incarnating Christ he intends precisely "the multinational corporation" that "build[s] manufacturing or other facilities in other lands in order to operate there." He speaks of the "grace" in these corporations and refers to these multinational corporations as not only "incarnational" but also "sacramental." This is Catholic liberalism at its worst. Novak's terminology does not help us understand the theological significance of either of our fictional corporations, but merely functions as a legitimating discourse that prevents the proper theological task of discerning faithful and faithless forms of exchange. Novak offers impoverished dogma.

Milbank helps us describe the corrupt practices of the shrimp and lobster plant as a violation of the charitable exchange that is a Christian ontology. This ontology can only be known through the historically contingent mediation of the Church, but that does not limit its political and social implications to the Church alone; for it remains an ontology, even if it lacks a foundation outside historical mediation. And what other kind of ontology is there? As I hope to show, capitalism itself assumes a different kind of ontology, historically mediated via a stoic theology.

MacIntyre helps us name the corrupt practices of the lobster plant as a violation of the virtue of justice, and thus also a violation of Catholic social teaching on the just wage. Both Milbank and MacIntyre might have more difficulty in identifying the virtue present in the water meter corporation, for it too occurs only within systems of capitalist exchange they both find uncharitable and unjust. How might they account for the genuine goodness of this corporation, given the heretical status they attribute to capitalist forms of exchange? Perhaps they could argue that, given the ontological claims the historical practices of Christianity entail, we should not be surprised that cooperation is more basic than competitiveness even in a corporation operating within a capitalist context. Peace and harmony are more basic to our being than vice, violence, and competitiveness. Catholic social teaching reminds us of this fact, even if it does not provide any guarantee that embodying the ontological priority of peace will ensure higher profits. Like the Church's teachings on biological reproduction and just war, its assumptions about harmonious cooperation and just wages are to be embodied because they bear witness to God's good creation, not because they "work" in a world still characterized, even at the end of history, by rebellion against God. Both Milbank and MacIntyre seem to suggest that some remediation for injustice can be found by conceding to workers just wages, which would include some ownership in the very corporation their labor makes possible; they maintain a socialist vision—although neither would present that socialist vision in Marxist terms or accept uncritically the labor theory of value. In fact, they both recognize that capitalist exchanges assume and require liberalism's cultural assumptions—particularly about the individual and the separation into separate spheres of religion, politics, and economics.[26]

Milbank and MacIntyre view critically the history within which the modern corporation has emerged because it is a history inextricably linked with modern, liberal assumptions that render Christianity marginal. This history assumes that what is "natural" can be viewed in terms of the primacy of the individual will and its exchanges. So "value" becomes the dominant mode of thinking not only about economic exchanges but also about morality. "Values" are choices persons make, which in economic terms give rise to the "value" of a product. Our willingness to part with so much money for a certain amount of a product becomes its "value." This "value" economy appears to be natural but it is not. It is instead the result of a particular history and moral tradition in which people are first constructed as "individuals" who make choices. "Value" rests upon the consumer's "choice," which when freed and unregulated produces the greatest "benevolence" or harmony for society. Although this is viewed as "natural" or the work of some "invisible" hand, it is actually a form of stoicism that emerged in seventeenth- and eighteenth-century moral philosophy. It will appear "natural" only when we refuse to historicize its own development and look at the practices—particularly the practices of the modern corporation and its legal commitment to maximize stock profits—that perpetuate this particular moral tradition, a tradition that cannot be squared with the Thomist tradition or, for that matter, any Christian tradition that assumes a confessional theology in which Christian dogma and Catholic social teaching matter at least as much as seventeenth-century British and Scottish moral philosophy. To refuse to situate the modern corporation in terms of its moral history and tradition is to be unable to understand it well.

Stoic theology or Catholic social teaching

I have suggested the relatively noncontroversial thesis that no definitive account of the "real" exists apart from a particular historical language. This may seem to be a trivial truism that concedes far too much to skepticism, but that is not my intention. Instead, what I hope to show is that any social analysis of the reality of the lobster and water meter plants will always-already come to us through language such that no easy distinction is possible between a sphere ruled by a natural causality explainable via natural laws and another sphere ruled by freedom and in which morality and theology prevail. It is Kant's "third antinomy" (which has other precursors in the philosophical tradition) that makes this kind of division of intellectual labor possible.[27] And once we adopt the "linguistic turn" (Hamann-Herder-Humboldt in continental philosophy or Frege-Wittgenstein in the English tradition), this kind of division can no longer be safely assumed. No "social fact" exists without its narratibililty via language.

Two dominant theological languages seek to render intelligible the kind of economic exchanges found in the lobster and water meter corporations.[28] Inasmuch as the corrupt practices of the former are read as a "social fact" that is necessary within a progressive development (either within capitalism itself or from mercantilism to capitalism or even as a stage in the transition from capitalism to socialism), then the theological language that makes such a "social fact" appear will be Adam Smith's stoic theology. But if one sees these exchanges under the aspect of the language of Catholic social teaching, a radically different "social fact" emerges.

Smith's stoic theology helps us understand why some persons justify the sacrifices Guarifuna men and women make for the sake of others' fast-food consumption. It assumes his "doctrine of unintended consequences." When Smith argues that "by pursuing his own interests" an individual "frequently promotes that of the society more effectually than when he really intends to promote it," he drew on his earlier notion of a stoic doctrine of providence.[29] For as he argued in his *Theory of Moral Sentiments*,

> The ancient stoics were of opinion, that as the world was governed by the all-ruling providence of a wise, powerful, and good God, every single event ought to be regarded as making a necessary part of the plan of the universe, and as tending to promote the general order and happiness of the whole: that the vices and follies of mankind, therefore, made as necessary a part of this plan as their wisdom or their virtue; and by that eternal art which educes good from ill, were made to tend equally to the prosperity and perfection of the great system of nature.[30]

To argue that the unjust situation of the shrimp and lobster plant is a necessary "social fact" contributing to the future development of the Guarifuna people is thus to accept Smith's stoic theology. It is to accept the idea that there is an economic providence intrinsic to social reality whereby sacrifices are required by some for the sake of a future development that will justify those sacrifices. This idea makes capitalism both a kind of theodicy and an eschatology. It is not theologically neutral.

Smith's implicit theology cannot be an option for Christian theologians, especially for those operating within the tradition of Catholic social teaching, with its longstanding commitment to the just wage and the concept of intrinsic evils—which is to say that some actions can never be undertaken even on the assumption of a greater future benefit because such actions cannot be turned toward God, who is humanity's chief end. This teaching only makes sense if, as John Paul II has stated, we need not assume a tragic world in which every good done to someone entails an evil done to someone else. The exceptionless moral norm, of which the just wage teaching is an example, only makes sense against the backdrop of a Christian theology in which our lives are to be obedient to Christ's. We can take the risk of obedience and not simply think of all actions in terms of cost/benefit ratios because Christ has shown us what a true and good performance of humanity is. We understand creation, incarnation, and the "natural" only by examining Christ's life. Any theology that plays one of these themes against another part of the Christian story—that proceeds as if the incarnation can be discussed without also discussing the Crucifixion and eschatology, or as if creation can be understood without Christology—vivisects the body of Christ.

If reading "social reality" through Smith's stoic theology is a necessary feature of capitalist exchanges, as I think it is, then should Christians pursue a socialist vision? Is it proper to see the relationship between owners, managers, shareholders, and workers as a clash of interests only to be remedied when workers own the means of production (for what else could we mean by socialism)? This too seems to conflict with Catholic social teaching, for it continually presents social reality not as fundamentally antagonistic, but as ontologically peaceable. If socialism assumes that all that binds us together is power, then like capitalism, it must be rejected. Manipulative power-relations may be the social bonds we have inherited, but—if Catholic social teaching is correct—the clash of interests such relations represent is not intrinsic to social reality. It is, rather, a sign of rebellion against God's goodness, a sign that, oddly enough, results from a historical tradition that presents itself as a putatively neutral, objective, rational, and ahistorical social analysis. This very analysis requires the positing of a "social fact" in which social relationships are reduced to power—both in theory and in practice—so that they can then be regulated.

Rejecting the reduction of all social relations to manipulative power exchanges is part of reconstituting new social practices. For theory and practice, like fact and value or nature and freedom, do not constitute autonomous realms. The reason I think Christianity must continue to be open to socialism in a way that it cannot be open toward capitalism is not because of socialism's historical performance. McCann and Stackhouse are correct to call us to repent of any kind of "scientific socialism" that seeks to rationalize struggle and antagonism via an immanent providential theology. The very fact that a corporation like our water meter plant can survive within capitalism demonstrates other possibilities for work that need not assume a stoic natural theology in which vice more than virtue contributes to the common good, and in which a fundamental antagonism rules us all. If socialism holds forth the possibility that workers can share ownership in their labor in a noncompetitive system in which the interests of owners, shareholders and workers need not—by some necessity of a natural social fact—be pitted against each other, then yes, Christianity must continue to hold forth the possibility of socialism and work for the abolition of capitalism.

But to ask the question of who owns the means of production is still to assume that the most persuasive social analysis we have is the labor theory of value. That assumption goes beyond the dogmatic task theologians must pursue. Other questions are more important. What moral norms does the Christian tradition present as those which direct our exchanges to God's goodness? And what is the cultural context within which exchanges take place? Can it permit reading the world as if what is most real is the teaching we have received in the Christian tradition? Christology and ecclesiology, not the theories of any social science, require that we be concerned about how the necessary exchanges of the modern corporation instruct us in theological teachings that will not let us remember the name of God well. The "corporation" must not usurp the *corpus verum* and the global market must not be confused with the Catholic Church.

5

The Unfreedom of the Free Market

William T. Cavanaugh

T here is a gap between dual perceptions of the market economy
that seems to be getting wider in the age of globalization. On
the one hand, we are told that we live in an era of unparalleled freedom of choice. As the last few state barriers to free markets crumble,
we see opening up all around us an infinity of opportunities for work
and consumption. On the other hand, there is a profound sense of
resignation to fate in attitudes toward the market. The process of
globalization seems to have advanced beyond anyone's control. Managers sigh that their decisions are subject to the impersonal control
of "market forces." The popularity of "Dilbert" cartoons bespeaks a
cynicism about the instrumentalized and bureaucratized nature of
corporate employment. Consumers feel besieged by marketing and
surveillance, and feel powerless in the face of enormous transnational
corporations disconnected from the communities in which they live.
We hear rumors that our shoes are made by children and other exploited laborers, but we have no idea how we would begin to resist.

The argument of this essay is that there is a fundamental connection between these two types of perceptions. In the ideology of
the free market, freedom is conceived as the absence of interference
from others. There are no common ends to which our desires are
directed. In the absence of such ends, all that remains is the sheer
arbitrary power of one will against another. Freedom thus gives way
to the aggrandizement of power and the manipulation of will and de-

sire. The liberation of desire from ends, on the one hand, and the domination of impersonal power, on the other, are two sides of the same coin.

If this is the case, then true freedom requires an account of the ends of human life and the destination of creation. I use St. Augustine to help make this argument. There is no point to either blessing or damning "the free market" as such. What is required is a substantive account of the ends of earthly life and creation, so that we may enter into particular judgments of what kinds of exchanges are free and what kinds are not.

The Empty Shrine

When is a market free? According to Milton Friedman, the central problematic of economics is how to ensure the cooperation of free individuals without coercion. The answer, says Friedman, was provided by Adam Smith, who saw that, in the absence of external coercion, two parties enter into exchanges because it will be mutually beneficial for them to do so, *"provided the transaction is bi-laterally voluntary and informed."*[1] No exchange will take place unless both parties benefit.

> So long as effective freedom of exchange is maintained, the central feature of the market organization of economic activity is that it prevents one person from interfering with another in respect of most of his activities. The consumer is protected from coercion by the seller because of the presence of other sellers with whom he can deal. The seller is protected from coercion by the consumer because of other consumers to whom he can sell. The employee is protected from coercion by the employer because of other employers for whom he can work, and so on. And the market does this impersonally and without centralized authority.[2]

State authority is necessary to maintain law and order and enforce voluntarily created contracts, but the state must not interfere in the market, and in fact may be called on to prevent such interference. If individuals are voluntarily entering into exchanges from which both parties expect to benefit, then the market is free.

This is a fairly conventional definition of a free-market economy. It hinges on the insistence that exchanges be voluntary and informed. With regard to information, exchanges are not free if one party deceives another, say, by selling a house without divulging a severe termite problem. Barring such deception, however, Friedman is confident that the price system in a free-market economy transmits all the information needed to make exchanges informed. Indeed, "The price system transmits only the important information and only to the people who need to know."[3] Producers of wood do not need to know why demand for pencils has increased or even that it has increased. In order to increase production, they only need to know that someone is willing to pay more for their product. At the other end, the increased price of pencils tells consumers to wear their pencils down to stubs before buying new ones. They don't need to know why the price of pencils has increased, only that it has.[4] It is the same for the relationship between employer and employee; the price system applies in equal measure, because wages and salaries are the prices of labor, and the employer-employee relationship is an exchange of labor for money.

Besides being informed, a free-market exchange must also be voluntary. What this seems to mean, first, is an absence of external coercion. The chief culprit here is the state. In a free-market economy, the state does not interfere. No one threatens dire consequences if one party decides not to enter into a particular exchange. In a voluntary exchange, each party enters into the transaction in the expectation of gain and not in the fear of punishment. Second, then, voluntary exchanges are based upon each party's wants. They need not want the same kinds of things; wrestling videos and rosaries can be freely exchanged for each other. There need be no agreement at all on the nature of desire for a voluntary exchange to take place. A market is free if people can satisfy their wants (within legal limits, of course), even if there are utterly incommensurable ideas about what people ought to desire. As Friedman says, a free-market economy "gives people what they want instead of what a particular group thinks they ought to want. Underlying most arguments against the free market is a lack of belief in freedom itself."[5] And freedom itself, in Friedman's account, is pursuing whatever you want without interference from others.

Two corollaries follow from this conception of voluntary exchange. The first is that freedom is defined negatively, as freedom *from* the interference of others, especially from the state. Freedom is what exists spontaneously in the absence of coercion. This approach is agnostic about the positive capacities of each party to a transaction—for example, how much power or property each party has at his or her disposal. To be free, it suffices that there be no external interference.

The second is that a free market has no *telos,* that is, no common end to which desire is directed. Each individual chooses his or her own ends. As Friedrich Hayek says, "this recognition of the individual as the ultimate judge of his ends"[6] does not mean there can be no common action among individuals, but the ends on which such actions are based are merely the "coincidence of individual ends"; "what are called 'social ends' are [in the free-market view] merely identical ends of many individuals—or ends to the achievement of which individuals are willing to contribute in return for the assistance they receive in the satisfaction of their own desires."[7] To claim that desires can be ordered either rightly or wrongly to objectively desirable ends has no place in a free market. To stake such a claim within the market itself would be to interfere in the freedom of the market. As Michael Novak says, democratic capitalism—of which a free market is a crucial component—is built on the explicit denial of any unitary order. There is no common *telos* or "sacred canopy" above the diversity of desires, only an "empty shrine" or "wasteland" where common goals used to stand.

> The "wasteland" at the heart of democratic capitalism is
> like a field of battle, on which individuals wander alone, in
> some confusion, amid many casualties. Nonetheless, like
> the dark night of the soul in the inner journey of the mystics,
> this desert has an indispensable purpose. It is maintained
> out of respect for the diversity of human consciences,
> perceptions, and intentions. It is swept clean out of
> reverence for the sphere of the transcendent, to which
> the individual has access through the self, beyond the
> mediations of social institutions.[8]

That is, the transcendent is not denied but preserved in the freedom of each individual to pursue the ends of his or her choice.

If ends are chosen and not received, on what basis are these choices made? On the basis of "wants" or "preferences" or "desires." From where do these come? Free-market economists are agnostic on this question. It may be unanswerable, and it does not matter anyway. Milton and Rose Friedman make a distinction between the "real wants or desires of consumers" and artificial wants supposedly created by advertising. They believe that advertising succeeds not by creating artificial wants, but by appealing to real wants. "Is it not more sensible to appeal to real wants or desires of consumers than to try to manufacture artificial wants or desires? Surely it will generally be cheaper to sell them something that meets wants they already have than to create an artificial want."[9] As an example, the Friedmans cite the success of automobiles that change models year after year over those like the Superba that did not. If unchanging models were "what consumers *really* wanted, the companies that offered that option would have prospered, and the others would have followed suit."[10] How do you tell the difference between real wants and artificial wants?

William T. Cavanaugh

Simply by noting what people in fact choose. If they choose something, they must have a real want for it. From where do real wants come? It does not matter. All that matters for a market to be free is that individuals have real wants and can pursue them without the interference of others, especially the state.

Augustine on freedom and desire

An examination of Christian thinking on voluntary action renders suspect the ideas that freedom can be adequately defined negatively and that freedom requires no objective ends. I will take as my principal guide St. Augustine of Hippo, arguably the classic source of Christian reflection on freedom and desire. Augustine was forced to wrestle with these questions in controversy with both the Pelagians, whose account of free will seemed to render God's grace unnecessary, and the Donatists, whose schism from the Catholic Church raised questions of using coercion to reunify the fold. These controversies may at first seem far removed from the dynamics of market economies, but Augustine represents the heart of Christian reflection on freedom and desire, and is thus directly implicated in any Christian attempt to answer the question, When is a market free?

With regard to the first corollary, freedom in Augustine's view is not simply the absence of external interference. Augustine's view of freedom is more complex; freedom is not simply a negative freedom *from,* but a freedom *for,* a capacity to achieve certain worthwhile goals. All of those goals are taken up into the one overriding *telos* of human life, the return to God. In the words of the famous prayer that opens the *Confessions,* "you have made us for yourself, and our heart is restless until it rests in you."[11] Freedom is therefore fully a function of God's grace working within us. Freedom consists in being wrapped up in the will of God, who is the condition of human freedom. Being is not autonomous. All being participates in God, the source of being.

Autonomy in the strict sense is simply impossible, for to be independent of others and independent of God is to be cut off from

Being, and therefore to be nothing at all. To be left to our own devices, cut off from God, is to be lost in sin, the negation of being. For the Pelagians, in order to be convicted of sin and rewarded for righteousness, human freedom must be in some sense "external" to divine grace. Freedom then becomes a kind of human power, and sin is an exercise of such power. For Augustine, on the other hand, sin is not a power but a weakness. In his anti-Pelagian treatise *The Spirit and the Letter,* Augustine uses the metaphors of slavery and sickness to discuss the nature of sin. "How, if they are slaves of sin, can they boast freedom of choice?"[12] Or again, "by grace comes the healing of the soul from sin's sickness; by the healing of the soul comes freedom of choice."[13] Sin is not subject to free choice, properly speaking. The alcoholic with plenty of money and an open liquor store may, in a purely negative sense, be free from anything interfering with getting what he wants, but he is in reality profoundly unfree and cannot free himself. To regain freedom of choice he cannot be left alone. He can only be free by being liberated from his false desires and moved to desire rightly. This is the sense in which Augustine says "freedom of choice is not made void but established by grace, since grace heals the will whereby righteousness may freely be loved."[14] Freedom is something received, not merely exercised. To determine if a person is acting freely, much more is therefore required than to know whether or not a person is acting on his or her desires without the interference of others. Others are in fact crucial to one's freedom, in Augustine's view. Slaves or addicts cannot, by definition, free themselves. Others—the ultimate Other being God—are necessary to break through the bonds that enclose the self in itself. A community of virtue is needed in which to learn to desire rightly.[15]

On display here is a fundamentally different view of desire from that held by the Friedmans. Augustine does not assume that individuals simply have wants that are internally generated and that subsequently enter the social realm through acts of choice. Nor does he assume that desires are simply real because people have them, nor that what one *really* desires is fully transparent and accessible to oneself. For Augustine, desire is a social product, a complex and multidimensional network of movement that does not simply originate within the individual self, but pulls and pushes the self in different directions both from within and from without the person. In his famous examination of his theft of pears as an adolescent, he repeatedly draws attention to the social nature of the act: "Yet had I been alone I would not have done it—I remember my state of mind to be thus at the time—alone I never would have done it. Therefore my love in that act was to be associated with the gang in whose company I did it. Does it follow that I loved something other than the theft? No, nothing else in reality because association with the gang is also a nothing."[16] Here Augustine points to the social nature of desire, the origination of desire both from within and from outside of the individual self. Augustine also points to the "unreality" of his desire. The object of his desire, because it is not oriented to the true end of human life, is literally a "nothing," or better, a privation. His desire is not endowed with reality simply by the fact of experiencing it and choosing on the basis of it. Furthermore, the whole affair—and desire itself—is not simply transparent to us mortals whose bodies are battlegrounds of competing loves: "Who can untie this extremely twisted and tangled knot?" The answer is God. Only through the sheer grace of God is Augustine able to continue on to say, "My desire is for you," that is, my *real* desire is for God.[17]

All of this indicates that there are true desires and false desires, and we need a *telos* to tell the difference between them. The second corollary of free-market economics we identified above is that freedom is maximized in the absence of a common *telos*. A market is free if individuals are free to choose their own ends based on nothing more than their own wants. To the contrary, in his controversy with the Donatists, Augustine argues that freedom in fact depends not on the autonomy of the will but on the end to which the will is moved. I do not wish to defend Augustine's justification of the use of civil authority to compel the Donatists to rejoin the Catholic fold. What is interesting about the way Augustine argues in this matter is his conceptualization of the relationship between freedom and coercion. For Augustine, the most important question is not whether the will has been moved externally or internally. The most important question is rather to what end the will has been moved.

Augustine acknowledges that no one can be forced to be good against his or her own will. Nevertheless, since he does not assume that mere negative freedom of the will from interference is a good in and of itself, he believes that the individual will can legitimately be moved from outside itself to reexamine its ways.[18] According to Augustine, many of the Donatists had long been prevented from examining the Catholic case by complacency, fear, ignorance, and indifference. Their wills had become entrenched in habit; they were "held prisoners by the force of old custom."[19] What was needed, therefore, was for their wills to be moved from without. Just as Christ "coerced" Paul to cause his conversion, God's grace often works upon us despite our own will for our own profit.[20] In Augustine's thought, we desperately need not to be left to the tyranny of our own wills. The key to true freedom is not just following whatever desires we happen to have, but cultivating the right desires. This means that the internal movement of the will is not a sufficient condition for freedom; we must consider the end toward which the will is moved. "[W]hat is important to attend to but this: who were on the side of truth, and who on the side of iniquity; who acted from a desire to injure, and who from a desire to correct what was amiss?"[21] In the case of the Donatists, the "whole question, therefore, is whether schism be not an evil work."[22] For this reason, according to Augustine, Christ added "for righteousness' sake" to the beatitude, "Blessed are they who are persecuted."[23] The cause of the persecution makes all the difference.

Does this mean that the end justifies the means? In places it seems as if Augustine is saying so.

> When good and bad do the same actions and suffer the same afflictions, they are to be distinguished not by what they do or suffer, but by the causes of each: e.g., Pharaoh oppressed the people of God by hard bondage; Moses afflicted the same people by severe correction when they were guilty of impiety: their actions were alike; but they were not alike in the motive of regard to the people's welfare,—the one being inflated by the lust of power, the other inflamed by love.[24]

Nevertheless, Augustine makes no separation between ends and means. He counsels moderation in dealing with the Donatists, and refuses to allow deception in bringing them back to the fold. Furthermore, Augustine rejects the use of judicial torture in dealing with the Donatists, and limits the means used to those available to schoolteachers—beating with canes. "For he whose aim is to kill is not careful how he wounds, but he whose aim is to cure is cautious with his lancet; for the one seeks to destroy what is sound, the other that which is decaying."[25] The images from education and medicine here are deliberate. In pedagogy the will of the students must often be redirected, sometimes forcefully, for them to learn. In medicine, pain is sometimes produced for the sake of healing. In both cases, however, the means must be proportionate to the end in order for good to be achieved.

I believe that Augustine was wrong in his choice of means for dealing with the Donatists. Nonviolent witness is a far more faithful means of persuasion. Nevertheless, Augustine's broader point about the relationship of desire to ends is important, and goes to the heart of our discussion of the freedom of the free market. The point is this: the absence of external force is not sufficient to determine the freedom of any particular exchange. In order to judge whether or not an exchange is free, one must know whether or not the will is moved toward a good end. This requires some kind of substantive, and not merely formal, account of the true end or *telos* of the human person. Where there are no objectively desirable ends given, and the individual is told to choose his or her own ends, then choice itself becomes the only thing that is inherently good. When there is a recession, we are told to buy things to get the economy moving; what we buy makes no difference. All desires, good and bad, melt into the one overriding imperative to consume. We all stand under the one sacred canopy of consumption for its own sake.

And yet, Augustine says, desire for objects cut free from their source and end in God is ultimately the desire for "nothing." In Augustine's vision of the great chain of being, all things that exist are good, but only insofar as they participate in God, the source of their being and the source of all good. To pursue the lower things on the chain of being for their own sake, to forget their source and their final end, is to sever the link that holds them in being, at which point they begin to slide back into the nothingness from which the *creatio ex nihilo* summoned them.[26] For Augustine, sin is committed when "in consequence of an immoderate urge towards those things at the bottom end of the scale of good, we abandon the higher and supreme goods, that is you, Lord God, and your truth and your law."[27] This is not just a matter of wanting too much; it is a matter of wanting without any idea why we want what we want. To desire with no good in mind other than desire itself is to desire arbitrarily. "I abandoned you to pursue the lowest things of your creation. I was dust going to dust."[28]

Augustine presents a remarkably sympathetic account of the person in this condition, for even in the pursuit of lower things, Augustine spies the inchoate groping for the true end of human life. Even murder is committed out of love, but it is love for some lower good that has become detached from its true end.[29] All such loves are disordered loves, loves looking for something worth loving that is not just arbitrarily chosen. "I sought an object for my love; I was in love with love."[30] Augustine would have no problem recognizing the pathologies of twenty-first-century advanced industrial countries, in which it is estimated that shopping addiction claims more than 10 percent of the population, and 20 percent of women—more than drugs and alcohol combined.[31] People buy things—anything—to try to fill the hole that is the empty shrine. Once the things are purchased, they become ephemeral "nothings," and the shopper must head back to the mall to continue the search. With no objective ends to guide the search, the search is literally endless.

Libido dominandi

Even if Augustine is right about the need for objective ends to guide the will, the question remains, who is to say what those ends are or should be? There is no doubt that Augustine's view can be taken in a very paternalistic direction: *We* know what you *really* want, and we are going to organize society accordingly. I have no intention of endorsing such a view. This is the specter of a socialist command economy that free-market advocates rightly reject. Free-market advocates would rather that individuals make their own mistakes. That some will make bad choices is inevitable, but it is far better to give individuals the freedom to damn themselves than to subject everyone to a power that is no more guaranteed than the individual will to choose well.

Nevertheless, the idea that this type of economy is free is also problematic, for it assumes that the abolition of objective goods provides the conditions for the individual will to function more or less autonomously. The reality is quite different. For as Augustine sees clearly, the absence of objective goods does not free the individual, but leaves him or her subject to the arbitrary competition of wills. In other words, in the absence of a substantive account of the good, all that remains is sheer arbitrary power, one will against another. This is what Augustine calls the *libido dominandi,* the lust for power with which Pharaoh was possessed. Without the idea that some goods are objectively better than others, the movement of the will can only be arbitrary. Persuasion in this context can only reflect the domination of one will over another. The will is moved by the greater force, and not by any intrinsic attraction to the good. The difference between authority and sheer power has been eliminated.

In this section I want to look at some of the ways that power in the market actually functions. In the absence of any objective conception of the good, sheer power remains. The prevailing models of business strategy recognize this fact and are unsentimental about it. For example, on the one hand, marketing is put forward to the broader public as the provision of information about products so that consumers may make choices that are both informed and voluntary. Here consumers are depicted as autonomous and rational, perfectly sovereign over their choices of products and ends. On the other hand, marketing presents itself in-house to its practitioners and clients as a machine fully capable of creating desire and delivering it to its intended goal. These two aspects of marketing are two sides of the same coin; marketing can manipulate desire successfully in part because of its success in convincing the broader public of consumers that their desires are not being manipulated. Richard Ott's popular marketing text *Creating Demand* is one example of the two faces of marketing. His introduction extols the consumer as king and declares the impossibility of manipulating consumers. The rest of the book is a detailed analysis of how to use the latest in psychological research to create desires by targeting consumers' subconscious impulses.[32] Not surprisingly, businesses expect more for their billions of dollars in marketing expenses than the mere purveying of objective information to the consumer.

In fact, most contemporary marketing is based not on providing information but on associating products with evocative images and themes not directly related to the product itself. Non-commodifiable goods such as self-esteem, love, sex, friendship, and success are associated with products that bear little or no relation to these goods. The desire for these goods is intensified by calling into question the acceptability of the consumer,[33] what General Motors' research division—in a reference to changing car models each year—once called "the organized creation of dissatisfaction."[34] This shift in the twenti-eth century from product-oriented advertising to buyer-centered ap-proaches has been extensively documented, and is recognized not just by critics of the advertising industry but by its practitioners as well. As one marketer promises, advertising creates emotional bonds between consumers and products; it is about "creating mythologies about their brands by humanizing them and giving them distinct per-sonalities and cultural sensibilities."[35] The efficacy of these approaches is augmented by the fact that most of us believe ourselves to be im-mune to such approaches. This sense of immunity is fostered by an entire genre of anti-advertising advertising, which either "exposes" the process of advertising itself (Sprite: "Image is nothing. Obey your thirst") or advances the notion that, by buying the product in ques-tion, one will not be conforming but rather following one's own path (Taco Bell: "There's nothing ordinary about it.")

It is of course true that advertising does not work on each indi-vidual as a lobotomy does. Tracing cause and effect is difficult. The individual does not react like a programmed zombie upon being ex-posed to effective advertising. As Michael Budde puts it, being sub-jected to advertising is more akin to playing poker against an oppo-nent who, unbeknownst to you, has already seen, through a slightly blurred mirror, the hand you are holding. You still exercise free will, but the dynamics of power have shifted because the situation is set up to advance the interests of others.[36] This imbalance of power hap-pens in two related ways. First, surveillance ensures that the balance of information is decidedly in favor of the marketer. Not only do mar-keters withhold information about a product from consumers, or di-vert their attention to evocative images unrelated to the product itself; marketers also gather extensive information about individual consumers and target their efforts based on this disequilibrium of knowledge. Erik Larson details this phenomenon in *The Naked Con-sumer: How Our Private Lives Become Public Commodities*. Larson began research for the book when, a few days after the birth of his second daughter, a sample of Luvs diapers showed up on his doorstep, courtesy of the Procter & Gamble Corporation. His eldest daughter had already received birthday greetings, just days before turning one, from a marketer on behalf of several corporations, including Revlon and Kimberly-Clark selling toddler-related merchandise. Larson describes how information on our purchasing patterns, births, deaths, political views, educational levels, credit histories, pet ownership, hobbies, illnesses, and so on is harvested from credit-card records, bank statements, hospital records, the websites we visit, our answers to surveys, frequent buyer cards, even filmed records of our shopping habits in stores. Such surveillance has become incredibly sophisticated: a flyer for "OmniVision," a system developed by a consumer intelligence service called Equifax, boasts, "We think we know more about your own neighborhood than you do, and we'd like to prove it!"[37]

The second way that marketers produce an imbalance of power is through the use of the information gathered from surveillance to saturate consumers' social environment. The average person is exposed to thousands of advertising images every week. Virtually everywhere we look or listen—television, radio, websites, newspapers, magazines, billboards, junk mail, movies, videos, t-shirts, buses, hats, cups, pencils, gas-pump handles, walls of public restrooms—is saturated with advertising. As one observer puts it, what the record reveals is an almost total takeover of the domestic informational system for the purposes of selling goods and services."[38] To pretend that the consumer simply stands apart from such pervasive control of information is to engage in fantasy.

Marketing is not the only area in which the logic of sheer power is manifest. Another is the concentration of power in enormous transnational corporations through mergers and acquisitions. The last two decades have seen an intensification of mergers and acquisitions as large corporations seek to outdo their rivals through the increase of their size and market power. The result is such behemoths as AOL

Time Warner and ExxonMobil. In industry after industry, a few huge corporations dictate patterns of production and consumption. In the meatpacking industry, for example, four giants handle 80 percent of the beef production in the United States, leaving small farmers and ranchers powerless to influence pricing or even determine how their cattle are raised. Independent bookstores and department stores have shut down in legions in the face of Barnes & Noble and Wal-Mart. Some argue that here the sovereign consumers have spoken; they simply prefer Barnes & Noble and Wal-Mart to smaller, less "efficient" operations. If this is the case, however, king consumer has paradoxically used his freedom to restrict his freedom, since now there are fewer choices available, and he is increasingly faced with the prospect of frequenting the same few chain stores whether he likes it or not. Rather than celebrate the growth of enormously powerful corporations as the manifestation of consumer freedom, it is more realistic to examine the ability of concentrated economic power to control patterns of consumption.

More severe than the asymmetrical power relations between corporation and consumer are the disparities of power in the exchange between employer and employee. In 1980, the average CEO made 42 times what the average production worker made. By 1999, the ratio had risen to 475 to 1, and it continues to rise.[39] Why do executives pay themselves so much? In part, because they can. Top executives serve on each other's boards of directors, and there is an expectation that they will keep up with increases in each other's pay packages. As the owners of capital have gained power, labor has lost power. Only 13 percent of American workers now belong to unions, and "Right to Work" legislation in twenty-nine states has made union organizing extremely difficult. A crucial factor in the atrophying of labor power in the United States has been the ability and willingness of corporations to shift production overseas, where they can and do pay wages as low as 30 cents an hour. Capital can move freely across national borders, but labor cannot. Factory workers in Massachusetts know that the threat of moving operations to El Salvador or China hangs over every negotiation with management, and the mere existence of such a threat suffices to weaken their bargaining power.

"Rosa Martinez produces apparel for U.S. markets on her sewing machine in El Salvador. *You* can hire her for 33 cents an hour." So goes an advertisement, paid for by USAID, in the textile trade journal *Bobbin.*[40] Why do companies pay such low wages? Again, because they can. Transnational corporations are able to shop around the globe for the most advantageous wage environments, that is, those places where people are so desperate that they must take jobs that pay very poorly, in many cases wages insufficient to feed and house themselves and their dependents. In other words, it is considered good business practice to maximize the disparity of power between employer and employee, in order to increase the profit margin of the corporation. All of this is done in the name of "free" trade. As Augustine saw, in the absence of any substantive ends, what triumphs is the sheer lust for power. The one and only end is profit, the aggrandizement of the corporation. This end is served precisely by the minimization of employees' freedom.

"Because they can" is not the end of the story, however, for most managers of corporations would reply that they act as they do because they must. When managers lament the displacement and suffering caused by closing factories that pay living wages and opening others that do not, they are not just being disingenuous, nor are people who make such decisions *ipso facto* bad people. When they blame the move on necessity, they recognize that in a very real sense the "free" market does not leave them free to act in ways they might believe to be just. In the search for cheap labor, managers often appeal to a sense of fate. They feel they have no choice in the matter, because they assume that, given the prevailing logic of free exchange, consumers will want to maximize their own gain in any transaction by paying the lowest price possible for a product. In a world of consumption without ends, it is assumed that the consumer will want to maximize his or her own power at the expense of the laborer, and the manager feels unfree to resist this logic, lest his or her own corporation fall victim to competition from other corporations that are better positioned to take advantage of cheap labor.

More than consumers, however, it is stockholders who drive the search for cheap labor. As Peter Drucker, Michael Naughton, and others have observed, over the last twenty years the tremendous concentration of stock in institutional investment plans—mutual funds, pension plans, insurance companies, etc.—has shifted the power dynamics of publicly traded corporations. Institutional investors have put tremendous pressure on executives to maximize returns for their clients. At the same time, offering stock options to executives has been the favored tool for ensuring that the interests of the executives and those of the stockholders coincide. As a result, executives have strong incentives to favor the concerns of stockholders over those of other stakeholders, such as employees and communities.[41] Who owns corporations—the question of property on which Friedman and others are generally agnostic—plays a crucial role in the dynamics of power.

When market forces alone are not enough to discipline the labor force, political coercion has often been brought to bear, supposedly to protect free markets from interference. As the examples of China, South Korea, Singapore, Taiwan, and Myanmar indicate, authoritarian regimes are perfectly compatible with "free"-market economies, where a disciplined labor force is considered attractive to business. The economies of many Latin American nations were "freed" of state interference through a series of military dictatorships in the 1970s and 1980s. As Uruguayan writer Eduardo Galeano remarks about this period, "people were in prison so that prices could be free."[42] Milton Friedman himself made a highly publicized visit to General Pinochet's Chile in 1975 to help guide the reconstruction of the economy under Chilean economists known as "Los Chicago Boys," students of Friedman and Arnold Harberger from the University of

Chicago. In published remarks, Friedman counseled General Pinochet to ignore his image abroad as a human rights abuser and focus on curing Chile of "statism."[43] Friedman also declared publicly that the Chilean economy needed "shock treatment."[44] To those thousands subject to torture by electricity under Pinochet, Friedman's words were a chilling confirmation of the link between the disciplining of labor and the freeing of capital.

Judging when a market is free

Is Rosa Martinez free? If we take Friedman's definition at face value, then we might answer yes. Her decision to take a job making clothes for American markets is presumably both informed and voluntary, provided she was not deceived about the kind and amount of work she would be doing, and the hourly rate at which she would be paid. Presumably no one forced her to take the job, and no one would prevent her from leaving it. Both Rosa Martinez and her employer entered into this exchange in the expectation of benefiting from it. The employer expected to increase profits by paying low wages, and Rosa Martinez expected an improvement over starvation.

The problem with this view is that it pretends to be blind to the real disparity of power at work here while simultaneously stripping away the ability to judge an exchange on the basis of *anything but* sheer power, since any *telos* or common standard of good has been eliminated from view. Nothing necessarily connects the employer's desires to Rosa Martinez's desires. In Friedman's view, to ask if this exchange serves the common good, or if it is just, is irrelevant to the question of whether or not the exchange is free; we may only ask if each party is entering into the exchange expecting to gain something for their own individual interests that they would not have gained had they not entered into the exchange. Considerations of goodness and justice seem to apply only to the capitalist system as a whole. Friedman and other free-market advocates argue that capitalism as such is the best system based on its ability to give people what they want. A system allegedly based on individual rights is thus ironically justified by a utilitarian justification of the system as a whole, to which individuals and their freedom are sacrificed.

Some free-market advocates may wish to argue, on the other hand, that the exchange with Rosa Martinez is not free, but an aberration in the free-market system that will work itself out if the market mechanism is given time to operate. Similar claims could be made for all the examples I gave above under the heading "Libido dominandi"; none are examples of the true functioning of the free market, and the market mechanism will protect against coercion if given time and allowed to function without interference.

However, in order to judge which exchanges are truly free and which are not, one must abandon Friedman's purely negative and functionalist approach to freedom and have some positive standard by which to judge. If we admit that Rosa Martinez's exchange with her employer is voluntary and informed, yet still want to claim that it is not truly free, we must be able to muster an argument based on some standard of human flourishing and the ends of human life that is being violated by her working for less than a living wage. In other words, once we admit that freedom defined strictly negatively is inadequate, we are pushed toward a recognition that Augustine was right; to speak of freedom in any realistic and full sense is necessarily to engage the question of the true ends of human life.

Yet such ends are precisely what free-market advocates would banish from the definition of the free market. To enter into judgments about the freedom of particular exchanges, we must abandon Friedman's definition of a free market, and also abandon any claims for the goodness of "*the* free market" as such. There is no point to claims that "capitalism produces freedom" unless one wants to claim that "whatever economic exchange produces freedom is capitalism," in which case one has simply uttered a tautology. The key point is that the freedom of each economic exchange is subject to judgment based on a positive account of freedom, which must take into account the good ends of human life.

Let us consider some examples. Reporter Bob Herbert visited a factory in El Salvador that makes jackets for Liz Claiborne. The jackets sell for $178 each in the U.S.; the workers who make them earn 77 cents per jacket, or 56 cents an hour. The factory is surrounded by barbed wire and armed guards. A worker interviewed after her twelve-hour shift told of being unable to feed herself and her three-year-old daughter adequately. He daughter drinks coffee because they cannot afford milk. Both mother and daughter suffer fainting spells. David Wang, president of Mandarin Co., which runs one of the plants in El Salvador, admitted to Herbert that the wages are inadequate: "If you really ask me, this is not fair." But then he offered a lesson in "free" trade. "In the United States, if you want to buy a Honda Civic, you can shop around and always you will find cheaper ones." This is what the clothing companies were doing, according to Wang. "They are shopping around the whole world for the cheapest labor price."[45]

Contrast this situation with the Mondragon Co-operative Corporation based in Spain, founded by Basque priest Jose Maria Arizmendiarrieta in 1956. Mondragon employs 60,000 people, and has annual sales of manufactured goods in excess of three billion dollars. What makes Mondragon extraordinary is that it is based on the principles of distributism, the idea—itself based on papal social teaching and promoted by Hilaire Belloc, G. K. Chesterton, and others—that a just social order can only be achieved through the just distribution of property and a recognition of the dignity of labor. Mondragon is entirely worker-owned and worker-governed, based on a system of one vote per worker. At Mondragon, they believe that labor hires capital, instead of capital labor. Their capital comes largely from a worker- and community-supported credit union. The highest-paid employee can make no more than six times the lowest-paid. Ten percent of surpluses are given directly to community development projects. Not only is the company successful and the laborers highly satisfied with their work, but the communities in which Mondragon plays a significant part enjoy lower crime rates, lower rates of domestic violence, higher rates of education, and better physical and emotional health than neighboring communities.[46]

By Friedman's standards, both the Salvadoran worker and the worker at Mondragon are free. If we allow ourselves to judge freedom on the basis of the true ends of human life, on the other hand, it becomes obvious that the Salvadoran woman is little better than enslaved, and the Mondragon worker is afforded the opportunity for true freedom. We must enter into particular judgments of this kind if "freedom" is not to be used as an empty slogan to cover over the depredations of naked power. Mondragon is founded on the recognition that true freedom requires careful consideration of what is required for human flourishing, which requires consideration of the ends of human being. As Belloc wrote, "Economic freedom can only be a good if it fulfills some need in our nature."[47]

> Economic freedom is in our eyes a good. It is among the highest of temporal goods because it is necessary to the highest life of society through the dignity of man and through the multiplicity of his action, in which multiplicity is life. Through well-divided property alone can the units of society react upon the State. Through it alone can a public opinion flourish. Only where the bulk of the cells are healthy can the whole organism thrive. It is therefore our business to restore economic freedom through the restoration of the only institution under which it flourishes, which institution is Property.[48]

The link between property and freedom is a crucial one. Free-market advocates tend to be agnostic on the question of ownership; barring external interference, an exchange is formally free even if all one person has to exchange is his or her labor. But as the example of Rosa

Martinez makes plain, having no ownership can make one little better than a wage slave. For Belloc—and much of the Catholic tradition on property going back to Aquinas—the ownership of property is natural to human beings and allows them to develop their own capacities.[49] Property is thus essential to human freedom. However, here freedom is not construed negatively. The ownership of property is not about power, and the wide distribution of property is not about a greater equilibrium of power. Rather, property has an end, which is to serve the common good. The universal destination of all material goods is in God. As Aquinas says, we should regard property as a gift from God,[50] a gift that is only legitimate if it is used for the benefit of others. Aquinas therefore sanctions private ownership only insofar as it is put to its proper end, which is the good of all: "man ought to possess external things, not as his own, but as common, so that, to wit, he is ready to communicate them to others in their need."[51] Absent such a view of the true end of property, freedom means being able to do whatever one wants with one's property, and property can become nothing more than a means of exercising power over others.

Let us consider two more examples, this time relating directly to consumption. When one buys a steak in a large chain grocery store, according to Friedman, all the information one needs to make a free decision—assuming that the steak is not simply defective or contaminated—is conveyed by the price. The true story behind the shrink wrap, however, is more consequential than Friedman would have us believe. A calf might spend the first few months of life eating grass on the range, but typically the rest of its short life is spent in a feedlot, ankle deep in manure. By nature cattle are equipped to turn the grass that grows naturally on arid land into high-quality protein. To let cattle graze is considered inefficient these days, however, because it takes longer. Today's cattle go from 80 to 1,200 pounds in just fourteen months on a crash diet of corn, protein supplements, and drugs. They are given hormone implants—banned in Europe—to promote growth. Their calories come from corn, which is cheap and convenient, but depends on the use of lots of petroleum products, and wreaks havoc on their ruminant digestive system, designed for grass. The only way to keep cattle from dying of bloating, acidosis, and abscessed livers on a grain diet is to give them steady doses of antibiotics. Still many strains of bacteria survive. We used to be able to count on the fact that such bacteria, raised in a cow's neutral-pH digestive tract, would be killed off by the acids in the human stomach. Now that the cow's digestive tract has been acidified by a corn diet, however, acid-tolerant strains such as E. coli have developed that, when found in our food, can kill us. When the cattle are slaughtered, they are caked with feedlot manure, which is where the E. coli reside. Rather than alter their diet or keep them from living in their own feces or slowing down the processing speed of the slaughter lines (all considered inefficient and impractical), the meat is sprayed with disinfectant solution and irradiated. Then it is shrink-wrapped and sent to your local supermarket.[52]

The meat is cheap, but the social costs are not included in the price. Each head of cattle requires about 284 gallons of oil in its lifetime. As Michael Pollan says, "We have succeeded in industrializing the beef calf, transforming what was once a solar-powered ruminant into the very last thing we need: another fossil-fuel machine."[53] Runoff from the petroleum-based fertilizer has traveled down the Mississippi and created a 12,000-square-mile "dead zone" in the Gulf of Mexico. Extensive use of antibiotics has led to resistant strains of bacteria. And scientists believe that hormone use has contributed to dropping human sperm counts and sexual abnormalities in fish. One cattleman interviewed by Pollan commented, "I'd love to give up hormones. If the consumer said, We don't want hormones, we'd stop in a second. The cattle could get along better without them. But the market signal's not there, and as long as my competitor's doing it, I've got to do it, too."[54] It is hard to imagine how this signal would be generated, however, for the system is designed to keep the origins of beef a mystery to the consumer.

Contrast this with E-Z Acres farm in Elko, Minnesota. When I buy beef from Jon and Lisa Zweber, I know that it is grass-fed, having been raised on pastureland behind their house. They use no hormones or antibiotics. When I buy beef from E-Z Acres, it is a free exchange. All the information I need is available and transparent, and the exchange contributes to the flourishing of the Zwebers, their local community, my family, the cattle, and the environment. My exchange with the supermarket is less than free. The information I need is not readily available to me; before I read Michael Pollan I had only the vaguest sense of how beef is typically raised. The ranchers and feedlot workers chafe under the compulsion of market forces beyond their control. All the while, their profit margin is made ever narrower by the four conglomerates that dominate the meatpacking industry. And the overall effect of the system on the environment and on rural communities has been devastating.

Conclusion

Is this a call, then, for state intervention in the market? No. It is a false dichotomy to limit the possibilities to either requiring state intervention or blessing the unfettered reign of corporate power. Neither state intervention nor its absence ensures the freedom of a market. There is no point to making broad utilitarian claims about the benefits of "*the* free market" as if we could identify a market as "free" merely by the absence of restraint on naked power. Giving free rein to power without ends is more likely to produce unfreedom than to produce freedom. There is simply no way to talk about a really free economy without entering into particular judgments about what kinds of exchange are conducive to the flourishing of life on earth and what kinds are not.

Though my purpose in this essay has not been to go into detail about the specific ends of human work and material possessions, the Christian tradition provides a wealth of reflection on these matters.[55] I believe it would be counterproductive to expect the state to attempt to impose such a direction on economic activity. What is most important is the direct embodiment of free economic practices. From a Christian point of view, the churches should take an active role in fostering economic practices that are consonant with the true ends of creation. This requires promoting economic practices that maintain close connections among capital, labor, and communities, so that real communal discernment of the good can take place. Such are spaces in which true freedom can flourish.

6

Individualism, the Market, and Christianity: Can the Circle Be Squared?

Samuel Gregg

Apilgrim journeying to the Holy Land in the thirteenth century would have found himself walking tremendous distances along old Roman roads, his only respite from the loneliness and hardship of the trek coming when he passed through one of the growing number of large towns throughout Europe. Anxious to observe his religious duties, the pilgrim would no doubt seek to visit the primary church of such towns, perhaps hoping to pay homage to the particular saint associated with the city.

As he hurried to pray before seeking shelter for the night in a local monastery, the pilgrim would perhaps observe the marketplace located outside the church. Most days, hundreds of merchants, shopkeepers, and craftsmen would gather there to buy and sell goods. Wandering among shops owned by traders, mercers, haberdashers, and goldsmiths, hearing the shouts of "silk," "wine," and "French cloth" uttered in a cosmopolitan range of accents, the pilgrim may have wondered if he had not stumbled into an eastern bazaar or Baghdad *souk*, rather than a world steeped in Christian belief.

Yet the fact remains that once we look beyond the myth of the Middle Ages as a time of ignorance, fear, and misery, we see that the first major expansion of commerce and market exchange in the West occurred during a period of history in which Christianity was regnant throughout Europe. Hitherto, merchant activity had been confined to

small groups of family traders, often Jewish by faith or origin. But in
the high Middle Ages, internally autonomous trading towns and cities
became a regular feature of the European landscape. These commercial centers varied in size from the great Italian and Flemish cities to
numerous small towns of Germania. They also differed between those
focused on long-distance trade (such as Venice, Lübeck, and Genoa),
those producing for export, especially of cloth (Florence, Cologne,
Amsterdam) and metal (Augsburg), and the great majority of smaller
towns engaged in local trade. The commercial population typically
included small retailers, independent craftsmen, merchant-entrepre-
neurs, bankers, producers of luxury goods, and landlords.[1]

For the great majority of Christians, this commercial activity
was not problematic. Indeed, in developing the Church's teaching on
the subject of usury, medieval scholastics contributed significantly
to expanding the amount of capital available for investment.[2] The
fact that most marketplaces were located near churches—typified by
the enormous square outside medieval Milan's cathedral—indicated
that neither merchants nor clergy found anything theologically in-
congruous about commerce. Nor was the Church blind to the benefits
flowing from the growth of market exchange, such as the emergence
of town constitutions, criminal codes, the minting of currency, as
well as the suppression of lawless nobles and the practice of ven-
detta. Moreover, trade expansion did not lessen people's attention to
the needs of the poor. Merchants and traders became major contributors to church almshouses and hospitals.

While there were conflicts between merchants and priests in
commercial towns, numerous clergy played an integral role in the
economic life of these cities. New religious orders such as the Friars,
Beguines, and Brethren of the Common Life developed a spirituality
and ministry peculiarly suited to such environments. Bonds—evident
in guild chapels, market religious festivals, and the adoption of pa-
tron saints—developed between religious and commercial life. Church
schools that answered the need of merchants for literacy, accounting

skills, and legal proficiency became common throughout Italy and the Holy Roman Empire.

There is, however, a less benign side to this story. Throughout the Middle Ages, there were sporadic explosions of violence against merchants, traders, and private property holders. Sometimes these were sparked by instances of brutal treatment of peasants. At other times, they contained a specifically religious impetus, with wild itinerant preachers, often from Franciscan backgrounds, denouncing trade and property ownership as sinful. These episodes sometimes resulted in temporary collapses of order, mass pillaging, and the murder of nobles, merchants, clergy, and peasants alike. It goes without saying that the suppression of such uprisings was equally brutal.[3]

This contrast between Christians engaged with and ministering to those involved in trade and the distaste of other Christians for commerce is not limited to the Middle Ages. Every day, millions of Christians engage in the free exchange of goods and services. Yet some Christians insist that there are deep tensions between the actions and intentions associated with what is often called a "market economy" and the demands of Christian faith. Some Christians insist, for example, that market economic orders facilitate materialistic cultures. Throughout the twentieth century, the proposed remedies of some Christians to these perceived problems have ranged from the advocacy of mixed economies to the outright collectivist propositions of some liberation theologians.

Often associated with these signs of Christian unease with the market economy are concerns about what is often called "individualism." In such cases, individualism is usually defined primarily as an attitude characterized by self-idolatry and a tendency to ignore what Christianity identifies as clear moral obligations on the part of each person to others.

Any discussion of these matters should begin by noting that there is significant room among Christians for prudential disagreement about the most optimal set of economic arrangements for any one society. Beyond adherence to certain principles, there is nothing in the Gospels or Christian tradition that mandates any one economic system. Certainly, these principles may indicate that certain economic systems, such as the command economy (in which the state alone controls all capital and the means of production), so deeply denigrate human dignity that no Christian may support them. Nonetheless, the precise formation of the economic system is not a central matter of Christian faith and morals. Christians cannot equate matters such as belief in Christ's divinity or the prohibition against the intentional killing of human beings with differing opinions as to whether the state should control 20 or 30 percent of a nation's gross domestic product.

On many economic issues, choice is between not only good and bad options but also a range of good options, some of which are incompatible with one another but compatible with Christian teaching. In many cases, the discernment of *how* a modern society can attain a good end may depend on empirical and prudential judgments reasonably in dispute among people equally well-informed by principles of Christian teaching. Having surveyed the available evidence and informed themselves of the relevant Christian principles, some Christians may conclude that universal healthcare is best realized by a predominantly state-funded system. Other Christians, having examined the available evidence and informed themselves of the same principles, may conclude that private health insurance, with the state providing a safety net, is the best approach. In any event, it should be acknowledged that there are many policies that Christians can advocate in order to realize such a goal while remaining in good standing with the Christian community.[4] The theologian Germain Grisez is surely correct to say that, in such cases, people should not propose their opinion as the Church's teaching.[5]

But having made these qualifications, the question remains: Is it possible for "individualism" and "the market" to be reconciled with the creed professed by those who believe that Jesus Christ is the way, the truth, and the life? Much of the answer depends upon the meaning given to these terms. Some interpretations of individualism and what constitutes a market economy are irreconcilable with orthodox Christian belief. No seriously orthodox Christian is likely to claim that people have no responsibilities to others beyond contractual obligations. There are, nevertheless, a variety of bases upon which a rapprochement of Christianity with "individualism" and "the market" may be attempted. One is the Christian vision of what man is, that is, a Christian anthropology.

A Christian anthropology

An indispensable reference point for a Christian anthropology of man is the Genesis account of Creation. This defines man in terms of our most fundamental relationship to God—the relation of image and likeness. "Let us make man in our own image, in the likeness of ourselves" (Gen 1:26). Man's creation is announced with an emphasis that is absent from the creation of other creatures. The essential difference between man and the other creatures is reinforced when God makes man the steward of all creation. This call to stewardship is not based primarily on man's physicality or the characteristics that he shares with the rest of the visible world. Rather, it is based on man's specific likeness to God which is derived from his spiritual relationship with God.

Thus, God's call to man to assume stewardship over the earth is not a call to sheer power and domination. "God saw that it was good" (Gen 1:10, 12, 18, 21, 25). This divine "seeing" is in every way primary, because it creates being and good. Human seeing and human doing are thus always secondary because they always encounter preconstituted value. For while man is called "to fill the earth and subdue it" (Gen 1:28), his task of dominion is defined in terms of a conditional superintendence (cf. Gen 2:15)—it must be used in accordance with the original intention of God. This is why, after investing man with the dominion of stewardship, God warns man not to eat "of the tree of knowledge of good and evil" (Gen 2:17). Man's stewardship is not therefore to be understood as absolute sovereignty; it does not give us the authority to use other persons or creatures according to arbitrary human preference. Instead, man should freely act in accordance with God's law. "The human mind plans the way, but the Lord directs the steps" (Prov 16:9).

Christians also believe that man's knowledge of his own dignity receives its final revelation in the person of Jesus of Nazareth. In Jesus Christ, God entered human affairs in an unrepeatable way, becoming one of the multitude of actors in human history but at the same time unique. The Incarnation reminds us that nothing, except God, surpasses the dignity of man. Each human person is made in the image of *the* Image that God gives us of himself—his own Son: He who is "the image of the invisible God" (Col 1:15).

The life of Christ also reminds us of the profound significance of human action, reason, and will. Jesus did, after all, think with a human mind, love with a human heart, act by human choice, and work with human hands. Through the Incarnation, man re-learns the deep esteem that all should have for the human person in his totality—his body, intellect, will, conscience, and freedom to live in truth. It is not enough, then, to define man solely as an individual of the species. There is something more to each individual, a particular richness and perfection, which can only be brought out by the word "person." For each individual as a person has a specific inner life; this is man's spiritual and moral life, and it revolves around truth and goodness. It is therefore as a person that each individual has value in himself. Hence, to speak of man as a person does more than convey the notion of the individual; it also recognizes each human individual as a creature desired for himself by God.

The fact that each individual is a person means that all of us have been graced with qualities that allow us to enter into relationship with God and to act as stewards of God's creation. These qualities are *reason* and *free will*. Both are aspects of each individual's spiritual dimension, precisely because they are attributes found in the inner self.

Yet, proceeding as they do from God's creative act, man's interior gifts of free will and reason do not necessarily set individuals on the path of attempting to free themselves "from" God. They can also direct him to the way of integral freedom that comes from living in truth. The dignity proper to each individual, the dignity presented to us both as a gift and as something to strive for, is inextricably bound up with truth. Truthful thinking and truthful living are indispensable components of that dignity.

But how does the human person come to know what is true and act accordingly? Christianity teaches that the fullness of truth is to be found within divine revelation. There are specific dogmas of Christianity, such as the Trinity, that cannot be explained by reason alone. Nonetheless, as John Paul II observed in his encyclical *Fides et Ratio*, "Faith is in a sense an 'exercise of thought'; and human reason is neither annulled nor debased in assenting to the contents of faith, which are in any case attained by way of free and informed choice."[6] Moreover, Christianity also proposes for everyone's acceptance on faith a number of propositions—such as the existence of God—which are also accessible by reason. St. Paul referred to this when he spoke of "pagans who never heard of the Law but are led by reason to do what the Law commands. . . . They can point to the substance of the Law engraved on their hearts—they can call a witness, that is, their own conscience—they have accusation and defense, that is, their own inner mental dialogue" (Rm 2:14–16).

Human reasoning about truth, especially moral truth, does not therefore involve people somehow creating "their own" moral order or "their own" truth. Instead, it takes the form of people attaining ever-deepening knowledge of the *unchanging* truth about good and evil. The process, however, by which each person can conform to the moral law is through human choice and action. To cite Boethius, Christians believe that, while *persona est rationalis naturae individua substantia*,[7] neither man's rational nature nor his individuality expresses fully the completeness contained in the concept of the person. It does not sufficiently underline the significance of human *acts* for each individual.

Man is only man when he is the author of his own advancement. A basic human need of each individual is to *act*, responsibly, and on one's own initiative. As soon as we reflect on human actions, we see that their uniqueness is derived from their moral significance. Morality constitutes their intrinsic feature, and it is not to be found in the actions that characterize other created beings. The acts of animals, for instance, lack a moral dimension because animals are not persons. Indeed, a conscious human act is an ethical experience for each individual because it is an act of free will. "God left man in the power of his own counsel" (Sir 15:14). This power of self-determination is based on reflection and manifested in the fact that man acts from choice. This makes each individual his own master, but also responsible for his actions before God: "He himself made man in the beginning, and then left him free to make his own decisions. If you wish, you can keep the commandments, to behave faithfully is within your power" (Ec 15:14–16).

Understanding the moral dimension of individual action helps us face another truth of human anthropology that, for Christians, cannot be ignored. Although God created all, and it was good, Genesis reminds us of the *mysterium iniquitatis*: the deep interior rupture that sin creates within man. "If we say we have no sin, we deceive ourselves, and the truth is not in us" (1 Jn 1:8–9). People who reject this are those who think themselves perfect, such as the Pharisee in the parable, or who imagine that no one could be better than themselves, such as Jean-Jacques Rousseau, who, in his *Confessions,* summons his peers to the Last Judgment and challenges them to produce one personal record more honorable than his own.

From the beginning, Christianity has proclaimed that, although man was made by God in a state of holiness, man abused his liberty from the onset of history. As Genesis indicates, it was not God who withdrew from man, but man from God. The man and the woman committed the error of attempting to seize for themselves the knowledge of the tree of good and evil (cf. Gen 3:1–24), that is, the error of seeking the power of deciding for themselves what is good and what is evil. Satan portrays God as a liar envious of man's knowledge of good and evil. Beguiled by such suggestions and desirous to become "like God," the man ate of the fruit. No sooner had he done so than his flesh rebelled against his reason. In the words of Thomas More: "And so entered death at the windows of our own eyes into the house of our heart, and there burned up all the goodly building, that God had wrought therein."[8]

In sinning, man made a claim to complete moral independence from God by refusing to recognize his status as a created being and seeking instead to become the Creator. Thus, as Augustine wrote, sin is "love of oneself even to contempt of God."[9] Insofar as they flow from individual human choice, sinful acts are not mere elements of transitory behavior. They contribute to shaping an individual's life, for in every sinful choice, each person makes himself guilty, regardless of whether one feels guilt or not. And that person remains guilty until he has a real change of heart, by freely choosing to repent. Sin, then, is always the result of an act of personal freedom. Christianity acknowledges that psychological, social, and cultural factors can condition the manner in which individual persons make their choices for good or evil. Yet while they can limit moral responsibility and constrain freedom, these influences should not be understood in ways that obscure the deeper reality—that sin is an integral part of the truth about man because the human person is a free moral actor. To acknowledge the reality of sin is to acknowledge the reality of freedom. This truth cannot be disregarded in order to place the blame for individuals' sins on external factors such as structures, systems, or other people. To do so would be to deny the person's freedom, which is also manifested—though in a negative way—in each individual's responsibility for the sins that he commits.

Man's propensity to sin means that individuals constantly struggle between acting in the ways that they know that they ought, and being drawn towards doing what they ought not. In St. Paul's words: "I have been sold as a slave to sin. I cannot understand my own behavior. I fail to carry out the things that I want to do, and I find myself doing the very things that I hate" (Rm 7:14–15). This anthropological truth has profound implications for Christian reflection on the social order. John Paul II's 1991 social encyclical *Centesimus Annus* explains this point particularly well:

> [M]an, who was created for freedom, bears within himself the wound of original sin, which constantly draws him towards evil and puts him in need of redemption. Not only is *this doctrine an integral part of Christian revelation;* it also has great hermeneutical value insofar as it helps one to understand human reality. Man tends towards good, but he is also capable of evil. He can transcend his immediate interest and still remain bound to it. The social order will be all the more stable, the more it takes this fact into account and does not place in opposition personal interest and the interests of society as a whole, but rather seeks ways to bring them into fruitful harmony.[10]

Human sin also indicates that while each person must struggle towards the perfection to which Christ calls us, there is no possibility of building an earthly utopia. Wounded by sin, man almost inevitably causes damage to the fabric of his relationship with others and with the created world.

The damage that individual choices for sin do to others as well as ourselves points to the final element of Christian anthropology relevant to this discussion: the truth of man's social nature. To paraphrase Pierre Manent, we are and wish to be individuals, but we are also *human* individuals.[11] Divine revelation makes clear the full significance of the human person's social character. Genesis stresses that God did not leave man as a solitary creature. "It is not good for man to be alone" (Gen 2:18). If man is to know himself, he must encounter other human persons. Hence, from the beginning "male and female he created them" (Gen 1:27). The most intimate form of reciprocity thus came into being, as man as male came to a new self-awareness with the appearance of man as *female*. The man instantly recognized his essential unity with this other human: "This at last is bone of my bones, flesh of my flesh" (Gen 2:23).

This companionship of man and woman produces the primary form of interpersonal communion. Man and woman were made for each other. This does not mean that God left them half-made and incomplete. Rather, God created them to be a communion of individual persons, in which each is "helpmate" to the other, for they are equal as individual persons and complementary as masculine and feminine. Although different, they are equal in dignity, and they are interdependent because they are unable to fulfill themselves as *isolated* individuals. Social life is not something added onto man. Through his dealings with others, each individual can shape himself as the person-that-he-ought-to-be.

There is a certain resemblance here between what Christians understand as the unity of the Trinity, and the communion that Christians believe that people should establish between themselves. The Trinity is not reducible to its members considered in their distinction from one another. The divine persons, united in their mutual communion, are God, and God is perfectly one in his reality, goodness, and love. Yet the three divine persons really are distinct individuals, not merely parts of a larger whole. Their distinct personhood is in no way diminished or lessened by the fact that together they are the one true God. The Council of Toledo summarized this in the following manner: "In the relational names of the persons, the Father is related to the Son, the Son to the Father, and the Holy Spirit to both. While they are called three persons in view of their relations, we believe in one nature or substance."[12]

Given that the person is social by nature, it follows that the good of each individual person is related to the *common good,* a common good that in turn can only be defined with reference to the individual person. As defined by the Second Vatican Council, the common good is "the sum total of social conditions which allow people, either as groups or as individuals, to reach their fulfillment more fully and more easily."[13] It follows that advancing the common good involves each human person supporting others as they seek, through free choice and action, to participate in those "fundamental human goods"[14] that are at the core of human flourishing, as well as providing others with the necessary autonomy that they need to use their reason to identify and then freely actualize these goods as the fruit of their own deliberation, judgment, choice, and action. In this light, the meaning of the evangelical commandment to love takes on fresh meaning, as it involves individuals intending and assisting the choice of others to participate in moral goods, thereby making the flourishing of others an aspect of their own flourishing.

Autonomy and truth

The preceding outline of a Christian anthropology of man provides a sound basis for assessing which understandings of individual autonomy and the market economy are compatible with orthodox Christian belief. Those conceptions of individual autonomy which deny, for example, that each human being has a social nature, or that human liberty should be understood primarily as the liberty to choose to live in truth, are incompatible with orthodox Christian belief about what man is. Equally incompatible are those versions of individualism primarily informed by an atheistic vision of man or any philosophical system that reduces humans to the status of mere pleasure-machines.

If, however, "individualism" means an appreciation of the role of individual choice in enabling a person to choose the good, assume responsibility for himself, and thereby fulfill himself as a person, then this understanding of individual autonomy simply expresses a truth about man that Christianity has always affirmed. Likewise, an "individualism" that upholds the principle that the individual, though possessing a social nature, may never be subsumed into the state or any other social organization, is simply underlining a principle long upheld by orthodox Christianity. Though one is reluctant to quote *Centesimus Annus* again, its critique of socialism summarizes these points in a succinct manner. If people are to be truly free, the encyclical states, they must recognize that man is, by virtue of being a person and the author of moral acts, responsible for himself:

> The fundamental error of socialism is *anthropological* in nature. Socialism considers the individual person simply as an element, a molecule within the social organism, so that the good of the individual is completely subordinated to the functioning of the socio-economic mechanism. Socialism likewise maintains that the good of the individual can be realized without reference to *his free choice, to the unique and exclusive responsibility which he exercises in the face of good or evil.* Man is thus reduced to a series of social relationships, and the concept of the person as *the autonomous subject of moral decision* disappears, the very subject whose decisions build the social order.[15]

Though this is obviously a scathing assessment of socialism, the moral anthropology of man from which this critique proceeds may also prove disconcerting to some of a rather non-socialist bent. Building a socio-economic system that denies that man, as a person and author of his acts, possesses the unique capacity of free choice, is folly. But this does not mean that choice itself is man's moral reference point. Free choice is exercised "in the face of" good and evil. Hence, for Christians, freedom is *not* about doing whatever one "feels like," but is rather about doing what one ought in light of the truth. That is why

Centesimus Annus defines free choice as a responsibility. Reference to truth links the individual person's natural capacity for freedom with the acquisition of responsibility.

In more than one commentator's view, this linkage brings us to the heart of the conflict between Christianity and certain versions of individualism.[16] The disquiet felt by some identified with the latter is captured in the much-quoted closing sentences of Milton Friedman's commentary on *Centesimus Annus:* "I must confess that one high-minded sentiment, passed off as if it were a self-evident proposition, sent shivers down my back: *'Obedience to the truth* about God and man is the first condition of freedom.' Whose 'truth'? Decided by whom?"[17] These words suggest that Friedman is skeptical of the idea of metaphysical truth and wary of anyone claiming that they know *the* truth. Such attitudes tend to typify most post-Enlightenment approaches to such questions. As Joseph Ratzinger comments: "The modern attitude towards truth is summed up in Pilate's question, 'What is truth?'"[18] Christianity, by contrast, regards discernment of truth as the very purpose of the human intellect, and free obedience to the truth about God and man as the prerequisite to each individual's attainment of true freedom.

For freedom is more than being—to use the title of Friedman's famous book—"free to choose." Paradoxically, there is a resemblance here between Friedman's view of the essence of a free society and Karl Marx's own dream of freedom. The state of the future communist society would make it possible, Marx claimed, "to do one thing today and another tomorrow; to hunt in the morning, fish in the afternoon, breed cattle in the evening and criticize after dinner, just as I please."[19] In both cases, freedom is understood as the right to do whatever we wish and to refrain from anything we do not wish to do. Each individual's choice—informed or otherwise—becomes the only principle of action. A radical primacy of the will, of individuals exercising their rights without any reference to the context of the moral life, thus emerges, "liberated" from the essence of distinctly human ends.

The problem with such positions is that they exclude any reference to reason. How free is man's will if he cannot reason in a non-instrumental way about the choices he is to make? Or, to cite Ratzinger:

> Is an unreasonable will truly a free will? Is an unreasonable freedom truly freedom? Is it really a good? In order to prevent the tyranny of unreason must we not complete the definition of freedom as the capacity to will and to do what we will by placing it in the context of reason, of the totality of man? And will not the interplay between reason and will also involve the search for the common reason shared by all men and thus for the compatibility of liberties?[20]

From this standpoint, the issue of freedom and individual autonomy is intimately related to the question of the will's link with reason, and the nature of reason considered within the totality of man. Not surprisingly, the Christian vision of man directs us to rather different conclusions than those of Friedman and Marx when it comes to understanding the *end* of individual autonomy. The purpose of individual freedom, for the orthodox Christian, is to know the truth and then achieve the self-mastery that each individual may realize by freely actualizing that which is truly good for man. The individual who constantly acts in this way is free in the fullest sense of the word. As the Deuteronomic verse puts it: "I set before you life or death, blessing or curse. Choose life, then, so that you and your descendants may live" (Dt 30:19). Thus does Christianity extend free choice to the infinite.

A type of market

If certain understandings of individualism find echoes in a Christian anthropology of the person, is the same necessarily true for the market economy? The market economic order is, after all, incomprehensible without its emphasis on individual choice in the production and purchase of material goods and services. This reality is sometimes obscured by a tendency to speak of the "market" as if it were an anonymous conglomerate that exerts its own will.

Certainly, there is an "abstract" dimension to market economies in the sense that they are premised, as the mainly Christian economists of the *ordo liberal* school stressed,[21] on widespread acceptance of certain rules and institutions. These include the law of contract and private property rights. But though essential, such rules and institutions remain ancillary to what is truly central to market exchanges: human persons, human choices, and human acts. If one accepts as a matter of orthodox Christian belief that God created each person to choose the truth freely and that the human person ought therefore to be free, then a free economic order—a market—is surely part of the order of human freedom. As observed by the Catholic philosopher Rocco Buttiglione: "The smallest element of the free market is a contract, the encounter of the free will of two human beings. They must both be free, for if they are not there can be no contract, and thus no free market. In this way, the law on contracts that stands at the very basis of a free-market economy is a law that presupposes human freedom."[22] Buttiglione justifies the market not by the fact that it is the most efficient system for allocating scarce resources, but rather because it is a moral requirement of a social order that takes the idea of freedom seriously by allowing people to assume responsibility for themselves in the economic sphere. Through contracts, we make ourselves the authors of particular obligations and acquire responsibilities. We also place limits upon our own tendency to act on whims.

Similar arguments were made by the Lutheran *ordo liberal* economist Wilhelm Röpke. History illustrated, he insisted, that only a market economic order had proved able to give individuals the necessary scope for free choice in the material realm. Hence, we should not be surprised to see Röpke explaining in 1953—at the height of Keynesian programs in the West and statism in the communist world—that "my opposition on technical grounds is that socialism, in its enthusiasm for organization, centralization, and efficiency, is committed to means that simply are not compatible with freedom."[23] Röpke also argued that, to the extent that choice in the economic realm remained free, it helped to keep individual persons from being subsumed into artificial collectives. In addition, market economic orders assisted individuals to recognize that freedom was demanding, and therefore helped to forestall the perennial temptation to abdicate freedom and become dependent on the state.[24] "My fundamental opposition to socialism," Röpke wrote, "is to an ideology that, in spite of all its 'liberal' phraseology, gives too little to man, his freedom, and his personality; and too much to society."[25] In these words, we hear distinct echoes of Alexis de Tocqueville's warnings about the potential for the citizenry to enter into a Faustian bargain whereby the state relieves people of responsibility for taking care of themselves, in return for which people give up their freedom. This "soft despotism," as Tocqueville called it, is surely contrary to the Christian vision of the free man and free society.

Neither Buttiglione nor Röpke believe that the market is in itself sufficient for human freedom. Their case, however, for an essential compatibility between the market economic order and the Christian vision of man is further strengthened once we take into account the reality of sin. An essential assumption of the free market is, as Adam Smith observed, that people tend to pursue what they regard as their self-interest. This "self-interest" need not be selfishness. Indeed, a true understanding of the greatness that God offers to each person who chooses to follow Christ suggests that selfishness is not at all in any person's ultimate interests. The market does, however, take into account the fact that man is not God; that he cannot, as Friedrich Hayek observed, know everything; and that he is forever divided between knowing what is good, and being drawn towards the false attractions of evil. Those who seek to ground a social order in *what man really is* would be imprudent to ignore this.

The question may, however, be asked: If the market economic order reflects, in part, the workings of each individual's self-interest, does this not implicitly restrict our capacity to build the authentic communities of love demanded by Christianity? Does it not distract people from establishing those conditions that assist others in fulfilling themselves that Christians call the common good?

Well, yes and no. The pursuit of self-interest and market competition suggests that commercial activity cannot be expected to mirror, for example, the life of that first *communio personarum* that we call the family. To this extent, commercial relations tend not to embrace the degree of self-giving that occurs, for example, in family life. Christianity has, however, always recognized that different forms of communities have naturally different purposes. It is therefore unreasonable to expect them all to be like the family or the nation-state. The jurist and philosopher John Finnis distinguishes a variety of relationships, such as "business," "play," and "friendship," all of which are embodied, to varying degrees, in any form of community.[26] The relative strength of these relationships within any one form of community makes all associations naturally conducive to certain activities and outcomes, and less conducive to others.

At the same time, the market economy does promote many material and social developments that contribute to the common good. Leaving aside their effective provision of the material basis required by any group of humans for existence, market economic orders do allow individuals to serve each other—albeit often indirectly—through the process of exchange. The market order also brings people from very different backgrounds into contact, while simultaneously reducing the potential for conflict by softening the intensity of political life. In an echo of Montesquieu, Tocqueville claimed:

> Trade is the natural enemy of all violent passions. Trade loves moderation, delights in compromise, and is most careful to avoid anger. It is patient, supple, and insinuating,

only resorting to extreme means in cases of absolute
necessity. Trade makes men independent of one another.
[I]t leads them to want to manage their own affairs and
teaches them how to succeed therein. Hence it makes
them inclined to liberty but disinclined to revolution.[27]

Tocqueville was not, however, naïve. In *Democracy in America,* he
noted that the commercial republicanism generated by the market
sometimes facilitates conditions that Christians call "occasions of
sin." But on the other hand, we should not underestimate the extent
to which commerce can also be conducive to the realization of virtue. Buttiglione reminds us that the entrepreneurial acts that drive
market economies can encourage the development of virtues such as
prudence, industriousness, courage, and loyalty.[28]

Nevertheless, for all the moral and material benefits that market transactions as well as their associated rules and institutions
bring to the social order, few Christians would consider the market
economy in itself to be a sufficient basis for a society conducive to
people's efforts to live in truth. Contractual justice is important, but
it is not enough. Indeed, at times, being a Christian means making a
choice for the good that we know will result in economic failure.
Christians therefore increasingly look to the cultural dimension to
ensure that individual choice and the market are grounded in a moral
ecology that reflects the truth about man.

The priority of culture

Christians convinced that their religious beliefs can be reconciled
with the market order and respect for individual autonomy invariably
emphasize the need for humans to be immersed in a particular type
of moral culture. Unfortunately, what they mean by "culture" is often
left unspecified. Only in recent decades have Christians devoted significant intellectual attention to its meaning. This is perhaps a result
of an awareness that a greater understanding of culture can facilitate

evangelization in not only the developing world, but also in the increasingly aggressively secularist cultures that characterize the West.

In a general sense, the word "culture" embraces everything through which people develop their many bodily and spiritual qualities. The formation of a culture thus requires the involvement of human creativity and intelligence. Human action is at the root of human culture. Plants and animals live and act, but have no culture. Culture is *from* man, since man's actions are uniquely creative of it. Culture is also *for* man since it is the way in which we come to know what we are to a greater degree. Man and his actions are thus the measure of culture, and consciousness of what man ought to be ensures that man does not become the prisoner of any one culture.

At the same time, human culture may be expressed and objectified in various products, practices, and institutions that, in their turn, influence man. These include not only material objects, but also the different ways of living that arise from our diverse manners of using things, laboring, expressing ourselves, forming customs, establishing laws, and cultivating our minds. In this sense, legal and state institutions are an expression of culture. Moreover, in most cultures, we discover profound reflections about man, his interior life, and his knowledge of God. Cultures may also, however, embody errors and the failure to recognize evil in their midst over long periods of time. Christians must thus constantly ask themselves: What is the image of man that underlies and is proclaimed by different cultures? What space does this image give to the truth of faith and the interior life?

The free choices we make in the economic realm are not somehow isolated from those actions, customs, and institutions that constitute the totality of human culture. If, therefore, individual choices are informed predominately, for example, by a moral ecology of materialism or what many Christians call the culture of death, then their acts will reflect materialistic priorities and concerns. Yet the same logic suggests that if individual choices are influenced by a moral ecology grounded in a vision of man as the *imago Dei,* then we may have greater confidence that such choices will be directed to the realization of moral good.

If we accept this analysis as true, the question becomes one of *who* should play the critical role of shaping the culture. Virtually all serious Christians would affirm that the family and the Church have indispensable roles to play in this regard. The family is the most formative influence on the lives of most people, and Christian teaching from the very beginning has given a special place to the family. The Church constitutes the Body of Christ that spreads the saving message of the Gospel and anticipates the Kingdom of God that is to come. Evangelizing human culture is essential to its mission.

More controversial is the role of law and state authority. A bond created by liberty is obviously preferable to one created by constraint. A "coerced free choice" is a contradiction in terms, precisely because such actions lack a self-determining dimension.[29] This is not an argument, however, for never preventing people from acting in certain ways. Few people, save anarchists, would hold that the use of coercion in the social order can never be justified. One need only read the letters of St. Paul and St. Peter to see that Christianity has always recognized that there are instances in which the state may exercise coercion. Christians sometimes, however, disagree among themselves, and certainly with many secularists, about the appropriate forms of state coercion, the conditions in which it may be justly exercised, and the institutions that may enact it.

Several points are at issue here. The first is an argument between two broad schools of jurisprudential thought. One is what Robert P. George calls the "central tradition."[30] This maintains—with Aristotle, Aquinas, and Kant—that there is truth; that people can know it through reason; that they can conform their lives to it through free will; and that the law plays a legitimate role in guiding people towards knowledge of truth and self-realization of the good. Opposing the central tradition are those such as Nietzsche and Sartre who believe that there is no truth, or at least none that humans are capable of knowing, as well as modern liberals such as John Rawls and Ronald Dworkin who argue that individual rights should be identified and political and legal institutions designed, to use Dworkin's phrase, "without employing any particular conception of the good life or of what gives value to life."[31]

The legitimate fear of liberals such as Dworkin and Rawls is that mixing truth-claims with the power of the state is a recipe for the unjust circumscription of individual autonomy. The problem is that such liberals may underestimate the extent to which the preservation of freedom itself depends on truth-claims. Without truth-claims, there is *nothing* to which we can morally and politically appeal in order to defend freedom. For if there is only opinion—your opinion, my opinion, everyone else's opinion—but no official recognition of truth, then there is no inherent reason that slavery should not be seen as the same as liberty, or coercion the same as equality. If all opinions are equal, then we must conclude that Edmund Burke's views, for example, are only as valuable as those of Joseph Stalin. If every preference is valid simply by virtue of being freely chosen, then it would be possible to state, "the Nazis cannot be held accountable for their choices because they acted according to their own preferences, they showed real commitment to what they believed, and who in any case is to judge that what they did was wrong?" In such an atmosphere, political debates cease to be a matter of reasoned discussion of the truth of people's views. Instead, politics becomes a question of who is able to provide their opinions with greater legislative weight. The truth about the good is not as great a threat to liberty as Rawls and Dworkin suppose. The absence of truth, however, certainly is.

A more fundamental problem with the type of argument for individual autonomy posited by Dworkin is that it is grounded on the claim that everyone enjoys what he calls "the right to moral independence." This right is in turn based on what Dworkin refers to as the abstract right to equality. Though Dworkin nowhere explains from where this right is ultimately derived (a perennial problem for most secularist jurisprudence), he defines it as the right to be treated by the state with "equal concern and respect."[32] The state violates this right to equality whenever it restricts individual freedom on the ground that one citizen's conception of the good life is superior to another's.[33]

Many commentators—both secular and Christian—have underlined the problems underlying this argument. It is not, for example, self-evident that a legal concern for the morality of individual persons indicates any form of disregard for those persons whose preferred conduct is restricted. In fact, such legal restrictions, Finnis comments, "*may* manifest, not contempt, but a sense of the equal worth and human dignity of those people, whose conduct is outlawed precisely on the ground that it expresses a serious misconception of, and actually degrades, human worth and dignity, and this degrades their own personal worth and dignity, along with that of others who may be induced to share in or emulate their degradation."[34] A similar view emerges in the writings of the liberal jurist Joseph Raz. He contends that reasonable laws to protect socially valuable institutions, such as monogamous marriage, far from diminishing individual autonomy, *advance* autonomy by protecting morally valuable options for choice. He also insists that the value of autonomy is realized by human beings in choosing between *good* options. The good of autonomy therefore, in Raz's view, "supplies no reason to provide, nor any reason to protect, worthless let alone bad options." Raz even states that "autonomously choosing the bad makes one's life worse than a comparable non-autonomous life."[35]

If it is the case that law exists to facilitate conditions that allow all to fulfill themselves by freely actualizing moral goods, then, *in principle*, Christians should not object to the law shaping the moral ecology and therefore individual choices in an appropriate manner. The precise form assumed by such shaping is, however, likely to be a matter for prudential judgment rather than authoritative teaching in the great majority of cases.

In forming such judgments, Christians are likely to be influenced by their view of the modern world—a world profoundly marked
by an emphasis on individual choice and the spread of market economic orders. Perhaps in unprecedented ways, Christians today are
rather divided in their view of this world. Some embrace it uncritically
and essentially reject the notion that being a Christian requires one
to make, on occasion, choices that may run counter to secular priorities. Such has been the path of "liberal Christianity." The relentless
self-destruction of churches most influenced by such thinking over
the past thirty years appears to illustrate its futility.

Then there are those Christians who wish to retreat into a fortress church—one that rejects the world and may even, in some cases,
be afraid of the world. Given the anti-Christian mindset that tends to
characterize much of the consciously secularist cultures of parts of
Western society, this position is comprehensible. For the orthodox
Christian, Jesus Christ is the way, the truth, and the life, and in
many instances, Christians live in societies where the world belittles
this way, disdains this truth, and destroys life. Why, then, should
Christians care about individual autonomy and the market economy
in the modern world?

The answer is that, for all its flaws, the world of man is one that
God loved so much that He gave his only Son to redeem it. Though
Christ and his Church will always be a sign of contradiction to the
world, it is in this same world that Christians have been called to
build the communities of love and self-giving that anticipate the Kingdom that will come when Christ returns in glory. This means that
Christians should rise to the challenge of redeeming concepts such
as individual autonomy and the market economic order, and plant
them in deeper soil than what is offered by secularist ideologies. The
concept of individual freedom finds deep echoes in Christian belief,
not least because Christianity affirms the *reality* of individual choice,
and its profound implications for man's development as a person.
Christianity also insists that humans are, in part, material beings,

charged with the responsibility of exercising dominion over the created world and able to acquire moral good in all their freely willed actions—including those that occur in the economic realm. Just as the Christians of the Middle Ages opened themselves to the possibilities of commerce and sought to evangelize a changing society, Christians in the modern world should remember the Lord's call to "be not afraid" so that they may persuade people to expose the reality of their unique capacity for choice to the possibility of transcendence—and the Truth that this transcendence embodies.

7

The "Bourgeois Family" and the Meaning of Freedom and Community

David Crawford

Proponents of Anglo-American liberalism often make two complementary claims. First, liberal institutions, including the free market, offer intermediate communities, such as the family, the resources and environment necessary to fulfill their autonomous roles. Hence, the family depends in large part on these liberal institutions for its complete social flourishing.[1] Second, they argue that liberal institutions also depend on the family for their proper functioning and survival. The family is the place where the virtues are inculcated. Thus, defenders of liberalism argue that the family is vital to the proper functioning of liberal culture itself.[2] The two exist in a kind of mutual interdependence, a symbiotic relationship, as it were. "It seems impossible," Michael Novak tells us, "to imagine the democratic governance, a free economy, and a liberal culture apart from the much disdained bourgeois family."[3]

Is this deep symbiosis real? In order to address this question, we must first address the thorny issue—an issue that is essential both to the liberal proposal and to the idea of family—of the relationship between freedom and community. Central to the idea of the free market is the notion of liberty. Defenders of liberalism understandably tend to emphasize the freedom presupposed by the very idea of the "free" market, and the interconnection between "economic liberty" and "political liberty." We hear of the "structure of freedom," by which is meant the variety of forms liberty takes in a liberal society—economic, political, cultural, and so forth. Less often addressed is the nature of freedom itself and the sense of community it implies. Closely associated with the free-market sense of freedom and community is the central concept of "self-interest," variously referred to as "virtuous self-interest," "rational self-interest," or "self-interest rightly understood."[4] As a general matter, freedom means, for liberalism, the ability to pursue what one sees as one's own best interests.

This essay will argue that the dual claims recited above—family is necessary for the liberal economy, and the liberal economy preserves and nurtures the family—are far from unambiguous. At base, the question comes down to the nature of freedom and community, as it is conceived by free-market economics, on the one hand, and as it is embodied in the family, on the other. Thus, this essay will discuss—within the limited confines of a short work—the "structure of freedom," but that term will indicate here the interior meaning of freedom itself.

"Self-interest" or "self-gift"?

"Self-interest rightly understood." We might begin our discussion by briefly recalling the celebrated statement of Adam Smith regarding the butcher, the brewer, and the baker. Unlike many types of animals, who survive as individuals in their natural state, Smith observes, the human person "has almost constant occasion for the help of his brethren." However, "it is in vain for him to expect it from their benevolence only." Rather, he must engage their "self-love in his favour, and shew them that it is for their own advantage to do for him what he requires of them." Indeed, this is the core meaning of economic exchange, the "bargain" and the contract. "It is not from the benevolence of the butcher, the brewer, or the baker, that we expect our dinner, but from their regard to their own interest. We address ourselves, not to their humanity but to their self-love, and never talk to them of our own necessities but of their advantages."[5] For our

purposes, at least two important ideas are expressed here. First, the flourishing of the human person requires a community of others who are able to supply, through exchange, his needs. Second, this community of others finds its genesis in the free acts of individuals, each attempting to realize his own interests.

While critics of liberalism often decry its individualistic tendencies, Smith begins his examination of the "causes of the wealth of nations" with a certain view of the relationship between the individual and the community. His first observation is that the human person needs a community of others, unlike some animals who lead solitary lives. He requires for his very survival "the help of his brethren," who supply the needs he cannot supply himself. Hence, for example, Michael Novak is able to speak of liberalism's "communitarian" character. Of course, the crucial point of the passage is that this community is a community of mutually coinciding self-interests. As we shall see in a moment, this fact raises the important question of whether liberalism can account for non-self-interested communitarian relations, and what these relations would mean within a liberal framework.

For the moment, however, we should grant that there are many ways in which self-interest is more complicated and less suspicious than some of its detractors have acknowledged. It is true that "virtuous self-interest" should not be equated with "narrow selfishness." Certainly, the concept of the "self" in "self-interest" is already an abstraction. "Self-interested" economic choice is more often exercised on behalf of a family than it is for the "individual" as such.[6] The "self" contained in "self-interest" is therefore, often, a "familial self." It is also possible to interpret self-interest broadly, to include actions and behaviors that do not at first strike us as characteristically "self-interested," at least not in the common sense of the term. Thus Novak tells us that "self-interest of a sort is the propellant of a mother's love even unto death for her child, as it is the propellant of love of one's own nation and the defense of the values one holds dear."[7] Elsewhere, quoting Milton and Rose Friedman, Novak claims that self-interest, thus broadly understood, lies at the root of the "self-sacri-fice" of philanthropists and religious who minister to the needs of the poor or serve as missionaries to convert the heathen to the true faith.[8] Novak's and the Friedmans' intention is not to "unmask" a secret "egoism" (again, at least in any normal sense of the word) buried in motherly love or philanthropic and missionary zeal. Rather, the intention is more benign: "self-sacrificial" actions realize values people hold dear, and therefore, in the broader sense, often consti-tute a realization of "self-interest." To the extent that these are good values, the people who hold them dear and act accordingly are what we call morally good people.

But does the association economic liberalism presumes between virtuous self-interest, freedom, and community preclude the possibil-ity of genuinely disinterested actions? Presumably liberal institutions can accommodate different actualizations of freedom. We should not immediately conclude that Novak, for example, has simply reduced charity to "virtuous self-interest," however broadly construed, al-though, as we shall see, he does leave it less than intelligible. In fact, Novak tells us that self-interest is one of, but "not the sole motive of religious men. . . ." He notes that Christianity appeals both to self-interest (the fear of damnation, the reward of bliss) but also to the "sacrifice of personal interests to the 'consummate order of all created things,' as willed by God." The latter "motive is nobler and deeper," but the "former is persuasive and more popular. . . . Both come from God."[9]

A fundamental claim of liberalism is that it leaves individuals a zone of liberty in which they can follow through on their religious beliefs without undue interference. Thus, to be consistent, liberalism would not seem to demand that all community and freedom be grounded purely in "self-interest." Religious communities, for example, are grounded in love, which is distinct from pure self-interest, if it is authentic. Perhaps an argument could be made, based on what has already been said, that the "nobler and deeper" relations of religion necessarily find themselves at the heart of the family. Recall the argument for the broader, "familial" meaning of "self" just recited. If this argument is to be supported, if the "familial" sense of "self" just mentioned is not simply to collapse back into a mere extension of a purely individualistic (and therefore "selfish") sense of "self," there must be a hard core of true *disinterestedness* contained in family relations. Realistically, it would seem, all human relations contain some "mixture" of self-interest and disinterest. Presumably, then, even economic exchange relations could contain a "nobler and deeper" element. Indeed, Novak suggests that all actualizations of freedom contain this mixture of self-interest, because of man's fallen condition. To attempt to extirpate this feature of behavior from the human heart would be to fall into dangerous utopianism. Hence, liberalism simply attempts to harness the energy resulting from man's fallen state to produce as much good as possible. And yet "nobler and deeper" motives may still be found, at least in theory.

The polarity between freedom and community. As we have seen, Adam Smith begins with a simple observation: people acting in the world are primarily motivated (or appear to be primarily motivated) by "self-love" or "their own interest." This observation might appear simply to reflect the way things really are. Certainly the reality of "self-interest" cannot be gainsaid.[10] At first glance, therefore, it might seem unproblematic. Indeed, defenders of liberalism often emphasize the "concreteness" of the liberal proposal, by which they mean its empirical and practical orientation. Nonetheless, at the heart of the notion of economic self-interest is a tacit understanding of the nature of freedom and community as such, an understanding that we all too easily presuppose without examination.

Although liberalism doubtless sees community as crucial to human realization, its conception of community arises within an understanding of freedom that remains, for all that, fundamentally "indifferent" to it. This assertion requires some explanation. The free market claims to say nothing concerning what the human person should desire or how he should use his freedom. It simply purports to set up a framework in which whatever is subjectively valued may be realized so far as this realization is consistent with public order. It is this framework that supports the idea of an "ordered liberty." Indeed, liberalism links community to conditions of scarcity in the economic realm, to the need for securing person and property in the political realm, and so forth. Community, therefore, remains a "by-product" of human freedom's actualization toward fulfillment in conditions of material scarcity. Liberalism views community as possessing a primarily instrumental and external relation to human freedom.

This is apparent when we consider that, insofar as a good can be realized without enlisting the help or engaging the self-interest of another, a community of interests will not arise, according to the liberal model, and therefore, following the logic of liberalism, no community *at all* will arise with respect to that good. After all, to enlist the help of another through an appeal to his self-interest always bears a cost to the economic actor. In order to enlist his aid, I will always have to settle for something less than I might have wanted initially, although this possible community of action might have produced a (perhaps intangible) common good. And therefore, by the very nature of the liberal proposal, the choice to avoid entering into community in situations that do not realize self-interest would be a valid actualization of my authentic freedom. Either possibility (entering/not entering into community) would be an equivalent actualization of freedom—not necessarily *morally* equivalent, but equivalent in the sense that either would constitute an equivalent engagement of the very nature of freedom itself. Conditions of scarcity and the need for security mean that communities will arise *in fact* from the free activity of individuals. These conditions and needs therefore impose a kind of external necessity upon community. But this is simply another way of restating the basic problem: community remains in this sense "accidental" or "external" to freedom. In this crucial sense, then, freedom is conceived as ontologically "indifferent" with respect to the other, and therefore with respect to community. Or put differently, freedom has been abstracted from—as we will argue below—its interior relation to community.

The hallmark of this version of freedom and community, which is the liberal version, is that it depends on minimal interference in individual choices made to realize subjective values. Freedom is not originally ordered from within, according to this view, toward anything or anyone in particular. Rather, it takes its outward direction from the recognition of some good it can attain in relation (or not in relation) to the other (i.e., through exchange or cooperation, or through the rejection of such exchange or cooperation). In other words, the basic notion of self-interest conceives human freedom and action, at least for purposes of the public, economic order, as fundamentally constituted in the ability to choose among various objects of economic activity, either in concert with others or (conceivably) on one's own. But this means that freedom is always basically "self-centered," and only secondarily or functionally "other-centered."

The discussion thus far has already suggested the extent to which liberalism conceives community instrumentally.[11] While it is true that this does not render all activities merely "selfish" or even morally vicious, it does give rise to certain issues. The person who stands before me is conceived as an object through whom I am enabled to realize some good, or some value that is important to me (i.e., "subjectively"). The one who stands before me, although he too is understood to have received a benefit, therefore becomes instrumentalized to my achievement of the value that is important to me. And this is true even of the most benevolent and exalted activities. Hence, for example, the work of a religious sister for the benefit of the poor is intelligible as an instrumentalization of the poor to her own moral excellence or "holiness," or to the realization of her values, or to her vision of the world, etc. However "beneficial" to others or the common good, however "selfless" the activities of self-interest may appear, contained at their core is a false sense of "self-centeredness."

The attempt to overcome a purely "self-regarding" understanding of freedom by broadening the concept of "self-interest" is therefore quite limited in its success. Instead of penetrating to the core of human desire and freedom, it merely broadens the horizon of "self-interest" both in terms of the "self" (to include within the "self" the family, for example) and in terms of "interest" (to include within the idea of "interest" the advancement of subjective values that seem—objectively—"disinterested"). The centrality of "self-interest" is not denied; rather, it is heightened. Indeed, the more broadly we interpret the idea of "self-interest" in our attempt to show its benignity, the more problematic it becomes, precisely because the effect is to broaden its significance beyond the confines of strictly "economic" activity. The free market rather quickly is taken as paradigmatic for a broad range of human communities, from the most mundane to the most sublime. The more broadly we interpret the idea of self-interest, the more it appears to possess a kind of sufficiency for explaining human behavior in general and, therefore, the more it begins to disclose itself as an *anthropology,* with specifically theological and philosophical implications.[12]

But even if we attempt to confine the significance of self-interest to the economic order, the ambiguity remains. In fact, to fix upon self-interest as the first principle of economic activity is to have made a fundamental decision about the nature of human freedom and community, and this decision possesses, however invisibly, untold consequences. The attempt to defend self-interest by defining it more broadly simply brings this ambiguity to the surface.

The abstraction of freedom from community leads to another closely related problem. As we noted, relations grounded in "disinterested" self-gift lie outside the liberal framework, which is unable to account for such "disinterested" engagements of freedom, except by reinterpreting them in terms of "self-interested" motivation. If the broadening of the sense of "self" to include a "familial self" seems to require a presupposed "irreducible core" of disinterestedness, this core still remains beyond the horizon of liberal rationality. This core remains, in other words, simply an abstract and formal possibility of human choice.

What is unclear and what cannot be resolved within the liberal horizon, therefore, is how these two objects of human freedom, the "sacrifice of personal interests" and the realization of self-interest, relate to each other. To the extent liberalism has already offered its own interpretation of freedom and its own anthropological vision, such actualizations of freedom appear to be merely private and, finally, *ir*rational. They tend to be marginalized as reflecting mere "religious motivation," and, to the extent they constitute obedience to a religious norm, they tend toward an alienating "moralism."

Freedom and love. What the liberal model of community and human exchange does not adequately recognize is the way in which freedom itself is priorly given, and because given, is "rooted in" and possesses the interior structure of givenness. In other words, liberalism does not have a proper conception of the priority of the other in freedom's very inception and structure. Liberalism is unable to account on its own principles for the relationship between self-realization or fulfillment and the structure of human reality grounded in gift. From this follows a host of consequences for the family. Most importantly, it calls into question whether so-called intermediate, nonliberal communities such as the family can avoid progressively accepting the abstraction of freedom from love, and thereby avoid taking on the instrumentalist relation of freedom to community offered by liberal institutions.

Freedom as gift

I would like to propose an alternative interpretation of the relationship between freedom, community, and love, one that attempts to avoid the abstractions just outlined. In this alternative view, *freedom arises within an original relationship among persons and therefore always contains the interior structure of community*. If liberalism supposes that community arises out of an initial act of freedom, the present proposal suggests that freedom always arises within an original community. In order to unpack and support this claim, we must retrace freedom, at least as it occurs in the unique situation of the family, back to its primordial moment in creation *ex nihilo*. In other words, before we can really address the nature of human freedom—whether it precedes and thus first creates community, or whether freedom arises as itself always already *inside* community—we must arrive at an ontology of the person. Of course, community, however it is conceived, is constituted by relations among persons. The question is how we understand the nature of these relations, where we locate them in human being, and therefore, where we understand freedom to arise with respect to these relations. In order to grapple with this issue, it is necessary to look at "relation" and "community" in the most fundamental sense possible.

The very idea of creation *ex nihilo* implies that the constitutive relations of community are written into creaturely existence at its most fundamental level. As David Schindler has argued, creaturely being does not first possess itself in an original act of existence (*esse*), which only then enters into relations (in a second act, *agere*) through creaturely freedom and activity.[13] Rather, relation is written into the most primitive level of being itself. In other words, creation *ex nihilo* indicates that creaturely "receptivity," hence "relation," is *ontologically* anterior to either self-possession or the creaturely activity of self-communication. Moreover, the human vocation to communion with God is given to the creature, and informs his nature and the meaning of his existence prior to any activity he might undertake. A similar idea is expressed by Joseph Ratzinger when he points out that the very meaning of "person" is grounded in the concept of "relation." The human person both comes "from," and is made "for," communion with God and others.[14] Creation *ex nihilo* therefore tells us that the "in-itselfness" of the creature, his self-possession in free acts, is always constitutively located within the prior reality of his being both "from" and "for." Both of these thinkers emphasize, therefore, that the relations that make the community already implied in creation not only precede any action of the creature, but shape the original nature of his freedom as well.

As Schindler suggests, this issue of where "receptivity" first arises in creaturely being is crucial for our understanding of freedom.[15] If the fact that the human creature is a "person" means that "relation" (that is to say, "community" in the deepest sense) is anterior to his "in-itselfness," indeed in-forms his very nature and existence, then personal freedom itself must be "interiorly" and "from its beginning" structured within these constitutive relations. Its very nature must be originally, and therefore fundamentally, relational, not only in the sense that it is structured toward and can only complete itself in reaching out to establish relations (a fact that is only partially accounted for by liberalism, according to which freedom remains originally "indifferent" to relation), but in the sense that freedom itself is, in its origin and in its very "logic," a *gift*, and therefore arises within a prior community (a fact that is *not at all* accounted for by liberalism). Freedom, therefore, is structured in its original meaning as both coming from and moving toward communion.[16] In its most basic order, then, freedom is *from and for* God and other creatures in God.

Now before we move on to discuss further the implications of the foregoing for the family, we must discuss the sense in which liberalism's placement of "self-interest" at the heart of community touches on an important truth, a truth that must be respected if we are to give an accurate account of freedom. As we have seen, liberalism places freedom, and therefore the human dynamic toward self-realization, prior to community, which means that community is conceived as a product—and not a necessary one—of the self-interested exercise of freedom. Liberalism, in other words, abstracts freedom from community and love. This problem arises not so much from the reality of self-interest as such, which Novak is quite right to insist cannot be extirpated from the human heart, but from the fact that liberalism gives self-interest priority in the constitution of human community.

In order to see this more clearly, we need to consider again the alternatives to the instrumentalization of community for my supposed self-interest and the alienation implied by "selfless disinterest." Liberalism, as we have seen, precisely because it abstracts freedom from community and love, simultaneously falls prey to both of these tendencies. The foregoing discussion of creaturely freedom, on the other hand, suggests that there is an interior relationship between gift and fulfillment, with priority given to gift. Human realization occurs insofar as the "other" possesses a certain priority in the search for self-realization. Thus, we must "make space" for the "other," a space that preserves the integrity of the "other" as a person, even while it is precisely within this space (which is necessarily reciprocal) that a mutual belonging is realized. The consequent interior relationship between human self-realization and self-surrender is not just a "mixture" or arbitrary juxtaposition of opposing elements. Rather, human fulfillment is found in the communion of persons itself, and this communion is only realized, paradoxically, in the space opened up by mutual self-emptying. Hence the relationship between personal fulfillment and self-gift is intrinsic and interior, with fulfillment ("self-interestedness") being realized always and most basically in self-gift ("disinterestedness").

We have now laid the groundwork for a response to the liberal abstraction of freedom from community and love. Freedom does not preexist community as a "neutral" foundation that may *then* be given the form of other-directedness or self-directedness, self-interestedness or "disinterestedness" (however virtuous or vicious). Rather the communal character of freedom is ontologically situated at the core of what authentic freedom really *is*. Creaturely freedom is first "given" in the act of creation and from within the community implied by creation. It is important to note, therefore, that community is not primarily the result of a possible use of freedom, as liberalism suggests. On the contrary, it indicates the deepest capacity of human fulfillment. If liberalism tends to marginalize self-giving actualizations of freedom—for example, by characterizing such acts as stemming from "religious motivation"—freedom as conceived within creation *ex nihilo* locates self-giving at the heart of what it means to be human. Because self-surrender is built into man's very being, it cannot be an alienation of his freedom.

More directly relevant to our present topic, however, is the priority of relation and community implied in the family itself. It is often pointed out that the family is a "nonliberal" community. That this is true is brought to light by the recognition that the family immediately implies questions of ultimacy, questions from which liberalism has in principle prescinded. Familial relations exist prior to any movement of freedom. Parents, children, and siblings do not enter into the community of the family on the basis of a simple exercise of their freedom, let alone by means of a bargain or an exchange, unless we posit the most extreme fiction in which the child, as a bargaining agent, is thought to preexist his conception, birth, and growth toward rational maturity. In other words, no one "chooses" to be a child, brother or sister, grandmother or grandfather, aunt, uncle, or cousin. These are human relations which are simply "given." We can embrace or run away from these relations, but we cannot choose for or against them *ab initio*. Our freedom arises within these relations as the capacity to ratify and fulfill what has already been given.

The human person always exists within a communion of others that both precedes and follows him. He is born, and hopefully welcomed, into a given family, with given parents, siblings, and grandparents. He finds himself, from the beginning, with a given name, cultural and social situation, a "mother tongue," a largely "given" set of beliefs and presuppositions about the "meaning of life," and so forth, all of which are inescapably mediated by the family community and the larger community in which it participates. The human person is given his personal history—the "story" of who he is, where he comes from, and where he is going—by these communities. Even if members of the family are physically absent or, indeed, were never known, they constitute part of the personal origin of the human person. They stand at the origin of his "I." The human person is awakened, is given his "I," in the encounter with these others, that is to say, in this "first" community that is the original condition and mediator of his existence.

Nor can the relationship between husband and wife be reduced to the sum of their acts of freedom. In their vows, their act of consent to marriage, husband and wife "receive" each other as "gift," and in so doing they receive more than each of them could ever really choose. At the very least, the interior implication of their sexual complementarity—another "given"—is the child, a "good" that can never be reduced to themselves. The child, as a spiritual, personal *creature*, is *pro*-created—that is to say, in conceiving their child, the parents cooperate in God's act of creation.[17] The child possesses an origin and a destiny beyond the horizon of the parents' experience, expectations, or choice, an origin and a destiny that he is called to ratify and direct with his own freedom and in love. The child and the spouses themselves always constitute a gift beyond imagination, a "more than can be chosen."

Of course, spouses and parents are often not overtly motivated by this transcendence. But however deficient the motivations of individual family members, the very idea of family carries with it this objective meaning. In this reception of "more than can be chosen," the spouses' freedom is genuinely engaged. In other words, while it is true that the marital community of husband and wife is grounded in their free consent, this freedom cannot exist apart from an original and prior set of relationships. Community and the relationship of sexual complementarity give marriage an origin and destiny that always entail this "more than can be chosen."

The distinction between the alternative senses of freedom should be clear. According to the liberal model, community (and by implication, perhaps, the family) is the product of an initial act of freedom. According to the creational model, on the other hand, it is relation (hence, community) which gives rise to freedom itself.[18] Both the liberal and the creational models, therefore, presuppose a polarity between freedom and community. The liberal model places a certain priority on freedom. The free actor could choose to act self-interestedly or perhaps "disinterestedly." He could enter into an economic relationship to realize a mutual benefit, or he could, perhaps, realize his interests without such a community. On the other hand, the creational sense of freedom and community places a priority on the communal pole—as the anterior conditional and original order of freedom. According to this latter view, freedom arises within the relationship with others who engage our capacity for mutual belonging. Each viewpoint implies a certain understanding of the basic relationship between freedom and community. The liberal model sees freedom as fundamentally "indifferent" or unstructured. Community is necessary, but accidentally and instrumentally so. Love becomes trapped between a self-love and a selfless love that cannot be inwardly reconciled, which results in the simultaneous extremes of instrumentalization and self-alienation. For the creational model, freedom relies intrinsically on relation and hence on community. The creational model therefore sees freedom as structurally ordered within community. It follows from this that fulfillment comes in relation to the other, which in turn implies a necessary "making space" for the other in an act of self-gift.

In sum, then, creaturely freedom retains (and this is what constitutes its "integrity") its rootedness in the gift of being, expressed in the form of creation *ex nihilo*. Hence, it does not possess an indifferent relationship to the other, or to the alternatives of self-gift and self-interest, or to some mixture of the two. Rather, it is internally ordered toward "self-surrender" as its very fulfillment.

The inversion of freedoms

The foregoing argument points to why the liberal conception of freedom and community provides an inadequate model for the family. It would locate, at the heart of the family, an abstraction of freedom from community and love, an abstraction of the human longing for self-realization and fulfillment from the interior self-giving moment of freedom and moral action.

Defenders of the free market may object, however, that I have been begging the question all along. They will counter that liberalism does not in fact purport to offer an anthropology or anything so exalted as a hermeneutic of the "person" or even his "freedom." Rather, the goal of Anglo-American liberalism is to offer the material resources and liberty necessary to enable self-realization, whatever understanding of freedom, community, and love is (privately) embraced. In other words, liberalism merely purports to offer the context and the conditions in which the "deeper" sense of freedom I have just outlined (or any other version of "freedom") may be enacted, based on private belief, within the family. Thus, liberal institutions provide those very mechanisms that guarantee to the family its liberty to embody the creaturely sense of freedom and community discussed above. At the same time, the fact that liberal institutions depend for their survival on the moral character inculcated by the family shows that liberalism is at least not hostile to the family. Why isn't it good enough simply to acknowledge a mutual dependence between the liberal structures of society and the reportedly nonliberal structures of the family? Why can't there be parallel senses of "freedom" and "community," one relating to the private sphere of the family (the domain of self-giving love) and the other relating to the public sphere of the market (the domain of virtuous self-interest)?

A recent book by Jennifer Roback Morse seems to suggest, in fact, that this parallelism is quite possible to maintain.[19] Morse implicitly draws a sharp distinction between the self-interested, contractual relations of the public sphere and the self-giving relations of the family. She is deeply concerned with the fact that, increasingly, the family has taken on the model of contractual relations, resulting in what she calls the "laissez-faire family." However, Morse is intent on defending the legitimacy of the liberal (or, indeed, libertarian) model in the political and economic arenas.[20] She thus implicitly accepts the disjunction between a so-called private ethic of love (i.e., the domain of personal-familial love) and a public ethic of "virtuous self-interest" (i.e., the domain of economic and political affairs). Of course, this contrast between the private and public spheres of human action is not based on a facile belief in their easy separation. Like Novak, Morse argues that familial relations grounded in love are necessary for the proper functioning of liberal institutions. The family is necessary for the inculcation of civic virtues and the trust necessary for the public sphere: " . . . both the economy and the polity are, in some way, held together with love. The love of a parent for a child allows the child to learn trust. This trust allows the child to learn a great many things that an economy needs for its smooth functioning: delayed gratification, impulse control, cooperative behavior, promise keeping. A self-governing political order requires self-restraint and forbearance as well. People cannot take advantage of every opportunity to use the political system that comes their way, or the system will collapse."[21] And it is clearly also the case that the health of culture and society has a strong impact on the health and viability of the family in innumerable ways. Morse eloquently explains the failure of social welfare policy and its role in undermining family relations.

But has the basic ambiguity regarding the relationship between freedom and community been resolved? The implication of Morse's thesis, like that of Novak's, is that liberal institutions constitute a minimalist and neutral ground in which human destiny may freely (albeit, privately) work itself out. Hence, for Morse and Novak, the problems facing the family today in its relations with the broader society are essentially due to poor individual choices and declining morality. However, to accept virtuous self-interest as the first principle of economic activity is already to have made a fundamental decision about the nature of human freedom and community. As we shall see in the remainder of this essay, this decision possesses, however invisibly, tremendous consequences, since economic exchange is already a fundamental form of community, a form of community that profoundly molds society itself. Certainly, as Morse holds, the family cannot be abstracted from the broader economic and social order. But once she has accepted the priority of gift with respect to family relations, how can she finally avoid either accepting its priority with respect to the public order or settling for an incoherent anthropology?

The problem, of course, is that the "liberty" offered to the family by liberalism is already shaped by certain assumptions regarding what freedom most fundamentally is. Liberalism, in purporting to provide the basic context in which the familial sense of community may be embodied, has already separated freedom from community and love. Thus, the question-begging charge noted above presupposes the liberal view of freedom and community as fundamental, since it regards the liberal sense of freedom and the creational sense of freedom as alternative actualizations. It presupposes, in other words, that freedom in fact precedes and is neutrally situated with respect to the alternatives of the familial and political-economic senses of freedom. But this very presupposition assumes, as the context in which these alternatives are presented, an underlying and "basic" sense of freedom that is, in fact, liberal. It supposes that the proposed familial sense of freedom is an alternative that individuals can adopt or not, when the possibility and implications of such a choice are precisely what is at issue.

Therefore, if it is granted that a domain of liberal freedom can coexist in harmony, let alone in a symbiotic relationship, with the creational freedom implied in the idea of family, the question of the fundamental nature of freedom and community has already been decisively answered in a liberal way. Familial freedom will always be re-proposed, in such circumstances, according to a more general and basic liberal sense of freedom, that is to say, as a possible actualization of freedom within a more basic liberal framework. While appearing to secure the family's liberty to constitute a certain type of community, therefore, liberal institutions in fact displace the familial or creaturely sense of freedom with their own abstract conception of freedom. Liberalism re-proposes the family as the "bourgeois family. Thus, an inversion takes place, in which the family tends to mimic the structures of the free market, even while the role of the family, as the most fundamental "cell" of society, is to instill its nonliberal sense of freedom and community into the public order.

This inversion's effect is most obviously manifest in the role defenders of the free market assign to the family. The inculcation of virtues supposedly necessary for the long-term survival of liberal institutions will necessarily require an inculcation of a liberal (or "bourgeois") sense of virtue. Liberals are certainly right to argue that the family is necessary and vital to the health of society and the economic and political culture. They are also right to point to the importance of the family in the inculcation of virtue. The question arises, however, as to what sort of virtue the family is called upon to inculcate. Christian critics have sometimes noted that the defenders of liberalism too often conflate the "virtues" called for by liberal institutions—"'hard work, diligence, discipline, attention to detail, frugality, and the systematic (not sporadic) cultivation of willpower'"—with "Christian virtue."[22] The argument of this chapter, however, suggests a further point: neither should we conflate "liberal virtues" with what is most fundamentally human. As a general matter, the virtues may be seen as shaping or ordering and, therefore, cultivating authentic freedom. But if liberalism has subtly but profoundly transformed the meaning of freedom by abstracting it from community and love, then in principle the virtues liberal institutions will seek from the family will be shifted accordingly. Hence the "new morality" of liberalism, emphasizing "industry, savings, the acquisition of wealth, upward mobility, and economic rationality,"[23] will tend to be placed prior to the idea of community and love, rendering the latter "voluntaristic" in character. The implication will then be that the family also is a "voluntaristic" community.[24]

As the burden of the neoconservative argument concerning the place of the family in society shows, the family and political-economic institutions cannot be hermetically contained in separate spheres. If the education and moral formation provided by the family are necessary for liberal institutions to survive, it is also true that liberal institutions will place certain demands on the sort of moral education—the shaping of human freedom and its relation to community—the family provides. Indeed, the discussion of how the family can offer moral formation often amounts to a reduction of family-inculcated moral character to an element of self-interested economic behavior. In such discussions, Christian defenders of liberal economics may mean, for example, that unbridled "self-interest" is inadequate to fully explain economic choice,[25] that it fails, in other words, to maximize economic or political good in the long run, unless the addition of moral constraint is made to serve as a limiting factor. They may mean, for example, that virtue is necessary in order to avoid falling into a race to gain short-term goods when, in fact, all would be benefited by a disciplined holding out for a greater, long-term good. Or they may mean that the familial inculcation of character serves an auxiliary role with respect to self-interest itself. The economic actor must have prudence, justice, fortitude, and temperance, for example, actually and fully to realize his self-interest. Alternatively, they may mean that the economic actor needs a proper alignment of subjective preferences and objective values to know what really is ontologically, objectively good for him. Should he, for example, pursue pornography or fine art?[26]

Is there not, in each of these cases, however, a subtle instrumentalization of virtue to self-interest, which remains, in this sense, "pure" and interiorly unqualified by the creaturely freedom embodied in the family? However "charitable" moral action might appear in these circumstances, it will still, at its heart, be grounded in an instrumentalization of the other, an other now subordinated to my "virtuous" interests. In this sense, liberal institutions such as the free market call on the family to project itself into culture and society by inculcating moral character grounded in a conception of freedom and community that amounts to a denial of what is properly familial.

More fundamentally, however, the instrumentalization of the family to free-market ends presents a rather easy slide in which family relations themselves are reinterpreted in terms of free-market principles. In fact, once the fundamental meaning of freedom is interpreted along liberal lines, all relations are necessarily reinterpreted voluntaristically, precisely because, set against a background of the liberal meaning of freedom, they are no more than mere personal choices, or "alternative engagements of freedom." Increasingly, then, family relations are evaluated in terms of self-interest—"Am I getting what I want in this relationship?" Self-gift, on the other hand, becomes less and less comprehensible precisely because it has become a purely "religious" question. When put in this way, the act of self-gift becomes irrational, and to that extent marginalized, until it can be reinterpreted along liberal lines. However much liberalism might purport to hold out the possibility of a private realization of a "nobler and deeper" sense of freedom and community, the fact is that it has already rendered that freedom incomprehensible in terms of human values.

In sum, the implications for the family of the "abstraction" of freedom from community and love are profound. Inevitably the family, a "nonliberal" community, begins nevertheless to adopt a liberal sense of freedom and community and its attendant set of abstractions. This tendency can be seen, as a practical matter, in many sorts of difficulties facing the family today, difficulties that neoconservatives such as Novak and Morse, to their credit, have attempted to combat: the relaxation of cultural and legal standards regarding divorce, the characterization of a mother's relationship with her fetus as a matter of "choice," the gradual erosion of the identity and meaning of the family, the almost complete acceptance of nonmarital cohabitation, the sense that each individual member of the family begins with a set of "rights" that preexist and generally trump whatever claims the family community as such may have, and so forth.

Finally, the argument I have offered here suggests the way in which the liberal conception of freedom and community skews the meaning of the economy itself. Liberalism depersonalizes the economy and abstracts economic activity from the family, in which its original meaning lies (οικος= house, household, family; οικονομια=the running of a household). The family is viewed as a voluntaristic consumer unit that functions within a mass, consumer economy. The human person is replaced as the fundamental economic protagonist on the one hand by the "person" qua legal fiction (the corporation), and on the other hand by the mass-market figure of the consumer.

I would like to conclude with a final thought. Defenders of liberalism grant that the classical liberalism of the Anglo-Scottish Enlightenment did not devote much discussion to the family. Perhaps this was because writers such as Smith could simply take the vitality and importance of the family as a natural institution for granted in a way that contemporary writers cannot.[27] Novak, on the other hand, recalls what they were writing against, viz., government *by* the family in the feudal system. Since that time, "political theory, economic theory, and moral theory—preoccupied with the individual and the state—have systematically neglected the social vitality of the family." He cautions, however, that at present, when "the traditional family is under relentless attack," "we are driven to face directly what our forbears neglected or took for granted." The argument of this essay casts doubt, however, on the idea that the Enlightenment writers' reserve concerning the family can be fully explained by the historical context in which they wrote. As Stanley Hauerwas has remarked, it was an aim of Smith, at any rate, "to show how the weakening of familial ties would increase the necessity of sympathy between strangers and result in cooperative forms of behavior that had not previously been realized."[28] It is not that families would cease to exist, but they would be transformed into the image of the exchange relations that underlie liberal societies. In fact, this is precisely what we are seeing today, with the triumph of the "bourgeois family."

8

Making Room in the Inn: Why the Modern World Needs the Needy

Jennifer Roback Morse

The self-sufficient, autonomous individual is at the heart of modern America's understanding of itself. Democratic political institutions depend on the free and informed participation of citizens. The free market relies on contracts and exchanges among independent and equal participants. Modern culture celebrates the individual, both as the basic and the ultimate unit of society.

However, some people are legitimately dependent on others. Children are profoundly, if temporarily, dependent on their parents. The elderly and the sick are dependent on others. The seriously disabled and the mentally ill are permanently dependent. Does the presence of these people threaten the modern ideal of self-sufficiency?

Until now, the modern world has had a tendency to marginalize the needy. This is both unwise and unnecessary. We can incorporate the needy into a vision of a society of free and responsible individuals by facing the fact of dependency and the need for community as squarely as we face the fact of self-interest and the need for autonomy. If we insist that the free person needs only self-interest and self-sufficiency without solidarity, we will marginalize the needy and dehumanize ourselves.

We are afraid to look too closely at dependent people because they remind us that our own consciousness is a contingent fact. The rational faculty is a gift that allows us to think and to choose. This gift of rationality makes our freedom and autonomy possible. But it is a mistake to view our rationality as the source of our value or dignity as persons. Our autonomy and rationality is vulnerable. Opening this question will ultimately strengthen, not weaken, the overall case for a free society.

The legitimately dependent

There are and always will be people who are dependent on others through no fault of their own. Human beings are born as helpless babies, and our species has a long period of dependency. In fact, we might say that dependency is the one truly universal human experience. Nothing like "fault" is involved; the helplessness of infancy is simply a fact.[1]

When we become ill, we are dependent on healthy people to take care of our needs in various ways. As we age, we require the assistance of others. Some futurists might imagine that the steady march of technology will eliminate this problem of dependence. But this belief is naïve. While technology has certainly lengthened the useful life of most people, technology cannot entirely banish the needs of the sick or the elderly for assistance from others. The very complexity of modern medical care means that an incapacitated individual needs the help of other people simply to take advantage of the technology.

Pharmaceutical regimes, for instance, can be exceedingly complex. AIDS patients need sophistication and diligence to take their complicated combinations of pills correctly. Many elderly people need help in managing their life-enhancing medications. Chemotherapy, while life-extending, is exhausting and debilitating. The cancer patient who must face this treatment completely alone is at a serious disadvantage compared to a person rich in relatives. Even accessing health care in the first place can be a daunting experience. A healthy and robust person can become overwhelmed navigating the bureaucratic maze of HMOs, insurance companies, and government services.

An isolated sick person will certainly have a difficult time obtaining the services he needs.

Virtually everyone has periods of partial or complete dependency. Some people, however, are more permanently or seriously dependent. They come into the world with mental or physical impairments that render them permanently dependent on others to some degree. Other people fall victim to accidents, strokes, or illnesses that leave them partially or completely disabled. Mentally ill people, sufferers from Alzheimer's disease, people who have had brain injuries—these are people who may have begun their lives with every prospect of independence. But because of no fault of their own, they cannot be contributing members of society without sustained assistance from others. Indeed, the extent of their dependency raises the question of whether "contributing to society" is really the proper way to understand their role.

Thus, the problem of the legitimately dependent cannot be finessed or argued away. There is no possible reconstruction of the social, economic, or political system that will eliminate the helplessness of infancy. The experiences of illness and old age, while not universal, are certainly widespread enough that we can say that this kind of temporary or partial dependency is legitimate and unavoidable. The only way to eliminate it would be to execute people at the first sign of infirmity.

The ubiquity of unavoidable helplessness points to the possibility that dependency is not peripheral to the social order, but is rather somehow central to it. We modern Americans take understandable pride in our self-sufficiency. Our jealous guarding of our political and financial independence keeps us both free and prosperous. We have created for ourselves an uplifting vision of free and equal adults making trades among themselves. But it is not the whole story about the human condition. We need to find a way to incorporate our experience of neediness into our more general vision of ourselves as free and responsible people.

How we marginalize the needy

In modern America, there are three primary methods by which we distance ourselves from the needy and the intellectual and ideological problem that they pose for us. First, we define them out of existence. We change the terms of the discussion so that those who are apparently dependent are really just as autonomous as everyone else. Second, we commercialize their care. We pay other people to take care of them so that we don't have to look too closely. Finally, we have developed elaborate justifications for ending the lives of those who are dependent on us. In other words, if all else fails, we kill them.

Redefining the needy as autonomous. Our reinterpretation of childhood offers a dramatic illustration of how we have redefined our terms so that people are not really needy, but autonomous. Social critic Robert Bellah once wrote, "[F]or highly individuated Americans, there is something anomalous about the relations between parents and children, for the biologically normal dependence of children on adults is perceived as morally abnormal."[2] Accordingly, many Americans have tried to manage this cognitive dissonance by re-imagining children, even infants, as competent and autonomous.

We have, for example, steadily lowered the age at which children are permitted to do a larger and larger number of things. Children are entitled to "free expression" in the form of clothing and writings inside public schools. Some people even advocate that children should have the right to sue their parents. Children are permitted to procure medical advice and care for themselves, so they can have access to contraception and abortion without the knowledge or guidance of their parents.

We have also largely given up on efforts to shape children's behavior and preferences, evidently believing that children's impulses are basically sound. Many opinion-makers have convinced themselves that children are naturally moral creatures who are ruined by the adults who attempt to civilize them.[3] Children's authentic selves will emerge if only adults leave them unfettered. Children should not be introduced to norms of behavior and collective knowledge bound up in customs of long usage. Rather than being initiated into culture, children should be protected from it.

Some parents have come to view their children not so much as dependents who need protection and guidance, but as learning machines who need input and stimulation. Even the infant is said to be "competent." We are told that babies are insatiable data gatherers who naturally want to be good. Dr. Spock informs us that "good manners come naturally." This will surely come as a surprise to many parents and grandparents.[4]

We have also come to believe that children are competent to handle the disruption that adult behavior inflicts on them. If their parents are unhappy, children will be able to handle a divorce. The parents may not be tough enough to handle the disappointments in their marriage, but the children are resilient enough to handle the disruption of a broken home.

It is as if we have literally applied the idea of the "noble savage" to childhood. Unfortunately, as a matter of plainly observable fact, children are not noble savages whose most pressing need is to be left alone. An infant left alone will die. Children need guidance and instruction if they are ever to be able to use well the freedom that our society ultimately wants them to have as adults.

Children are not the only group of people whom we have redefined as autonomous. We have come to treat the mentally ill as though they were equipped to use the Bill of Rights and as though their decisions were rational. Numerous observers have come to the conclusion, for instance, that many of the people described as "homeless" are actually mentally ill people who have been "deinstitutionalized."[5]

Both the Left and the Right have conspired in this process of redefining the mentally ill. From the Right, people such as Thomas Szasz stress individual responsibility and autonomy. Szasz argues that debilitating mental illness is as mythical as witchcraft. There are only "problems in living." Szasz believes that everyone should be held accountable for their actions and not be excused based on invented claims of mental illness.[6]

From the Left, communist-turned-anarchist-turned-deconstructionist Michel Foucault "boldly equated sanity and madness," claiming that the concept of sanity is socially constructed.[7] Indeed, for Foucault the insane are often the most sane of all, since they at least recognize the insanity of our culture for what it is. "Radical therapists" take this one step further. They believe that through a transformation of the capitalist system all those who currently appear to be mentally ill will become healthy, functioning members of the utopian society.

Even schools of thought within mainstream psychiatry have been unable to grasp fully the importance of severe mental illness. Freudians saw mental illness and mental health as a continuum, with most people having some degree of mental impairment. It is significant that the doctors who held this view typically had psychiatric practices treating neurotic middle-class patients. The average psychoanalyst seldom encountered schizophrenics, manic-depressives, or autistics. These chronically ill people could seldom hold even minimal jobs, and certainly could not afford to pay for expensive psychoanalysis. They were much more likely to be hospitalized in state hospitals tended by public health psychiatrists, who were (and are) not the most prestigious members of their profession.[8]

These three disparate groups, the libertarian Right, the anti-capitalist Left, and segments of the psychiatric community itself have something in common: They all see the mentally ill person as a special case of the ordinary person, and avoid the problems posed by the more seriously impaired mentally ill person. Likewise, each of these groups envisions a solution to the "problem" of "mental illness." These solutions are simple to state, if expensive or even radical to implement.

Szaszians see the problem as one of people engaging in unusual behavior who need to be held accountable for problems they cause others, but who do not necessarily need medical intervention. Radical therapists see the problem as one of a corrupt capitalist system that drives people crazy and needs to be overthrown. The "Mental Health Bar," the legion of civil liberty lawyers who represent the mentally ill, resemble the radical therapists and ex-patients in evidently believing that mental illness is created more by society and failed treatments than by any physiological process. The people described as mentally ill would be fine if only society would provide them with housing and acceptance.

Likewise, the solution of a substantial segment of the psychiatric profession has been to advocate an extensive and expensive network of "preventive mental health services." In the 1950s and 1960s, some psychiatrists dreamed of a world made well by their services. After the race riots of the '60s, Dr. Leonard Duhl, who became chief of planning at the National Institute of Mental Health, described this vision as follows:

> The city . . . is in pain. It has symptoms that cry out for relief. They are the symptoms of anger, violence, poverty and hopelessness. If the city were a patient, it would seek help. . . . The totality of urban life is the only rational focus for concern with mental illness. . . . Our problem now embraces all of society and we must examine every aspect of it to determine what is conducive to mental health. . . . [T]he total society needs a mental health treatment program.[9]

Unfortunately, there was not the slightest evidence that psychiatry had any competence to prevent the social and economic problems plaguing Dr. Duhl's society.

In 1963, Congress authorized the establishment of a system of Community Mental Health Centers, ostensibly designed to supplement the state hospitals and establish community-based preventive services. But as the programs actually developed, they were ill-equipped to deal with the problems of the seriously, chronically ill patients who had been housed in the state hospitals. The focus turned out to be more on "preventive services" than on serving the seriously ill people recently released into the community.[10]

Indeed, some participants in the process later admitted that passing the Community Mental Health Centers legislation required that this population be discussed in only the vaguest terms. Too great an emphasis on the extensive needs this population would have in the community would have scuttled the legislation. Some psychiatrists spoke in almost messianic tones of the benefits that freedom alone would have for the currently hospitalized. According to one advocate of preventive psychiatry, "In the past twenty years, we have come to the realization that most of the symptoms of the chronic deteriorated psychotics who crowd the back wards of our mental hospitals are produced by the pathogenic environment in which we incarcerate them rather than by the mental disorder which led to their admission."[11] In other words, serious mental illness is the product of social conditions, and could be cured by the proper restructuring of society. The mentally ill do not have a disorder that requires unique, specific treatment or care from others.

This ideological position masks the true condition of the mentally ill person's impairment. Damage to the brain can impair a person's ability to think and choose. Our system of civil liberties assumes that people have the ability to reason. Some of the mentally ill potentially have the use of their rational faculties, but only if they take appropriate medication. Yet mental health law has evolved to the point that no one can compel them to take medication or to be committed to any kind of institutional care. The legal system offers seriously mentally ill people the right to live on the street, but not the right to treatment. The families of the seriously mentally ill have the right to take care of their loved ones in their own home, but they have no right to keep them there against their will. As a result, the home becomes a mental institution staffed by untrained family members who never receive training, assistance, or even a day off.[12]

Some self-styled advocates of the homeless chide the American public for lacking the generosity necessary to care for the homeless adequately. But stinginess is not the issue here. The problem is that we would prefer not to look too closely at the problem of mental illness. According to recent estimates, about a third of the chronically homeless population have either schizophrenia or bipolar disorder (manic-depressive illness).[13] Describing the issue as "homelessness" suggests that the primary issue is a material problem of adequate housing. If only we could find a place for these impoverished people to live, if only the neighborhoods would be more welcoming, if only the government would commit more resources, the problem of homelessness would be solved.

But the residents of neighborhoods where the homeless live don't complain about poor people without shelter. They complain about people wandering the streets muttering to themselves, urinating in public places, eating out of garbage cans, starting inexplicable fights or leaving trash and filth wherever they go. The people in these neighborhoods can see that these mentally ill men and women inhabit a different reality, that they need something more profound than housing. And they know that there is nothing compassionate or respectful about letting people roam the streets with their needs for human solidarity unmet.

Any one of us could get a bump on the head that would leave us without the use of our rational faculty. Any one of us could have a stroke or contract Alzheimer's disease. We would then need the kind of help that some of the seriously mentally ill or brain-damaged people need. To face this vulnerability is uncomfortable, to be sure, because it challenges our understanding of ourselves. We are rational beings capable of making responsible choices. But we need not be, and may not be forever. The mentally ill remind us, if we allow them, that our ability to think is a gift that, like all gifts, is not of our own making.

Commercializing dependent care. Our second avoidance strategy is to pay other people to take care of the dependent. Contrary to the complaints of some on the Left, Americans are prepared to pay to take care of the needy. It is the needy themselves that we fear. But we do not fear the needy because they are the "Other," the scapegoat that societies invent to create social cohesion among the "Included." Rather, modern Americans fear the needy because they remind us of the interior tension between our official ideology of independent individualism and the reality of temporary or permanent dependence.

The welfare state provides a highly visible and pervasive example of this avoidance strategy. Advocates claimed that state funding would regularize and systematize the care of the poor. In the process, however, it removed the care of dependent people from the messy, personal realm and moved it into the sanitized, bureaucratic realm. One of the key impacts of the bureaucratization of poverty relief has been to remove the face-to-face contact between the poor and the donor. The donor has become an impersonal taxpayer rather than a real person. The recipient has become a client of state agencies, not a neighbor in need.[14]

Advocates of an expansive welfare state viewed this as an advantage. No more would the stuffy church ladies demean the poor with arrogant offers of help accompanied by sneers of disdain for their behavior. The poor could preserve their dignity if they received their entitlement from a government office that would ask only a minimal number of antiseptic questions.

Large numbers of people acquiesced in the transformation of social charity into public charity. The encounter with the needy is one that many, if not most, people would prefer to avoid. Paying someone else to do it allows donors to feel that they have fulfilled their moral duty, while at the same time allowing them to avoid direct encounter with the poor.[15]

In a somewhat different way, the trend toward paid childcare has also contributed to keeping dependent people at arm's length.

Paid childcare has moved children out of the home and into the care of hired strangers. The public arguments in favor of this shift have been two: first, mothers need to work because of economic necessity, and second, women are entitled to work because their personal dignity requires it. The opponents of this shift have argued both that the need for daycare is exaggerated, and that daycare is harmful to children in various ways. Neither side has paid particular attention to the point I want to make: turning childcare into a business shields parents, and society more generally, from confronting the full scope of their children's dependence.

With daycare, the care of children becomes one more commodity, another household expense. The reality that infants are helpless is much less immediate if one only has to face it for part of the time. Caring for a newborn around the clock, on the other hand, reveals just how profound our initial helplessness is.

Paying people to take care of children transforms the relationship between parents and children in a variety of ways. Parents become consumers of childcare services. They thus conceptualize their role as selecting the most suitable service provider, where "suitable" can take on many possible meanings. Kay Hymowitz reports, for instance, that some parents try to locate people who can provide proper intellectual stimulation for their baby's developing brain. The baby can be left with anyone, as long as the baby is stimulated according to the parents' instructions.[16]

Even if parents have a perfectly reasonable understanding of what is "suitable," the transformation from parent to consumer has subtle consequences. The primary business of parenthood is not economic, but relational.[17] The irreplaceable job of parents is to build a relationship with their children. But you can't pay someone to have a relationship with you. How much less can you pay someone to have a relationship with a third party, namely, your child?

With the weakening of the relationship between parents and children comes the concomitant empowering of childcare "experts."

By experts, I mean not only daycare providers, but also people who study children and their needs as a profession. Many parents, not just working parents, rely increasingly on advice from these professionals. But while child-development scholars may provide valuable information about specific aspects of child development, they are unlike ordinary parents in some crucial respects.

To begin with, these professionals spend their working days with other people's children. Teachers spend all day with a large number of children, while psychologists, clinical and research alike, spend small amounts of time with particular children. Their conclusions are thus based on observations of large numbers of children for relatively small amounts of time, and under controlled conditions. Parents, on the other hand, know their particular children well enough to know whether the study or approach of the experts is truly applicable. Parents, and only parents, are positioned to see the larger picture of their children's behavior, abilities, strengths, and weaknesses. If parents, then, delegate too much of their child's care to others, this big picture will not really be seen by anyone.

This distinction between the scientific knowledge available to experts and the specific, localized knowledge available only to parents or other intimates is reminiscent of Nobel Prize–winning economist F. A. Hayek's distinction between explicit and tacit knowledge.[18] Hayek argued that no team of technocrats could centrally plan an economy because they would be unable to gather all the knowledge held by the millions of individuals in the system. These numerous individuals would be unable to fully articulate every relevant fact that they knew. Nonetheless, Hayek showed that ordinary people can make good economic use of this tacit knowledge without ever being able to explain what they are doing or why. Similarly, parents know far more about their own individual child than they can fully explain or articulate, whereas a brief encounter with a child may very well conceal as much as it reveals.

Besides, at the end of the working day, all these professionals go home to their own homes and families. They are never held accountable for the consequences of what they tell parents to do or not do. Because they don't have an ongoing, personal relationship with the children they observe, they don't have to live with the results of their advice. Likewise, the parent who primarily pays others to take care of a child doesn't really have to live with his or her decisions: the caregiver does. It is all too easy to pass off the care of a difficult child to paid caregivers, rather than to engage in the "tough love" or "patient love" part of parenting.

Every one of these disadvantages of paid care stems from the same source: the commercialization of a personal relationship. Much of the argument between the Left and the libertarian Right has focused on whether government should finance daycare. Libertarians argue that the market can provide all the childcare people really want and need.[19] This argument, however, concedes too much to the statist, corporatist mentality. Government-provided childcare also uses the market, because the government pays people to take care of the kids. The difference between market-provided and government-provided childcare is not as great as the difference between personal care by a family member and impersonal care provided by a paid stranger.

Similarly, the care of the dependent elderly has been commercialized and moved out of the family. Many people will say, "I don't want to be a burden to my children." Of course, no one wants to be a burden to anyone. On the other hand, no one wants to go through their final illness and death all alone, at least when actually faced with that reality. It is difficult for us to face our own descent into helplessness and ultimate demise. It is difficult for our loved ones to face it as well. But we are better off if we do face it, because it is a fact.

Taking care of the routine needs of an incapacitated person's body is a demanding, sometimes disagreeable activity. Often, an infirm or elderly person's needs can be so great that round-the-clock care is needed. A family may very well want to hire help, just to ensure that everyone in the family receives good care.

But this approach to hired help is quite different from that we encounter when the sick or aged person is passed off to paid care providers. In the first case, the person is still embedded within the family's nexus of love and care. In the second, the family creates distance between itself and its infirm member. They try to tell him that they can't give him good enough care, and that he will be better off in some kind of facility. And sometimes, that is the truth. But often, there is an unwillingness to become engaged with the dependent person and his infirmity.

We kill dependent people. The care of the dependent elderly brings up a final way that we distance ourselves from people who cannot take care of themselves: we kill them. Two prevalent attitudes combine to make this legalized killing seem justified. First, the logic of dependence and independence means that the dependent appear to be of no value. Second, our Anglo-American emphasis on legal rights and obligations obscures the other kinds of duties and relationships that define the truly good society.

This combination of ideas lies behind the impulse to take innocent life. The independent have no legal or moral obligations to the dependent. The dependent have no intrinsic value. No one has an obligation to take care of an infirm elderly person, to assist him, to alleviate his pain, to help make his life seem worthwhile. Similarly, the child in the womb is dependent on his mother. She is not obligated to take care of him. He can't take care of himself. He has no intrinsic value. Therefore, the child must die, if his mother wishes it.

Even our attitudes toward disabilities reflect this combination of views. Many people see nothing wrong with prenatal screening for serious disabilities, with the consequent abortion of fetuses with detected abnormalities. But this doesn't solve the problem of the dependent. It simply removes the problem from view. The philosophy underlying this strategy is that the solution to the disabled person's problem is to end his life before it begins.

We have even come to the point where some argue for a "right not to be born." A recent case in France awarded damages to the parents of a disabled child because the doctors should have told them of the abnormality so that they could abort. This is a radical avoidance strategy.

The role of the needy in the debate between capitalism and its critics

Some critics of capitalism view the poor as a challenge to the very foundations of the decentralized market order. The economic system, with its cutthroat competition, causes some people to be dependent or to live on the edge of survival. These critics have called for radical changes in the entire economy, including the nationalization of key industries, massive entitlement programs, and highly progressive tax codes.

Defenders of capitalism have responded that the care of the needy can be best accomplished using the basic instruments of the market and private property, combined with an active private charitable sector. These defenders observe that the market system has a far better track record of raising people from poverty than schemes for centralizing the economy. They observe further that there is plenty of room to enlarge and enhance the charitable sector.

Unfortunately, framing the debate as an argument between capitalism and its critics, or between socialism and its critics, has been singularly unhelpful to the poor and other needy people. Socialists were inclined to expand the definition of the dependent in order to buttress their case for a radical restructuring of the economy and society. The Left expanded the definition of entitlement by moving away from the distinction between the "deserving poor" and the "undeserving poor." Loosening this distinction was part of the effort to undermine the wage-based capitalist system. This blurring of categories served a dual political purpose: it expanded the set of potential clients of the welfare state, and it demonized as insensitive or uncaring anyone who attempted to exclude people from benefits based on their behavior and character.

But there is no need to rehearse this debate over the relative merits of capitalism and socialism for the poor. For the presence of dependent people does constitute a challenge to American individualism, just not the kind of challenge most critics have so far articulated. Capitalism has given millions of people a far higher standard of living than they could have obtained under any other economic system. Of concern is not the economic system per se, but the wider philosophical framework of individualism within which capitalism is most often defended.

Both the critics and defenders of capitalism have done a disservice to the poor by reducing the problems of the needy to economic problems. The critics of capitalism are mistaken if they believe that there is some potential economic reform that will eliminate the problem of dependency. And the defenders of capitalism have been mistaken in accepting these terms for the debate. No matter how the economic system is structured and restructured, some people will still be dependent on others. Transferring money to the profoundly dependent does not address their need for human relationships and personal care.

Curiously enough, many of the Left's preferred solutions to social problems amount to replacing an interdependent human relationship with an impersonal bureaucratic relationship. For instance, many on the Left argue that mothers could be independent of men if only the state provided a generous enough safety net for single mothers. But this policy doesn't end the dependence of the mother and her child. It only transfers their dependence to the state. Instead of being interdependent with a husband and father who provides an actual human relationship, the lifestyle Left proposes that women and children be dependent on the state.[20]

Likewise, many of the radical therapists seem to think that mental illness will disappear if only the legal and economic system could be substantially reformed. But the need of the mentally ill for the assistance of others will not go away. Giving a seriously sick person the right to live on the street denies their need for human solidarity.

In this respect, dependent people do challenge the American ethos of individualism. Their presence threatens the underlying contractual structure of American life. A person who cannot take care of himself is not part of the economic system. Is there a place for such a person within the society based on a market order? If a person is unable to participate in the governing and choosing process of democracy, is he somehow a rebuke to the system itself?

These questions point to why conservative and libertarian calls for an expanded charitable sector are unlikely to be successful taken by themselves. Unless we are willing to challenge this utilitarian view of the needy, we are not likely to get many volunteers to help them. We need to expand our vision of the free society beyond the nexus of exchange. Without this expansion, our appeals for an increase in the private charitable sector will ring hollow to many.

It is true that our free society depends on individual choice and responsibility. The economic and legal systems rest on the assumption that people have the capacity, and indeed the right, to make independent choices for themselves. This system of free enterprise, constitutionally limited government and culturally sanctioned individualism works reasonably well for most people most of the time. It has produced a society with a higher standard of living and greater amount of personal freedom than any system that has ever existed.

We often defend this system because it upholds the dignity of each individual person. Tacit in that defense, though, is the unspoken claim that a person's dignity depends on the ability to think, choose, and make and keep commitments. But this tacit defense is not quite good enough. It cannot take account of situations in which recognizably human creatures are unable to choose and behave rationally.

Some thinkers have redefined "human" in order to avoid this difficulty. In their view, only creatures capable of moral choice and rational thought are fully human. Therefore, humans without these capacities do not have the same sets of rights as others, and in some theories, they have no rights at all. But this redefinition is inherently dangerous, since anyone could be at least temporarily unable to take care of himself and unable to think.

The solution, then, is not to turn away from the problem of dependency, but rather to confront it directly and embrace it. Directly facing the problem will allow us to see both that our understanding of our free society needs to be modified, and that the problem of caring for the dependent is solvable within that modified understanding.

The humane alternative to impersonal bureaucracy and radical individualism

Advocates of minimum government need not avoid the issue of dependence. The case for a free society does not depend on the claim that everyone behaves like rational economic man at all times. The case for limited government and free markets simply depends on the claim that these institutions do a better job of enhancing the freedom, dignity, and prosperity of more people, more of the time, than any known alternative. Advocates of the free society would serve their cause better by confronting the issue of dependency head-on, rather than waiting for others to bring it up.

There are three implicit presumptions behind the American version of individualism. These unexamined presuppositions create a set of interlocking problems that conspire to keep the needy at a distance. The first is the narrowly utilitarian view that limits us to thinking that only someone who contributes economically has a place in society. The second is the undue emphasis on legal rights and obligations to the exclusion of claims and duties that are not legally enforceable, but nonetheless culturally demanded.

Finally, and most basically, there is the scientistic presupposition that this sort of argument must be conducted without broaching the questions of value, justice, truth or goodness.[21] But if we limit our discussion to allegedly value-neutral categories, using semi-scientific language, we will neglect some of the most promising options for understanding how to deal with dependent people in a humane way.

Utilitarianism and economic value. In the Anglo-American tradition of liberty, utilitarian arguments play a prominent role. If we view the problem only through the lens of usefulness, narrowly construed, we will quickly come to the conclusion that the person who is dependent is not useful to anyone.

Economists infer the values of goods based on people's willingness to pay. An economist might say that productivity in the market is too narrow a definition of an object's or a person's economic worth. Economists would point to many situations in which people willingly give up profitable market opportunities for the sake of some objective that they value more highly. Mothers, for instance, may very well (and very rationally) value time spent taking care of their children more highly than time spent in the market for wages. They demonstrate by their decisions to stay home that time with children is valuable, even though no money changes hands.

So the economists' interpretation of utilitarianism suggests the following question about dependent people: Do we view them as valuable for some reason other than their ability to produce consumer goods or services? Are we willing to sacrifice other kinds of goods for their care? The economists' variant of utilitarianism, willingness to pay, illustrates that the problem for dependent people lies squarely with how the rest of society views them. Thus, by reformulating our thinking about dependency and neediness, we point toward one possible solution.

The dignity of the person in the free society. The free society undoubtedly produces many visible benefits. Free markets bring greater prosperity to more people than any alternative economic system. Democratic, participatory governments aggregate the preferences of larger numbers of ordinary people more effectively than alternative forms of government. The rule of law preserves the rights and dignity of ordinary people more effectively than alternative legal systems.

But why do we consider these characteristics to be good? We consider giving people what they want a good thing because we trust people to have reasonable wants, and we want people to be happy. We want people to be protected from the arbitrary encroachments of the state because we believe that each individual has an intrinsic dignity worthy of such protection. In short, the philosophical principle behind the utilitarian reasons for valuing the free society is that each human being has an intrinsic value that no one has the right to trample. This emphasis on the intrinsic value of each person is one of the reasons to argue for personal, not corporate, responsibility for the needy. Face-to-face encounters are more likely to be rewarding for both the recipient and the donor, and more likely to safeguard the intrinsic dignity of both.

The main business of society is more than business and the politics that supports it. The main business is to recognize and protect the dignity and value of each and every human being, no matter how lowly. That is and always has been the distinctive mark of the modern Western liberal society. There is no hereditary class consisting of people intrinsically more valuable than others. Every person, no matter how poor, has a right to participate in the political system, has the right to the protection of the laws, and has a right to make a living unencumbered by unreasonable restrictions. Indeed, this set of convictions about the individual is the modern world's most appealing feature.

This is the premise behind the premise, so to speak. And if we really believe that each person has intrinsic value, we have available to us a dramatic way to prove it: We must attend to the needs of people who have no productive value, people who cannot ever contribute to society in any ordinary economic sense.

Legal rights and obligations vs. cultural rights and obligations.
The Anglo-American tradition of liberty is strongly framed in terms of legal rights and obligations. The most basic of the American rights are negative rights, that is, rights that require other people to refrain from doing something, e.g., killing, stealing, or committing fraud. But these negative rights confer no positive obligation on anyone to do anything for any particular person, including radically dependent persons.

The problem of the needy combines legal and cultural elements. The cultural element is the decision about what constitutes a person's "usefulness" to the rest of society. Large segments of American culture presume that a person's ability to contribute economically is the primary measure of his social usefulness. Large numbers of us also presume that a person's abilities to think, make decisions, and choose rationally are at the heart of his humanity. And if we have already decided a dependent person is not useful, and that usefulness is the measure of a person's legal rights, we will be reluctant to create a legally binding right to care.

But we have more decisions to make about dependent others than can be settled through legal means. For instance, we might support a set of cultural norms that endorse and celebrate the decision to care for the weak. We might create institutional arrangements, outside of the government, that make it easier for people to do so. We might make movies and write plays and books that sneer at people who abandon the weak. We might even inconvenience ourselves to do this work, when it presents itself to us in the form of a relative or friend who becomes incapacitated.

All of this requires, however, that we reassess our understanding of the dependent. If we define "usefulness" too narrowly, we will not be able to convince ourselves that dependent others have enough value for us to extend ourselves to them. If we believe that our legal obligations exhaust the sum of our social obligations, we will be unwilling to take any personal responsibility for dependents.

Scientism, truth, and goodness. Robert Nelson has argued that economic analysis, and the public policy analysis based on it, usually has embedded within it deep philosophical and even theological presuppositions. He argues that we would have more constructive policy conversations if we were willing to acknowledge these assumptions, rather than cover them with a patina of scientific-sounding jargon.[22] I am willing to take up Nelson's challenge. I believe that we have a potentially devastating intellectual problem in dealing with dependents. American individualism, rationalistic economic thinking, and excessive legalism combine to make it all but impossible to find socially acceptable reasons for caring about people who are legitimately dependent upon us. This is devastating because it makes us all vulnerable.

There is no need here for any pretense of value-neutrality. An ethic of caring for the needy is both true and good. It is true to the extent that it is grounded in observable and undeniable realities, and it is good to the extent that it helps us grow in happiness, maturity, and, ultimately, in our humanity. In short, an ethic of dependent care is consistent with human nature.

An ethic of care: How it is true

The first reason to face the issue of dependency is that it is simply a fact. Facing reality has always been one of the strong suits of the philosophy of freedom. Advocates of the free market understood that it was a fool's errand to abolish private property and reorganize the entire economy as if it were one big happy family. When socialists tried to eliminate the instinct for self-interest and self-preservation by destroying economic incentives, it was free-market economists who pointed out that such a vision was doomed. Economics has been successful as a science because it is based on the undeniable fact that people are self-interested and respond to incentives in a systematic and predictable way. This is also the reason that free societies work reasonably well.

But this is not the only truth about human nature. It is equally true that we are dependent, all of us some of the time (during infancy), and some of us all of the time (the disabled and the elderly). The fact of dependency creates an unavoidable need for human solidarity and interdependence.

It is also true that we have a desire to contribute to others, as well as to something good that extends beyond ourselves. This desire is as much a part of the human condition as the self-interested impulse economists spend so much time talking about. Indeed, we might suppose that this desire is the basis of the attraction felt by many to various socialist projects, however poorly conceived. We will not lose the advantages of individual motivation and effort by acknowledging this fact.

An ethic of caring for the dependent is realistic in that it is based on these enduring facts about the human condition. We cannot reasonably expect to ever abolish human dependency. Nor can we expect that people will stop caring about their infirm or dependent relatives. Nor, finally, can we assume that family members will never need some assistance from the wider community.

We come into the world as helpless babies. We leave the world as helpless dying persons. We need other people. To put it simply, we need love.

The law of the gift

The radical alternative to both impersonal bureaucracy and atomistic individualism is the law of the gift. This approach begins with the person in quite a different situation from the autonomous, choosing self. Instead of positing an initial presumption that each individual is a rational agent endowed with rights and freedom, it starts with the idea that each human life is a gift. Our own life is a gift to us; the lives of others are gifts to them, and ultimately, to us. Likewise, our capacities, including our capacity for rational thought and choice, are gifts.

With this approach, we lose none of the advantages of the legal rights and obligations perspective. Our lives, talents, and capacities are still "ours" and can be understood in the familiar property-rights sense. No one else has the right to take our lives or exploit our talents. Every person owns himself and his endowments in much the same way as in the private-property image of the self. I still have no more right to help myself to other people's gifts than I would to help myself to their real or moveable property.

The gift perspective also preserves the universality principle that is so important to the Western philosophical and legal tradition. Not only am I a gift to myself, so is every other person a gift to him or herself. There is still a powerful egalitarian impulse in the gift approach. Although we may differ in our gifts and talents, each one of us is still a gift as much as any other. We cannot sensibly view one person as a solution and another as a problem. There is a level at which no one really has reasonable bragging rights. I didn't create my intellect, my health, or my family background any more than I created my own life. The gift perspective helps us to see that each of these talents and endowments was entrusted to us and is not of our own creation.

Thus, the gift perspective maintains crucially important features of our Western system of legal rights and obligations. But at the same time, it provides us with several unique advantages.

First, viewing the person as a gift helps us to have a more realistic understanding of human dependency. We can more easily see that our crucial talents and abilities are contingent, not necessary, facts. I am an intelligent person. I need not have been, and I need not remain so. I am a healthy person, but I need not have been, nor am I guaranteed to continue to be healthy. I have the ability to help others. But I may not always have that ability, and indeed, I may one day be in need of the assistance of other people. Realizing all of this makes it easier to embrace our own periodic dependency on others—and more difficult to reject the dependent others in our midst.

The second advantage of viewing the human person as a gift is that this perspective inspires an attitude of gratitude. It is harder to go through life feeling cheated if one continually reminds oneself that one's entire life is a gift that need not have been given. The modern obsession with "fairness" quite often takes the form of self-pity: "I could have achieved as much as so and so, if only I had had his advantages in life"; "I could really make something of myself, if only the world were more fair, so that I could have had an equal chance." If we remember that our lives, our talents, our relatives are not of our own making, we are less apt to feel sorry for ourselves.

This suggests yet another advantage of the gift perspective. Seeing people as gifts provides us with an antidote to the extreme forms of competitiveness that sometimes mar human relationships. Competition can be constructive as an accountability mechanism in economics. But competition can be destructive in human relationships. It spurs us to spend our time and psychic energy comparing ourselves with others, even in situations that are not really commensurable. If I regard myself as better than the other person, I walk around feeling superior and smug. If I regard myself as worse than the other person, I walk around feeling inadequate and incompetent. Neither smug superiority nor dejected inferiority is a generally reasonable attitude.

But if I see my life as a gift, the question of who is better than whom becomes much less troubling. After all, I didn't earn my life. Neither did the other person earn his. Our relative talents and abilities are not really a reflection of our intrinsic merits. Thus, we can focus more upon what we choose to do and not do with what we have been given, rather than worrying about who has more or less. What we choose to do and not do is the essence of our moral blameworthiness or praiseworthiness in any case. Reminding ourselves that our lives are gifts has a way of short-circuiting that entire destructive line of interpersonal comparisons.

In addition to these advantages, there comes a surprising change in how we see the radically dependent person. We now see other people not only as gifts to themselves, but also as gifts to us. This gives us a perspective from which to appreciate the helpless.

It is easy to see how someone useful to me could be regarded as a gift. But people who are useful in the ordinary sense receive some form of compensation within the world of exchange. The person who fixes my car does me a great service that I could never perform for myself. In this I can (and do) marvel and take delight, and my expressions of gratitude and awe are no doubt satisfying to my mechanic. He nonetheless expects to be paid.

But the person who can perform no service for me, how can I see that person as a gift? We can edge toward an answer by looking at how people ordinarily respond to a newborn baby. A room full of people watching a tiny sleeping baby will regard it as the most fascinating creature in the world. An economist might subsume this question as a category of capital investment: we value the potential for life and productivity that a newborn child represents. A sociobiologist might say that we are hard-wired to feel drawn to the infant's neediness because the survival of our own genes depends on it. But to me, at least, these sound more like rationalizations than real reasons. And even if they are completely true from some grand evolutionary perspective, these accounts tell us very little about how we ought to evaluate our own attraction to the newborn, and whether and to what extent we ought to cultivate that feeling.

The newborn baby draws out our ability to care for another person in a more intense way than we experience in almost any other situation. The fact that my baby counts on me in a radical way forces me to look inside myself to find the resources to meet his needs. I find out how much I can give, how much sleep deprivation I can stand, how much love I am truly capable of. I do not maximize an existing, known utility function. I discover that my happiness can be enhanced in ways that I had never known existed.

Babies also point us to the deeper realities of human existence: our vulnerability, fragility, and ultimate demise. We need our parents for our very survival. We can't really do anything for them, except be cute, smile, and make them laugh. Infancy is the realm of the pure gift. It is possible that a mother nursing a newborn baby is performing a complicated calculation that her action will result in a secure old age for herself. Possible, but not likely. More likely, she is entering into the world of pure love. She nurses the baby because her body cries out to nurse. The baby is certainly not involved with a convoluted series of exchanges with his parents. Our parents make the First Move in the game of life. We come to trust that the world is a safe place, fit for our existence, and that we ourselves deserve to live.

In taking care of my baby, I learn to see my own vulnerability in a different light. I realize that some of my discomfort at that vulnerability stems from a fear that the universe will not respond to my neediness, that no one will take care of me. I do not really trust that anyone will be there for me in my time of need.

How does this help us understand the value of the adult dependent? For the mind steeped in utilitarianism, the natural question to ask is, "Of what use are the infirm, the mentally ill, and the old?" The answer is that such persons allow me to enter into the world of trust, the world of gift.[23] The helpless person invites us to enter into the realm of unconditional love, a realm that we all need to inhabit at least some of the time.

The mysterious and paradoxical God of the Christians

Here is a specifically Christian vision, though it can be hoped that it will have some appeal to non-Christians as well. Those who have been steeped in the Christian tradition are surely familiar with the injunction to see the face of Jesus in the face of the poor and suffering. Even those not steeped in Christianity can realize that this Western culture of ours has been profoundly influenced by this concern for and attention to the weak. [24]

The examples are numerous. Mother Teresa used to say that she and the sisters should see Jesus in the distressing disguise of the dying people on the streets of Calcutta. Some of her houses have a chalkboard in the entryway, showing the number of people who had come into the home on a given day, and the number who had died. At the bottom is written the phrase, "This, we do for Jesus."

Jean Vanier is a priest who has founded a series of homes for the mentally disabled. People come to live among the disabled and care for them. The most severely disabled have a full-time assistant who lives with them, taking care of their bodily needs. Young people come from all over the world to staff this network of 120 communities in twenty-nine countries. Why do they do it? Jean Vanier explains:

> I can witness that many young volunteers who come to our communities live an experience of transformation. Jesus is waiting for them in the poor and the weak. They discover something fundamental about being human and being a follower of Jesus.
>
> First of all, they gradually discover their own hearts, their own deepest selves. People with learning disabilities are crying out for affection, faithful friendship and for understanding. They have a mysterious way of breaking down barriers around people's hearts. They awaken what is deepest within us, our hearts and our desire for relationship. . . .
>
> Many young volunteers come to our communities wanting to do good to the poor, but what they discover is that it is the weak and the poor who are healing and transforming them, leading them into compassion. . . .[25]

Christianity has made attentiveness to the weak a hallmark of the civilization it inspired. But an ethic of care for the needy is based on universal truths. The weak really do call out to our hearts, if we let them. We know this through our experience with babies. We civilize them and they civilize us. We humanize them, and they humanize us. That experience is universal, and can be generalized to other dependents. More than that, we too were once completely dependent on others for our very survival. We may once again be so dependent. In addition, our ability to produce takes on new meaning when other people are dependent on us. We work harder when our work is motivated with love. Perhaps that is why married men with children have always earned more money than single men. It is not just that employers show favoritism to fathers. It is that fathers themselves are more intensely motivated.

This perspective can help provide some insight into the potential contributions of the "faith-based" social service agencies now part of the public policy discussion. Many analysts have come to appreciate the role that religious faith plays in motivating charitable activity. Many analysts have also discovered that religious commitment plays a valuable role in instilling virtues and habits that keep people out of certain kinds of trouble. I would add one further contribution of religion to the care of the poor and needy. The Christian religion and the Jewish tradition on which it is based help people to find value and meaning in the care of the dependent in the first place.

The Christian religion and the culture it has created help people discover the part of themselves that can respond to the neediness of others. Although Christianity is not essential to this transformative process, it is certainly helpful. We do not usually enter this realm of the gift automatically, or untutored. We need to have it brought to our attention.

The Christian understanding of love has a crucial role to play in expanding the vision of the free society. "To love is to will and to do the good of another." This understanding allows an individual to expand his notion of self-interest to include the good of someone else.

People do not make this leap automatically, but most people are capable of it. They need some support, direction, and guidance. Religion plays a crucial role in helping people see what values are worth pursuing.

Judaism very quickly interpreted the prohibition on killing to include a positive duty to aid the weak. "Love your neighbor as yourself" is first a Jewish commandment. Christianity expanded the definition of neighbor to include anyone in need. Each religion instills real meaning into the care of the dependent. It is not simply the promise of everlasting life that motivates people to care for the weak. The Judeo-Christian tradition also provides the belief that the activity is intrinsically worth doing, and leads to the human person's highest fulfillment.

Nico and his grandma

I have had the opportunity to learn this truth in the last couple of years. I have had a couple of "special needs" people living under my own roof, my son and my mother-in-law.

I have written about my adopted son before. My husband and I adopted him from a Romanian orphanage when he was two and a half years old. He had a variety of problems and challenges, resulting from those years in an orphanage. Those were warehouse years for him, years outside the world of love and interpersonal connection.

We wondered whether he would ever learn to love or attach himself to anyone. We were pretty sure he was making progress along those lines, but we had the opportunity to find out just how much progress when my husband's mother became seriously ill. Nico was then twelve years old.

My mother-in-law was diagnosed with breast cancer at about the same time we (finally) realized that she had Alzheimer's. Her judgment, memory, and ability to take care of herself were deteriorating rapidly, and at exactly the time that her illness made her even more needy. We told ourselves that we wanted to honor her independence as long as possible. That was only part of the truth. We also did not really want to admit that the mind of this wonderful person was fading away before our eyes.

It finally became apparent that she needed to move in with our family. As we looked around the house, the most suitable room for her was Nico's bedroom. It was the closest to our own bedroom, and close to a bathroom. We would have to reorganize the house, which meant moving Nico into a more public room than he was used to.

We told Nico that Grandma really needed to live with us, and that in particular she needed his room. Naturally, he resisted this idea, as any twelve-year-old boy might. He asked if there was some-place else she could live. I told him that the realistic alternative for her was a nursing home. He asked the obvious question, "What's a nursing home?" I told him (in a truly inspired moment of mother-hood), "A nursing home is an orphanage for old people."

He paused just long enough for his eyes to grow wide. Then he said, "No way." He gave Grandma his room cheerfully, without any further hint of complaining.

Our son and daughter got to help take care of Grandma during those last six months of her life. She was a lovely, delightful person, easy to take care of. I made a game of it for the kids. I would summon them by clapping my hands and calling, "Elves, I need some elves. Grandmama needs a tissue," or whatever it was she needed. The kids would come running, tumbling over themselves to be the first one to bring Grandma whatever it was. She never failed to laugh at this, and the kids never failed to be pleased with themselves.

Grandma took a turn for the worse while Nico and I were away on a trip to Switzerland and Washington, D.C. My husband called to tell us that she could no longer swallow; we should be prepared for the worst. When we got home, it was unusually hot and humid, and the family was keeping wet towels around Grandma's neck, trying to feed her ice chips to suck on. Nico went right to her room and began talking to her about our trip. She couldn't say much, but she smiled at him. I stayed with her and watched as the kids went outside to play together. Nico showed his sister his favorite souvenirs, a noisy cow horn from Switzerland and a kazoo in the shape of a duck's beak from "D.C. Ducks."

The kids just happened to play and make their noises right outside Grandma's window, where she could see them. She was happy just to watch them and listen to their noise. They just happened to bring their board game into Grandma's room and play at the foot of her bed. I didn't tell them to do it. They didn't talk about what they were doing. But it was obvious: they wanted to be near Grandma because it would make her happy to see them there. Our nine-year-old daughter is naturally empathetic: was it her idea? If it was, Nico surely didn't object. At any rate, the two of them intuited that it was good for them to be near a dying woman whom they loved.

It might seem that they were doing her a service, and that she got all the benefits in this situation. She plainly took pleasure just in being close to these children. She didn't look very good. In fact, her appearance was a bit alarming. She was dying. She couldn't do anything for herself. What was she ever going to do for them?

But they got to know that they were of value to her simply by being there. They didn't have to do anything to be important to her and to be loved by her. They received the experience of being valued simply because they exist. That is as close to unconditional love as a person can get this side of heaven.

Surely, this experience of unconditional love is crucial for the foundation of a healthy personality and sense of self-worth. Certainly, that is how a mother wants her children to feel. What could I have done that would have conveyed that message any more powerfully than their grandmother did on her deathbed?

Ultimately, this is the contribution of the dependent to the rest of us: they teach us how to love, and be loved.

Fame is fleeting, love is eternal

As it happened, my first book was published during my mother-in-law's final months. While I was juggling doctors' appointments, coordinating respite providers, and trying to keep everybody comfortable, I was also doing radio interviews and writing op-ed articles for book publicity. In all that flurry of both kinds of activity, I noticed a difference in how they each felt.

I loved doing the radio shows. I enjoyed the attention that my book received. But I noticed that after each program, book review, or speech, I was immediately looking forward to the next one. I can't say I was ever really satisfied. No matter how well I did, or how many books sold that particular day, I was always wondering why I hadn't done better, or when the next event would be.

It is a peculiarity of one of the economists' first axioms: more of a good is always preferred to less. We don't teach the students the feeling that goes along with that axiom. To the extent that more really is preferred to less, the consumer is never really satisfied, but is rather always striving for more.

But in taking care of Grandma, I had an experience where more is really not preferred to less. In fact, the phrase doesn't have any meaning in the context of such a situation. No one "prefers" to have their loved ones die. It is not an experience that anyone "chooses" in the usual sense. But given that everyone does die, we have preferences about how and where our loved ones die. I wouldn't have wanted Grandma to die anywhere else but in our home.

Although there were many times when the tasks were disagreeable, I wouldn't have wanted to miss out on having her with us. I had a sense of peace about the whole experience, since it was obvious to me what my first priority had to be. The book would be there later, but our time with Grandma was limited. Book publicity got squeezed in around the edges of baths and doctors' appointments. My only regret is that we didn't move her in sooner, and that we brought too much hired help into the home.

As I reflected on these two experiences, publishing a book and taking care of Grandma, I remembered the old story about the Roman conquerors. When the laurel wreath was placed upon their heads, to the accolades of the cheering crowds, slaves would whisper in their ears, "Fame is fleeting."

I'm still chasing the fame. I still like to look at each new review and feel a moment of enjoyment. I still always wonder when the next one will come out, and why there wasn't a better one in a bigger publication. But when I look back on taking care of Grandma, I feel a profound satisfaction. Having her in our family those last six months of her life was a self-contained, complete experience that nothing will ever replace.

Conclusion

The vision of the free society must be humanized. We can do this in part by facing the reality of human dependence, along with the reality of human autonomy. We can build up a free society by embracing those who are legitimately dependent on us. We can take personal care of our own children, so they know they are loved and that the world is worth being part of and contributing to. We can take care of the disabled so that we have the opportunity to take a vacation from the world of exchange and live in the world of the gift at least some of the time. We can take care of the elderly and help them to know that they are loved, and that their lives have meaning and value. Surely this is a project worthy of a great and prosperous nation.

9

International Markets, International Poverty: Globalization and the Poor

Daniel T. Griswold

Globalization has been a blessing for the world's poor wherever it has been allowed to work. Like all manifestations of change and economic progress, it has caused disruptions to established patterns of life, but most of the change has been for the better for the large majority of people it has touched. Globalization—that is, the liberalization of international trade, investment, and migration, and the resulting integration of national economies—has spurred higher growth in poor nations that have opened themselves to the global economy. That higher growth has raised living standards, reduced poverty, and narrowed the income gap between the advanced economies and those poorer nations that have made peace with globalization. Along with its economic blessings, globalization has fostered individual freedom and responsibility, promoted a "race toward the top" in labor and environmental standards, and encouraged the spread of more representative government and respect for human rights.

All of those assertions directly contradict the claims of the anti-globalization movement. On their websites, in their publications, and at their sometimes-violent protests (prior to September 11, 2001, anyway), anti-globalization critics assert that the poor of the world are the principal victims of globalization. They claim that globalization exploits the poor by creating low-wage jobs, widening the gap between rich and poor, and stoking a "race to the bottom" in which poor countries lower their social standards to attract cost-conscious and increasingly mobile international capital.

This chapter will demonstrate, from theory and experience, that the protesters are tragically wrong and that globalization, combined with internal market reforms, offers the best hope for the world's poor. Because of the real-world benefits it delivers to the poor, globalization is not merely good economics but also morally sound, upholding biblical principles of justice, peace, and individual moral worth.

The morality of free trade

Free trade is consistent with a Judeo-Christian moral view. Nowhere does the Bible condemn trade *per se,* either within or across international borders. The Old Testament prophet Ezekiel did warn the citizens of Tyre, the bustling Mediterranean port city of his day, "By your great skill in trading you have increased your wealth, and because of your wealth your heart has grown proud." But even when the Bible speaks harshly of the "merchants of the earth," it is not international trade itself that comes under condemnation, but the intent and the character of the traders. Trade is not the sin, but dishonest scales, greed, indulgence in luxuries, and the temptation to pride that can come from wealth. In this respect, trade is no more sinful than technological discoveries or hard work.

Solomon's Temple could not have been built without international trade. When constructing the temple, Israel traded wheat and oil to King Hiram of Tyre in exchange for skilled labor and cedar logs from Lebanon. Trade was part of Solomon's splendor: In First Kings we read, "The king had a fleet of trading ships at sea along with the ships of Hiram. Once every three years it returned, carrying gold, silver and ivory, and apes and baboons."

Free trade affirms the God-given right of individuals to enjoy the fruits of their own labor free from coercion. To support free trade is to oppose an unjust form of redistribution known as protectionism. Protectionism is stealing, a violation of the Eighth Commandment and other prohibitions against theft. It takes from one group of people, usually a broad cross-section of consumers who are forced to pay higher prices, and gives the spoils to a small group of producers whose only claim to the money is that they would be worse off under open competition.

Free trade meets the most elementary test of justice, giving to each person sovereign control over that which is his own. As Frédéric Bastiat wrote in his 1849 essay, "Protectionism and Communism," "Every citizen who has produced or acquired a product should have the option of applying it immediately to his own use or of transferring it to whoever on the face of the earth agrees to give him in exchange the object of his desires. To deprive him of this option when he has committed no act contrary to public order and good morals, and solely to satisfy the convenience of another citizen, is to legitimize an act of plunder and to violate the law of justice."[1]

Free trade encourages individuals to cultivate moral virtues. To be successful in a free and open marketplace, producers must serve their fellow human beings by providing goods and services others want and need. In the 1991 papal encyclical *Centesimus Annus,* Pope John Paul II observed that a market system encourages the important virtues of "diligence, industriousness, prudence in undertaking reasonable risks, reliability and fidelity in interpersonal relationships, as well as courage in carrying out decisions which are difficult and painful but necessary."[2]

Free trade promotes cooperation and tolerance across racial, ethnic, and religious divides. Historically, those cities and countries at the forefront of international trade were also among the most open and tolerant societies of their day. Venice in the 1400s and the Dutch Republic in the 1600s, the leading commercial centers of their eras, provided freedom and legal protection to Jews and other religious dissenters. They learned to welcome people of differing religions and races because intolerance was, among its other shortcomings, bad for business. Today, societies open to trade are more likely to safeguard freedom of religion and speech and political pluralism (a point to be treated in more detail later in the chapter).

Early Christian and pagan thinkers even argued that international trade could be seen as part of God's plan to encourage good will and understanding among nations. This early view of trade has come to be called the "Doctrine of Universal Economy," a belief that God spread resources and goods unevenly throughout the world to promote commerce between disparate nations and regions. In the fourth century A.D., the pagan Libanius expanded the doctrine more fully, declaring: "God did not bestow all products upon all parts of the earth, but distributed His gifts over different regions, to the end that men might cultivate a social relationship because one would have need of the help of another. And so He called commerce into being, that all men might be able to have common enjoyment of the fruits of earth, no matter where produced."[3]

Two giants of Christian thought, the Catholic Thomas Aquinas and the Protestant John Calvin, each understood the prudential value of international trade. In his *Summa Theologiae,* Aquinas acknowledged "a certain debasement" connected to trading, but concluded that trading for profit, "though not implying, by its nature, anything virtuous or necessary, does not, in itself, connote anything sinful or contrary to virtue."[4] Calvin warned against the pride and dishonest gain that can come with trade, but was on the whole positive about its contribution to mankind: "Navigation [trade] cannot, indeed, be condemned on its own account; for by importing and exporting articles of merchandise, it is of great advantage to mankind. Nor can any fault be found with this mode of intercourse between nations; for it is the will of God that the whole human race should be joined together by mutual acts of kindness."[5]

In sum, expanding the liberty of people to engage in global commerce is entirely consistent with Judeo-Christian thought. Globalization encourages individual virtue and respect for the rights and property of others. It fosters cooperation across borders, oceans, and cultures. And, as we shall see, it can be an effective instrument to feed and clothe the world's poor.

Globalization and growth

Globalization benefits the world's poor through a powerful dynamic: Nations that open themselves to the global economy tend to grow faster economically than those that isolate themselves. The resulting growth lifts a rising share of their populations out of poverty, creates the domestic wealth necessary to raise environmental, labor, and general living standards, and creates conditions more conducive to political pluralism and respect for human rights. Those may seem to be tall claims, but they rest on two centuries of economic thought and experience.

Globalization and its handmaiden of free trade promote growth by allowing a greater division of labor in the world. International trade allows nations to produce more of what they are relatively efficient at producing, trading their surplus production for those goods that people in other nations are more efficient at producing. Adam Smith noted two centuries ago in his classic study, *The Wealth of Nations*, that an individual family that insisted on producing all its own clothing, shoes, furniture, and food would consign itself to poverty. The same applies to nations. Larger markets through globalization allow a finer division of labor and a greater degree of specialization, raising productivity and living standards.

Free-trade theory was strengthened further in 1817 when British economist David Ricardo first explained comparative advantage. The key insight of his theory is that nations can benefit from free trade even if people in other nations are more productive in producing everything. What matters is not *absolute* advantage in productivity between nations, but what people are *relatively* more productive at producing compared to other products they could produce. If Americans are twice as productive at making t-shirts as people in Bangladesh but are twenty times as productive at making civilian aircraft, it will still be to the advantage of both countries for Americans to specialize in producing aircraft and buy their t-shirts from the Bangladeshis. Comparative advantage means there is a place under the free-trade sun for every nation, no matter how poor, because people of every nation can produce some products relatively more efficiently than they produce other products.

The blessings of open trade and globalization apply all the more to poor nations, conferring on them a "latecomer's advantage." First, poor nations that engage in globalization can dramatically expand the size of markets for both their producers and consumers. Consumers gain access to a much wider range of goods and services at more competitive prices, raising the real standard of living for most workers. For people in poor countries, especially, trade provides advanced goods—TVs, cell phones, medical equipment—and financial services that would otherwise be impossible or prohibitively expensive for them to produce on their own. Domestic producers gain access to a wider range and better quality of intermediate inputs at lower prices, and those that export enjoy a quantum leap in economies of scale by serving global markets rather than only a confined and underdeveloped domestic market.

Second, poor countries that open themselves to international trade and investment gain access to a much higher level of technology. Rather than bearing the cost of expensive, up-front research and development, poor countries can import the technology off-the-shelf, embodied in such products as pharmaceuticals and electronic hardware and in new capital machinery that raises productivity. Hybrid seeds and new medicines are raising nutrition levels and extending lives in poor countries. Subsidiaries of multinational companies also bring with them new production techniques and employee-training that add to the host nation's stock of human capital.

Third, engagement in the global economy provides additional capital to fuel future growth. Most less-developed countries are people rich and capital poor. Access to global capital markets allows poor countries to raise the level of domestic investment and to accelerate their pace of growth. Inward foreign investment can finance more traditional types of infrastructure, such as port facilities, power generation, and an internal transportation network, just as British capital helped to finance America's network of canals and railroads in the nineteenth century. But just as importantly, multinational companies can provide more efficient telecommunications, insurance, and banking services. Cellular telephone networks, for example, allow poor villagers in remote areas to bypass antiquated and unresponsive government landline monopolies. As many poor countries are discovering, an underdeveloped service sector retards growth in other sectors of the economy. A poor country that closes its door to foreign investment or fails to maintain sound domestic policies will forfeit the immense benefits this inflow of capital can bring.

Finally, engagement in the global economy encourages governments to follow more sensible economic policies. Sovereign nations remain free to follow whatever economic policies their governments choose, but globalization has raised the cost that must be paid for bad policies. With capital more mobile than ever, countries that insist on following anti-market policies will find themselves being dealt out of global competition for investment. As a consequence, nations have a greater incentive to choose policies that encourage foreign investment and domestic, market-led growth. And by creating a more hospitable climate for foreign investment, governments in less developed countries usually create a more friendly business climate for local producers and entrepreneurs.

For all those reasons, poor nations that open themselves to trade and investment typically grow faster than other poor nations that keep themselves closed. Of course, other factors play a role in determining a nation's rate of growth, so the link between openness and growth is not perfect, but the empirical evidence strongly indicates that openness is good for growth.[6] The annual *Economic Freedom of the World* report, published by the Fraser Institute in Canada, found that nations that were in the top quintile of trade openness from 1980 to 1998 enjoyed real per capita GDPs that were more than seven times greater than those in the bottom quintile and grew nearly five times faster (see Figure 1).[7]

Consider the tale of two African island nations, Madagascar and Mauritius. From the early 1970s through most of the 1990s, Madagascar followed an economic policy its government described as "Christian Marxism." That path led the government to nationalize industries, control domestic markets, and close its borders behind high tariffs. The result was stagnant growth, and pervasive, persistent poverty, malnourishment, and illiteracy. Nearby Mauritius, in contrast, engaged itself in the global economy by establishing an export-processing zone in 1972 to woo foreign textile producers from Hong Kong and other East Asian countries. Taking advantage of access to American and European markets, Mauritius rapidly expanded its trading sectors, becoming globally competitive in a labor-intensive industry that played to its comparative advantage. As a result, Mauritius pulled away from Madagascar by virtually every measure of well-being: By 1998, its annual per-capita income had reached $3,690, compared to $250 in Madagascar; 22 percent of its residents owned phones compared to 6 percent in Madagascar, and literacy had reached 100 percent compared to 45 percent in its poor neighbor.[8]

Pope John Paul II, in his 1991 encyclical on the morality of a market-based economic system, noted the connection between free markets and growth: "Even in recent years it was thought that the poorest countries would develop by isolating themselves from the world market and by depending only on their own resources. Recent experience has shown that countries which did this have suffered stagnation and recession, while the countries which experienced development were those which succeeded in taking part in the general interrelated economic activities at the international level."[9]

Figure 1:   Trade Openness, Income, and Growth

Graph A

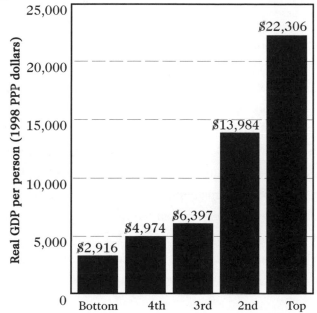

Trade Openness Index (1980-1998) Quintiles

Graph B

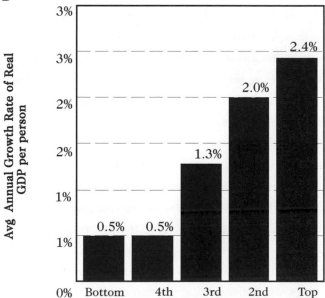

Trade Openness Index (1980-1998) Quintiles

Trade liberalization alone will not guarantee more growth. Economic openness must be accompanied by internal reforms such as a noninflationary monetary policy, secure property rights, economically rational regulation, a transparent and rule-based legal system, government spending restraint, and a tax system that allows workers to enjoy the fruits of their labors. Some nations that have opened themselves to the global economy have run into economic troubles, not because of globalization, but because of lagging domestic reforms. In East Asia in the late 1990s, South Korea, Thailand, and Indonesia experienced steep downturns because of growing doubts about opaque domestic financial systems dominated by politics. More recently, Argentina has suffered recession and mounting foreign debt because of profligate government spending and a legal system that stifles entrepreneurial activity. While trade reforms do not guarantee growth, they make growth more likely when combined with other market reforms.

Lifting the lot of the poor

People of faith cannot in good conscience ignore the condition of poor people, either in their own communities or in distant countries. A persistent theme of the Bible, from the Old Testament through the New, is concern for the lot of the poor. Believers are commanded to not discriminate against the poor in their courts, churches, or friendships. We are not to oppress the poor by denying them the ability to provide for themselves. We are commanded to help those in desperate need, through direct charity and by allowing them to harvest the "gleanings" of our own abundance.

Jesus Christ told his disciples, "The poor you shall have with you always," and that statement is no less true today (in absolute numbers, anyway) than it was two thousand years ago. Despite dramatic advances in living standards in the last two hundred years, at the turn of the millennium, an estimated 1.2 billion people in the world were still living in what is defined as absolute poverty—the equivalent of one dollar per day or less. These people lack the necessities of life that people in the West have come to take for granted: access to electricity, clean drinking water, minimum daily nutrition and calories, elementary education, and basic medical care.

The disparities between rich and poor countries can be appalling. Diseases that have almost disappeared in the West, such as tuberculosis, diarrhea, polio, meningitis, malaria, river blindness, and leprosy, are common and deadly in poor countries. In the richest fifth of countries, fewer than five babies out of every thousand births will die before their first birthday; in the poorest fifth, the infant mortality rate is 200 out of every thousand. Millions of children in poor countries die each year from bacterial pneumonia, whooping cough, polio, diphtheria, tetanus, measles, and from dehydration caused by diarrhea. Vitamin A and iodine deficiencies inflict blindness and mental retardation on hundreds of thousands of children each year. Another 170 million to 400 million are infected annually by intestinal parasites such as hookworm and roundworm, which stunt physical and mental growth.[10]

Blame for the suffering of the world's poor cannot be pinned on globalization. Poverty, disease, and death were even more prevalent in the decades that preceded the latest round of globalization. Indeed, absolute poverty has been the lot of the vast majority of mankind for all but the most recent two centuries of human history. In the last three decades, measurable progress has been made in most poor countries in nutrition levels and life expectancy, and against infant mortality and poverty, nowhere more so than in those countries that have embraced globalization. In fact, during the last generation, more progress has been made in reducing poverty and raising living standards in poor countries than during any previous period in history. In less developed countries, life expectancy has increased from fifty-five to sixty-five years. Incomes per person have doubled. Infant mortality rates have been cut in half. The proportion of children attending school has risen from less than half to more than three-quarters.[11]

The most dramatic progress against poverty has been in those poor countries that have moved most decisively to open themselves to the global economy. More open and competitive markets have raised rates of growth, lifting incomes for poor families as well as the non-poor. Better paying jobs have been created by foreign direct investment, especially in labor-intensive industries such as apparel and other light manufacturing. Such jobs typically pay wages that are much higher and offer benefits and working conditions that are much better than what locally owned producers offer.[12] Lower trade barriers have brought the price of a wider range of consumer goods—cellular telephones, refrigerators, motorbikes, TVs, and VCRs—within reach of lower income families. Better jobs and higher incomes have raised health standards and allowed more kids to attend school.

Benefits to the poor are most visible in countries that have opened themselves to globalization. In China, two decades of economic reform and trade liberalization have raised growth rates, quadrupled real wages, and reduced the number of people living in absolute poverty by more than 100 million.[13] Chinese economic reform has been, quite simply, the greatest antipoverty program the world has ever seen. Since 1991, poverty rates have also fallen sharply in Vietnam, India, and Uganda—all formerly closed economies that have liberalized their domestic and trade policies in the past decade. In none of those countries was poverty reduced primarily through foreign aid, internal income redistribution, or outside economic and political pressure, but through internal market reforms and globalization. A 2001 World Bank study found that "the only countries in which we have seen large-scale poverty reduction in the 1990s are ones that have become more open to foreign trade and investment."[14] In the two decades since 1980, the study could not find a single example of a poor country that had closed its markets and at the same time closed the income gap with the rich countries.[15]

An April 2002 study on trade and poverty by Oxfam International, while critical of multinational companies and other aspects of globalization, nonetheless concluded, "History makes a mockery of the claim that trade cannot work for the poor. Participation in world trade has figured prominently in many of the most successful cases of poverty reduction—and, compared with aid, has far more potential to benefit the poor.[16]

How globalization raises standards

Critics charge that globalization encourages a "race to the bottom" in environmental and labor standards. They argue that multinational companies, in a never-ending quest to cut costs and increase profits, roam the planet looking for countries with the least restrictive regulations and lowest wages. The governments of poor countries are thus encouraged to keep standards low so as not to frighten away footloose foreign investment. And to prevent capital from fleeing to low-standard countries, so the theory goes, Western governments face relentless pressure to lower their own standards. The trouble with that scenario is that there is little in theory to support it and virtually no evidence.

When Western multinational firms invest in less developed countries, they typically bring higher standards, not lower standards. For reasons of internal efficiency as well as public perception, multinational companies expect similar standards from their affiliates, whether operating in less developed or advanced economies. Thus, multinational companies tend to impose higher standards on their overseas production plants than those of domestically owned and operated companies, thus raising average standards in the host country. And for most industries, the cost of complying with labor and environmental standards are so small as to make them relatively unimportant in choosing where to locate.

If low standards and low wages were the dominant factors driving investment flows, as the race-to-the-bottom thesis assumes, then we would expect poor countries to be capturing most foreign direct investment from developed countries. Yet the low social standards endemic to less developed countries do not seem to confer any observable advantage in attracting foreign direct investment. The overwhelming majority of foreign direct investment comes from and flows to developed countries with similarly high wages and high labor and environmental standards. Those nations in the world today with the highest labor and environmental standards are invariably those with the highest incomes and the most open economies. Globalization and the development it spurs lead not to a race to the bottom, but to a race to the top.

That improvement includes the most emotional of labor standards—child labor. Child labor of the worst kind is a fact of life in the world's poorest countries. According to the International Labor Organization, an estimated 250 million children between the ages of five and fourteen were working in less developed countries in 1997, nearly half of them full-time and to the exclusion of school.[17] Children who are deprived of an elementary education are likely to be condemned to perpetual poverty, and society as a whole loses the benefits of a more educated and productive population. Yet for many Third World families living on the edge of subsistence, the alternative to child labor is not school but starvation.

The overwhelming majority of child laborers toiling in poor countries work in sectors far removed from the global economy. More than 80 percent work without pay, usually for their parents or other family members, typically in subsistence farming.[18] Most other child laborers work for small-scale domestic enterprises, typically non-traded services such as shoe shining, newspaper delivery, and domestic service.[19] A report by the U.S. Department of Labor found that "[o]nly a very small percentage of all child workers, probably less than five percent, are employed in export industries in manufacturing and mining. And they are not commonly found in large enterprises; but rather in small and medium-sized firms and in neighborhood and home settings."[20]

As with labor standards in general, trade and globalization are not part of the problem of child labor but are in fact a necessary part of its alleviation. As household incomes rise, especially wages paid to adult females, fewer families face the economic necessity of sending their children to work. Studies confirm that labor force participation rates by children aged ten to fourteen decline significantly with rising GNP per capita.[21] Child labor rates also fall as a nation's population shifts from rural agricultural areas, where child labor rates are relatively high, to urban centers. The most objectionable forms of child labor are most commonly found in rural areas of poor countries, areas that are the farthest removed from the reach of global trade and investment. As trade expands and incomes rise, more parents can afford to send their children to school rather than to work.

Through the same dynamic of development, globalization is also enabling poor countries to raise their environmental standards. Openness to trade and investment allows less-developed nations to import the latest technology to help control pollution in the most cost-effective way. By encouraging competition, globalization helps reduce wasteful consumption of resources. Multinational companies that set up operations abroad tend to follow higher standards of pollution control than those followed by the domestic companies in the host country. By promoting development, globalization makes it easier for less developed countries to afford pollution-controlling technology. When incomes and education levels rise, citizens are more likely to demand more effective regulation of pollution. That explains why the most stringent environmental laws in the world today are maintained in developed countries that are relatively open to trade.

Development by itself can have a mixed impact on the environment. All else being equal, an economy that produces more of exactly the same goods and services in exactly the same way will produce more pollution. But development changes not only the size of an economy but also its composition and its level of technology. More sophisticated technology can mean cleaner production processes and more affordable and effective pollution abatement. As nations progress to a higher stage of development, they tend to move away from more resource-intensive activities such as mining, agriculture, and heavy industry, and into light manufacturing, information technology, and services. And as incomes rise, households rely less on wood as a fuel, lessening pressure to harvest forestland. As a study by the OECD on globalization and the environment concluded, "There is some evidence that, once a country begins to industrialize, trade liberalization helps to make the structure of its economy less pollution-intensive than in those countries whose economies remain relatively closed. In particular, freer trade seems to promote the transition from heavy resource-processing sectors to light manufacturing ones (at least at middle income levels)."[22]

Of course, open trade and economic growth alone do not lead inevitably to higher environmental and labor standards. Absent clearly defined property rights, government regulation is usually necessary to protect common air and water resources from pollution that can endanger the public's health. Government action may also be necessary to eliminate forced labor, the exploitation of children, and market distortions caused by anticompetitive practices, whether by industry or labor unions. But the evidence is clear that economically sound regulations are perfectly compatible with an open economy.

Conditions in less developed countries can strike Western observers as unacceptable if not appalling. But two points need to be considered. First, wages and working conditions are likely to be even worse in non-trade-oriented sectors, such as services and subsistence agriculture, sectors that have been largely untouched by globalization. Second, poor working conditions in those countries are not a new phenomenon but have always been a chronic fact of life. "Sweatshop" conditions persist today not because of globalization, a relatively new phenomenon, but because of previous decades characterized by protectionism, inflation, economic mismanagement, hostility to foreign investment, and a lack of legally defined property rights.

Globalization is not the cause of bad working conditions but the best hope for improving them.

Globalization and equality

Another indictment of globalization is that it has bred rising inequality in the world, both within nations and among nations. Critics argue that even if globalization has made some people and nations richer, rising inequality has morally tainted the whole enterprise. What they imply is that even if the lot of poor people and poor countries may be improving *absolutely,* globalization has failed because the lot of the poor has worsened *relatively.*

Inequality in the global economy is in fact a mixed story. By some measures it has been rising, but by others it has been falling. Inequality has indeed risen among nations. The income gap between the world's poorest countries and the world's richest has been growing steadily for decades, and is far greater today than it was a century ago. The story of inequality within countries is more complicated, with inequality rising in some countries and falling in others. Even if rising inequality were broadly true, two important questions would remain: To what extent is globalization responsible, and is the inequality it may have caused necessarily a bad thing?

The charge that globalization has widened the income gap between rich and poor countries is half right. Globalization has fostered faster growth in those poor countries that have expanded trade with the rest of the world, allowing them to close the gap with the richer countries. But globalization cannot be justly blamed for the lack of growth in those countries that have rejected it. An important study by David Dollar and Aart Kraay of the World Bank found that the economic fate of less developed countries that join the global economy is starkly different from the fate of those that remain relatively isolated. Dollar and Kraay divided the less developed world into two categories: "globalizers," which are those countries that have experienced rapid increases in trade and foreign investment during the past two decades, and non-globalizers, which have experienced declines in trade and foreign investment in the past twenty years. Among their major findings was confirmation that globalizing poor countries have indeed grown faster than the non-globalizers, and faster than the world's advanced economies. "Thus, the globalizers are catching up with the rich countries while the non-globalizers fall further and further behind."[23]

Another major finding by Dollar and Kraay was the lack of any connection between a nation's growth rate and its level of domestic inequality. Less-developed nations were as likely to see inequality fall as rise during periods of growth. In fact, the incomes of the poorest 20 percent of a nation's population rose on average at the same rate as the rest of the population. If globalization can spur faster growth, as the evidence indicates, then the poorest segments of society in the globalizing country will typically benefit to the same degree as everyone else. "The fact that increased trade generally goes hand-in-hand with more rapid growth and no systematic change in household income distribution means that increased trade generally goes hand-in-hand with improvement in well-being of the poor," they concluded.[24]

In addition, to pursue equality as the Holy Grail can pose a moral hazard as well by arousing unhealthy feelings of resentment and envy. An exclusive focus on equality can turn attention away from mutual gains from trade and toward an obsessive comparison to, and resentment of, people and nations that have achieved higher productivity and incomes. Economic egalitarianism pits one group against another, based on the false assumption that one country's poverty can only be explained by another's wealth. Such a worldview assumes that global wealth is an exogenous given, like manna from heaven that has been distributed unequally and without regard to merit, and thus, in the name of justice, must be redistributed more equitably. In such a zero-sum world, nation is pitted against nation and one ethnic group against another, since one group's gain must by definition be another's loss. In the past, that mindset has stoked ethnic violence against minorities such as Jews and overseas Chinese who have historically been traders and merchants with above-average incomes.

Making equality the sole measure of success quickly leads to a moral absurdity. Consider this thought experiment: Which world would be morally preferable, one in which everyone earned $1,000 a year, or one in which half the population earned $2,000 a year and the other half earned $20,000? If equality were the dominant goal of policy, the first world of universal poverty would be preferable to the second in which everyone was better off absolutely but some people were much better off than others. Yet the second world is, roughly speaking, the one that globalization has helped to create. Through trade, integration, and market reforms, an expanding number of nations have managed to escape widespread poverty to join the ranks of middle- and upper-income nations. And many nations that have failed to participate in globalization have seen absolute living standards rise, even though they have fallen further behind relative to other nations.

History itself poses a challenge to the egalitarian standard. According to estimates by economic historians, world income was much more equally "distributed" a thousand years ago. Absolute poverty was almost universal in the year 1000, with GDP per capita averaging $435 (in 1990 dollars). Early death from starvation and disease was ubiquitous, with average life expectancy a mere twenty-four years. Incomes across regions and continents of the world were roughly the same, with people in Asia, the world's richest region at the time, living on the equivalent of $450 per capita per year and people in the Americas, Russia, and eastern Europe, the world's poorest regions, living on $400. A thousand years later, every region of the world is better off absolutely, but the general advance of living standards has been marked by dramatically rising inequality. In Africa, the poorest region in the world today, per-capita GDP is more than three times greater than it was a thousand years ago. Huge disparities arise from the fact that inhabitants of western Europe produce forty times more GDP per capita than they did a millennium ago, those of

Japan fifty-one times more, and those of North America and Australia sixty-five times more.²⁵ Can anyone argue that the world of uniform poverty that was mankind's lot a thousand years ago is morally preferable to our world of far greater wealth but far greater inequality?

To blame globalization for the widening income gap between the richest and the poorest countries is akin to blaming education for the growing income gap between college graduates and high school dropouts. Our response should not be to condemn globalization, but to find ways to spread its benefits to a widening circle of humanity. In the words of U.N. Secretary General Kofi Annan, in a May 2000 speech to the Millennium Forum in New York City, "I believe the poor are poor not because of too much globalization, but because of too little—because they are not part of it, because they are excluded."²⁶

Tilling the soil for human rights

Globalization and the development it has spurred have created a more hospitable climate for civil and political freedoms. The economic openness of globalization allows citizens greater access to technology and ideas through fax machines, satellite dishes, mobile telephones, Internet access, and face-to-face meetings with people from other countries. Rising incomes and economic freedom help to nurture a more educated and politically aware middle class. People who are economically free over time come to want and expect to exercise political and civil liberty as well. Catholic social thinker Michael Novak identified this as the "Wedge Theory": "Capitalist practices, runs the theory, bring contact with the ideas and practices of the free societies, generate the economic growth that gives political confidence to a rising middle class, and raise up successful business leaders who come to represent a political alternative to military or party leaders. In short, capitalist firms wedge a democratic camel's nose under the authoritarian tent."²⁷

The interplay of economic openness and political and civil freedom is admittedly complex, and the question of causation remains unsettled, but the two phenomena are clearly linked. In the past twenty-five years, as an expanding share of the world has turned away from centralized economic controls and toward a more open global market, political and civil freedoms have also spread. Since 1975, the share of the world's governments classified by Freedom House as democracies has risen sharply, especially since the late 1980s when globalization began to gather steam (see Figure 2).[28] Many of these new democracies are low- and middle-income countries that have simultaneously liberalized and opened their economies.

When we compare countries according to their economic openness and their degree of political and civil freedom, the connection becomes even more evident. People who live in countries relatively open to international trade and investment are far more likely to enjoy full political and civil liberties than those who live in countries that are relatively closed. Among the top two quintiles of nations ranked according to their economic openness,[29] 90 percent are rated "Free" by Freedom House and not a single one is rated "Not Free." In the bottom quintile of openness (i.e., those with the most closed economies), fewer than 20 percent are rated "Free" and more than half are rated "Not Free" (see Figure 3). In other words, countries that maintain a relatively open economy are more than four times more likely to be free of political and civil oppression than countries that remain closed.

Recent decades have witnessed dramatic examples of how economic freedom and openness till the soil for civil and political reform. Twenty years ago, both South Korea and Taiwan were military dictatorships without free elections or full civil liberties. Today, thanks in part to economic growth and globalization, both are thriving democracies where citizens enjoy the full range of civil liberties and where opposition parties have won elections against longtime ruling parties. In Mexico, more than a decade of economic and trade reforms helped lay the foundation for the historic July 2, 2000, election of the opposition candidate Vicente Fox, ending seventy-one years of one-party rule by the PRI. Internal economic reforms and the North American Free Trade Agreement helped to undermine the dominance of the PRI over Mexican political life. Alejandro Junco, publisher of the opposition newspaper *Reforma,* noted after the PRI's historic defeat, "As the years have passed, and with international mechanisms like NAFTA, the government doesn't control the newsprint, they don't have the monopoly on telecommunications, there's a consciousness among citizens that the president can't control everybody."[30]

Even in nominally communist China, economic reform and globalization give reason to hope for political reforms. After two decades of reform and rapid growth, an expanding middle class is experiencing for the first time the independence of home ownership, travel abroad, and cooperation with others in economic enterprise free of government control. The number of telephone lines, mobile phones, and Internet users has risen exponentially in the past decade.[31] Tens of thousands of Chinese students are studying abroad each year. This has to be good news for individual freedom in China, and a growing problem for the government. A recent study by the Chinese Communist Party's influential Central Organization Department noted with concern that "as the economic standing of the affluent stratum has increased, so too has its desire for greater political standing." The study concluded that such a development would have a "profound impact on social and political life" in China.[32]

While genuine political reform has been absent so far in China and dissent is still brutally suppressed, its economic reforms have opened the door for evangelization. More than one hundred Western missionary organizations are active in China. Those organizations have distributed millions of Chinese-language Bibles in China. Thousands of Christian workers who are tent-making as English teachers or some other occupation are able to minister to the growing body of believers in China. All this would have been unthinkable twenty-five years ago when China was still isolated from the global economy.

Globalization and economic development do not guarantee political reform in China or anywhere else, but the track record of economic

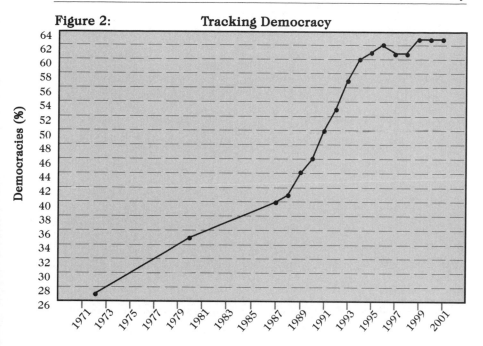

Figure 2:   Tracking Democracy

Figure 3:   **Trade Openness and Political Freedom**

Countries open to trade are far more likely to be politically free

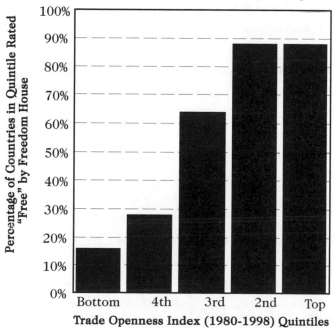

engagement is far more promising than the failed record of sanctions and economic isolation. Four decades of an almost total U.S. embargo against Cuba have yet to soften Fidel Castro's totalitarian rule. Sanctions against Iraq and Burma (a.k.a. Myanmar) have only worsened the condition of the very people we are trying to help without bringing any progress toward democracy and freedom. The folly of imposing trade sanctions in the name of promoting human rights abroad is that it deprives people in the target countries of the technological tools and economic opportunities that can help to free them from tyranny.

For the past two decades, globalization, human rights, and democracy have been marching forward together, haltingly, not always and everywhere in step, but in a way that unmistakably shows they are interconnected. By encouraging globalization in less developed countries, we not only help to raise growth rates and incomes, promote higher standards, and feed, clothe, and house the poor; we also spread political and civil freedoms.

An agenda for reducing global poverty

How should our concern for the poor and our understanding of the global economy translate into action? It is not enough to merely march in the streets or write to members of Congress. The apostle James reminds us that it is moral folly to see another person "naked and destitute of food" but to pass them by with only a greeting of "Depart in peace and be warm and filled." We must do more. We must "give them the things which are needed for the body." We must support practical, prudent, and proven policies that will enable people to lift themselves out of poverty and to set their countries on the path of self-sustaining development. To help achieve those ends, we must:

Encourage trade and internal market reforms in less developed countries. The liberating lesson in all this for less developed countries is that their economic fate is largely in their own hands. Convergent growth does not depend primarily on foreign aid or other favors from the more advanced economies, but on adopting market-friendly policies and institutions. The most important steps poor countries' governments can take to raise rates of growth and reduce poverty are to respect the rule of law, secure rights to private property, pursue sound monetary policies, cut nonproductive government spending, and, of course, open their markets to international trade and investment. When pursued with consistency and commitment, market reforms lead to higher growth rates and all the benefits that growth and development bring.

Open rich-country markets to poor-country exports. Countries tend to protect their least competitive industries, and the rich Western nations are no exception. The highest trade barriers in the West are typically against exports that are most important to people in poor countries—textiles, labor-intensive manufactured goods (such as clothing and shoes), and agricultural good, (such as sugar, fruits, and vegetables). On average, advanced countries impose tariffs on imports from poor countries that are four times higher than tariffs on imports from other advanced countries.[33] By opening their markets to free trade from poor countries, Western nations would be doing themselves a favor by lowering the costs of goods for their own citizens and delivering substantial income to workers and farmers in poor countries. In fact, the annual cost imposed on poor countries by rich-country trade barriers is more than double the amount the rich countries donate in foreign aid.[34] As a corollary, rich-country governments should drop any demands that poor countries raise environmental and labor standards as a condition for market access; imposing such sanctions would have the perverse effect of denying poor countries the necessary means to raise incomes so that they can afford higher standards.

Relax intellectual property rules, especially as applied to life-saving drugs. The vast majority of people in poor countries simply cannot afford to pay the patent-protected price for many drugs that could prevent disease and save lives. The potential lost sales from the relaxation of patent rules in most poor countries would be so small that the economic loss to Western pharmaceutical companies would be minimal. Yet for a cost of pennies per person, lives can be saved and lifetime disabilities avoided. Rules on intellectual property negotiated through the World Trade Organization threaten poor countries with sanctions if they do not enforce Western-style intellectual property laws—laws inappropriate for their less advanced stage of development. WTO rules also impose a regulatory burden on poor-country governments that many of them simply cannot afford. Those rules should be relaxed to reflect the economic realities that characterize most poor countries.

Allow more migration from poor countries to rich countries. Migration is mutually beneficial, providing rich countries with additional labor and human capital, and returning important benefits to the home country. As the World Bank economists Dollar and Kraay note, "Migration from poor locations is the missing factor in the current wave of globalization that could make a large contribution to reducing poverty. . . . Most migration from South to North is economically motivated, and it raises the living standard of the migrant while benefiting the sending country in three ways. First, it reduces the South's labor force and thus raises wages for those who remain behind. Second, migrants send remittances of hard currency back home. Finally, migration bolsters transnational trade and investment networks."[35]

Reserve foreign aid for true emergencies. Foreign aid has failed to raise living standards and encourage self-sustaining growth in those poor countries that have received it. In fact, government-to-government transfers tend to centralize power in the hands of corrupt rulers, who use the aid for their own enrichment, to buy friends through patronage, and to undertake grandiose public works projects with no lasting economic value. Foreign aid, including below-market-rate loans from the International Monetary Fund (IMF) and World Bank, tends to delay needed economic reforms by shielding Third World governments from the full impact of their economic mismanagement. For all these reasons, the $1 trillion in foreign aid (measured in 1985 dollars) that rich countries have lavished on poor countries in the last fifty years has failed to promote a sustained rise in living standards.[36] Instead of pouring good money after bad, aid-donating countries should reserve foreign aid for true emergencies such as impending famines or outbreaks of disease. Wherever possible, aid should be distributed directly to the people it is intended to help, and should be distributed through voluntary nongovernment relief organizations that are more closely attuned to the needs of people on the ground.

Relieve poor countries of their bad debts without throwing good money after bad. Those poor countries that cannot repay past loans should simply be declared in default, like any other bankrupt debtor. Their creditors should be left to absorb the losses and lessons, whether private lenders or government lenders such as the IMF and World Bank. Any debt relief should be extended with a clear-eyed understanding of its limitations. Supporters of the Jubilee 2000 campaign have argued that absolving the most highly indebted poor countries of their obligations would free up their domestic resources for education, public health, and economic infrastructure. But unless market reforms are implemented and domestic institutions fixed, the new money made available by debt relief will in all likelihood be squandered just as the old money was. Previous rounds of debt relief have failed to spur growth or raise living standards in the countries that have received it.[37] Absent serious reforms, any new concessionary government-to-government loans will only put the borrowing country back in the hole, setting the stage for yet another round of default and relief.

Conclusion

The persistence and pervasiveness of global poverty can seem over-whelming, but we have reason to hope that real progress can be made in improving the material conditions of millions of people. Only a few centuries ago, life for just about everybody was, to borrow the famous phrase of Thomas Hobbes, "solitary, poor, nasty, brutish, and short." But for a growing minority of nations, meager subsistence has been transformed into general affluence. Those nations that are the most materially prosperous in the world today are invariably those that are the most engaged in the global economy. Those nations have blazed a path that can lead millions of people out of grinding poverty.

Of course, progress is not measured solely by gross domestic product per capita. Man does not live by bread alone, but people do need bread, nowhere more so than in those parts of the world that remain desperately poor and cut off from the global economy. Just as it would be a moral mistake to focus exclusively on GDP per capita as a measure of progress, it would be equally mistaken to dismiss concern for it as immoral materialism.

Not long ago I was invited to critique an anti-globalization video before an audience of college students. Among its many talking heads was a rock singer who lamented that globalization was turning us all into materialist consumers who care only about buying a new pair of shoes and ignore what really matters in life. It reminded me of a recent newspaper article I had seen about an export-oriented clothing factory that had just opened in the desperately poor country of Madagascar. One of the barefoot workers at the factory, clearly excited about her new job, was asked what she planned to buy on her first regular payday. Without hesitation, she replied, "Shoes."[38]

10

Wealth, Happiness, and Politics: Aristotelian Questions

V. Bradley Lewis

The dynamic capitalist economy is emphatically a modern phenomenon. Its modernity is manifested in many ways, although
three are most important for my present purposes: (1) its relationship
to modern economic science, itself an attempt to abstract and explain a class of economic phenomena by reference to law-like gener-
alizations based on the notion of utility; (2) its association with technology and with modern natural science more generally; and (3) its
close connection to the characteristic political arrangements of modern times, the nation-state distinguished from society.[1] That there is
any such thing as economic "science" is, of course, controversial;
however, I shall not be concerned with contesting that notion here.[2]
My concern is to understand the specifically modern character of the
market and just what we should make of it if, as many think, the
modern project is itself subject to serious criticism. I shall not argue
this latter point, but rely on it as a hypothesis, some of the reasons
for which will become evident.

I want to pursue this question by looking at a representative—
the representative—premodern philosopher of human affairs, Aristotle.
My reasons for considering Aristotle in particular are several. First,
much valuable work in moral and political philosophy has in recent
years returned to Aristotle in an attempt to understand and remedy
defects in modern moral philosophy.[3] Part of the reason for this return

is the resistance of Aristotle's account of human life to the characteristically modern attempt to compartmentalize life into different spheres. This resistance is a source of recovery for any notion of life as a meaningful unified whole and is, in one sense, precisely what makes Aristotle premodern. Second, Aristotle is, more than any other premodern philosopher, a thinker whose work "preserves the perspective of the citizen or statesman" or even is "the fully conscious form of the 'common sense' understanding of political things."[4] A third and related reason for considering Aristotle is that he is representative of the Greek discovery of political philosophy, and thus he saw political phenomena with a clarity unmediated by the succeeding tradition of social and political thought.[5] Fourth, the philosophy of Aristotle was integrated into Christian moral theology in its classic form, achieved during the High Middle Ages, and came to influence the tradition of specifically Catholic social teaching.[6] So Aristotle's views are still important to a properly Christian concern about moral and political questions.

Aristotle's account of the place of wealth in human affairs is infamous in some circles and has often been thought to show just how ignorant Aristotle was of economics.[7] He is often closely associated with notions like that of the just price and with harsh criticisms of usury. Concerning the former, Aristotle has usually been misread, and concerning the latter his views have usually been distorted.[8] But neither of these issues is my concern here. My focus is on the moral and political context of wealth in Aristotle's broad "philosophy of human affairs."[9] While Aristotle cannot be fruitfully read as discussing what we think of as "economics," he is certainly concerned with the larger human context of wealth. I want to try to understand precisely why he urges the strictures he does on what we would call economic growth. My answer to this inquiry will reveal an important connection between Aristotle's discussion of wealth and his theory of final causality, a theory that is central to his natural philosophy and ethics. This account has the benefit of showing just what we have given up in adopting the modern economic view of wealth. What we might do about that loss is another question, about which I will say a few things in my conclusion.

Rational and Political Animals

Classical political philosophy did not recognize the modern distinction between ethics and politics. Instead it held that man was by nature a political animal (*Nichomachean Ethics* [*NE*] 1097b11; *Politics* [*Pol.*] 1253a2, 1278b19), one whose nature contained the potential for a kind of perfection that could only be attained in the political community called the *polis*. That perfection, which Aristotle called *eudaimonia* and which, since Anscombe, has often been translated into English as "flourishing," he defined as rational activity of the soul in accordance with the virtues of both character and thought (*NE* 1098a7–18; *Pol.* 1332a7–10) and made the pursuit of it the highest aim of the *polis* (*NE* 1103a14–b6; *Pol.* 1280a31–b8, 1334a11–40).[10] Even in the *Nicomachean Ethics,* Aristotle refers to the inquiry therein, one usually classified as moral or ethical, as "a kind of politics" (*tis politikê, NE* 1049a18–b11). The word *polis* is usually translated "city-state," and this translation is not incorrect. Nevertheless one must take care not to confuse the "city" part of city-state with modern cities or the "state" part with modern states. The *polis* was much smaller than modern cities and thus much smaller than modern nation-states.[11] The issue of size is not accidental, for it bears on the ability of the *polis* to perform the sorts of tasks Aristotle thinks it by nature should perform.

One can approach this question of scale from two directions, genetic and analytical. In the first book of the *Politics,* Aristotle offers a genetic account of the city, that is, an account that shows how the city naturally grows out of more primitive forms of human community: the community of man and woman, the household, and the village. There are, however, two other, related approaches to the city in the *Politics.* In the third book, Aristotle provides an analytical account that breaks the city down into its component parts and focuses on the form of composition (*eidos tês suntheseôs*, 1276b6–7) of the citizens, another name for which is "regime" (*politeia*, 1276b1–15). In the seventh book, Aristotle discusses the city from the perspective of the *best* regime, itself intelligible from the perspective of the most choice-worthy way of life (1323a14–16). Let us first consider the genetic account and then the two analytical accounts.

Even in the specifically genetic account of the city, teleology is crucial. The *polis* is a community (*koinonia*), and every community is established with a view to some good (1252a1–3). The city is natural in the way that all human affairs are natural, that is, mediated through the human capacity for rationality. There is a natural drive among human beings to move towards the community of the *polis,* but it also requires intelligent work (1253a29–31).[12] Moreover, the *polis* is the type of community that pursues the most authoritative (*kuriôtatos*, 1252a5) goods, or those goods the pursuit of which is most distinctly human. The prior forms of community are the community of man and woman ordered to the continuation of the species, the household (*oikos*) ordered to the satisfaction of everyday necessities (1252b12–14), and the village (*komê*), which arises out of the household and encompasses many households related by kinship. The *polis* emerges from the village, and while it may initially seem that the difference between the two is merely one of degree, it is much more significant and transforming.

The move from the household to the village provides for a kind of primitive division of labor and thus for a kind of social development. However, the extent of this development is limited by the village's basis in kinship. One can see this in Aristotle's speculation that the familial nature of the village explains the rise of political monarchy: "for in every household the eldest is king, and because the offshoots of the household were ruled in the same way in virtue of their common descent" (1252b20–22). Age is a kind of natural claim to authority—even more so where people are related by blood.[13] Yet, as natural as the village is, in one sense, it is not the highest stage of political development. The *polis* is superior inasmuch as it provides for self-sufficiency (*autarkeia*) for a life beyond mere necessity. However, it does more than this.

Aristotle famously writes that man is by nature a political animal. Even though other animals live in groups and even evince a kind of division of labor, only human beings are properly political. The political nature of humans is related to the human capacity for rational speech (*logos*) as distinct from mere voice (*phônê*). While the latter can be used to express pleasure and pain, only the former can render clear what is advantageous and disadvantageous, just and unjust, good and evil (1253a7–18). In other words, only in the city, as distinct from the household or village, does man's capacity for rational argument become fully actualized. The root of authority in pre-political communities is authority based on age and kinship. Communal decisions are the province of, as it were, the alpha males. The properly political community, however, transcends kinship: it requires multiple kinship groups to join together under the banner of the city. But that creates a dilemma: How does one come to agreement on the advantageous and the disadvantageous, the just and the unjust, what is good and what is evil when there are multiple authorities each with a claim to rule in their own kinship groups? There must be some way to settle on community decisions that is not simply dependent on the personal authority of hereditary chieftains.

Rational argument offers a way out of this dilemma. In Plato's *Laws,* the Athenian stranger, like Aristotle, describes the origin of cities as the coming together of clans, each "possessing both its eldest who rules, and its own particular customs because it has lived apart." Moreover, "the laws of each are necessarily pleasing to them, while the others are less so." This is the origin of legislation (*archê nomothesias*): "those who have come together are compelled to choose certain men common to them who look over the customs of all the clans and, having picked out the ones they find especially agreeable for the community, display them clearly and present them for the

245

approval of the leaders and chiefs."[14] What I want to suggest is that in both of these accounts the capacity for rational argument is spurred on by (not simply originated by, or else it would never exist) the need to establish political institutions and laws that can be justified before communities formerly bound by kinship. In other words, men who come together in larger political groupings than those ordered by blood ties negotiate their common life through *logos*.

Of course, once rational argument has been actualized, it can transcend the conditions that actualized it. It is for this reason that philosophy emerges, not just anywhere, but out of the culture of cities, and also why Aristotle describes man as both a political animal and a rational animal.[15] The two are in fact the same: man first displays his capacity for rational argument in the city. That is to say, man is a political animal because the city is the goal (*telos*, 1252b32–33) of his association and it is precisely in the context of the city that his rational nature reveals itself. Therefore, the distinctively human work (*ergon*) of rational action is manifest in the *polis*. And thus was the human perfection Aristotle called *eudaimonia,* "flourishing," understood as the end intended by political community and its most important instrument, the law. Law was the principal way that the city aimed to make its inhabitants flourish. This brings us to the second approach to the city, which is complementary to the genetic approach: the analytical, which has two aspects.

The analytical approach to the city starts not with the question of how or whence the city arose, but rather with the question of which elements make a city. It proposes that the most important element is the body of citizens, but who counts as a citizen (*politês*), defined as one who shares in judicial decisions and is eligible to hold political office, is determined by the regime (*politeia*, 1275a1–5). The regime is variously described by Aristotle as "an arrangement of those who live in the city," "an arrangement of a city with respect to its ruling offices, particularly the one that has authority over all [matters]. For what has authority is everywhere the governing body, and the governing body is the *politeia*," and "the way of life (*bios*) of a city" (1274b38, 1278b8–10, 1295a40–b1). These descriptions indicate that even though *politeia* is often translated as "constitution," it means much more than this. *Politeia* suggests the ethos of a community, and it connects this ethos with the ethos of the ruling group.[16] Ultimately, Aristotle, like Plato, held that some kind of mixture of the claims of different groups was necessary to produce a sufficiently stable *polis*. But the issue of ethos remained important, as we can see by looking at Aristotle's discussion of the best regime.

Any adequate investigation into the best regime must, Aristotle holds, first determine what is the most "choice-worthy way of life" (*hairetôtatos bios*, 1323a14–16). In reviewing this topic Aristotle offers a kind of précis of his account in the *Nicomachean Ethics* of the relationship between human flourishing and the virtues. This account is itself a version of natural right, a fact signaled from the start of the discussion in Aristotle's reminder that there is an order of human goods that places goods of the soul first, goods of the body second, and external goods third (1323a24–b21; cf. *NE* 1098b12–20).[17] This amounts to the same thing as Aristotle's famous definition of *eudaimonia* as rational activity of the soul in accordance with the virtues in a complete life. To live well is to engage in a life of action on the basis of reason, that is, action that has its source in the ends specified by the moral virtues and the means specified by practical wisdom.

It is central to Aristotle's political theory that the *polis* has as its aim the inculcation of the virtues through the instrument of law. Legislation in general must look to the formation of habits and thus cover the whole of life (e.g., *NE* 1099b29–32, 1102a7–13, 1103b3–6, 1129b14–25, 1179b20–1180a24). Similarly, Aristotle writes that the purpose of the *polis* is not simply what modern liberal regimes take the purpose of the state to be, namely the establishment of internal peace and defense against external enemies, but the promotion of living well (*Pol.* 1280a31–1281a4), and the best claim to rule in the best regime is one based on virtue and aiming at the virtue of one's fellow citizens (1283a23–26, 1284a1–3, 1323b29–1324a13). The most important task of the *polis,* then, is moral education, and the measure of its success is the measure of a *polis*'s goodness (*NE* 1129b24–25).

Given this essential moral-educational task, the best regime for the *polis* requires certain presuppositions, which Aristotle outlines in the seventh book of his *Politics*. The foremost of these presuppositions concern the size and type of the city's population and territory. Aristotle's remarks on both of these topics reflect the task of the *polis*. The population of the best city must be large enough to allow for the self-sufficiency requisite for living well—that is, it must be conducive to noble actions and leisure (1326b7–9; cf. 1252b29, 1281a1, *NE* 1097b7–17)—but it must not be too large. How large is too large, and why should it be necessary to suggest such an upper limit on population? Some have suggested that these considerations are not important in Aristotle's political philosophy and perhaps result from his inability to transcend the classical Greek political institutions with which he was most familiar.[18] Aristotle, however, indicates that he knows about larger political communities (Persia) and disapproves of them for substantive reasons.

First, a large multitude would be unable to receive good laws. The reason for this seems to be that law aims to order the people, and there is an optimum relationship between the amount of material and the type of order it can receive. It is one thing to legislate for a relatively small community, the general character of which one can know, and another to legislate for a much larger human group that is, of necessity, basically anonymous. Ordering a large multitude would, Aristotle suggests, be the work of a god. Perhaps, then, it is no accident that many rulers of large political units both before and after Aristotle did in fact claim for themselves divinity or close connection to the gods.[19] Second, Aristotle suggests that too large a population could not support a regime, and thus he asks, "who will be its herald unless he have the voice of Stentor?" (1326b7). This concern suggests that what Aristotle questioned was the ability of a great multitude to engage in serious political deliberation. Finally, Aristotle writes that the citizens and rulers of a city must pass judgment on matters of justice and distribute offices according to merit. However, in too large a city it would be impossible for citizens or rulers to know one another's characters, and so such tasks would be impossible. This last point is more complicated than it first appears and has at least two important dimensions.

First, it is related to the previous point about deliberation and, in particular, deliberation about the city's most important work, education. The two tasks of the citizen are participation in judicial decisions and service in political office. The former task involves making determinations about guilt, innocence, and what Aristotle calls "corrective justice" in the *Nicomachean Ethics*. The latter involves making political decisions, but also lawmaking itself. Moreover, filling political offices requires citizens to assess the fitness of candidates to serve. All of this requires judgments about the character of rulers and subjects. Such judgments can only be made in the presence of the kind of information one could gather through one's own experience. The most crucial political virtue is practical wisdom (*phronêsis*), and it seems unclear the extent to which *specifically practical* wisdom can transcend man's other, more physical capacities. Surely it can in some ways, but Aristotle seems to want to keep the two close when he concludes his discussion of size by saying that "the best limit (*horos*) for the city is this: the furthest that the excess of numbers for securing a self-sufficient life can go that can be well seen at once (*eusunoptos*, 1326b22–25). There is a sense in which the practical intelligibility of the political community is related to man's natural capacities of perception as well as deliberation. This relationship between limit and intelligibility is crucial in the issue of the size of the city, and is also important for Aristotle's account of wealth, as we shall see below.

There is a second and broader dimension that concerns the intelligibility of actions that are right according to nature. The good for human beings, *eudaimonia,* requires that they live together in cities, for it is in this context that the range of human capacities and excellences becomes manifest. Living together, however, requires that humans live according to certain rules and standards. No political community can flourish (and the flourishing of individuals requires flourishing communities) where citizens do not trust one another and cannot reasonably anticipate complex cooperative activity with one another over time. Such trust and such relationships require that they behave in regular ways and that they simply refrain from some actions, for example, killing or wounding one another, stealing from one another, and other violations of trust like lying and adultery.[20] Any reasonable man can see that the consequence of not refraining from such activity is the depletion of trust that makes long-term complex cooperative activity among persons possible. In very large societies, however, these consequences are less apparent, and the relative anonymity of many inhabitants renders their relationships thinner and their sense of communal obligation more evanescent. This is another reason the size of communities seems important to Aristotle (and to Plato, as well).[21] Modern nation-states are very different sorts of political units and have a much greater difficulty intelligently and effectively doing the work Aristotle assigns to the *polis*. All of these considerations are related to modern economic practices, of course, since states must support huge populations, must utilize mass communications technology, and must acquire vast military means to defend themselves. Indeed, modern technology and economics make the modern state possible, but on Aristotle's view, they at the same time drastically alter the state's moral character.[22]

Now, all of this discussion of the best regime needs to be qualified in light of Aristotle's own political realism. As noted above, Aristotle ultimately thought that some mixture of elements from different regimes offered the best hope for a stable *polis* that embodied as much of the best regime as was practicable under given circumstances.[23] This orientation is important to emphasize in any Aristotelian approach to politics. At the beginning of the fourth book of the *Politics,* Aristotle writes that a student of politics must study the best regime, the one most in accordance with what one would pray for, but, knowing that its establishment was impossible for most peoples, one should also study what regime is best under a variety of circumstances, how different regimes are preserved and improved, and what regime is "most in harmony with every city" (1288b21–1289a7; cf. *NE* 1135a4–5). The account of the polis offered above outlines those conditions that, as Aristotle says, "one would pray for," and thus abstracts from many complicated political realities, but however rarely realized in practice, it *is* a standard. Indeed, it is in many respects an ideal standard derived from the citizen's experience of and hopes for political practice.[24]

Acquisition natural and unnatural

We now need to look at how wealth fits into this account. Aristotle's discussion of the economy has sometimes been considered an early and highly unsuccessful attempt to "discover" the market. It was the great merit of Karl Polanyi's pioneering paper on Aristotle's economic thought to show against this view that, for Aristotle, economic transactions are "embedded" in more general human communities.[25] It is important to notice that Aristotle's most extensive remarks on economics appear in the first book of the *Politics* and, moreover, are contained within his discussion of the household. Indeed, the primary theme of this discussion concerns the relationship between the art of running a household (*oikonomikê*) and the art of acquisition (*chrêmatistikê*), both of which are set within the context of the art of governing a *polis* (*politikê*). Of these three arts, *chrêmatistikê* is the most perplexing, since it is characterized by a real and persistent ambiguity. The root of the ambiguity is, I believe, that *chrêmatistikê* concerns the acquisition of wealth, and wealth, while necessary to individuals, households, and cities, is a means to some end and not an end in itself (*NE* 1096a5–7). Wealth and its acquisition, like all human affairs, must be related to man's natural capacities and relationships in a way that supports *eudaimonia*. It is precisely the tendency of modern economics (and other social sciences) to see its object as autonomous, value-free, and perhaps even reducible to non-human causes that Aristotle's account rejects.

While the most well-known, and perhaps infamous, aspect of Aristotle's economic thought concerns his condemnation of interest income (1258b2–8), it is another aspect that is most important and, I wish to argue, of enduring relevance. Part of the confusing character of the economic discussion in the *Politics* stems from Aristotle's use of certain terms. He begins with the term *ktêtikê,* usually translated as "ownership" or, more literally and clumsily, as "the art of property." This term refers most generally to the art of acquiring *and using* the property necessary to the maintenance of the household and the city. Indeed, Aristotle writes that wealth (*ploutos*) is a "multitude of tools" for household management and the political art (1256b37–39), an art that, one should recall, has as its purpose the making of citizens who are "good and capable of noble actions" (*NE* 1099b29–32), and *ktêtikê* itself has as its end "self-sufficiency for living well" (*autarkeia pros agathên zôên,* 1256b32). Living well, of course refers to *eudaimonia* or flourishing, a life of rational activity in accordance with the virtues. Self-sufficiency with respect to flourishing is a crucial limit to the acquisition and use of wealth for Aristotle.[26] He then moves to using primarily the more controversial term, *chrêmatistikê,* usually translated as the "art of acquisition," "business," or "moneymaking." The more general *ktêtikê,* which is in the service of household management, is, Aristotle writes, "according to nature" (*kata phusin,* 1256b26–27). *Chrêmatistikê*, on the other hand, is either according to nature or contrary to nature, depending on its place relative to the household or the political art. That distinction will be important shortly.

Interestingly, most of the discussion in *Politics* 1.8 concerns not property in general, but a highly specific sort of property, food.

This is important for a number of reasons: first, food is absolutely basic to the survival of any living creature (*NE* 1097b33–1098a1; *On the Soul* 413a20–b1, 416b14–20). Second, for most living things, there is a very close relationship between their means of sustenance and their way of living more generally. Food is the first type of property, and it crucially affects the way different species live. This distinction is said to be the work of nature (1256a19–22a26). Initially, Aristotle only mentions animals, distinguishing the carnivores, herbivores, and omnivores, but one is already led to ask about human beings. Human beings can fit into any of these three classes. However, the connection between food and way of life seems unclear. Certainly, nonhuman animals' ways of life are driven by their food needs, and perhaps early human ways of life were similarly determined by nature. But now it is the other way around: our way of life drives our food production. We are less determined than determining in this respect (and often determine in ways opposed to good health and reason).

This inversion is suggested in the sequel, where Aristotle explicitly discusses human beings and divides them into classes. There are nomads, hunters, farmers, and those who utilize a mixture of these three. Now one can imagine human beings whose way of life is radically determined by food supply of a particular type. The BaMbuti pygmies described by Colin Turnbull lived in relatively small and highly mobile bands related by kinship precisely because they were hunter-gatherers.[27] Nomads and hunters are rather like this: they go where the food is. Settled agricultural peoples, however, are a bit different. For one thing, their way of life involves more complex arts than those of hunters and nomads. Moreover, an agricultural life means staying in one place, cultivating it, and usually developing relationships with neighboring peoples with whom one can exchange goods. But the farmers Aristotle has in mind here must be quite primitive. Following this classification of human ways of life, Aristotle says that these are the ways of life that have their work in "what is spontaneously grown" (*autophuton*, 1256a40–41), and *not* procured through exchange or trading. The lives of such people are determined by need (*chrea*, 1256b6).

But the need is satisfied: "property like this is manifestly given by nature itself to all" (1257b7–8). Aristotle describes the ways in which newborn animals are supplied with nourishment in the very circumstances of their birth or by their mothers. "As a result (*hôste*)," Aristotle writes, "it is similarly clear that with respect to things grown (*genomenois*), we must suppose (*oiêteon*) plants to be for the sake of animals and animals for the sake of humans" (1256b15–17). "If," he continues, "nature makes nothing either incomplete (*ateles*) or in vain (*matên*), then she has necessarily made all things for human beings" (1256b20–22). The reasoning here could certainly be construed as fallacious.[28] It seems to work this way: since nature has given plants and animals a means to nourish themselves at the expense of lower-order beings, this must be understood in connection to the discernible hierarchy of beings with respect to their maintenance that matches the natural hierarchy of beings with respect to their natural work as described in *Nicomachean Ethics* 1.7 (*ergon, NE* 1097b22–1098a7). An important part of this sort of argument, however, goes unspoken: that the natural whole acts to order itself through the internal operation of each thing's form, that it can be conceived of as a kind of coherent whole such that we can, perhaps metaphorically, attribute to it something *like* intelligence as distinct from chance. Aristotle certainly makes similar remarks elsewhere (e.g., *NE* 1099b20–25, cf. *Physics* 197a30–32, 199b30–32, *Meta.* 1075a11–25).

This metaphor is immediately affirmed in the sequel, where Aristotle returns to the *art* of property as naturally part (*kata phusin meros*) of the *art* of household management. *Ktêtikê,* then, is an art that by nature serves the higher arts of household management and politics and provides for their self-sufficiency, and self-sufficiency here is "for the good life" (*pros agathên zôên,* 1256b32). Moreover, the good life has with respect to property the character of a limit (*peras*). Wealth is a "multitude of tools" (*organôn plêthos*) for the domestic and political arts (1256b36–37). If the animals had the arts, one might say that there was an art of property proper to animals that concerns food exclusively, and that it is more complex with respect to human beings. The difference, of course, would be that with respect to animals the art is simply nature itself, understood as a spontaneous but intelligible process. It was perhaps thus with the early humans, but with Aristotle's reintroduction of the domestic and political arts we are back to civilized man.

In the ninth chapter, Aristotle specifically addresses *chrêmatistikê*, giving an account of its origins and criticizing one version of it. As mentioned, the word *chrêmatistikê* is often misleadingly translated as "business" or "moneymaking," which is not so odd, since the term is used in more than one sense. Clearly, the literal meaning derived, as Finley pointed out, from *chrêmata* ("goods," "property") and the suffix *-ikos* (used to form abstract concepts) is "the art of acquiring [property]."[29] In this primitive sense it is the art that corresponds to the even more abstract "provision" (*porisasthai*) as distinct from "use" (*chrêsasthai*), the latter of which Aristotle earlier associated with household management and politics (1256a11–13), so that, as Aristotle said, acquisition is ministerial to (*hupêretikê*, 1256a5, 1258a34) household management. Property in its most basic sense (food!) is the subject of chapter eight. I will, for sake of brevity, translate *chrêmatistikê* as "acquisition."

So we are back to the original question about the relationship between household management, politics, and *chrêmatistikê*, although now we will focus on this last term in detail. The basic difference between the two senses of the term is indicated by Aristotle towards the end of the chapter. There is a type of acquisition and, indeed, wealth that is according to nature (*kata phusin*) and is proper to household management. Another kind is not, but is rather associated with commerce (*kapêlikê*).[30] This latter type is said to be mostly concerned with money (as opposed to *chrêmata*) and as such is without limit (1257b17–24). Later the two are distinguished as the necessary versus the unnecessary types of acquisition, and again they are contrasted with one another in terms of nature and limit. The natural, limited, necessary type is referred to as proper to household management and concerned with food (1258a14–18). The discussion begins and ends with the notion of limit (*peras*, 1257a1, 1258a18), although in the last passage, the term *horos* (literally, a boundary marker) is used. I want to come back to this, but first we need to double back and look briefly at the transition from natural to unnatural acquisition, which partly explains the bad connotation the term generally has.

Aristotle initially refers to *ktêtikê* simply and suggests that there is another type of this art of property that comes about not through nature, but through "a certain experience and art" (1257a3–4). Aristotle goes on to explain what he means by stating that any type of property has two uses, one proper to the object (*oikeia*), the other not. The first relates to use and the second to exchange (*metablêtikê*). Exchange is itself a kind of use, and one that, although not proper to the object, is not at all unnatural: "in some things human beings have more than is sufficient and in others less" (1257a15–17). Aristotle is here describing a kind of barter (*allagê*), which he associates with primitive men and barbarians. By the end of this discussion, though, Aristotle is already associating what he treated above (and will treat again at the end of the chapter) as neutral, *chrêmatistikê,* as associated with commerce (*kapêlikê*). The way from the initial meaning to the central one leads through the invention of money.

Money arose, according to Aristotle, out of the need for exchange of goods beyond the boundaries of the city. The point of acquisition here remains self-sufficiency, but when that required trading goods between households and, more importantly, between cities, necessity gave birth to money, "for not all things that are naturally needed are easy to carry around." So people agreed for purposes of exchange to substitute something useful and malleable—metals—for ordinary goods. Eventually the amounts of exchange material became symbols and took on a life of their own as money. And from this necessary exchange (*allagê*) came the kind of *chrêmatistikê* called *kapêlikê* (1257b1–2), the activity of the *kapêlos* or trader (often used with a pejorative connotation), which aimed to amass as much money as possible.[31] This is why acquisition is usually associated with plain moneymaking.

From Aristotle's perspective, however, there are two problems with this kind of acquisition, both of which stem from any understanding of property the central case of which is money. First, money is essentially a conventional marker: "altogether a thing of law and by nature nothing" (1257b10–11). The very name, *nomisma*, indicates the conventional character of money, as does our word "currency." It can be changed in more or less radical ways, including both the forms of money or the value (cf. *NE* 1133a29–31). Aristotle emphasizes the point by mentioning men who are rich in money but lack necessities like food. For us, a more powerful image might be those photographs of people just after the First World War taking sacks and even wheelbarrows full of money to buy bread.[32] The root of this criticism is the very basic point that money is a means and not an end in itself (cf. *NE* 1096a5–7).[33]

The second problem is more complex and involves the notion of limit mentioned above. While this idea may look perplexing at first, it links up Aristotle's account of wealth with his general moral and political philosophy and, moreover, with his philosophy of nature and metaphysics. Natural acquisition concerns household management. Unnatural acquisition concerns commerce (*kapêlikê*) and not the production of goods in any way, only the exchange of goods. Unnatural acquisition, then, is exchange, and exchange "seems to be about money" (1257b22), for, Aristotle continues, "money is the element (*stoicheion*) and limit (*peras*) of exchange (*allagê*)" (b23). This formulation is a careful one: the term for exchange is the most neutral of those used by Aristotle.[34] The specificity indicated in the formulation is in the element and limit of this type of exchange. By element Aristotle indicates that money is the most basic and irreducible starting point of this type of exchange, while property is the basic element of natural acquisition.[35] This formulation again ascribes to money a strangely evanescent quality: it is conventional and in any case only *stands for* what is really good. Money is also the limit.

Limit (*peras*) is crucial here: the term and its opposite (*apeiros*) occur fourteen times in the rest of chapter nine. Aristotle's most detailed discussions of the concept of limit are, as one might expect, contained in the *Metaphysics,* and he treats it in the context of his defense of final causality.[36] Final causality is one of the four forms of causality (the "for the sake of which," *ou heneka*) in Aristotle's natural philosophy, along with material, efficient, and formal causality.[37] It is crucial to his teleological view of nature and human affairs. In *Metaphysics* a 2, Aristotle argues against the possibility of an infinite series of causes. The final cause (*to heneka*), he states, is an end (*telos*). If there is a last final cause, the process is not infinite (*apeiron*). But if there is none, then there is no final cause. Moreover, "those who maintain the infinite series eliminate the nature of the good without knowing it." Limit, in this sense, is necessary to intelligibility. The intelligibility Aristotle is most concerned with here is theoretical,[38] but he also suggests a more practical implication: "no one would try to do (*prattein*) anything if he were not going to come to a limit (*peras*); nor would there be intelligence (*nous*) in things; the man having intelligence always acts for the sake of something, and this is a limit (*peras*), for the end (*telos*) is a limit" (*Meta.* 994b9–16).[39] This impression gains strength in light of the definition given of limit in *Metaphysics* a 17.

There we are given four meanings of limit: (1) the end or last point (*eschaton*) of each thing; (2) the form of things that take up space; (3) the end (*telos*) of each thing, meaning principally the "that towards which" (*to heneka*) of movement and action (*kinêsis kai praxis*), which he identifies with the final cause (*to heneka*); and (4) the substance (*ousia*) of each thing, which is identified with its essence (*to ti hên einai*). Essence is the limit and object of knowledge. Aristotle concludes: "evidently, therefore, limit has as many senses as beginning (*archê*), and yet more; for the beginning is a limit, but not every limit is a beginning" (*Meta.* 1022a4–13). Again, the notion of limit is linked to final causality with respect to both understanding and action. The point is reinforced by the reference to *archai*, which can be both explanatory principles and the beginning points of practical reason associated with the good (*to agathon*) and the noble (*to kalon*), that is, the final causes of action, "for the good and the noble are the beginning both of knowledge and of the movement of many things" (*Meta.* 1013a21–23). The inquiry that has as its specific objects the good and the noble is *politikê* (*NE* 1094b14–19).

With respect to practice, limit would seem to serve two functions. First, it makes action intelligible to an external observer by pointing to its purpose and completion, that is, by reference to final causality; second, and closely related to this, it guides the conduct of the actor by its connection to the end or goal of action, that is, by reference to a final cause. These two things are closely related, since for Aristotle the theoretical and practical perspectives on action use the same terms.[40] In this account of practical reasoning, reasons are causes in a nonreductive way. Limit, then, is a characteristic of intelligibility. Why is this important in thinking about money?

Money, Aristotle says, is the element and limit of exchange. He goes on to state that "the wealth that comes from this acquisition [that is, *chrêmatistikê* that is against nature] is without limit (*apeiros*)" (1257b23–24). The immediate implication here would be that unnatural acquisition is unnatural precisely because it is unlimited and thus unrelated to a final cause in a way that is intelligible. It is thus unnatural because irrational and irrational because unlimited. Aristotle goes on to discuss such acquisition in terms of its status as a kind of art (*technê*, suggested earlier at 1257a5); "each of the arts is unlimited with respect to its end (for that more than anything is what they wish to produce)" (1257b25–27). Just before this remark he had given the example of the medical art, saying that it was unlimited with respect to health. Clearly, he cannot mean that there is simply no limit in the art, for, as we have just seen, that would make it unintelligible. It makes more sense to read him as meaning that the arts as arts tend not to look beyond the ends internal to them. They can induce a kind of tunnel vision that excludes limits proper to the wider context of human affairs and practical reason. In the *Apology of Socrates,* Plato has Socrates observe that manual artisans (*cheirotechnai*), because they had knowledge of some things, deemed themselves "wisest in other things, the greatest things."[41] Just because one is expert at some art does not make one expert at all arts or in the wider context of practical reason as a whole. And this is especially the case with acquisition, Aristotle suggests, given its particular object, money. To see the world from the perspective of the acquisition of money is to see it in a highly distorted way. This raises a larger question about the relationship of the many arts to the human good.

In his treatment of the intellectual virtues in the sixth book of the *Nicomachean Ethics,* Aristotle makes it clear that prudence (*phronêsis*) is the virtue most important to right practical reason, and one that transcends the spheres of the arts: "it seems that the prudent man is able to deliberate nobly concerning what is good and expedient for himself, not partially, for example, what conduces to health or strength, but what conduces to the good life as a whole" (*NE* 1140a25–28). Art (*technê*), by contrast, concerns production in some discrete sphere and not action (*praxis*) as such. Prudence is particularly associated with managing households and cities (*NE* 1140b10–11), but its political character is actually the more heavily emphasized by Aristotle. "Politics (*politikê*) and prudence are the same disposition (*hexis*), although their being is not the same" (1141b23–24). He then goes on to distinguish two types of politics: the "architectonic" art of legislation (*nomothetikê*) and ordinary political deliberation. This is important because *politikê* was the name given to the inquiry into the human good as a whole by Aristotle in the very first book of the *Nichomachean Ethics* (*NE* 1094a18–b11), where its object was said to be "the highest good attainable by action" (*NE* 1095a15–17).

The problem with unnatural acquisition is that it accepts no limitation beyond its own purposes: it maximizes its object without limit, and it is precisely this characteristic that can put it at odds with the human good as such, since the good for human beings itself is a limit and limits other sorts of pursuits (cf. *NE* 1094b5–7). While those who devote themselves to unnatural acquisition increase money without limit (1257b34), those who engage in the natural type do not, and paradigmatic for the natural type of acquisition is the art of household management. Household management, Aristotle writes, is often confused with unnatural acquisition since both use acquisition (*chrêmatistikê*, 1257b36) and thus property, but in different ways. Household management does not have the same end as unnatural acquisition, which is increase (*auxêsis*, b38). But the work (*ergon*) of household management does concern the acquisition of property, the use of which conduces to living well (*eu zên*, 1258a1), an end that limits acquisition (1258a14–18).

That this is so is indicated by Aristotle's explanation for why those engaged in unnatural acquisition pursue increase without limit. Their disposition is explained by "their seriousness (or zeal, *to spoudazein*) for *living,* but not for living *well* [my emphasis]; and since their desire is unlimited (*apeiron*) they desire an unlimited amount of things that produce it" (1257b41–1258a2). There is even a tendency among those who aim to live well to be carried away by the potential for wealth to support their enjoyment. They subordinate all excellences to acquisition, distorting the arts for profit, making "all of them into *chrêmatistikê*" (1258a2–14). Aristotle's main point, then, is that the final cause of human action, the subject of practical reason and the arts of politics and household management, must be seen as the limit on acquisition. Acquisition limited by the overall good of living well and the constitutive arts of household management and politics is natural, since it supports the proper work of human beings and its completion in the final cause of human action, *eudaiomonia*.

This point can be more clearly seen by contrasting it with a modern account that often seems self-consciously and diametrically opposed to Aristotle's, Thomas Hobbes's *Leviathan* (1651).[42] The very subtitle of the work, "The Matter, Forme, and Power of a Commonwealth Ecclesiasticall and Civil," signals the disappearance of final causality, a disappearance emphasized in the mechanistic metaphor for both man and commonwealth proposed in the introduction. In the anthropology that constitutes Part I of *Leviathan*, Hobbes first defines the terms "good" and "evil" by reference to the individual appetites and aversions of people, "for these words of Good, Evill, and Contemptible, are ever used with relation to the person that useth them: there being nothing simply and absolutely so; nor any common Rule of Good and Evill, to be taken from the nature of the objects themselves."[43] What individuals are drawn to is a result of the physical constitution of their bodies and their educations. Men do pursue happiness (Hobbes calls it "felicity"), but that is defined as "continuall successe in obtaining those things which a man from time to time desireth."[44] The point is emphasized later with remarkable bluntness: "the Felicity of this life, consisteth not in the repose of a mind satisfied. For there is no such *Finis ultimus,* (utmost ayme,) nor *Summum Bonum,* (greatest Good,) as is spoken of in the books of the old Morall Philosophers."[45] Rather "Felicity is a continuall progresse of the desire, from one object to another; the attaining of the former, being still but the way to the latter. The cause whereof is, That the object of mans desire, is not to enjoy once onely, and for one instant of time; but to assure forever, the way of his future desire." This leads Hobbes to "put for a generall inclination of all mankind, a perpetuall and restless desire of Power after power, that ceaseth onely in Death."[46]

For Hobbes there are final causes neither in nature nor in human life. Each man pursues the desires determined by the construction of his body and his learned preferences. The beginning of motion in human action is a kind of good, but radically reduced and individualized. Happiness is simply continual progress in getting what one wants, and the one generalization that follows from this is an infinite desire for *means*. Indeed, for Hobbes, even this individual desire for the good is not solid enough to build a political theory on, since the objects of desire are innumerable and men compete for the finite means of obtaining them. So he takes his stand on the one thing that all men agree is evil, violent death and the fear of it. Thus, at the bottom of Hobbes's account is merely living, not living well, and since the desire for living is infinite, men desire an infinite amount of the things that produce it (cf. 1257b41–1258a2).

I have argued above that Aristotle's understanding of wealth is integral to his ethics and political philosophy and that all of these subjects must be understood in light of concepts central to his philosophy of nature. The reason many students of ethics and political philosophy have turned to Aristotle is a sense that his account of the moral life still explains the common sense view of morality and human things generally in a more adequate way than does modern thought. This view requires, however, that one take seriously the entirety of Aristotle's ethics, including his views about wealth. One could, of course, as Hobbes did, simply reject the Aristotelian view of all these things. The consequences of that are quite clear.

Conclusion

Aristotle's criticisms of commerce are sometimes thought to reflect an aristocratic snobbery or prejudice against trade as an occupation. But, as Meikle has pointed out, there is not much real textual evidence of this (there is much more in Plato).[47] As I have tried to show above, Aristotle's case is a moral case, one grounded in a larger theory of human nature that prominently includes the notion of final causality. It is of a piece with the rest of his "philosophy of human affairs," and related to his natural philosophy. Those who have a stake in the continued relevance of other Aristotelian ideas—for example, his accounts of practical reason, the virtues, and the idea that there is a natural horizon for moral and political institutions and practices— must take it seriously. But what does taking it seriously mean?

Before getting to that I need to recognize three objections that have doubtless already occurred to the thoughtful reader. The first concerns the role of slavery in Aristotle's account. Does not his economic thought in some sense presuppose not only the existence, but also the natural justice, of slavery? While the role of slavery in the classical Athenian economy is a matter of scholarly dispute, this need not detain us. Aristotle's very distinction between natural and conventional slavery in *Politics* 1.4–6 is subversive of slavery as conventionally practiced in all historical eras that we know about. Moreover, his discussion of naturally justified slavery seems to suggest that its occurrence is so rare as to be politically and economically negligible.[48]

The second objection concerns the place of natural teleology in Aristotle's philosophy of human affairs. The rejection of teleology is a central feature of modern science and this would seem to cast doubt on the important place of final causality in Aristotle's approach. This is a large issue about which one can say at least this much: (1) some kind of teleology does seem to be viable in some parts of natural science, especially in biology; and (2) the abandonment of teleology entirely in favor of reductionism certainly leads to very difficult questions of self-reference, which seem to render unintelligible not just ordinary practical reason, but the scientific and philosophical enterprises as such.[49] Moreover, it seems possible to understand teleological explanations in ways not vulnerable to the most obvious logical objections to making ends causes.[50] So even if modern scientific theory and practice was right to reject aspects of Aristotle's teleological apporach, there is a case to be made for its continuing importance at some level of understanding and even explanation.

Finally, there is an obvious objection, related to the first two, grounded in the centrality of the ideal of liberation in modern culture. I mean by the "ideal of liberation" a number of things, but especially the claim that we ought to pursue maximal personal freedom through political institutions, economic practices, and the scientific conquest of nature through technology. While there are various more or less radical ways to interpret this ideal, there is no doubt that it is importantly different from what one finds in classical thought.[51] About this, one can say first, that part of the origin of this view is theological and becomes less intelligible once the supernatural destiny of human persons has ceased to be the crucial context for human freedom; second, that the political program associated with the ideal is partly a salutary strategy for defending the human person against the extraordinary power of specifically modern political and economic institutions like the nation-state and the limited liability corporation, both of which emerge from the rejection of key parts of the classical view. Yet, at bottom, there remains a principled disagreement about the human good and thus about the project of liberation as it is now understood. The ideal of freedom as "doing as one pleases" was one that Aristotle thought a particular danger of democracy (*Pol.* 1310a26–36, 1317b10–17), and in its extreme manifestations it has been a source of concern to modern friends of democracy like Tocqueville. And the part of the ideal related to modern technology and the project of the conquest of nature was similarly worrying to the Greeks, especially Plato, who associated it with an imprudent desire "to have things happen in accordance with the commands of one's own soul," a desire that leads "everyone who sees something big, with a lot of power and strength" to "immediately feel that if only the possessor knew how to use a thing of such quality and magnitude, he would perform many amazing deeds and become happy."[52] This sort of desire the Greeks associated with tyranny and tragedy. They offered as an alternative the importance of limit and moderation.

Taking Aristotle's views about wealth, politics, and happiness seriously means at least taking seriously the claims of limit and moderation. What else might it mean? This question raises further, very difficult questions that lie beyond the scope of this essay. I want to close, however, by suggesting at least a few other ways in which we might take Aristotle's views about economic and moral life seriously. Obviously, there is no point in recommending some attempt to return to premodern life. Such a thing is doubtless impossible in itself, and even imagining any large-scale attempt to do so brings to mind visions of all the odious impedimenta of other modern mass political upheavals. Attempts to use the power of the state to implement antimodern political programs are themselves one of the most terrible manifestations of political modernity. While some kinds of small-scale experiments in founding communities like the *polis* are imaginable, one must say about them at least two things: first, they will be the exception and not the rule of social life and, second, they would have to live under the protection of modern states that refrain from claiming to represent the goods of *polis* life. This is a tall order and unlikely, but not impossible.[53]

There are more obvious ways of taking Aristotle's account seriously in thinking about some of our own practical problems. Aristotle's account can, I think, be utilized in constructing theories and generating hypotheses that can guide the work of an Aristotelian social science.[54] One of the problems that could fruitfully be considered by such a science would be the extent to which modern market economies have the results Aristotle suggests with respect to important practices and institutions. It has been suggested many times that the increasing presence of the market in society tends to promote moral relativism and secularization. It is easy, on Aristotelian grounds, to see how this might be the case: the pursuit of money without limit distorts ordinary moral perceptions and encourages one to focus on utility or means. This activity tends to overtake or colonize the goods internal to traditional practices and mores and to see practices and relationships as inherently temporary and defeasible. And all of this could be expected, of course, to be manifested in a lack of human happiness or flourishing even amidst great material prosperity.[55] While some social sciences have indeed suggested that the marketization of society depletes "social capital" without replacing it, others have argued that the market necessarily creates its own social capital.[56] I can think of at least two cases that might challenge the latter conclusion. The first concerns marriage; the second concerns universities.

In a recent inquiry into the values of contemporary Americans, Alan Wolfe interviewed twenty-five people in each of eight communities around the United States. In one chapter he describes a "postloyalty world" in which his respondents seemed to provide evidence that the values of the contemporary market have come to influence the practice of marriage. This is especially true in the wake of the highly flexible corporate model of postindustrial society and the loss of job security this model has entailed. In summarizing some of his findings, Wolfe writes, "We like to believe that the loyalty taught in families will carry over everywhere else. More likely, the emphasis on putting one's own interest first taught in the economy will carry over into family life." He continues:

> When business firms treat workers as disposable commodities, the last thing on their minds is that their actions could have an effect on the divorce rate. Americans started divorcing one another long before the current wave of corporate downsizing, but there is nonetheless a relationship between workplace disloyalty and marital disloyalty that runs throughout the comments of our respondents. The moral maxim learned in the world of business comes down to the proposition that if you can no longer trust your company, you have no choice but to trust yourself. Because America is a business civilization, one in which every institution finds itself conforming to the logic of profit when it has another ostensible purpose, it is an easy temptation for people to apply the same moral maxim to the family. The American divorce rate is high for a reason.[57]

Wolfe's point is not simply about personal behavior, but about social pressures that derive from the extent to which business and its values have come to dominate social life more generally. The point is quite Aristotelian: "the life of business (*chrêmatistikê*) is constrained (*biaios*)" (*NE* 1096a5–6). Even before the current wave of economic restructuring, industrialism rendered the household a largely irrelevant unit economically. Bound by ties of sentiment divorced from practical reinforcement, part of the glue that held traditional families (and thus society on an Aristotelian view) together seemed to be lost.[58]

The other example I have in mind concerns universities. One could mention the extent to which marketing and fundraising have come to dominate the concerns of university administrators to the point of influencing curricula and other policies. But what I have in mind is the suggestion by James Burtchaell, in his study of the "disengagement of colleges and universities from their Christian churches," that the secularization of such institutions was abetted by financial considerations, especially the desire for federal funding to enable them to compete with secular institutions in fields that attracted students. This lust for lucre seems to have led to changes in such schools' core curricula and religious affiliations.[59]

Protecting the autonomy of such institutions and practices that challenge the predominant views of modern life is not only good in itself, but good for modernity, since it opposes the tendency of pluralism to slide into homogenization and provides resources for self-criticism. Another example might be policies that protect the existence of small farms. There is a long tradition of agrarianism in the United States that stretches from Jefferson's ideal of a republic of smallholders through the Vanderbilt agrarians of the mid-twentieth century and the more recent social criticism of Wendell Berry and Victor Davis Hanson's defense of the family farm. Though Jefferson's agrarianism was combined with an enlightenment view of nature, there are real resonances with Aristotle's thought in the work of the more recent agrarians like Berry and Hanson, both of whom defend not just an economic form, but a way of life and a view of nature.[60] There is a specifically Christian appropriation of these themes in the school of distributist political economy exemplified in G. K. Chesterton's *What's Wrong with the World?* (1910) and Hilaire Belloc's *The Servile State* (1912).

These are only suggestions. Obviously, to satisfactorily sort out the question of how the market has undermined human happiness, and in what specific ways it has done so, demands a great deal of empirical work. But such work is always informed by theoretical principles, and Aristotle's discussion of wealth in the context of human flourishing is a framework that could generate useful research and suggestions for just what we can realistically do to build the kind of economic and political life that promotes human flourishing.

11

"We Are Not Our Own": George Grant's Critique of Science, Technology, and Capitalism

Arthur Davis

*I remember being gripped in the sheer presence of the booming,
pulsating place which had arisen since 1945. What did it mean?
Where was it going? What had made it? How could there be any
stop to its dynamism without disaster, and yet, without a stop,
how could there not be disaster?*

—George Grant, returning to Toronto in 1960

Most Americans will need a brief introduction to George Grant
(1918–88),[1] the Canadian moral and political philosopher who
stormed the public mind in 1965 when he published *Lament for a
Nation,* and by any measure one of the twentieth century's most
important and original critics of science, technology, and capitalism. In *Lament for a Nation,* Grant predicted and mourned the
gradual incorporation of Canada within a vast, American-sponsored
technological-capitalist North American empire. Grant opposed the
Vietnam War and seemed to many Canadians to speak with extraordinary authority about their moral and political difficulties.
He was a religious conservative and Platonist who grappled with
contemporary issues and engaged modern existential thinkers like
Sartre in the 1950s and Nietzsche and Heidegger in the 1960s and
1970s. Grant was critical of capitalism on moral grounds because

of its unleashing of greed. But he also criticized Marxists for their failure to respect individual freedom.

The term "Red Tory," which has become part of the Canadian lexicon, was coined to describe Grant's distinctively Canadian mix of conservative and social democratic political thought. Unlike some American conservatives, he did not see the state as the chief threat to individual liberty but rather as an essential instrument in the effort to counterbalance corporate power, maintain order, and preserve Canadian culture. Grant's great subject, in politics as well as in philosophy and religion, was the need for order or limits in a world that had embraced human freedom in the form of technological science, and had embraced corporate power as the means of improving the human condition. In *Lament for a Nation,* using the British and Canadian meaning of the word "conservative" rather than the American, he argued for "the impossibility of conservatism as a viable political ideology in our era," since our commitment to open-ended technological change was unlikely to change:

> The practical men who call themselves conservatives must commit themselves to a science that leads to the conquest of nature. This science produces such a dynamic society that it is impossible to conserve anything for long. In such an environment, all institutions and standards are constantly changing. Conservatives who attempt to be practical face a dilemma. If they are not committed to a dynamic technology, they cannot hope to make any popular appeal. If they are so committed, they cannot hope to be conservatives.[2]

For similar reasons, he argued that the Left could not and would not prevail—the conservative elements in socialism could not be reconciled with dominant liberal and technological principles:

To emancipate the passions is to emancipate greed. Yet what is socialism, if it is not the use of the government to restrain greed in the name of social good? In actual practice, socialism has always had to advocate inhibition in this respect. In doing so, was it not appealing to the conservative idea of social order against the liberal idea of freedom? Even if socialists maintain that their policies would lead in the long run to a society of unrestricted freedom, in the short run they have always been advocates of greater control over freedom. This confusion in their thought is the chief reason why socialism has not succeeded in the large technological societies since 1945. Western civilization was committed in its heart to the religion of progress and the emancipated passions.[3]

For the most part, then, Grant was gloomy about the possibility of changing the direction of his society because he was aware that most North Americans were very much "behind" the liberal economic and technological order. It has become the way we experience the world and ourselves. We pay allegiance to and affirm the profit, power, and methods of technology every day of our lives. But Grant believed that our delusions about our abilities and our progressive mission were perhaps driving us to destruction.

What gave Grant hope were the irreducible experiences of joy we still have, experiences not measurable in the terms of science and capital. We receive gifts of love and beauty in our own lives and are enraptured by the gifts of artists. We are given the strength to treat others justly and to rebel when we are treated unjustly. We are, however, finding it increasingly difficult to validate and sustain these experiences publicly, even though they remain a challenge to the modern account of human being as grounded in freedom as opposed to reverence.

We must turn to Grant's critique of modern science, as strange as that may seem, to discover what he thought was endangering these experiences of love, beauty, and justice, and his advice as to how we should respond. Grant said in 1969 that technology "is ourselves,"[4] meaning that we have become converts to the spirit of technology that generated modern science and has made technology and capitalism our civilizational destiny. Change will only occur when we change the technological way in which we see ourselves and the world. For Grant, nothing stood in the way of our adoption of a new perspective more than modern scientific practicality, which is rooted in the seventeenth-century revolution that made human freedom the ground of knowledge, rather than God and nature.

In the 1950s and the 1960s Grant entered into debates with empiricists and scientists about the human experience, always with the overriding concern of challenging their understanding of who we are, and of pointing to the blessings and limitations that are ours as human beings, blessings and limitations given us both by nature and history. How can we learn to receive and obey what is given? In the first section below, I will sketch Grant's critique of technology, which emerged out of his own experiences and debates, including his experience of the bombing of London, his conversion to a belief in God, his engagement with the philosophical empiricists while teaching in the 1950s, his encounter with scientists in the early 1960s, and finally his responses to the Vietnam War and the abortion debate. I will follow in section two with a discussion of Grant's mature critique of technology, which is also a critique of capitalism, especially as that critique is set out in "Thinking about Technology" and "Faith and the Multiversity," two of his final essays, which were published in *Technology and Justice* (1986). I will conclude with a summary statement of Grant's argument for obedience, reverence, and order as moderators of human freedom.

Experience, religion, and science

James Wiser in 1989 asserted that the key to understanding Grant was his concentration on experiences rather than doctrines.[5] Grant believed that we have come to misread or misconstrue our own experiences. One example would be the way we characterize morality as "values," as if morality concerned only subjective preferences as opposed to something given in the nature of things. Though we clearly experience morality as something given, Grant believed that the modern account of experience dictates that it be seen as subjective. We thus belong at the same time to two different worlds. In "The University Curriculum" he described the estranged "division" between the isolated "I" and the world of objects that results from the modern account of morality as "that division [which] has led us, in our very drive to universalise freedom, to build the acme of the objective society which increasingly stifles the spontaneity of those it was built to free. The division widens so that it has almost killed what little remains of those mediators—common sense, reverence, communities and art (perhaps even finally sexuality)—which are the means for us to cross the division separating ourselves and our habitations." Almost killed, but not quite. Such mediators persist and provide evidence that we are "sustained by all that is":

> [T]he fact begins to appear through the modernity which has denied it: *human excellence cannot be appropriated by those who think of it as sustained simply in the human will, but only by those who have glimpsed that it is sustained by all that is.* Although that sustainment cannot be adequately thought by us because of the fragmentation and complexity of our historical inheritance, this is still no reason not to open ourselves to all those occasions in which the reality of that sustaining makes itself present to us.[6] (emphasis mine)

Grant's experiences during the Second World War dislodged from his mind the optimistic humanism of John Stuart Mill and Dewey with which he had grown up. His father's life had been shortened when he was wounded in World War I, an event that led Grant to become a pacifist in his late adolescence. At Oxford when World War II broke out, Grant left the university to work for the Air Raid Precaution Service in the East End of London during the bombing raids of 1940–41. His job included recovering those wounded and killed by bombs, sometimes friends and loved ones. His experience of the horrors of war shook his faith in "the religion" of human progress. The Western world's descent into the cataclysm of two world wars led him to lose faith in the notion that the West was building a prosperous civilization of liberty and equal prosperity for all. Grant collapsed into near despair in England in 1941, but then came his sudden and startling conversion:

> The great experience for me was [World War II]. . . . [I] went into the English countryside to work on a farm. I went to work at five o'clock in the morning on a bicycle. I got off the bicycle to open a gate and when I got back on I accepted God. . . . I have never finally doubted the truth of that experience since that moment. . . . If I try to put it into words, I would say it was the recognition that I am not my own. In more academic terms, if modern liberalism is the affirmation that our essence is our freedom, then this experience was the denial of that definition, before the fact that we are not our own.[7]

Grant's conversion came soon after his experiences of the London Blitzkrieg. These two events, which he called "primals," led him to an all-encompassing judgment about the way things are. He described his conversion as a revelation of an eternal order that shelters and limits us and that is not constructed or governed by what happens in history. We belong to a whole we do not control, though we play an important part in it. We are free not because we are on our own but because we are part of a loving order. This insight led Grant to the conviction that we need now to regain a sense of the limits of our ability to make our own history. We must stop believing and claiming to be triumphant conquerors constructing either a sacred or a humanist paradise on earth; conversely, we must also stop considering ourselves solely responsible for what is wrong with the world.

Grant's new outlook resulted in a distinctive approach to moral and political questions. He insisted in lectures and class discussions that the assumptions underlying ancient religious and philosophical knowledge must be considered as having the same status as the assumptions informing modern philosophical and scientific knowledge, thus confronting the presuppositions of his students. His students, he knew, generally experienced the world from within the modern assumption that humans are historical agents free to make history, that they are "their own." Grant encouraged his students first to become aware that they *had* such assumptions, then to question their worth, and finally to think about their moral and political consequences.

Grant carried on a debate over many years with proponents of the predominant secular or empiricist account of the world and human relationships. In his doctoral thesis on the Scottish liberal theologian John Oman (1860–1939), Grant argued that Oman failed to communicate his religious account of experience effectively to the secular empiricists around him at Cambridge in the 1930s.[8] He failed, according to Grant, because he did not put God's creation of nature and humanity at the center of his argument. This tactical error was fatal, for his empiricist contemporaries had already adopted the secular faith, with its very different account of nature. Any argument about the nature of the whole would fall on deaf ears unless that basic starting point, the assumptions we bring to our experience of the world, was challenged.

As a result of what he saw as Oman's failure, Grant began to develop his own philosophic approach to our different assumptions about experience. He brought his own public and private experiences and his engagement with other thinkers into his lectures, and he encouraged his students to bring their moral and political deliberations into their learning as well. Grant argued for an approach to philosophy that helped students learn how to live in a changing world. He fought for the idea that reason can be practical, because it brings to light what is given, and he used Plato and Kant as the chief exemplars of this approach. He tried to refute empiricists like Bertrand Russell and Karl Popper at the level of logic and doctrine, arguing, for example, that Russell could not claim that practical reason is an illusion and then logically ask us to take his talk about morals seriously.[9] Russell wrote countless books on how to live, and Grant shared his pacifism; but Russell shared his opinions even though he had accepted the idea that reason is only an instrument that serves the passions, that "what ought to be" cannot be deduced from "what is." Grant hated the idea that philosophy had become, as he put it, "the errand boy" of science and business because it had abandoned practical reason.

But Grant knew that it was no more possible to go back to the Platonic or even the Kantian position than it was likely that religion would be recovered. He knew that Russell and others were not going to see the light, renounce David Hume, and reinstate practical reason out of a respect for logic. Moral philosophy, like religion, he believed to be fated to survive only in detached enclaves, dismissed and passed over as subjective opinion by the modern public.

Grant did succeed, however, in drawing attention to the fragility of modern moral principles after their religious and metaphysical grounds have been undermined. He argued that the empiricists were naïve to believe that people would continue to be decent after the destruction of their religious and philosophical traditions, and he pointed out that this result had even been predicted by John Maynard Keynes. In his recollections in "My Early Beliefs," Keynes recalled D. H. Lawrence's disapproval of Bertrand Russell, himself, and their Bloomsbury circle of friends, all of whom were under the spell of G. E. Moore's *Principia Ethica*.

We were among the last of the Utopians, or meliorists as they are sometimes called, who believe in a continuing moral progress by virtue of which the human race already consists of reliable, rational, decent people, influenced by truth and objective standards, who can be safely released from the outward restraints of convention and traditional standards and inflexible rules of conduct, and left, from now onwards, to their own sensible devices, pure motives and reliable intuitions of the good. . . . We were not aware that civilization was a thin and precarious crust erected by the personality and the will of a very few, and only maintained by rules and conventions skillfully put across and guilefully preserved. We had no respect for traditional wisdom or the restraints of custom. We lacked reverence, as Lawrence observed. . . . It did not occur to us to respect the extraordinary accomplishment of our predecessors in the ordering of life (as it now seems to me to have been) or the elaborate framework which they had devised to protect this order.[10]

Not only Bloomsbury progressivists but scientists as well were responsible for undermining sustaining religious and philosophical traditions, in Grant's view. In fact, the two were closely linked, since like the apologists of progress, scientists generally rejected the idea of natural limits to human endeavor. Grant was fond of arguing that David Hume's skepticism regarding natural human limits had helped to clear the way for science and capitalism. And seeing that science and capitalism were closely linked, he noted in all his 1950s talks the growing influence of "the expanding economy" and "the mass society." These developments, he argued, were accompanied by the hegemony of the scientific disciplines in the universities. Scientists were "confident about what they wanted their students to know" in a way that philosophers and others were not because scientists knew their studies were respected and backed by the established order.

In 1959, Grant interviewed a number of prominent Canadians on a national television program about religious belief. He became friends with one of them, a leading Canadian physicist, Keith MacDonald, who arranged for him to speak to his fellow scientists at the National Research Council about science and political philosophy. Grant asked the neurological scientists to examine the implications of their way of obtaining knowledge. He was especially concerned about their use of a mechanical model of the human brain. Science that describes humans in mechanical or behavioral means may not consistently take human beings seriously as beings with political intentions, a conception of man essential to political philosophy, or as beings that are ends in themselves, a conception essential to Kantian moral philosophy. The dominant paradigm of the neurological scientists, Grant said, was tyrannical in the sense that it implied that the sort of moral and political philosophy that provided human beings with dignity was subjective and spurious.

Many of the scientists in attendance were outraged. They did not see why or how they could be accused of contributing to tyranny. As Grant knew, they were hard-working scientific practitioners who did not make ambitious theoretical claims. On the other hand, he pointed out that leading scientists did make such claims. In his talk, he quoted K. S. Lashley, a Harvard neurophysiologist who had voiced the widespread reductionist view that for scientists, "Our common meeting ground is the faith to which we all subscribe, . . . that the phenomenon of behavior and of mind are ultimately describable in the concepts of the mathematical and physical sciences."[11] Such a view demonstrated that scientists, like businessmen, had for the most part not accepted the moral and political responsibility that came with their ascendancy.

MacDonald had revealed during his television interview with Grant that he experienced his individual, conscious self as quite distinct from the sort of knowledge he generated in his scientific work. Grant was struck by this Cartesian split, and he later urged MacDonald to write about the disjunction of the lonely subjective "I" from the measured "objective" world of science. He wrote to MacDonald that science should "teach one to come to terms with the world as it is, not as one wishes it to be." Grant was not opposed to modern science and he even declared it to be "true" in *English-speaking Justice* (1974). He objected rather to the ways in which it led to the weakened status of the truth that humans are fitted for moral and political life.

By making the effort to reach out to scientists, the new arbiters of what is true about things, Grant was communicating across a gulf seldom bridged in the multiversity, where everyone tended to work within the narrow confines of their own specialties. The same sort of gulf divided him from market economists and businessmen. But of the two groups he thought that the scientists were more likely to listen and possibly change, because "the scientist is the one most likely to recapture the meaning of the concept of limit. . . . Who better illustrates in the modern world the great dictum of Socrates that the wise man is the man who knows not, or is limited, than Einstein."[12]

The Vietnam War confirmed Grant's conviction that the English-speaking democracies, led by the United States and including Canada, had gone tragically off course. The war made it impossible to deny that "[t]he very substance of our lives is bound up with the western empire and its destiny, just at a time when that empire uses increasingly ferocious means to maintain its hegemony."[13] Later, in the 1970s, Grant became convinced that the struggle for abortion rights, led by the women's movement, provided further evidence that the technological society had gone off course and was headed toward "the triumph of the will." He lost some his supporters on the Left when he published "The Case against Abortion" in a national magazine in 1981. But he had already argued in *English-speaking Justice* (1974) that the United States Supreme Court had ruled wrongly in *Roe v. Wade,* and a limited circulation piece on abortion was written with his wife Sheila in 1976.[14] For Grant, legalized abortion showed that liberalism's failure to protect human beings against the imperatives of technology was the result of its loss of faith in the religious conviction that all human beings are created equal. He was not sanguine about the future portended by abortion. "If tyranny is to come in North America, it will come cosily and on cat's feet. It will come with the denial of the rights of the unborn and of the aged, the denial of the rights of the mentally retarded, the insane and the economically less privileged. In fact, it will come with the denial of rights to all those who cannot defend themselves. It will come in the name of the cost-benefit analysis of human life."[15]

The technological society

Grant said in 1970 that our most important task was to "expose the ignoble delusions of our public men—generally a mixture of technological progressivism and personal self-assertion—all that is left of official liberalism in the English-speaking world."[16] He argued that our North American civilization had fallen prey to the delusion that technology would solve all our problems and eventually make everyone free, equal, and prosperous. Those opposed to this view, according to Grant, had first to distinguish the true and useful from the false and delusory in modern science, and then to expose science's inadequacies publicly.

In "Thinking about Technology," a chapter in *Technology and Justice* (1986), Grant spelled out his mature understanding of technology and capitalism. He identified what he called "the dominant paradigm of knowing," taking up Kuhn's popular phrase,[17] and focused on the moral vision that helps to sustain that paradigm, paying special attention to the steep price our civilization has paid for having gone down the technological road. The essay appears bleak because its primary goal is to debunk the naïve and widely held view that technology is neutral, that we can use our tools, instruments, and systems for either good or ill—the idea, for example, that "the computer does not impose on us the ways it should be used." Grant believed, on the contrary, that technology opened up certain possibilities and foreclosed others. The belief that the modern scientific-technological project is neutral was false and needed to be refuted.

The paradigm of objective knowledge, according to Grant, promises us the ability to master and remake the world and ourselves. "Suffice it to say that what is given in the modern use of the word 'science' is the project of reason to gain 'objective' knowledge. And modern 'reason' is the summoning of anything before a subject and putting it to the question, so that it gives us its reasons for being the way it is as an object."[18] This seventeenth-century vision, which has generated the marriage of technological science and capitalism, has gradually gained widespread allegiance because of its breathtaking achievements and remains dominant, to the point where it informs "each lived moment" of our public and private lives and has become, in Grant's words, our civilizational destiny. We have come to view our world almost exclusively through the prism of science and capital, as if no other way of viewing it were possible.

Grant saw that modern scientific paradigm carried with it an aggressive practical agenda. In other words, what is usually called "pure" science was conceived and constituted with its application in mind; it does not reflect a nonutilitarian pure desire to know but is rather "folded towards making." As Grant put it, "That it has been so folded is expounded with consummate clarity in such writings as those of Bacon and Descartes, as they distinguished modern science from ancient science at the time of its very beginnings."[19] We might paraphrase or "translate" this Heideggerian phrase, "folded towards making," as "designed and constructed with application and control in mind." Grant was profoundly indebted to Heidegger for this point about the practicality of science. He agreed with Heidegger's argument that the technological spirit was inherent in the genesis of modern science: "Modern science's way of representing pursues and entraps nature as a calculable coherence of forces. Modern physics . . . indeed already as pure theory, sets nature up to exhibit itself as a coherence of forces calculable in advance [and] orders its experiments precisely for the purpose of asking whether and how nature reports itself when set up in this way."[20]

Capitalism

What did Grant think was the relation of capitalism to technology? The answer is that when he talked about technology mastering nature, including human nature, he thought of capitalism as an integral part of that system of mastery. This is important because it means that, for him, any attempt to engage capitalism or the market without understanding its technological character is going to fail. The scientific, economic, and political elements of the technological society work together because they are ruled by the same principle. Capitalism is "the great economic machine" by which the technological paradigm of knowledge "has been put into the world." "I have very little sympathy in any way for communism, or socialism as a total regime," confessed Grant. "But . . . [a] society whose whole end is making money is not going to be a good society.[21]

Because of his essentially conservative suspicion of capitalism, Grant attempted to engage the Canadian new Left movement in the 1960s. In a speech called "Protest and Technology," delivered at a University of Toronto teach-in in 1965, Grant applauded the movement for opposing the Vietnam War and for resisting the universities, governments, and corporations that supported it. But he also made clear that he thought the new Left's dreams of transforming capitalism and technology were "utopian":

> I find myself in agreement with the account the leaders of this movement give of the inhumanity of the institutions of North America. How can a conservative not feel sympathy with the outrage of the new left against the emptiness and dehumanization that this society produces?

. . . When the new left speaks, however, of overcoming these conditions by protest, I think they are indulging in dreams, and even dangerous dreams. The moral fervour that accompanies such dreams is too valuable to be wasted on anything but reality.[22]

The new leftists' delusion lay in their underestimating the allegiance of people to "the American system" and its agenda: "There is a lot of talk among the new left about the present system of society collapsing because of its internal contradictions. What signs are there of this collapse? The American system with its extension into Western Europe seems to me supremely confident and to have the overwhelming majority of its citizens behind it." The young, he thought, should abandon the goal of revolutionary transformation through activism, seek to understand the limits of a society committed to technology, question their own commitment to progress, continue to act with courage on behalf of justice, and work to create cultural space for spontaneity and thought not motivated merely by technological goals: "If protest is to be effective in this era, if we are to be successful in creating space for human spontaneity in the iron maiden of the technological apparatus we have created, then it is essential that those who are in the vanguard of the protest combine their action with the deepest and most careful thought."

In "Faith and the Multiversity," the second major theoretical essay in *Technology and Justice,* Grant goes on the offensive by asserting that the language of the dominant technological paradigm cannot adequately measure and describe our most important human experiences. He argues on behalf of "the experience that intelligence is enlightened by love," the definition of faith that he takes from Simone Weil.[23] This essay—perhaps Grant's most eloquent defense of the insight "that we are not our own," that we are loved and freed by what we are given—attempts to critique scientific objectivity by drawing attention to the universal human experience that we know our loved ones better *because* we love them, and that *because* we love them we also know better the places that we love. In other words, he forces us to confront the idea that our ability to know is improved, not distorted, by love. And love is necessarily opposed to the idea of radical human autonomy and self-sufficiency: "love is consent to the fact that there is authentic otherness. . . . When life becomes dominated by self-serving, the reality of otherness, in its own being, almost disappears for us. . . . In political terms, Plato places the tyrant as the worst human being because his self-serving has gone to the farthest point. He is saying that the tyrant is mad because otherness has ceased to exist for him. I can grasp with direct recognition the theological formulation of this: 'Hell is to be one's own.'"[24]

Our love of our children, often stimulated by their love for us, our love of particular places—such overwhelming experiences have no place in the formulae of objective truth that structure the sciences and the market economy. We love others and the things around us because they are beautiful. "The beauty of otherness" according to Grant, "is the central assumption in the statement, 'Faith is the experience that the intelligence is enlightened by love.'" Grant calls our attention to the fact that we cannot love people and places and consider them beautiful when we are analyzing them as objects. Nor can we consider the world and human beings beautiful if we think about them as resources: "certain rhetoricians used to say: 'Canada's greatest resource is its people.' That well-meaning sentence expresses what has been lost as well as found in modernity."[25]

Grant also defended the meaning of the word "good" in a world where it had been superseded by the word "free," where "free" means "free from interference." The language that speaks of the gifts of beauty and love goes together with the language that speaks of the good as something given rather than first produced by human beings. But in the modern scientific paradigm the conception of good has been dissolved into uncertainty.[26] The question about what is good for humans and nature has been consciously avoided by both scientists and capitalists.

Conclusion

George Grant drew our attention to the urgent need to respect limits, as well as the way in which the supersession of limits in the modern age is intrinsically related to the triumph of technological capitalism, which in turn represents the triumph of the unchecked human will. Being human is a mystery we cannot fully comprehend. It situates us inside a much larger whole than ourselves, to which we belong and within which we must live, and at the same time it frees us, leaving us responsible for building our communities and shaping our lives. This freedom is fraught with personal and political dangers, and can tend, as we have seen, toward the "freedom" of the tyrant for whom otherness has ceased to exist, and also toward the freedom that structures our technological science.

Grant spent years grappling with the question of how to "be good" in an age that more and more attempted to achieve human freedom and progress by conquering and transforming nature, including human nature. His work must be read as an effort to, in the words of W. H. Auden, "teach the free man how to praise."[27]

12

The Liberalism of John Paul II and the Technological Imperative

Richard John Neuhaus

It is no secret that when *Centesimus Annus* appeared in 1991 some of us viewed it not only as an important teaching moment but also as a vindication of our understanding of Catholic social doctrine. There was a great temptation to declare triumphantly, "I told you so." That temptation was not always resisted as it should have been. This contributed to a degree of polarization over the encyclical. Liberals who paid any attention at all to the document were not convinced of the demise of socialism and lifted up passages that they thought supported their collectivist dream. But, for the most part, liberals paid little attention. As with the other great teaching documents of the pontificate of John Paul II, the appearance of *Centesimus Annus* was for most liberal Catholics a nonevent.

The stronger polarization developed between certain conservatives and those called neoconservatives, the former accusing the latter of hijacking this pontificate, and *Centesimus Annus* in particular, in order to gain magisterial legitimation for what is called democratic capitalism or liberal democracy. The neoconservatives are described, and sometimes describe themselves, as advancing "The Murray Project," referring to the effort of the late Father John Courtney Murray to square Catholic teaching with the American democratic experiment. The conservative critics—for instance, Professor David Schindler of the John Paul II Institute in Washington, D.C.—accuse

Murray and those like him of selling out authentic Catholic teaching to a desiccated and desiccating liberalism.

Schindler writes in his book, *Heart of the World, Center of the Church:* "My argument, then, offered in the name of de Lubac and Pope John Paul II as authentic interpreters of the Second Vatican Council, has . . . two main implications. First, it demands that we challenge the regnant liberalism which would claim that it (alone) is empty of religious theory in its interpretation of the First Amendment and indeed of Western constitutionalism more generally. Secondly, it demands that we seek a truly 'Catholic moment' in America [as distinct from Richard John Neuhaus's 'Catholic moment'], understood, that is, not as another Murrayite moment but as a truly Johannine (John Paul II) moment. This means that we must expose the con game of liberalism which enables it, precisely without argument, to privilege its place in the public order."[1]

In his book, and repeatedly in the pages of the English edition of *Communio,* of which he is the editor, Schindler assaults the liberal "con game" in which he thinks some of us are complicit. I confess that I find this somewhat frustrating. In my experience, David Schindler is a friendly fellow. We have engaged our differences in both private and public exchanges, after which he ends up agreeing that there is no substantive disagreement between us. I always look forward to our next amicable conversation, and brace myself for his next public attack.

I do think there is an important difference between us. It is not, or at least it is not chiefly, a difference over Catholic theology. The difference, rather, is that Prof. Schindler and those who are associated with his criticism tend to put the worst possible construction upon the liberal tradition, and on the American cultural, legal, and political expression of that tradition. In doing so, I believe Prof. Schindler and his friends hand an undeserved victory to those who interpret the liberal tradition in ways that we all deplore. With John Courtney Murray, I suggest that our task is to contend for an interpretation and, where necessary, a correction of liberalism, in a way that is compatible with the fullness of Catholic truth. In what follows, I address chiefly the liberal polity, but of course the polity is influenced by scientific and technological dynamics that can, in some instances, challenge the primacy of the political. I will return to that later.

There is no doubt that the American experiment is constituted in the liberal tradition. Since we cannot go back to the eighteenth century and reconstitute it on different foundations, we must hope that the foundations on which it is constituted are not those described by Ronald Dworkin, John Rawls, Richard Rorty—and David Schindler. Toward the end of understanding the liberal tradition as consistent with Catholic truth, *Centesimus Annus* is an invaluable guide.

Liberalism, needless to say, is a wondrously pliable term. There is the laissez-faire economic liberalism condemned by Leo XIII in *Rerum Novarum,* and also by John Paul II. In American political culture that liberalism goes by the name of libertarianism, and, despite its many talented apologists, including Charles Murray (no relation to John Courtney), it has never acquired many adherents beyond what Russell Kirk called its "chirping sectaries." In the American context, extreme libertarianism remains in the largest part a thought experiment for college sophomores of all ages.

The liberalism so fiercely criticized today is not limited to libertarianism. At the hands of the critics, the republican liberalism of virtue and the communitarian liberalism of Tocquevillian civil society come off little better than libertarianism. David Schindler has good ecumenical company in attacking liberalism *tout court.* Stanley Hauerwas, a Methodist theologian at Duke University, has in books beyond number been assaulting, hammering, pummeling, and battering it with magnificent aplomb. Liberalism and all its ways and all its pomps have also taken a severe beating from Oliver O'Donovan, Regius Professor of Theology at Oxford. Despite his Anglican bias against what he calls "papalism," I most warmly recommend his book, *The Desire of the Nations: Rediscovering the Roots of Political Theology.*[2] It is not only a devastatingly convincing critique of a certain version of liberalism, but also a fascinating examination of what the idea of "Christendom" might mean in our moment of modernity's discontent.

We can summarize some of the salient points in the indictment offered by the Christian critics of liberalism and modernity (the two terms usually being more or less interchangeable). Whether it be the enchanted G. K. Chesterton, the near-magisterial Alasdair MacIntyre, the caustic George Grant, the swashbuckling Stan Hauerwas, the daring O'Donovan, or the melancholic David Schindler, the indictment tends to be much the same. Lest there be any misunderstanding, let me say that I find myself in warm agreement with the indictment of a certain kind of liberalism. The contention turns on what we mean by liberalism.

The first charge is that Christian thinkers have been too ready to trim the Christian message in order to accommodate the ruling cultural paradigm of liberalism. I definitely agree. That, however, is more accurately seen as an indictment of Christian thinkers, not of liberalism. If we are hesitant to declare in public that Jesus Christ is Lord, the fault is in ourselves. We cannot plead the excuse that liberalism made us do it. John Rawls or Richard Rorty or the Supreme Court, claiming to speak in the name of liberalism, may have intimidated us, but the fault is with our timidity.

Other points in the indictment of liberalism are variously expressed. It is charged that liberalism is purely procedural. Excluding the consideration of ends, liberalism claims to be only about means, but in fact disguises its ends in its means. Thus Father Murray's construal of the First Amendment as "articles of peace" is in fact—or so the indictment reads—a surrender to the inherently antireligious bias of liberalism. In short, the claimed "neutrality" of liberalism is anything but neutral. Liberalism, it is charged, is premised upon the fiction of a "social contract" that is, in turn, premised exclusively upon self-interest. Liberalism denies, or at least requires agnosticism about, transcendent truth or divine law, recognizing no higher rule than the self-interested human will. Liberalism's idea of freedom is freedom from any commanding truth that might impinge upon the totally voluntaristic basis of social order.

These liberal dogmas, it is further charged, are inextricably tied to the dynamics of capitalism. Liberal dogma and market dynamics are the mutually reinforcing foundation and end of a social order that is entirely and without remainder in the service of individualistic choices by the sovereign, autonomous, and unencumbered Self. The wages of liberalism is consumerism, and consumerism is all-consuming. The end result is what some critics call "liberal totalitarianism."

It is an impressive indictment, and it is supported by impressive evidence. Against each of the distortions mentioned I have written at length, as have others who are favorably disposed toward liberal democracy or, as some prefer, democratic capitalism. But that is just the point: one may argue that the indictment is an indictment of the distortions of liberalism. If that is the case, we are contending for the soul of the liberal tradition.

A personal word might be in order. In the 1960s I was very much a man of the Left. Not the Left of countercultural drug-tripping and generalized hedonism, but the Left exemplified by, for instance, the civil rights movement under the leadership of Dr. Martin Luther King Jr. In the latter half of the 1960s this began to change with the advent of the debate over what was then called "liberalized" abortion law. By 1967 I was writing about the "two liberalisms"—one, like that earlier civil rights movement, inclusive of the vulnerable and driven by a transcendent order of justice; the other exclusive and recognizing no law higher than individual willfulness. My argument was that, by embracing the cause of abortion, liberals were abandoning the first liberalism that has sustained all that is hopeful in the American experiment.

That is my argument still today. It is, I believe, crucially important that that argument prevail in the years ahead. There is no going back to reconstitute the American order on a foundation other than the liberal tradition. A great chasm has opened between the liberal tradition and what today is called liberalism. That is why some of us are called conservatives. Conservatism that is authentically and constructively American conservatism is conservatism in the cause of reappropriating and revitalizing the liberal tradition.

Toward that end, *Centesimus Annus,* as I said, is an invaluable guide. The document is often described as an encyclical on economics, but I suggest that is somewhat misleading. Certainly it addresses economic questions in considerable detail. One reason for that is that the encyclical is commemorating and developing the argument of *Rerum Novarum,* which was much and rightly concerned about the problems of the worker and the threat of class warfare in an earlier phase of capitalism. Another reason for the focus on economics is that the pope is addressing the situation following the Western-assisted suicide of the Soviet empire, and that empire had justified itself by a false ideology that reduced the human phenomenon to the economic dimension. In explaining why that ideology is false and in pointing the way toward a more promising future, it was necessary for the encyclical to pay close attention to economics.

It is more accurate, however, to say that *Centesimus Annus* is about the free society, including economic freedom. The discussion of *Rerum Novarum,* of the right understanding of property and exchange, and of the circumstances following the momentous events of 1989, culminates in chapters V and VI, "State and Culture" and "The Person Is the Way of the Church." When we consider the encyclical in relation to American liberalism, several cautions are in order. *Centesimus Annus* is not a freestanding text. It must be understood within the large corpus of this most energetic teaching pontificate and, beyond that, in the context of modern Catholic social doctrine dating from *Rerum Novarum*. Even further, it must be understood in continuity with the Church's teaching ministry through the centuries. Then too, we must always be mindful that the pope is writing for and to the universal Church.

Keeping these and other cautions in mind, however, one cannot help but be struck by how much *Centesimus Annus* is a reading of "the signs of the time" with specific reference to the world-historical experiences of this century. The encyclical is not historicist, in the narrow sense of that term, but it is firmly and determinedly located in a historical moment. And, while it is not a freestanding text, one can through this one text trace the controlling themes of this teaching pontificate. Although it is written to and for the universal Church, the Church in each place is invited and obliged to read the encyclical as though it were addressed to its own specific circumstance.

Moreover, I am confident that we as Americans make no mistake when we think that the American experiment is a very major presence in *Centesimus Annus*. After all, the Western democracies, and the United States most particularly, are the historically available alternatives to the socialism that so miserably failed. I think it true to say that in this pontificate, for the first time, magisterial teaching about modernity, democracy, and human freedom has a stronger reference to the Revolution of 1776 than to the French Revolution of 1789. It is, then, neither chauvinistic nor parochial to read *Centesimus Annus* with particular reference to the American experiment. On the contrary, it is the course of fidelity, made imperative by the duty to appropriate magisterial teaching to our own circumstance, and by the powerful awareness of the American experiment in the mind of the encyclical's author.

There is no more common criticism of the liberal tradition than that it is premised upon unbridled "individualism." *Centesimus Annus* speaks of the "individual" and even of the "autonomous subject" (13), but most typically refers to the "person." Citing the earlier encyclical *Redemptor Hominis,* John Paul writes that "this human person is the primary route that the Church must travel in fulfilling her mission . . . the way traced out by Christ himself, the way that leads invariably through the mystery of the Incarnation and Redemption."

He then adds the remarkable statement, "This, and this alone, is the principle which inspires the Church's social doctrine" (53).

This, and this alone. He writes, "The Church has gradually developed that doctrine in a systematic way," above all in the past century. Very gradually, we might add without disrespect. In the later encyclical *Veritatis Splendor,* John Paul pays fulsome tribute to modernity and its development of the understanding of the dignity of the individual and of individual freedom. Individualism is one of the signal achievements of modernity or, if you will, of the liberal tradition. Nor should we deny that this achievement was effected in frequent tension with, and even conflict with, the Catholic Church. One important reason for such conflict, of course, was that the cause of freedom was perceived as marching under the radically anticlerical and anti-Christian banners of 1789. It is a signal achievement of this pontificate that it has so clearly replanted the idea of the individual and of freedom in the rich soil of Christian truth from which, in its convoluted and conflicted development, it had been uprooted. Only as it is deeply rooted in the truth about the human person will the flower of freedom flourish in the future.

It is a mistake to pit, as some do pit, modern individualism against a more organic Catholic understanding of community. Rather should we enter into a sympathetic liaison with the modern achievement of the idea of the individual, grounding it more firmly and richly in the understanding of the person destined from eternity to eternity for communion with God. The danger of rejecting individualism is that the real-world alternative is not a Catholic understanding of *communio* but a falling back into the collectivisms that are the great enemy of the freedom to which we are called. As *Centesimus Annus* reminds us, "We are not dealing here with humanity in the 'abstract,' but with the real, 'concrete,' 'historical' person." The problem with the contemporary distortion of the individual as the autonomous, unencumbered, sovereign Self is not that it is wrong about the awesome dignity of the individual, but that it cuts the self off from the source of that dignity. The first cause of this error, says *Centesimus Annus,* is atheism (13).

"It is by responding to the call of God contained in the being of things that man becomes aware of his transcendent dignity. Every individual must give this response, which constitutes the apex of his humanity, and no social mechanism or collective subject can substitute for it" (13). The great error of both collectivist determinism and of individualistic license is that their understanding of human freedom is detached from obedience to the truth (17). Culture is a communal phenomenon, but it is in the service of the person's response to transcendent truth. In one of the most suggestive passages of the encyclical, John Paul writes, "At the heart of every culture lies the attitude a person takes to the greatest mystery: the mystery of God. Different cultures are basically different ways of facing the question of the meaning of personal existence" (24).

We are brought back to the remarkable proposition about the flourishing of the human person. "This, and this alone, is the principle which inspires the Church's social doctrine." This is not individualism in the pejorative sense, but it is commensurable with the modern achievement of the idea of the individual. It is commensurable with the constituting ideas of the American experiment, in which the state is understood to be in the service of freedom, and freedom is understood as what the Founders called "ordered liberty"—liberty ordered to the truth. And there are, as the Declaration of Independence declares, "self-evident truths" that ground such freedom and direct it to the transcendent ends of "Nature and Nature's God."

The theistic references of the Declaration are not, as some contemporary commentators claim, simply crowd-pleasing asides, but are integral to the moral argument of the document—and the Declaration is, above all, a moral argument. Moreover, such references must be understood in the context of the innumerable statements by all the Founders that this constitutional order is premised upon moral truths secured by religion. The American experiment is constituted by

a Puritan-Lockean synthesis that in recent decades has been bowdlerized to fit the secularist prejudices of our academic elites. It is imperative that we challenge the bowdlerized version of the founding
that has been fobbed off on several generations of students, from
grade school through graduate school, and take our American history straight.

It will be protested by some that this is mere "civic religion."
But we have missed the point of *Centesimus Annus* if we think there
is anything "mere" about sustaining a public order that acknowledges
the transcendent source and end of human existence. Of course such
formal acknowledgment provides only a very thin and attenuated theology, but it creates the condition within which the Church can propose a rich and adequate account of the human story. But that, it is
objected, is just the problem: In a liberal society the Church can only
propose its truth, putting the gospel on the marketplace as one consumer item among others.

This is a frequently heard objection, and we have to wonder
what people mean by it. Are they suggesting that the Church should
coerce people to obey the truth? In the encyclical on evangelization,
Redemptoris Missio, the pope says, "The Church imposes nothing,
she only proposes." She would not impose if she could. Authentic
faith is of necessity an act of freedom. If we fail to understand this, it
is to be feared that we fail to understand what John Paul calls the
principle which alone inspires the Church's social doctrine. The
Church is to propose—relentlessly, boldly, persuasively, winsomely.
If we who are the Church are not doing that, the fault is not with
liberalism but with ourselves. Although the Church's message provides a secure grounding for liberalism, liberalism is not the content
of the Church's message. It is simply the condition for the Church to
invite free persons to live in the communio of Christ and his Mystical
Body, which communion is infinitely deeper, richer, and fuller than
the liberal social order—or, for that matter, any social order short of
the right ordering of all things in the Kingdom of God.

Few things are more important to the free society than the idea and reality of the limited state. However much the courts and secular intellectuals may have denied it in recent decades, the American order is inexplicable apart from the acknowledgment of a sovereignty higher than the state. As in "one nation under God," meaning a nation under judgment. Christians understand and publicly declare that higher sovereignty in the simple proposition "Jesus Christ is Lord." It is not necessary for the state to declare that Jesus Christ is Lord. Nor, at least in the American circumstance and any foreseeable reconfiguration of that circumstance, is it desirable that the state declare that Jesus Christ is Lord. The role of the limited state is to respect the political sovereignty of the people who acknowledge a sovereignty higher than their own. As the encyclical states, "Through Christ's sacrifice on the cross, the victory of the Kingdom of God has been achieved once and for all" (25). That victory denotes the highest sovereignty by which the state is limited, and the proclamation of that victory is the most important political contribution of the Church. In a democratic society that has been effectively evangelized, citizens do not ask the state to confess the lordship of Christ. Their only demand is that the state be respectful of the fact that a majority of its citizens confess the lordship of Christ. We affirm not a confessional state but a confessional society, always remembering that the state is the servant of society, which is prior to the state.

The Church also makes an invaluable political contribution by insisting upon the limits of politics. The great danger, says *Centesimus Annus,* is that "politics becomes a 'secular religion' which operates under the illusion of creating paradise in this world. But no political society . . . can ever be confused with the Kingdom of God. . . . By presuming to anticipate judgment here and now, people put themselves in the place of God and set themselves against the patience of God." The power of grace "penetrates" the political order, especially as the laity take the lead in the exercise of Christian public responsibility, but there can be no pretensions that earthly politics will create the final right order for which our hearts yearn (25).

As in the liberal order, the ambitions of the state are checked by the democratic assertion of a higher sovereignty and by the limits of politics itself, so those ambitions are checked by diverse "sovereignties" within society itself. With Leo XIII, John Paul declares that "the individual, the family, and society are prior to the State." The state exists to serve and protect individuals and institutions that have priority (11). Human persons and what I have elsewhere described as the mediating institutions of society "enjoy their own spheres of autonomy and sovereignty," according to *Centesimus Annus* (45). These spheres of sovereignty are smaller than the state, but they are not lower than the state.

The striking modernity of the encyclical's argument is evident also in its understanding of the state. Unlike earlier formulations, the state is not situated within a hierarchy of authorities, descending from the rule of God to the rule of the lord of the manor. The argument of *Centesimus Annus* is profoundly democratic. Christ is sovereign over all, and that sovereignty is asserted by those who acknowledge the sovereignty of Christ. The unlimited state, whether based on Marxist atheism or the engineering designs of Enlightenment rationalism, aspires to totalitarian control. "Thus there is a denial of the supreme insight concerning man's true greatness, his transcendence in respect to earthly realities, the contradiction in his heart between the desire for the fullness of what is good and his own inability to attain it and, above all, the need for salvation which results from this situation" (13). The limited state is kept limited by the democratic assertion of the transcendent aspiration of the human heart.

In this connection, John Paul infuses the doctrine of subsidiarity with new vitality by the use of a most suggestive phrase, "the subjectivity of society." "The social nature of man . . . is realized in various intermediary groups, beginning with the family and including economic, social, political, and cultural groups which stem from human nature itself and have their own autonomy, always with a view to the common good" (13). In the free society, the state is one institution, one player, among others. It is an indispensable player in its service to all the other players, but it is subject to the subjectivity of society, and the subjectivity of society consists in free persons and free persons in community living in obedience to God and solidarity with one another. There is in *Centesimus Annus* and in other writings of this pontificate, I believe, a fresh and compelling theory of democracy that awaits systematic development by the next generation.

There must be a cultivated skepticism about the state if it is to be kept limited. "To that end, it is preferable that each power be balanced by other powers and by other spheres of responsibility which keep it within proper bounds" (44). Skepticism regarding the power of the state does not mean, however, skepticism about the purposes that the state is to serve. Quite the opposite is the case. Only when those purposes are clearly and unambiguously asserted can the state be held accountable. Section 46 of *Centesimus Annus* clearly and unambiguously challenges the point at which contemporary liberalism has most severely distorted the meaning of democracy in the liberal tradition. Here is the crucial paragraph:

> Authentic democracy is possible only in a state ruled by law, and on the basis of a correct conception of the human person. It requires that the necessary conditions be present for the advancement both of the individual through education and formation in true ideals and of the "subjectivity" of society through the creation of structures of participation and shared responsibility. [Then comes the vital passage.] Nowadays there is a tendency to claim that agnosticism and skeptical relativism are the philosophy and the basic attitude which correspond to

democratic forms of political life. Those who are convinced that they know the truth and firmly adhere to it are considered unreliable from a democratic point of view, since they do not accept that the truth is determined by the majority, or that it is subject to variation according to different political trends. It must be observed in this regard that if there is no ultimate truth to guide and direct political activity, then ideas and convictions can easily be manipulated for reasons of power. As history demonstrates, a democracy without values easily turns into open or thinly disguised totalitarianism.

The importance of this paragraph, and its pertinence to our American situation, can hardly be overestimated. The dogmatic insistence upon agnosticism in public discourse and decision making has created what I have called "the naked public square." People who, like the Founders, hold certain truths to be self-evident are today "considered unreliable from a democratic point of view." In a usurpation of power that indeed threatens a "thinly disguised totalitarianism," the courts have presumed to declare that the separation of church and state means the separation of religion and religiously grounded morality from public life, which means the separation of the deepest convictions of the people from politics, which means the end of democracy and, in fact, the end of politics. Thank God, we are not there yet. But it is the direction in which we in the United States have been moving these last several decades, and it is the real and present danger requiring those of us called conservatives to rally to the defense of the liberal tradition.

In contending for the soul of liberalism, we must be sympathetically alert to some of our fellow citizens who honestly believe that any appeal to transcendent truth poses the threat of theocracy. John Paul recognizes how widespread that misunderstanding is, and therefore immediately follows the above passage with this:

> Nor does the Church close her eyes to the danger of fanaticism or fundamentalism among those who, in the name of an ideology which purports to be scientific or religious, claim the right to impose on others their own concept of what is true and good. Christian truth is not of this kind. Since it is not an ideology, the Christian faith does not presume to imprison changing sociopolitical realities in a rigid schema, and it recognizes that human life is realized in history in conditions that are diverse and imperfect. Furthermore, in constantly reaffirming the transcendent dignity of the person, the Church's method is always that of respect for freedom.

Let it be candidly said that that has not always appeared to be the Church's method. We should not leave it to others to point this out. In *Tertio Millennio Adveniente (As the Third Millennium Nears)* and on many other occasions, the pope has candidly called upon Christians to acknowledge the ways that, individually and corporately, they have failed to respect the dignity and freedom of others. That acknowledgment must, however, be joined to two other propositions. First: When, in the name of democracy, transcendent truth is excluded from the public square, the result is "open or thinly disguised totalitarianism." Second: Democratic totalitarianism, which recognizes no higher truth than majority rule, creates a treacherously dangerous circumstance for minorities.

We could go on to examine other themes of *Centesimus Annus* that can be correlated with the liberal tradition, rejuvenating that tradition and turning it in more promising directions. There is, for instance, the connection between freedom and virtue, both personal and public, which must evoke intensified effort toward the evangelizing and reevangelizing of society. The stakes in that effort are very high, as John Paul sets forth with such urgency in *Evangelium Vitae*'s dramatic portrayal of the conflict between "the culture of life" and "the culture of death." But these and other questions are for another time. Indeed, as I have suggested, it will be the work of generations to systematically unfold and disseminate the remarkable teaching ministry of this pontificate.

Brief reference was made earlier to the dynamics of science and technology that can challenge the primacy of the political. Here the political is understood in Aristotle's sense of free persons deliberating the question of how we ought to order our lives together. In the view of many, that freedom and deliberation is increasingly undermined by what some view as the scientific and technological imperative. One thinks, for instance, of the impressive arguments of the French Protestant intellectual Jacques Ellul, with his powerful invocation of Karl Barth's "Nein!" to the determinisms of modernity, including the dominance of scientific and technological "progress." That emphatic No! resonates with Catholic social doctrine, and *Centesimus Annus* in particular, in their contending for the primacy of the political. At the same time, in contrast to Barth and Ellul, the spirit of Catholicism in relation to its host culture is not dialectical but dialogical, aimed at engaging and transforming the culture.

The threat of what Ellul calls the technological imperative is, it must be frankly admitted, not adequately addressed in *Centesimus Annus*. It is much more comprehensively treated in the encyclical *Evangelium Vitae (The Gospel of Life)* with specific reference to biotechnological developments as they touch on "the culture of death" that, in John Paul's understanding, is pitted against "the culture of life." A related set of questions is taken up in the encyclical *Fides et Ratio (Faith and Reason),* which underscores the gift and task of reason appropriate to maintaining the deliberation that marks authentic politics. In these and other teaching documents, it is fair to say that John Paul believes that the Church must contend for politics as such against all determinisms, whether ideological, economic, or technological. Without values—i.e., without reasonable and morally informed deliberation—all these dynamics "easily turn into open or thinly disguised totalitarianism."

One still hears it said that science and technology are neutral, capable of being used for either good or evil, and there is an important measure of truth in that. Increasingly, however, it is recognized that science and technology take on a life of their own, moving ahead step by step in obedience to a dogma of progress based upon what is undeniably, at least in a linear sense, progress. Efforts to check or hold accountable that apparently inexorable movement require a renewal of the political. In our circumstance, however, and especially in connection with reproductive technologies, cloning, eugenics, and related developments, explicitly moral challenges to such developments are disallowed as being "religious" in character and therefore, by definition, arbitrary and private. Morality and religion are curiously conflated (both by the secularist and the religious), with the unhappy consequence that the "ought" in the public deliberation that marks Aristotle's understanding of politics is effectively gutted.

It is a great merit of *Centesimus Annus* that it is attentive to the historical particularities of its writing. It forcefully addresses the ideas of economic determinism that drove the socialist totalitarianisms of the past century. In the years ahead, Catholic social doctrine must more effectively confront the threatening totalitarianism of science and technology. As things are turning out, our real and present danger today is not so much Orwell's *1984* as Huxley's *Brave New World*. A world made content by "soma" is not capable of deliberating how we ought to order our life together. The abolition of politics is at the heart of what C. S. Lewis called the abolition of man. In contending for the restoration of the primacy of politics, we have no better resource than the liberal democratic tradition. That insight, too, is part of "the liberalism of John Paul II."

I began with some comments on *Centesimus Annus* and what some call "The Murray Project." Nobody should try to usurp the authority of magisterial documents in order to advance particular intra-Catholic partisan arguments. Before the magisterium of the Church we are all learners. Our purpose must be *sentire cum ecclesia,* to think with the Church. I know that I have learned from and have been changed by *Centesimus Annus,* and I trust that will continue to be the case. In no way should the encyclical be interpreted as an unqualified affirmation of the American experiment. In many ways, it is a searing criticism of what that experiment has become under the influence of contemporary liberalisms. Yet I do believe *Centesimus Annus* is commensurate with the American liberal tradition, and in critical continuity with the great work of John Courtney Murray. I believe that is the case, and I hope that is the case, for we have not the luxury of imagining the reconstitution of this social and political order on foundations other than the liberal tradition.

As sympathetic as we may be to some of the determined critics of liberalism, we do well to remind ourselves that all temporal orders short of the Kingdom of God are profoundly unsatisfactory. When we survey the depredations and ravages of our social, political, and religious circumstance, it is tempting to look for someone or something to blame. It is easy to say, "Liberalism made us do it." But liberalism is freedom, and what we do with freedom is charged to our account. For American Christians, and for Catholics in particular, there is nothing that has been done wrong that could not have been done differently. Amidst the depredations and ravages of an American experiment that once exalted the human spirit, and may do so again, *Centesimus Annus* invites us to reappropriate and rebuild the liberal tradition.

Editor's Response

The Conundrum of Capitalism and Christianity

Doug Bandow

British historian Paul Johnson has called the twentieth century
"the age of politics." It was also a secular age. But faith did not
disappear. Rather, the object of worship changed. The reigning theology became statism, and government became god, charged with the
people's salvation.

Not that this religious experiment worked well. The age of politics unleashed untold death and destruction while solving few of
mankind's most vexing problems, including poverty. To the contrary,
all too often it was, and continues to be, government policy—usually
inadvertently, but sometimes intentionally—that created and/or ex-
acerbated social problems.

By the dawn of the new millennium the failure of politics to live
up to its grandiose promises was evident to all but a dispirited band of
zealots. Indeed, virtually no one any longer disputed that capitalism
had won the "bathtub" test. If one wants a prosperous society—with
resources available for the poor as well as the rich, with rising living
standards, with technological progress that does everything from heal
the sick to clean the environment—one needs a market economy. In
short, democratic capitalism and totalitarian communism battled for
most of the twentieth century, and history rendered its judgment.

Almost as dramatic, though not quite as complete, was the failure of the moderate welfare states, which suffered from bloated public budgets, imploding public pension systems, bulging jail popula-

tions, counterproductive work incentives, and hobbled national economies. Individuals, families, and communities were destroyed by authoritarian paternalism, with a panoply of disastrous social pathologies ensuing. Elected lawmakers and unelected bureaucrats in these systems murdered dreams rather than people, but they also found themselves losers in history's great trial.

Of course, officials of all ideological stripes in all political systems resisted accepting that their time had drawn to a bloody, calamitous close. They continued to fight to preserve their privileged positions, using whatever tools were available, ranging from the pork-barrel politics of democracy to the brutal repression of dictatorship. Some succeeded in maintaining political control, but usually due less to genuine public support than to the apparent lack of good alternatives.

Nevertheless, the global triumph of capitalism—and it has been a global triumph of staggering proportions—fails to fully satisfy the human spirit. If recent events demonstrate that socialism and other forms of statism do not work in practice, many idealists, especially religious activists, still believe that capitalism is immoral in theory. This line of criticism is ecumenical: Catholic liberation theologians dress Marxist class analysis in religious clothing, left-wing evangelicals equate markets with materialism, and mainline Protestants still retreat to the "social gospel."

At heart, Christianity poses a radical challenge to the appropriateness of every human action and institution. "Do not love the world or anything in the world," wrote the Apostle John in his first epistle. "If anyone loves the world the love of the Father is not in him. For everything in the world—the cravings of sinful man, the lust of his eyes and the boasting of what he has and does—comes not from the Father but from the world. The world and its desires pass away, but the man who does the will of God lives forever" (1 John 2:15–17).

Capitalism is therefore not exempt from scrutiny. It is an imperfect institution animated by sinful men, just like any other social organization. No matter how successful they may be, markets are not everything. They provide individuals with manifold opportunities, but they neither mandate virtue nor prevent poverty. They offer liberty, but they do not tell people how to use that freedom. Indeed, at many times in human history, many, many people have used their freedom in the market to do ill.

The potential for abuse is only likely to increase. By generating abundant wealth and spawning transformational technologies, capitalism has created new avenues for sin. Virtually everyone is but one click of the computer mouse or remote control away from images that degrade rather than affirm the dignity of the human person. Biogenetics is challenging the very nature of the human person. Although capitalism promotes virtue in some ways—rewarding thrift and hard work, for instance—it also multiplies temptations. The very wealth that it produces generates a centrifugal force in families and communities. And that wealth itself is distributed in a wildly unequal fashion. If poverty persists in wealthy countries, the unmet human needs in poorer states are staggering. Obviously the social agenda for any person of good will, and especially a Christian, remains long. The only question is how to effect reform.

This, then, is the conundrum faced by those concerned with both virtue and freedom. It is impossible to imagine a prosperous society that is not also free. Similarly, it is difficult to imagine a good society that does not simultaneously protect people's freedom to sin. But liberty obviously is not enough to make people good, end poverty, and ensure a Christian understanding of the human person.

These are the issues with which the authors of the present volume struggle. Most write as Christians. All desire to build a society that affirms virtue and empowers the poor. All recognize that doing so requires more than a liberal understanding of freedom, that is, freedom as the lack of coercion. All see the need to infuse social life, including the economy, with a Christian anthropology.

Yet the areas of common agreement do not preclude enormous disagreements. While dialogue is possible—as proved by the very existence of this volume, if nothing else—it will not be easy.

The central issues are simultaneously simple and complex. Perhaps the most fundamental social question is, does liberal economics inevitably undermine the Christian virtues? Is it neutral, serving as an empty vessel for whatever morals its participants bring with them; negative, posing an inevitable assault on family and community; or positive, encouraging such characteristics as honesty and thrift? There are economic questions, too: Why poverty in a world of wealth? Is economic liberty a boon or a bane for the poor and powerless, particularly in poor societies? Political questions logically follow: How much freedom? What kind of freedom? What institutions? What regulations? And, ultimately, at what point do theology and prudence require the state to restrict capitalist exchanges among consenting adults?

The socialist temptation

The harshest critics of capitalism suggest that a market economy is not just defective, but is fundamentally inconsistent with the Christian faith. For example, in the view of John Cort, the author of *Christian Socialism,* "a Christian could, not to mention should, be a socialist." He contends that "[t]he 'spirit of Christian love' cannot be reduced to a political imperative, granted, but it most certainly has a political dimension. Feeding the hungry and clothing the naked are not precisely identical with a systematic redistribution of wealth, but in the present situation, of gross inequality, obscene wealth and wretched poverty, they most certainly cry to heaven for both systematic and unsystematic redistribution." But despite Cort's emotional appeal to the "spirit of Christian love," the Bible does not specifically speak to the proper degree of governmental intervention in the economy. There is no explicit endorsement of any type of economic system in the Bible, no equation of capitalism or socialism with the Kingdom of God. Old Testament Israel placed some restrictions on debts, interest, and property transfers, but it allowed for relatively free economic exchange and obvious wealth inequality. The so-called Jubilee laws were tied to the Israelites' special status as God's people— it goes without saying that secular America is not a good analogue to theocratic Israel—and did not transfer property ownership from individuals to the state.

The Gospels and Epistles are similarly remarkably free of economic policy recommendations. Indeed, writes the late Paul Heyne, a professor at the University of Washington, "What we do find in the New Testament is an extraordinary disregard for almost everything in which economists are interested." In the absence of a holy ideology, then, the question is more subtle: What kind of economic system is consistent with Christian moral, and particularly biblical, principles?

D. Stephen Long surveys some of the literature on this issue and points, for one, to John Milbank. Long explains that for Milbank, "The gift God exchanges with creation through Christ must be the basis of all exchanges. Christianity opposes capitalism because the gift can never be reduced to a contract with nicely calculated profit/ loss ratios where individuals enter into exchanges without being fundamentally changed by those exchanges. The Christian life requires a gift economy in which a return is always expected—as it should be when one gives gifts—but never one that can be calculated such that the contract terminates and the relationship dissolves."

Catholic philosopher Alasdair MacIntyre, another thinker to whom Long points, makes a somewhat different claim. As Long explains, MacIntyre believes that the "injustices" of "commercial and industrial capitalism" are "both individual and systemic: individual, because capitalism rewards not virtue but vice, allowing vicious persons to benefit at the expense of virtue itself, systemic, because at the origin of all accumulation in capitalism are 'gross inequalities in the initial appropriation of capital.' Capitalism also pits workers against owners, and it refuses to acknowledge legitimate moral teachings on just wages and just prices."

Alas, such arguments can only be made by those who see all economic systems through a glass darkly, if at all. In fact, most participants in a market economy make decisions notable for their complexity and based on many variables other than material. Otherwise there would be no theologians living in a capitalist economy, no seminaries training former businessmen to be priests, no people marrying for love, no parents sacrificing for their children or children sacrificing for their parents. As Max Stackhouse and Lawrence Stratton write: "To hold that nothing more than material interests or the laws of survival or the drive to dominate others determines all that people do economically represents a thin, even cynical understanding of human nature."

At the same time, there has never been a socialist system that operated on any principle approaching "God's gift"; nor has any such system succeeded in suppressing human (class) conflict or in implementing anything bordering on "just" wages and prices. Indeed, if there is a system that encourages brutal materialism, turns politics into a winner-takes-all war for total social control, and discourages humane cooperation, it is socialism, along with less complete forms of political control over the economy. The competition is not between a capitalism that reflects human frailties and a socialism that reflects human perfection, but two imperfect systems. And history has dramatically demonstrated which system is more likely to murder, starve, impoverish, and oppress its own population.

This, then, makes Long's conclusion so curious. "If socialism holds forth the possibility that workers can share ownership in their labor in a noncompetitive system in which the interests of owners, shareholders, and workers need not—by some necessity of a natural social fact—be pitted against each other, then yes, Christianity must continue to hold forth the possibility of socialism and work for the abolition of capitalism." Yet socialism, by concentrating power and surrendering the economy to political control, intensifies social competition and conflict.

In fact, only in capitalist systems, in which the economy is owned and managed privately, does one find the sort of positive institutions that Long desires. Indeed, only a private economy provides room for nonconformists to create their own forms of human community, including business as well as social relationships that can operate on principles far different than the marketplace norm. Such approaches will arise only if Long and those who think like him convince people that their way offers a better expression of Christian or (more generally) humane values. And such approaches will find expression only if people have the freedom to act on their changing and perhaps unpopular values.

Controlling capitalists

More realistic than calls for socialism are critics' more limited arguments for taming rather than eliminating capitalism, arguments motivated by the belief that the profit motive must be chastened or reformed. It is common to hear calls for regulation and income redistribution along the lines of an enhanced but modernized welfare state.

In discussing capitalism it is important to distinguish a competitive market economy from systems that merely allow some private property ownership. Kleptocracies and crony capitalist regimes circle the globe; particularly obscene are many African and Latin American governments, which have long used political power to exploit their populations for the benefit of rapacious elites. Such systems are far closer to socialism than capitalism, however, since they involve pervasive government economic control. Open market economies are their antithesis.

Is there a biblical case for advocacy of the interventionist state in genuine market systems? Christ's message is clear: believers are not to place their faith in mammon or any of the other idols of this world. But while the Bible is long on injunctions involving man's relationship to God and his neighbors, as noted earlier, it says far less about the role of the state or economics. Just as there is nothing to suggest that the means of production should be placed in the hands of a coercive institution such as government, there is nothing to suggest doing the same with economic decision making. If there is an argument for doing so, it must be based on specific principles involving specific issues.

The plight of the poor

For instance, the most fundamental criticism of capitalism is that even with its seemingly complete victory there remains a prevalence of poverty amid plenty. In a world of seemingly exploding opportunity around the globe, far too many people have been left behind, even in the most advanced industrialized nations.

Yet liberal economics doesn't purport to solve poverty. It claims to reward economically those with economically valuable skills. Where such talents are not evident or exercised—whether through poor life choices, disability, or injustice—poverty will result. What is most striking, however, is that truly free market societies, in contrast to various statist systems, have performed best in enhancing the economic status of the vast majority of their citizens. Taiwan, for instance, has enjoyed a dramatic increase in literacy and life expectancy, and a more equal distribution of income, as it has expanded economically. In the U.S., those who are poor live far better than the bulk of the population in Third World nations. As Michael Novak observes, the assumption that non-capitalist systems offer better distributions of wealth "is clearly not true of the pre-capitalist Third World regimes of present-day Latin America, Africa, and Asia, in which inequalities of income are of enormous proportions, while for the poor opportunity scarcely exists. Nor was it true of communist societies, whose poor are now known to have lived in squalor and whose elites lived in closed circles of high privilege." Without production there is nothing to redistribute. Only in a capitalist economy may one meaningfully advocate private or public efforts to aid the needy.

Yet today the state does far more to harm than to help the poor. Indeed, much of the poverty in the U.S. is the result of government policy, often pursued at the behest of powerful special-interest groups. Labor unions back the minimum wage because it prices disadvantaged workers out of the marketplace. Occupational licensing makes it harder for poor people to enter a variety of trades, such as driving a cab. Trade barriers to protect privileged industries push up the cost of clothing, food, shoes, and a host of other goods. Antiquated building codes protect unionized construction jobs by increasing housing costs. Expansive government transfer programs enrich influential voting blocs—farmers, retirees, and the like—at the expense of the poor and middle class. And so on.

In a true market economy, those with the least influence can still gain access to economic opportunity. The more expansive government controls are, though, the more likely concentrated interest groups are to twist policy to their own ends—to the detriment of the most disadvantaged in society. This does not mean that the implementation of capitalism is enough for the creation of a just, and "Christian," society. Individuals and families, along with private mediating institutions—particularly charitable and fraternal associations, charities, and churches—play a critical role in helping those who, like the proverbial widows and orphans of the Old Testament, are unable to succeed in a market economy. Even public welfare programs are not intrinsically inconsistent with a generally free society, though the current system has proved to be socially destructive, subsidizing illegitimacy and family breakup and discouraging work and independence.

Christian responsibilities

Biblical theology clearly emphasizes the importance of voluntary, nonpolitical action. Christians are commanded to help the needy. Believers should demonstrate the same passion as did Jesus in reaching out to the poor, hungry, and homeless. All people should give generously. Perhaps no Scripture so sears the heart as Christ's pronouncement to the accursed: "I was hungry and you gave me nothing to eat, I was thirsty and you gave me nothing to drink, I was a stranger and you did not invite me in, I needed clothes and you did not clothe me, I was sick and in prison and you did not look after me" (Matthew 25:42, 43).

But the Bible includes no comparable injunction to use political authority to achieve these ends. People are to give financially, leave crops in their fields to be gleaned, ensure that their churches care for the needy, aid desperate sister congregations across the Mediterranean, and "do good to all people" (Galatians 6:10). The early Christians, at least in Jerusalem, shared their material goods with the needy in the community of faith. Yet no role for the political authorities is evident. In the Old Testament it is God who promises to do the judging, visiting good and bad consequences upon his people depending upon their obedience. Christ's followers appear never to have attempted to forcibly redistribute the assets of fellow believers, let alone non-Christians. Indeed, the Apostles consistently taught that giving was not mandatory, as it was under the law of the old covenant. Peter stated that members of the Jerusalem church had no obligation to sell their property and turn over the proceeds. Paul refused to command members of the Corinthian church to aid believers in Jerusalem. He makes a powerful appeal for alms, but emphasizes: "Each man should give what he has decided in his heart to give, not reluctantly or under compulsion, for God loves a cheerful giver" (2 Corinthians 9:7).

Of course, not everyone is a cheerful giver. What to do then?

The temptation to have government do the giving for them is obvious and understandable. Yet a faith that refuses to order its adherents to give not surprisingly provides little support for using the state to make others give. And the commandment against theft raises a caution about how easily coercive collective action might exceed its purported biblical authority. Indeed, today's mass-transfer state allows a multitude of special interests to loot the body politic—always in the name of the poor or the general public, of course.

Poverty, not income inequality

Thus, the case for political charity, if charity is the right word, is prudential, not theological. The biblical imperative is to help the poor. The prudential issue is whether this end can be achieved only with the involvement of the state (and if so, how much and what form of assistance is necessary). This is an important issue, hotly debated in state capitals and Washington, D.C., but it does not go to the essentials of liberal economics. One can simultaneously support a market economy and a government social safety net.

At the same time, one should not confuse the issues of poverty and income inequality. As Wheaton University economist Peter J. Hill argues, redistribution in this context "represents a harmful distortion of an appropriate and laudable human motive, a desire to help the infirm, the suffering, and the unfortunate." Poverty is a matter of overriding concern to the faith communities in both the Old and New Testaments. It is, indeed, impossible to imagine a serious biblical faith that does not incorporate provision for those in need.

Not so income redistribution. In any capitalist society—which distributes rewards based on economic, not moral, worth—incomes and wealth will range widely. Just as a market society does not purport to make all rich, it does not purport to make all equal. Yet income differences demonstrate nothing about levels of income or adequacy of income for those at the bottom.

Some clerics apparently see inequality per se as unacceptable. For instance, the British theologian Andrew Kirk claims that "[t]here is a Biblical imperative to redistribute wealth on a regular basis." Yet the Bible says nothing about the morality of income inequality. To the contrary, while filled with injunctions to care for the poor and needy, Scripture is notably silent on income redistribution. Oppression was rife in the Old and New Testament communities, but the problem was oppression; the resulting income inequality was only a symptom.

The Bible neither creates a personal duty to equalize wealth nor mandates government to engage in such a practice. Christians have a very clear duty to help the needy, but the Bible presents such transfers as a believer's obligation, not a beneficiary's right. In urging members of the Corinthian church to give generously, for instance, Paul pointed to the example of Christ, who "though he was rich, yet for your sakes he became poor, so that you through his poverty might become rich" (2 Corinthians 8:9). And the goal of such charitable transfers is not to equalize incomes, but to alleviate the recipient's physical poverty and promote the donor's spiritual growth. Paul instructed Timothy to command the wealthy "to be generous and willing to share. In this way they will lay up treasure for themselves as a firm foundation for the coming age, so that they may take hold of the life that is truly life" (1 Timothy 6:18–19).

Scripture also challenges all people to follow Christ rather than money; wealthy believers face an especially stiff challenge in avoiding the temptations posed by riches. But in the case of the rich young ruler, God's objective was not to reduce the man's income to achieve financial equality; the objective was to facilitate his salvation. "It is easier for a camel to go through the eye of a needle than for a rich man to enter the kingdom of God," explained Jesus (Matthew 19:24).

Nor does Scripture suggest that the biblical definition of justice includes redistributing income to promote equality. The rich are not to oppress the poor or acquire money through force, theft, or fraud; instead, the wealthy are to help the needy. There is no scriptural principle that mandates income transfers unrelated to procedural injustice or poverty alleviation. Even the Year of Jubilee is not about the redistribution of wealth but the redemption of family land. Sale prices were to be based on the number of years remaining until the Jubilee Year; in effect, the Bible provided for the leasing rather than the sale of God-given property. The underlying wealth of neither lessor or lessee was altered (Leviticus 25:14–17). In fact, God distributed the Promised Land unequally. The tribe of Joseph, for instance, complained that its allotment was too small (Joshua 17:14, 16).

Trite though the claim might seem, the most important equality is that of equality of opportunity and equality before the law. No biblical principle entitles one to possess as much as someone else possesses, irrespective of circumstance. What people are entitled to is the opportunity to seek as much as someone else and the legal protection of that opportunity.

The problem of envy

At least one powerful biblical principle should discourage forcible income transfers unrelated to helping the poor. Complaints about income distribution inevitably end up resting on envy. And redistributing wealth for the purpose of satisfying envy—where the issue is not that people lack shelter, but that their home isn't as big as someone else's—would seem to run afoul of the Tenth Commandment against covetousness: "You shall not covet your neighbor's house. You shall not covet your neighbor's wife, or his manservant or maidservant, his ox, or donkey, or anything that belongs to your neighbor" (Exodus 20:17). Indeed, writes Michael Novak, "the good Lord himself forbade covetousness five times in the Ten Commandments: envy is to be resisted."

Recall John's warning above about the dangers of loving the things of this world. A person who turns to government to seize the possessions of his richer neighbors, no less than a man who devotes his life to making money in the marketplace, has fallen in love with the world. Although religious advocates of redistribution may not be motivated by greed, the political demands that resonate in Washington, D.C., and across the nation in election years are consistently fueled not by a commitment to a just economic order, but by an angry demand that the candidate's potential supporters get a bigger share of the economic pie.

Nevertheless, are there prudential reasons to engage in widespread income transfers? For instance, Danny Collum, an editor of

Sojourners, once complained that "the gross inequalities of wealth and poverty in the U.S. are the natural result of a social, political, and economic system that places the maximization of private profit above all other social goals. The human, social, cultural, and spiritual benefits that would result from a more just distribution of wealth and power will never show up on the all-important quarterly profit and loss statement." The benefits of aiding the needy in improving social stability, if nothing else, are obvious. Not so the gains from engaging in sustained (inequality results from an ongoing series of free choices) and intrusive (the wider the redistribution, the tougher the enforcement necessary) campaign to ensure that no one earns more than anyone else, or some arbitrary level, or a multiple of some average figure, or whatever standard is set.

In the end, abstract income and wealth distributions say nothing about justice, fairness, poverty, or contentment. There is much injustice in the world. Many people the world over suffer the horrors of premature death, hideous suffering, and degraded lives. Many more reject God and the blessings that he has prepared for them. None of these result from the simple fact that some people are richer than others.

In fact, a focus on wealth distribution obscures the more fundamental issue of poverty. Compared with Bill Gates, the average middle manager in corporate America is little better off than a desperate refugee in the Sudan. Yet their situations cannot be compared.

The poorest people in a rich society are likely to be better off than everyone but the wealthiest in a poor society. Peter J. Hill compares India and the U.S., for instance. In relative terms, the poor in the former own more than the poor in the latter. But no serious Christian could suggest that the human needs in the latter are greater and require greater attention. What is a generous believer to do? Try to move middle-class Americans closer to their rich compatriots in order to improve abstract measures of income distribution? Or provide food, clothes, and shelter to those who have none?

Counterproductive politics

There are powerful practical reasons not to use political means to redistribute wealth. Poverty is a complex phenomenon because it has more than one cause. Its causes include not only personal infirmity and imperfect social structures; much poverty also results from poor individual decisions—drug use, criminal activity, premature pregnancy, excessive spending. And individual differences play an even greater role in generating income inequality.

Income will inevitably be unequal because people are unequal. At issue is not just natural ability but ambition and personal preference. If the larger social order, particularly the economic rules of the game, are just—and admittedly this is an important and controversial "if"—then the resulting economic distribution should not be regarded as morally suspect. Where inequalities result from injustice, the injustice should be addressed because it is unjust, not because there are inequalities.

Dubious also is the mechanism to be used to redistribute income. Defining poverty is hard enough. Even relative income and relative wealth can differ substantially (the elderly have more of the latter than the former). There is no moral principle defining what constitutes an appropriate income. Moreover, the demand for redistribution is in principle unending. So long as people are free to choose how much and where to work, where to invest, and how to spend what they earn, even if incomes were forcibly equalized today they would be different tomorrow and even more different the day after. After all, you could give away all of Michael Jordan's and Barbra Streisand's money today, and tonight people will make them rich again by voluntarily paying to watch them perform.

Moreover, forcibly redistributing income is itself socially expensive. As Hill observes, "The achievement of greater economic equality can only come with the creation of great political inequality. Only when the coercive power of government is extended into numerous private spheres of action can substantial gains in material equality be realized." This process will create disincentives to innovate and work. Some people get rich by entertaining the rest of us, whether by acting or throwing a football. Others do so by creating a product, such as a car or copying machine or software. In a fallen world, money is an important motivator, and we would all be worse off if people with special gifts were unwilling to put them to use because they were unable to reap a financial reward for doing so. Expropriating their earnings to satisfy the envy of a few would impoverish our culture and lower our standard of living—while making all of us less free.

Finally, human experience gives little reason to believe that those in the greatest need will either control the redistributive process or use it fairly. There certainly is scriptural reason to be skeptical of proposals to concentrate economic power in the government's hands. Most importantly, the Christian faith recognizes that all human institutions are flawed and that sinful men will act sinfully. Consider the Apostle John's vision in Revelation of a hideous "Beast" with expansive power, including power over people's economic affairs (no one could buy or sell anything without the Beast's mark).

Less apocalyptic but nevertheless equally striking is the prophet Samuel's warning when the Israelites ask God for a king:

> He will take your sons and make them serve with his chariots and horses, and they will run in front of his chariots. Some he will assign to be commanders of thousands and commanders of fifties, and others to plow his ground and reap his harvest, and still others to make weapons of war and equipment for his chariots. He will take your daughters to be perfumers and cooks and bakers. He will take the best of your fields and vineyards and olive groves and give them to his attendants. He will take a tenth of your grain and of your vintage and give it to his officials and attendants. Your menservants and maidservants and the best of your cattle and donkeys he

will take for his own use. He will take a tenth of your flocks, and you yourselves will become his slaves. When that day comes, you will cry out for relief from the king you have chosen, and the Lord will not answer you in that day. (1 Samuel 8:11–18)

This warning could be changed only slightly to describe democratic politics in most wealthy industrialized societies. The only difference is that in these democracies the king is periodically elected.

It must also be remembered that economic liberty is a prerequisite for other freedoms. Countries such as South Korea and Taiwan used market economies to prosper; demands for political reform then naturally grew with the development of a middle class no longer focused on avoiding starvation. Capitalist reforms in China have helped create a more prosperous population, which has grown increasingly restive under traditional communist political controls. Market-driven prosperity has also helped spread tools of freedom—computers, cell phones, faxes, automobiles.

Economic freedom also is important because it helps disperse power, allowing the development of private institutions—associations, corporations, think tanks, labor unions, universities, and churches, for instance—that can counterbalance state power. Private property is necessary for the exercise of many political rights. If you cannot buy a printing press or TV station, hire a hall, or sell newspapers, you have no freedom of the press. The personal computer, necessary for economic progress but a potentially devastating weapon in the hands of dissidents, was the great conundrum for communism.

Even the more moderate wealth redistribution practiced in the U.S. has tended to concentrate benefits on the politically dominant middle class and influential interest groups. Social Security and Medicare, for instance, overwhelmingly benefit the middle class. A range of programs, from loan guarantees to export subsidies to free services, underwrite businesses of all sorts. Welfare for middle- and upper-income people, who vote in greater proportions and fund campaigns to a greater extent, is much more expensive than is welfare for the poor.

Market sterility

Nevertheless, however sound the economics of market capitalism and however strong the argument that poverty and inequality do not constitute injustice, free markets embody a spiritual sterility that understandably bothers many religious people. Indeed, some contend that markets embody an anti-religious spirit. Argues Adrian Walker in this volume: "the claim that the market is neutral with respect to the question of the objective good of the person is nothing more than a cover for liberalism's imposition of a definite, decidedly liberal paradigm of economic freedom." As a result, he claims, "The shift from communion to contract effectively puts financial gain in the place of the objective good of the person as the immanent finality of economic exchange."

The claim is that the existence of the market predetermines people's mode of participation. Contends Walker: "So-called neutrality really means that a contractual exchange indifferent to the objective good of the person has been enshrined as the paradigm of economic freedom." Indeed, one form of poverty, he writes, is the "conception of oneself as having to produce on [instrumentalist] terms," a conception advanced by liberal economics. Similarly, British theologian Andrew Kirk contends that capitalism assumes "that the main purpose of man's life is the pursuit of happiness to be achieved by the constant expansion of goods and services" and that this pursuit is thereby "the basis of our daily political and economic life."

David Crawford applies the same lesson more broadly to the family: "While appearing to secure the family's liberty to constitute a certain type of community, therefore, liberal institutions in fact displace the familial or creaturely sense of freedom with their own abstract conception of freedom. . . . Thus, an inversion takes place, in which the family tends to mimic the structures of the free market, even while the role of the family, as the most fundamental 'cell' of society, is to instill its nonliberal sense of freedom and community into the public order."

These are serious charges. Undoubtedly, some people advocate a radical form of autonomy in which human and community bonds are few, if any. Crawford writes of a "liberal abstraction of freedom from community and love." This abstraction is, as Sam Gregg admits, a rejection of Christian anthropology. However, it is an abstraction that seems divorced from the real world, at best an analytic tool used to try to predict human behavior.

After all, few people in even the most market-oriented societies actually order their lives along such narrow economicist lines, concerned only with "restless profit-seeking," in Walker's words. Most people marry, raise children, go to seminary, forge friendships, volunteer their time, care for their elderly parents, and pursue hobbies for completely different reasons. Some explicitly and many implicitly are attempting to pursue the ultimate good. And many—if not as many as we would like—attempt to make their economic decisions conform to that pursuit. Liberal economics is not to blame for the fact that some do not try and others who try fail. If liberal economics was so effective in shaping behavior, its quasi-coercive mechanism should be visible and have more pervasive results.

Indeed, at some level even Walker seems to acknowledge that practical economic processes do not reflect the theoretical failures that he perceives: "To the extent that modern Western economies have in fact 'worked" and continue to 'work,' they have not done so for the reasons claimed by liberal economics, but rather because they unconfessedly rely on an integration of economic activity with a fuller sense of person and community that liberal economic theory nonetheless logically undermines." Similarly, although Crawford makes a highly specific claim about the impact of liberal economics on the family, he offers little explanation and few examples as to how this process works. Contrary to his contention that we have witnessed an "easy slide in which family relations themselves are reinterpreted in terms of free-market principles," most families continue to operate radically against market principles as social communes centered around loving relationships. If family economic enterprise is less common today, it has been less common in almost all modern societies, socialist, communist, and capitalist.

Indeed, coercive political-economic systems are far more likely to attempt to impose a non-Christian anthropology on families—consider the socialist collectivization of agriculture, even more relentlessly destructive of the family farm than market capitalism. As Crawford himself acknowledges in dissociating his "sense of community" from anything found within socialism or communism: "freedom arises in community because of its nature as a fundamental openness to another person, while community also requires freedom (because genuine community requires an active 'letting be' or 'making space'). In collectivism, on the other hand, freedom is simply subordinated to 'community.'"

Walker goes on to argue persuasively that the problem of poverty is very much one of meaning. But this lack of meaning has been evident in all systems and societies. Traditional agrarianism and materialistic communism no less than laissez-faire capitalism have left people believing themselves to be merely economic agents. The unseemly desire for wealth and material pleasure and a distressing lack of concern for the good and virtuous life reflect human, not economic, failings. Liberal economics allows, but does not mandate, the displacement of what Walker calls "the objective good of the person," or "ontological wealth." It is government, in fact, that is much more likely to be completely devoid of vital spiritual dynamics, which is probably the most important reason why political programs do so poorly in addressing poverty.

Much the same can be said in response to V. Bradley Lewis's application of Aristotle, particularly Aristotle's view of unnatural acquisition, to the economy. Lewis points to potential problems caused by economic practices regarding marriage and the university, though in the latter case he identifies the desire for federal funding, the very antithesis of free-market practice, as the problem. However, the broader issue he broaches is nothing less than modernity itself, and hence almost every contemporary economic institution. Suppressing liberal economics offers little hope for dealing with the problem of modernity, though. Lewis himself acknowledges that "[a]ttempts to use the power of the state to implement antimodern political programs are themselves one of the most terrible manifestations of political modernity."

The very necessity of the poor understanding the "fuller sense of person and community" of which Walker writes demonstrates not that liberal economics is at fault, but that it is not enough, just as government transfer programs have demonstrated that they are not enough (and, indeed, are often counterproductive) in helping the poor. Liberal economics merely allows people to think of themselves in a certain way; it does not make them do so, nor would making the economy illiberal cause them to cease doing so.

The curse of modernity

Although some economic institutions seem more characteristic of capitalism than socialism, the deeper human issues remain common to both. It is thus with "the shopping mall and the rest-stop Burger King" that Walker finds so objectionable. These institutions exist because people want them, not because liberal economics demands them. I have found the trappings of Western consumerism even among ethnic (and Christian) Karen living in primitive villages in the jungles of eastern Burma.

Thus, while confronting human sin is difficult in any society, in his essay Michael Novak demonstrates how liberal economics may aid in providing the right answers. We live in a global system that is increasingly organized along "liberal" lines. Yet it emphasizes the immaterial part of economic success more than ever before. It creates a form of solidarity with people who live thousands of miles away. At the same time, the concept of subsidiarity is gaining new life, as "today many diverse local forces are stirring and coming again to life." And the indisputable productivity of liberal economics is helping to alleviate the desperate material needs that so degrade the poor.

In another way, the market rewards honesty and trustworthiness. Although the corrupt will always find ways to enrich themselves, corruption in a market is usually exposed and punished. Entire companies, such as Arthur Andersen, were destroyed by employees, customers, and suppliers fleeing to more honest competitors. Similar, and even more pervasive, corruption has been much harder to root out in statist systems, for example, in companies run by well-connected elites in communist China or kleptocratic Third World regimes.

William Cavanaugh comes at liberal economics in a slightly different way. He views freedom as being more than the lack of coercion, putting forth the Augustinian notion of "freedom *for*, a capacity to achieve certain worthwhile goals." Few Christian advocates of the market would disagree. For instance, Sam Gregg also rejects the belief that choice alone defines our freedom: "Not surprisingly, the Christian vision of man directs us to rather different conclusions than those of Friedman and Marx when it comes to understanding the *end* of individual autonomy."

That freedom itself is a rich concept, encompassing much more than the lack of coercion, is not itself a critique of liberal economics. True, what has been called "the permissive society" has resulted at least in part from the spread of capitalism. Yet Singapore combines a market system with intensive social regulation, including a ban on chewing gum. In fact, the most serious challenge to a Christian anthropology comes from modernity in all of its manifestations. The twentieth century demonstrates that coercive, collectivist systems undermine pursuit of virtue and the good life much more than do capitalist systems. As Arthur Davis shows, even the "Red Tory" George

Grant was critical of socialist collectivism. Capitalism may be better at generating new technology, but that is not for want of trying on the part of socialism.

The fact that Christian theology teaches that there are worthwhile transcendent goals does not mean that human society would be improved by widespread economic coercion. Indeed, the state, even if it is so inclined, can only suppress public manifestations of sin, while it is the heart about which God is most concerned. Cavanaugh himself points to God rather than the state as the ultimate "Other" who frees us and expresses a preference for "nonviolent witness" as the best method of persuasion.

The solution, then, lies not with the defenestration of liberal economics, but in looking without the market to shape behavior within, to construct a better moral environment within which to nestle a capitalist system. How to think of the human person, what objectives to set as a priority, what balance to strike between the conditions of virtue and material profit—liberal economics will never offer its participants a Christian answer to such questions. It will never provide full Christian freedom. Yet, as Stackhouse and Stratton observe, "economic activity is always embedded in moral and religious convictions that are meaningful to economic actors, and in matrices of social institutions that are shaped both by such convictions and by material necessities."

Again, consider technology. Like all human creations it can be used for ill as well as good. Thus, technological progress should not be taken as an inevitable good, or even a likely neutral. Yet Stackhouse and Stratton show that Christianity has long embraced technology to advance the good. It is not progress, or even the accelerated progress under capitalism that threatens us, but the theological deracination of progress: "it is quite likely that technology could become a peril and not a resource for the human future if its spiritual roots are neglected as a regulatory moral guide to its use," they warn. Appropriately, theologians now are confronting technological issues more closely. Richard John Neuhaus points to Pope John Paul II's encyclical *Evangelium Vitae* ("The Gospel of Life"), which addresses biotechnology. Writes Neuhaus, "[T]he Church must contend for politics as such against all determinisms, whether ideological, economic, or technological."

Capitalist excesses

The unique features of capitalism seem most to upset serious Christians, including some of the contributors to this volume. For instance, one of the hallmarks of a relatively unregulated market economy is the abundance of goods and the conspicuous consumption that often ensues. It should come as no surprise to anyone who believes in original sin that some people will use their liberty to go grievously wrong.

Yet fecundity normally is not seen as an infirmity. The poverty produced by Marxism did not generate religiosity, for instance. Indeed, most collectivist systems have proved to be profoundly materialistic; political life in such societies always revolved around gaining access to a relatively small pool of consumer goods. Thus the avariciousness of the nomenklatura and the ruling elite and the ubiquitous lines in the one-time communist world. The average citizen of a socialist state does not care any less about possessing shoes, washing machines, VCRs, and cars than does an American; he is simply less able to satisfy his desires.

Related is the issue of freedom of choice. The very multiplicity of economic endeavors that so antagonizes critics of market economies is taken by some, including Wendell Berry, to mean that real choice does not exist. At the very least, it is said, not everyone has equal choices, and the options facing the poor in poor countries are often highly constrained. Britain's Andrew Kirk will not even admit that capitalism promotes liberty. A market economy, he writes, "certainly increases the freedom of some, but always and inevitably at the expense of the freedom of others."

Yet to suppress liberal economics would reduce freedom for all. It is no solution to the problem of poverty to deny people, especially the powerless, the few options provided by a liberal economy. It is especially scandalous for those living in the wealthy West to essentially tell, say, Chinese or Indian peasants, no matter how sick, poor, and vulnerable, to simply and happily accept whatever their local politicians deliver in the way of a local economy.

Another, related argument is that capitalism relies on destructive competition rather than constructive cooperation. Berry simultaneously denies that much competition exists in our economy and claims that it is characterized by a highly destructive war that inevitably yields only one producer. That analysis would surprise most automakers, fast food chains, health clubs, shoe stores, supermarkets, and other businesses, which day in and day out are surrounded by vigorous competitors. Perhaps Berry envisions a process occurring not over years, decades, or even centuries, but millennia.

Competition is obviously important to a market economy, and has been evident in most industries at most times—absent the sort of government protection ironically advocated by Berry. True, there are losers, else no company would go bankrupt, but competition has proved to be an extraordinarily valuable social tool. Private monopolies usually break down quickly due to competition, unless they have government support. Competition drives down the price of consumer goods, enabling even people of modest incomes to acquire clothing, food, and shelter. And competition has driven innovators to constantly seek to design better products that cost less.

Yet while competition is a pillar of capitalism, so is cooperation. For only through extensive cooperation—among entrepreneurs, customers, financiers, suppliers, and workers—can a business succeed. In a system of state control politicians can impose their dreams on reluctant citizens, empowering companies to force their products on reluctant buyers, to extract financial resources from reluctant citizens, to extract supplies from reluctant producers, and to mandate

work from reluctant employees. While money may seem a crass in-
ducement, it is less crass than coercion. Finally, many firms, in which
people group together voluntarily, generate an esprit de corps that
reflects a variety of nonmaterial values.

Another much-criticized aspect of capitalism is advertising, a
concern articulated in this volume by Cavanaugh. Yet while advertising may draw people towards particular kinds of goods and brand names
by letting them know of their availability, it is hardly necessary to
make people want things. As noted earlier, people routinely lined up
for goods in communist economies, and the ruling elites in communist countries gorged themselves on Western products. Moreover, advertising does not guarantee sales: huge companies have found that
even multi-billion-dollar marketing campaigns can leave money-los-
ing Edsels in their wake. Once-dominant and wealthy companies,
such as Montgomery Ward, frequently fail in the face of new competition. If the essential issue at the heart of the critique of capitalism is
materialism, then capitalism's "fault" is that it better meets material
demands, not that it generates such demands.

Spiritual answers from without

It is still necessary to find a spiritual answer, and that spiritual answer must come from without. Forcibly abrogating liberal economics
is not a realistic answer. Set aside all of the problems regnant with
political action. Political action won't occur without a dramatic
change in public attitudes, and if that occurs political action won't
be necessary. George Grant, for one, argued: "If protest is to be
effective in this era, if we are to be successful in creating space for
human spontaneity in the iron maiden of the technological apparatus we have created, then it is essential that those who are in the
vanguard of the protest combine their action with the deepest and
most careful thought."

That thought can, and should, be shaped by a Christian understanding of man. Richard John Neuhaus points to *Centesimus*

Annus, which, he writes, "is about the free society, including economic freedom." It is a document that almost all acknowledge is favorable towards—though not uncritically accepting of—a market economy.

Certainly D. Stephen Long is quite right in demanding that theologians not treat the current economic structure as self-legitimizing. They must, in Long's words, "pursue the dogmatic task that is theology." And if they do it well, we will all benefit. But to do it well requires an understanding of economics as well as theology.

Of course, Long argues that "[t]o read economics theologically is within the proper competence of the theologian. To read theology through the lens of an economist is not." True, yet the application of theology to economics is not so obvious as Long would have us believe. For instance, he offers the example of a Honduran company whose workers remain in poverty while its owners prosper. "This was (and is) clearly an unjust situation. No theologian (I hope) would intentionally defend these kinds of exploitative practices; for, insofar as God and Scripture still matter, these practices cannot be justified." Later he exclaims: "For those of us who stand within the Christian tradition, it is obviously wicked."

But it is not enough to simply pronounce the situation Long describes as unjust and wicked. In what way is it indefensible? How can the company's practices be said to be corrupt and the wages paid be said to be unjust? The mere fact that the owners are wealthier than the workers demonstrates nothing nefarious; that situation could have resulted from entrepreneurial insight and the honest investment of money fairly earned, resulting in the creation of a company that pays market wages as promised and benefits that may well exceed any comparable ones in the community, region, or even nation. Such an enterprise, operating in a sea of poverty, is no less "positive," to use Long's standard, than the typical firm operating in America. Nothing in the process he describes is necessarily unjust.

Charity versus justice

Nevertheless, the situation is unacceptable. Long rightly says that it should not be accepted as a "social fact." Our Christian conscience should cry out, but it should cry out for charity—the duty of those to whom much has been given to aid those in great need. The rich should give because God wants them to be obedient to him and generous to their neighbors, not because their possession of wealth means that they have sinned in their economic relations.

Indeed, one will have trouble finding God or the prophets applying Long's analysis to biblical conditions far more difficult than the ones he posits. There is much scriptural denunciation of injustice, but the injustice was not that rich people employed poor people, but that rich people exploited the poor, using their superior power to seize property, refusing to pay wages that were due, or levying tribute. The wealthy also refused to help the needy, but the biblical authors never describe this refusal as an inherent failure of capitalism to be remedied by turning ownership or control over to the king and his court. After all, more often than not the king and his court were the exploiters (or were in league with the exploiters). Samuel's warning to the Israelites well illustrates what would likely result by employing a political strategy for relief.

William Cavanaugh makes a different critique, complaining that the ability of transnational corporations to shift production demonstrates their disproportionate power compared with that of workers. Yet corporate "power" is in fact highly constrained by labor unions (consider the airline industry), the need for highly trained employees (consider software development), and the importance of a stable political and legal environment (consider the persistence of U.S. manufacturing, which has retained a stable share of GDP over the past thirty years, despite the availability of low-cost alternatives overseas). Moreover, this power, as he calls it, benefits the poorest workers in the poorest nations, unless he thinks that they would be better off remaining impoverished peasants or unemployed urban dwellers rather than workers in foreign-owned factories.

In fact, Daniel Griswold demonstrates how international commerce helps alleviate international poverty. Trade and investment that are free are consistent with Christian ethics and bring the isolated poor into the global circle of exchange. That the poor have fewer options than the rich does not demonstrate that trade is unfair, but that those concerned about the poor should help expand their opportunities—as do trade and investment. Powerful transnational corporations provide capital, transfer technology, offer training, and pay above-average wages.

Max Stackhouse and Lawrence Stratton bring similar arguments and evidence to bear on this issue. They cite economists Stephen Parente and Edward Prescott, who looked at the benefits of eliminating international trade barriers: "The gains from such practices are huge, not 1 or 2 percent, but 1,000 or 2,000 percent. There is no reason why the whole world should not be as rich as the leading industrialized country." Indeed, growth in the poorest countries accelerated faster than that in the industrialized world in the 1990s, which was the decade of globalization. Periodic financial crises should not obscure the escape of hundreds of millions of people, particularly in East and South Asia, from extreme, debilitating poverty.

This does not mean that the complicated, stressful, and disruptive process of development, in which societies move from being traditional to industrialized, is easy. To the contrary, as Stackhouse and Stratton acknowledge, the poor and powerless are often ill-prepared for change, and that change is best accomplished "when the other decisive spheres of civil society—educational, medical, political, legal, and especially religious—are also open, developed, and accessible to all." But to blame capitalism in general and globalization in particular for Third World poverty is to blame the primary engine of poverty relief.

Wendell Berry goes further, attacking most every feature commonly associated with industrial capitalism. As a screed that reflects profound philosophical and spiritual unease with modern economies, socialist as well as capitalist, his essay should cause serious reflection. As evidence of how some market critics blame statist policies, such as crop price supports, high military spending, and even war, on liberal economics, it should encourage market advocates to more carefully delineate what they represent. But as a blueprint for transforming society it falls far short.

Berry's charges are common but often contradictory, and they are usually disconnected from economic reality. For instance, the modern market economy has generated myriad benefits for mankind. Higher yields of lower-cost foods have made it easier to feed the starving poor throughout the world; the greatest enemy of peasant farmers in developing states is local governments that steal their crops, not foreign corporations that purchase them. Increasing productivity based on mechanization has reduced the cost of goods while allowing people to move into new industries, making all better off—otherwise living standards would not have improved so dramatically over the decades and centuries. These advances yield not just material wealth, but better health and safety, which is why infant mortality is falling and life expectancy is rising most quickly in poor nations.

Advances such as laser scanning are being used to preserve and repair archaeological and cultural treasures. Wealth and technology even yield better environmental protection, the ability to produce more food with less land, make more goods with less energy, drive more miles with less gasoline, and strain more pollutants out of lower emissions. Finally, however principled a philosopher like Berry may be, nothing in human experience in any government at any time suggests that his prescriptions would be adopted without the normal corruption intrinsic to any political process.

Repealing modernity

Indeed, what Wendell Berry wants to repeal is not capitalism, but modernity, since collectivist economics varies little from liberal economics in the areas that he criticizes. He is not alone—technology critic Jeremy Rifkin and others have extolled the virtues of the medieval world. What Berry seems to desire is the sort of community that existed in premodern times.

However, the perceived benefits of this sort of community cannot be considered without looking at its costs, now often lost in the rosy depiction of simple rural life, a life so hideous to those who lived it that they eagerly fled to the industrialized city in order to escape. It is easy today to advocate "neighborhood and subsistence" as long as the outside global economy supplies what would otherwise be unavailable. But such a local economy would be much more problematic without the escape hatch of a society informed by liberal economics surrounding it. As Stackhouse and Stratton observe, "free market systems compare favorably to hunter-gatherer, nomadic, subsistence, village, feudal, mercantilist, liberationist, or modern 'statist' systems of political economy" in providing "the best opportunity for individual human development and for increasing the social participation of groups living in poverty."

Moreover, modernity's excesses should be blamed not on corporations, the target of so many darts within and without this volume, but on people. It is the latter who shop at Wal-Mart, which Berry disdains, because it offers a better selection, at lower cost, than the small shops he prefers. People of moderate income are especially fond of Wal-Mart: the choices and low prices offered there obviously most benefit those who earn the least, just as protectionist tariffs most hurt the same people. It is ironic that someone as antagonistic towards business as Berry would advocate one of the tools advocated by business, especially large corporations, to help management and shareholders at the expense of lower-income American consumers and impoverished foreign producers.

Indeed, the entire effort to assess corporations theologically is problematic. There may very well be theological roots for the corporate form of association, as Stackhouse and Stratton argue. But like all human institutions, business enterprises have impacts both good and ill. Within them people can choose to exercise or not exercise the Christian virtues.

The relevant moral agent is the human being. Corporations do not act so much as people act. The challenge, then, is how participants in corporations should act. Even Long acknowledges that firms "can be a faithful form of discipleship." And the more faithfully firms are directed, the less likely that we will see develop the sort of problem to which Walker points: a raw and pure economism driving actors within the marketplace. But the temptation afforded by corporate enterprises is no different than the temptation afforded by small businesses, professional partnerships, nonprofit organizations, and even families. Participants in all these institutions need moral guidance that is not likely to be available from the market as such.

Perhaps the greatest threat posed by any modern economic system, socialist or capitalist (but especially capitalist), is the abundance of temptation it provides. The family and community are under attack, and certain attributes of industrial society, particularly the increased wealth and mobility that are its consequences, may undercut those institutions by multiplying arenas of individual choice, including arenas in which people may choose to do ill. This is another reason why religious leaders should emphasize that the exercise of freedom must reflect a broader understanding of the human person. For instance, Gregg writes of an individualism that "means an appreciation of the role of individual choice in enabling a person to choose the good, assume responsibility for himself, and thereby fulfill himself as a person." This sort of individualism "expresses a truth about man that Christianity has always affirmed."

Promoting two freedoms

The Christian truth about man is best promoted by defending the two different forms of freedom: liberty from coercion; and liberty to avoid sin and engage in worthwhile behavior, as Cavanaugh puts it. The importance of the second type of liberty is explored by Jennifer Roback Morse in her essay. How may one care for the needy, in this case a dying mother-in-law, in a liberal economic order? Contrary to what Crawford might fear and expect, Morse the free-market professor, relying on virtues instilled from outside the market order, chose love and family over profitable publicity tours and efficient institutionalized care.

In a similar vein, Gregg explains that

> [t]he free choices we make in the economic realm are not somehow isolated from all those actions, customs, and institutions that constitute the totality of human culture. If, therefore, individual choices are informed predominantly, for example, by a moral ecology of materialism or what many Christians call the culture of death, then their acts will reflect materialistic priorities and concerns. Yet the same logic suggests that if individual choices are influenced by a moral ecology grounded in a vision of man as the *imago Dei,* then we may have greater confidence that such choices will be directed to the realization of moral good.

However, what constitutes proper moral behavior often will not be as obvious as some market critics seem to assume. For instance, Cavanaugh complains that the market drives "the search for cheap labor." Yes, but it mandates nothing. Every day businessmen make nonmarket decisions, whether giving to a local symphony or keeping on staff a worker of declining productivity. Apparently Cavanaugh wants charity carried out under the guise of business—paying above-market wages, for instance.

There's nothing wrong with such an approach, but nothing mandatory about it either. There is no objective "just" wage. After all, consider the possible standards: what the richest industrialized economy pays, what the average industrialized economy pays, what is necessary for some local minimum individual standard of living, what is necessary for some local minimum family standard of living, what the average theologian thinks the average corporation should pay in the abstract, etc. Instead of expecting business to act charitably, it makes more sense to look outside the market and expect owners, shareholders, executives, and workers to fulfill their responsibilities as moral agents responsible to God, to share what they have been given with the less fortunate around them.

This human, rather than business, duty includes being better stewards of economic resources as consumers. Theologians could even make the case for the "idea of local economy" propounded by Wendell Berry. After all, he discourages his readers from thinking that the solution to what he perceives as an "environmental crisis" is political and advocates that his principles "be practiced not by our proxyholders, but by ourselves." Similarly, Cavanaugh writes, "From a Christian point of view, the churches should take an active role in fostering economic practices that are consonant with the true ends of creation." To do so is not contrary to capitalism, but fully consistent with it, since the economy is but a constituent part of a free society that seeks to provide space for the fulfillment of the full diversity of human goals.

It would be far better, then, to educate participants in the liberal economic order than to attempt to abrogate that order. Leaven freedom with truth. Yes, this remains seemingly unsatisfying, since, writes Neuhaus "the Church can only propose its truth, putting the gospel on the marketplace as one consumer item among others." But is there truly an alternative? Christians, and the Christian church, can use the broad freedom afforded by a liberal society to encourage the members of that society to embrace the richer, saving freedom of faith. But given a human history so filled with the horrors of statist rule, occasionally employed by religious authorities for their own ends, religious believers should not abrogate the one freedom in an attempt to impose the other.

Thus, Neuhaus warns against pitting "modern individualism against a more organic Catholic understanding of community." His objection is practical as well as philosophical: "The danger of rejecting individualism is that the real-world alternative is not a Catholic understanding of *communio* but a falling back into the collectivisms that are the great enemy of the freedom to which we are called." We must not allow politics itself to become an idol, "'a secular religion' which operates under the illusion of creating paradise in this world," as *Centesiumus Annus* warns. The dangers of such an approach are clear—if we have learned anything about power, it is that Lord Acton's aphorism that "power tends to corrupt, and absolute power corrupts absolutely" is true. A good society requires the political accountability and democracy of which Neuhaus writes, which are sustainable only in a liberal economic order in which a substantial civil and economic society exists that is able to counterbalance political power.

There is danger even in attempting to deploy more modest levels of coercion within a democratic polity. First, the resort to coercion typically mistakes the symptom for the disease. Two questions seem obvious: Are we less virtuous because we have become more free, and would becoming less free make America more virtuous? The answers to both questions would seem to be no.

The natural human condition, as taught in Christian theology and by historical experience, is not one of virtue. "There is no one righteous, not even one," Paul wrote in his letter to the Roman church, citing the Psalms (Romans 3.10). Our fallenness is why a transcendent plan of redemption is necessary.

But societies can be more or less virtuous. Did ours become less so *because* government no longer tried so hard to mold souls? Blaming moral shifts on legal changes mistakes correlation for causation.

In the area of sexual mores, for instance, America's one-time cultural consensus eroded during an era of strict laws against homosexuality, pornography, and even fornication. Cracks in this consensus led to changes in the law. In short, as more people viewed sexual mores as a matter of taste rather than morals, the moral underpinnings of the laws collapsed, followed by the laws themselves. Only a renewed moral consensus could allow the reestablishment of such laws.

But government is not a particularly good teacher of virtue. The state tends to be effective at simple, blunt tasks, like killing and jailing people. It has been far less successful at reshaping individual consciences. If one could pass the "right" laws, yes, there might be fewer overt acts of immorality or more acts of economic justice, as defined by capitalism's critics. But there would be no change in people's hearts. A country full of people lusting in their hearts who do not consummate that lust out of fear of arrest, or a country of greedy people forced to give up a bit more of their gains is scarcely better than one full of people left free to act on their sinful whims. It is, in short, one thing to improve appearances, but quite another to improve society's moral core. And God, Jeremiah tells us, looks at the heart (Jeremiah 17:10).

Indeed, attempting to forcibly make people virtuous would make society itself less virtuous in three important ways. First, individuals would lose the opportunity to exercise virtue. They would not face the same set of temptations and be forced to choose between good and evil. This approach might thereby make their lives easier. But they would not be more virtuous and society would suffer as a result. In this dilemma we see the paradox of Christianity: a God of love creates man and provides a means for his redemption, but allows him to choose to do evil. While true Christian liberty means freedom from sin, it also requires that more common form of freedom: the opportunity to choose whether to respond to God's grace.

Second, to vest government with primary responsibility for promoting virtue shortchanges other institutions, or "governments" in

Puritan thought, like the family and church, sapping their vitality. Private social institutions find it easier to lean on the power of coercion than to lead by example, persuade, and solve problems. Moreover, the law is better at driving immorality underground than eliminating it. As a result, moral and spiritual problems may seem less acute and people may become less uncomfortable, and private institutions may therefore be less likely to work as hard at promoting virtue and offering charity.

Third, making government a moral enforcer encourages abuse by majorities or influential minorities that gain power. If one thing is certain in life, it is that man is sinful. "There is no one righteous, not even one," states a biblical passage that bears repeating. The effect of sin is magnified by the possession and exercise of coercive power. Its possessors can, of course, do good, but history suggests that even in a democracy they are far more likely to do harm. All told, an unfree society is not likely to be a just or virtuous one.

The fact that government can do little to help does not mean that there is nothing it should do. Most important, public officials should adopt as their maxim "first, do no harm." Indeed, one of the great virtues of liberal economics lies in its illustration of how counterproductive government policies have subsidized poverty, family breakdown, and community destruction. The greatest economic injustice is often the abrogation of market opportunities that offer the greatest benefit for the poor and powerless.

Conclusion: The problem of humanity

In the end, the problem of humanity is not liberal economics, but humanity. All men are fallen and sinful; greed and envy are our inevitable lot, not the products of particular social systems. "When we survey the depredations and ravages of our social, political, and religious circumstance, it is tempting to look for someone or something to blame," writes Neuhaus. And with global capitalism triumphant, what better to blame than liberal economics? Yet the blame is misplaced.

Neuhaus's view is buttressed by the pope's words in *Centesimus Annus*. The pope's critique of Marxism is devastating: "The historical experience of socialist countries has sadly demonstrated that collectivism does not do away with alienation but rather increases it, adding to it a lack of basic necessities and economic inefficiency " (41). In contrast, he praises capitalism, including its reliance of entrepreneurship and profits. "When a firm makes a profit," he writes, "this means that productive factors have been properly employed and corresponding human needs have been duly satisfied" (35). All told, he argues, "the free market is the most efficient instrument for utilizing resources and effectively responding to needs" (34).

The pope remains vitally concerned about the poor, however, and believes that capitalism cannot be the sum of society. As Neuhaus puts it, "liberalism is freedom, and what we do with freedom is charged to our account." Which is why the pope emphasizes that individual freedom needs an "ethical and religious" core. This core makes liberal economics itself more successful. As Stackhouse and Stratton write, the social, cultural, and moral capital constituted in structures of accountability and education ensure that markets do what they do better, deliver more goods and services for less, and do so in a manner that is more fair and consistent with human dignity.

Of course, as obvious as I find these conclusions, many people dispute them. Several have contributed to this volume. Nevertheless, the resulting dialogue should help advance understanding on both sides. But it should be a start, not an end.

Worthy of further exploration is the very nature of liberal economics and capitalism. Most of the economies that parade around the world in capitalist dress are anything but open, competitive, free-market societies. Although all systems are imperfect and harbor injustice, the sins of crony or kleptocratic economies, irrespective of the existence of private property, should not be attributed to capitalism.

An equally significant area of disagreement among the participants is the issue of the impact of the global economy on poor countries. Are capital mobility, foreign investment, and international trade boons or banes? To answer that question requires an understanding of how countries develop, and what has caused some nations to be rich and others to be poor.

A related issue is the application of biblical notions of justice to economic outcomes. None of the contributors to this volume would disagree that much goes on in the world that offends human dignity. They disagree on how to characterize many economic outcomes. Is the low wage paid to an unskilled worker in an unstable nation where investment is insecure an injustice to be remedied through political action? Or an example of poverty to be remedied through economic growth combined with Christian charity? Global capitalism is seen as a problem in the first case and an answer in the second.

Perhaps most important, both sides can and should work together in response to Neuhaus's call to contend "for the soul of liberalism." To defend the importance of economic and political liberty is not to ignore the importance of transcendent truth. To the contrary, economic and political liberty are best protected in alliance with transcendent truth. This battle runs far deeper than the partisan control of Congress or the passage of a school prayer constitutional amendment. At issue are the beliefs and characters of people living in community with one another. If the liberal project is flawed—and it is, but it is not likely to be abandoned—then it behooves friends and foes to work together to try to repair it.

Is capitalism Christian? No. It neither advances human virtue nor corrects ingrained personal vices; it merely reflects them. But socialism and its weaker statist cousins exacerbate the worst of men's flaws. By divorcing effort from reward, stirring up covetousness and envy, and destroying the freedom that is a necessary precondition for virtue, noncapitalist systems tear at the just social fabric that Christians should seek to establish. A Christian must still work hard to shed even a little of God's light in a capitalist society. But his task is likely to be much harder in a collectivist one.

Editor's Response

"Homelessness" and Market Liberalism: Toward an Economic Culture of Gift and Gratitude

David L. Schindler

The title of this collection of essays suggests the thesis of my concluding reflection: wealth and poverty must be understood finally in terms of the destiny that defines the nature of man. This claim may seem innocent enough, since scarcely any of the authors in this volume would dispute it in this generalized form. And yet, as we will see, their assessments of contemporary market economies at least imply that the authors diverge widely in terms of how they understand the claim.

The task given the two editors of the collection was to gather writers who, against the general background of Christianity, would offer variant readings of free market systems relative to issues of wealth and poverty. The authors selected by Bandow are Hill, Novak, Gregg, Morse, Griswold, and Neuhaus; those by Schindler are Walker, Long, Cavanaugh, Crawford, Lewis, and Davis. The essays by Stackhouse and Stratton and by Berry, selected to supply further background material, more or less align with the first and second groups, respectively. My intention is to show how the thesis stated above serves as a fault line in differentiating these two groups. Notwithstanding many differences *within* the two groups of thinkers, each group differs as a whole from the other in the extent to which the ever-increasing global influence of the market economy is judged to be "a blessing for the world's poor" (Griswold), and this difference is governed above all by a difference in anthropology: in how the two groups understand the nature and destiny of man.

Thus we may say that the thinkers in the first group subscribe to varieties of judgments such as: "[c]ontemporary open, market-economy systems are, on the whole, good for poor people"(Stackhouse and Stratton); "the 'free market' usually provides the best opportunity for individual human development and for increasing social participation of groups living in poverty" (Stackhouse and Stratton); we have "a society with a higher standard of living and greater amount of personal freedom than any system that has ever existed" (Morse).[1] Every author in the second group would dispute such judgments in his own way. My own intended challenge[2] turns on the meaning assigned (more or less explicitly) to each of the judgments' key terms— for example, "open," "good," "free" or "personal freedom," "individual human development," "social participation," "standard of living," and indeed "poverty." My argument will be that these terms as used here in their economic context presuppose and are guided in crucially important ways (even if sometimes unconsciously) by some larger sense of the nature of man—of the human person in his or her totality.

Thus, in challenging the first group of thinkers' economic judgments, I mean to challenge the anthropological substance that is partially but decisively determinative of these judgments *already in their economic character.* Which is to say, I mean to challenge the first group's *claims about the market*, insofar as these claims themselves already express what seems to me a defective anthropology.

Now, in debates among Christians regarding market systems, the conventional assumption is that the contested issues are first economic in nature. Beginning with the idea that the purpose of economic exchanges is to produce wealth, we assume that properly economic questions are about how to realize that wealth most effectively, within the limits set by our common Christian eschatological and ethical framework. In a word, we understand an economic system as something conceived first on its own terms, to which theological or philosophical or cultural substance is then added.

This conventional approach to market debates, however, begs what we will see are the crucial questions raised by the differences between the two groups of authors: those questions, namely, which concern the original nature and purpose of "economic exchanges" and of "wealth." The conventional way of approaching these debates, in other words, begs the prior question of how man's *telos* anteriorly shapes (or should shape) the meaning of economics and wealth as such, and therefore ignores the sense in which an economic system itself already embeds, indeed *is* also, a theology and an anthropology and a culture.

My contention is thus that this collection's two groups of thinkers differ significantly as economists, but only as their respective economies themselves already express—at a more fundamental (though often implicit) level—different notions of Christianity and of humanity. The burden of my reflections is to show how this is so, and why it is crucial for us to understand how it is so as we engage the urgent problems, increasingly global in reach, regarding the market economy and its approaches to wealth and poverty.

It is of course beyond the scope of an introductory reflection such as this to mount a full-scale argument regarding the nature and destiny of the human being. Instead, Part I provides an outline of what I take to be an adequate anthropology. Part II indicates what this anthropology implies for an economy of gift and gratitude, in contrast to a liberal economic culture. Part III offers a technical review of the assumptions that establish liberal anthropology as "instrumentalist." In light of the argument of Parts I–III, and drawing on the writings of Pope John Paul II and also on Jennifer Roback Morse's own contribution to the present volume, Part IV describes and assesses our contemporary cultural problematic in terms of its underlying "instrumentalist" or "utilitarian" logic. Finally, Part V illustrates, in relation to several authors of the first group, how their economic proposals embody the substance of a liberal anthropology: how what are otherwise the genuine goods defended in those proposals—efficiency, creativity, freedom, productivity, and indeed things in relative abundance—express and contribute to this instrumentalism, that is, given the authors' liberal reading and despite what are their clear intentions to the contrary.

Before we begin, a methodological note: as I indicated earlier, the present collection of essays presupposes a background of Christianity, and my own argument unfolds within a definite reading of Christianity. It is essential to my reading of Christianity, however, that it make ontological claims about how things are. That is, the claims I make regarding the nature and destiny of the human being are meant to be in some significant sense accessible and indeed convincing, in their ontological meaning, to readers who do not share the Christian faith, even as I take Christian faith to be required for the claims to be fully accessible and convincing. The following text from Pope John Paul II indicates, in form and content, the relation between Christian faith and ontology (anthropology) I am presupposing here:

> Man cannot live without love. He remains a being that is incomprehensible for himself, his life is senseless, if love is not revealed to him, if he does not encounter it and make it his own, if he does not participate intimately in it. This . . . is why Christ the Redeemer "fully reveals man to himself [*hominem ipsi homini*]."[3] If we may use the expression, this is the human dimension of the mystery of the Redemption. In this dimension man finds again the greatness, dignity and value that belong to his humanity. . . .[4]

What is crucial for the integrity of the pope's statement is that its claim about love finds an echo, a resonance, in every human heart, not just in explicitly Christian hearts; and that it does so even as the claim retains its intrinsically Christian character—that is, even as the love about which he speaks is fully revealed only in Jesus Christ. My own argument unfolds in terms of man's encounter with love in the fact of his creation, hence in man's original reality as gift-eliciting-gratitude. And it presupposes with the pope that this creative love finds its full realization in the redemptive love of God revealed in Christ.

Clearly, the relation presupposed here between faith and philosophy/culture demands justification on its own terms.[5] The foregoing statement nevertheless suffices for the limited purposes of the present forum.

The Idea of "Home": Toward an Anthropology of Gift and Gratitude

My argument is that "homelessness" is the fundamental problem of a liberal economy. The term "homelessness" is taken here in its root sense as a matter of man's relation simultaneously to earth and to heaven. "Homelessness," in other words, refers to a lack of one's proper place in the cosmos, and not in the first instance to the condition of a discrete group of people living in the streets (though my argument presupposes that these two senses of "homelessness" are intrinsically related).

The dictionary defines "home" as "one's place of residence," "a familiar or usual setting," "a place of origin." To be "at home" is to be "relaxed and comfortable or at ease," as well as to be "in harmony with one's surroundings." The Latin term for "home" is *domus*," and "to domesticate" thus means to "bring into domestic use," or "to fit for domestic life." My argument presupposes that "home" and its attendant terms here receive their most proper meaning in terms of man's creation and destiny, of man's ontological beginning and *telos*. "Home" and "homelessness," in other words, refer most basically to the sense in which man is made to be in harmony with his earthly surroundings, in relation to God as his origin and end.

In a word, man is rightly said to be at home insofar as he realizes the relations that most profoundly constitute his being as a creature.

We can state this in more technical terms. First, each man to be sure is an individual. But each man is constituted in his individuality precisely in and by virtue of his relation to the creator—and redeemer—God. In the words of John Paul II, "relation to God is a constitutive element of [one's] very 'nature' and 'existence': it is in God that we 'live and move and have our being' (Acts 17:28)."[6]

The relevant point is thus that each man has his meaning as an individual only *from within this original and abiding ontological community with God.*

Second, this relation to God that is constitutive of the individual person includes relation to other persons: "[The] human person has an inherently social dimension which calls a person from the innermost depths of self to *communion* with others and to the *giving* of self to others . . . . Thus society as a fruit and sign of the social nature of man reveals its whole truth in being a communion of persons."[7]

In contrast to a common view in liberal societies, therefore, individuality and community in their primary meanings do not oppose but on the contrary presuppose each other. Individuality emerges *from within* community and is always already an expression *of* community, even as individuality itself conditions and is presupposed by the original meaning of community.

Third, "the first and basic expression of the social dimension of the person . . . is the married couple and family. . . . [The] partnership [*consociatio*] of man and woman constitutes the first form of the communion of persons." "The family is the basic cell of society." Elsewhere, John Paul II states that "the sexual difference constitutes the very identity of the person."[8] These assertions imply that familial or nuptial relations—that is, (aptness for) paternity or maternity, filiality, and the like—are intrinsic to the original and hence abiding identity of the person.

Finally, each entity of the world, as created, is intrinsically related to God and thereby in some intrinsic sense also to all other entities of the world. This original relation, or "community," of cosmic entities is meant to be lifted up and transformed into the service of human and indeed finally liturgical-eucharistic community, in and through the "flesh" and labor of man (St. Maximus the Confessor). It follows that space, time, matter, and motion are themselves, in their original and proper—i.e., creaturely—nature, apt for expressing and "containing" community.[9]

I said above that man is at home when he realizes the relations that constitute his being as a creature. We now see that these relations include relations both to God (above all) and (in some significant sense) to all creatures, and that they pass through and are mediated by familial relations. Man is at home, therefore, when he is rightly related to God, to others, and to the world in and through a family.[10] It is within these relations and in their right ordering that he finds his basic place of residence, or truly comes to rest.

Now, it is difficult to see how anyone, certainly any Christian, would object to these assertions in the schematic form in which they are expressed here. Surely no one in the first group of thinkers in this volume, all of whom vigorously defend the liberal market economy, would want to dispute the centrality of right relations to God, others, the world, and the family for realization of a person's health and wholeness—his fundamental "at-home-ness." And yet I propose to argue that the very conceptions of wealth and poverty prevalent in today's liberal market economy tend to prevent realization of this fundamental at-home-ness. The liberal market economy, in its very efforts to produce wealth and reduce poverty, tends of its inner logic to fragment a person's relations to God, others, the world, and the family, thus rendering man "homeless" in the deepest sense.

To justify these assertions, which may at first appear to be extreme, I must now explain how I am conceiving these relations of each individual man to God, others, the world, and the family.

The crucial point is to see what is implied in saying that these relations are *constitutive*. They are constitutive in that they are first *given to* man: they are entailed in the fact of his creation, his very constitution as a creature. The relations are not first *chosen by* man. In a word, the relations, and the original communities implicit in these relations, are *gifts* "before" they are *constructions*. This does not mean that the relations are not also in some essential way matters of freedom. It means—in a sense yet to be properly qualified—that these relations are *objects* of free choice only as already constitutive of the *subject* of free choice.

Clearly, there are significant differences among the types of community indicated in man's relations to God, others, the world, and his family. The community a man shares with his family, for example, differs in fundamental ways from the community he shares with all other human beings. The pertinent point is simply that these communities, despite and within what are their important differences in other respects, all share the fact of first being given *to*, and not *by*, man.

Furthermore, insofar as these relations are constitutive of man's being, they are necessarily presupposed in any and all of his actions. But this is just to say that man is structurally dependent *in* the very independence that characterizes his activity as an individual: he is dependent on the others to whom he is constitutively related (i.e., in different ways to God and to other creatures) in the very independence (creativity, self-determinateness, and the like) of his actions as entailed by his individuality.

These features of gift and dependence are essential to the idea of home rightly understood, and hence for the realization of man's at-home-ness.

A phrase drawn from the writings of Canadian philosopher George Grant puts the matter nicely. "We are not our own," he says, in words offered response to our cultural problematic. In other words, we belong to others. This of course does not mean that we do not belong also, and fundamentally, to ourselves, but that we belong to ourselves only in our original and continued belonging to God, and, after God, to our parents and indeed in some sense to the world as a whole. We truly "possess" ourselves, but only as we are also gifts from Another (and others). This is what it means ontologically to be a creature: to discover that we come to ourselves only *in* and *through* our selves' constitutive belonging to others (God, and other creatures in God).

Thus, it is not as though we start out dependent upon and belonging to others, and then grow eventually into an autonomy that leaves this dependent belonging behind. On the contrary, the fact of our createdness implies that we bear this relation of dependent belonging in the core of our being, however much, as we move from infancy to adulthood, there is a progressively deeper capacity for recuperating this relation in freedom.

Contemporary theologian Hans Urs von Balthasar sums all of this up well when he suggests that a creaturely ontology is best approached through reflection on the mother's smile.[11] A child's first experience of being comes through the smile and embrace of the mother, hence through the radiant presence of the goodness of another. The child's first experience of existence, then, is of being loved. It is an experience of existence itself as generous: as gift from another.

To be sure, the child is scarcely aware of this in any explicit fashion at the moment of birth! The relevant point, however, is that in time the child smiles back at the mother. Note what is happening here. The child's eventual smile is a *response* to the *generosity* of the mother: the mother's loving smile becomes effective in the child, evoking the child's smile in return, just as the rays of the sun penetrate the flower and evoke its bloom.

Hence, the child comes into existence and begins to realize his own existence only in and through the abiding, anterior presence of another, a presence that, precisely *because and insofar as it is generous*, reveals to the child *his own worth*.

We discover here the primitive structure of a creaturely ontology. We see that creaturely being, as gift-from-another, is defined most properly in terms of *being-as-response*. In its own proper being and activity, in its very independence and autonomy and individuality, the creature is anteriorly receptive of, dependent on, and in intrinsic community with, another.[12] Thus, receptivity and dependence are positive, not negative, features of our being.[13]

But we can take this further. For what the foregoing implies is that the most basic disposition of the created being in relation to the other (the world) is that of an *obedient and patient and contemplative wonder*, evoked by what may be called the *beauty* of the other. An obedient wonder: that is, a wonder that listens (*oboedire* [*ob/audio*]). A patient and contemplative wonder: that is, not in the sense of "passivity," but rather in the sense of an activity that is anteriorly responsive. Wonder, insofar as the being of the other—and of one's self—comes unexpectedly and surprisingly, or, in more traditional language, contingently. Evoked by the beauty of the other, insofar as it is the attractiveness of the other that always first elicits and indeed in a significant sense continues to bear the active response of the self both to itself and to the other.

In short, an ontology of being as gift-from-another entails, on the part of the being who is inescapably from his depths a receiver, a dependence taking the form of a contemplative wonder born of and sustained by the beauty of the other. I believe these features are accurately summed up in the word *gratitude*.

My contention, therefore, is that the ontology proper to a creature is an ontology of *being-as-gift* that elicits and is completed in *being-as-gratitude*.

Such an ontology of gift and gratitude enables us, in the face of the ever-present brokenness and evil in the world, to find a positive meaning even in *suffering*. Again, consider the mother in relation to her child. In conceiving and giving birth, she makes space for the other, in his otherness. This entails risk and vulnerability: in "letting the other be," she allows for the possibility that the child will abuse his freedom and reject or disappoint her, or indeed, more broadly, that the child himself will be subject to abuse and rejection and disappointment at the hands of the world. This possibility of suffering, or this anterior willingness to suffer, is inherent in the original *positive* meaning of being as gift and gratitude.

For Christians, the highest creaturely expression of this ontology of gift and gratitude that is from the beginning disposed to suffer is Mary in her *fiat* ("let it be done unto me"). Mary, in contemplatively-actively responding to God's initiative in grace, makes space for the incarnate Other, a space that is ready to endure, in the face of evil and with a gratitude eventually full of sorrow, even his crucifixion and death.

I have proposed that man is rightly said to be at home when he realizes the relations that constitute his being as a creature. We can now see, in more concrete terms, that man is truly at home insofar as he finds his identity inside the *constitutive belonging to others* (God, other creatures) summed up in gift and gratitude. Obversely, he becomes homeless, in the root sense, insofar as his identity falls outside of or is abstracted from this belonging—insofar as his relations to God and others become fragmented.

There is a common expression in English that "a man's home is his castle." The term "castle" adds to "home" the notion of wealth or riches, and with this we can now resume our larger theme. For I wish to suggest that home is rightly understood as a "castle" because and insofar as home is where the creature most truly *belongs*, where the creature comes to realize the richness of the relations that most profoundly and intimately constitute his being as a creature.

Wealth and poverty in their deepest and most proper meaning, in other words, signify being in relation and not being in relation, respectively, in the sense indicated by "home" and "homelessness."

This notion of wealth and poverty will no doubt appear arcane to some, but I invite the reader to ponder the ontological nature of the argument. For the precise point has been that the creature is understood in his truest *reality* as gift (from God above all, but also from others in relation to God), and that this reality can therefore be realized *as such* only through an abiding grateful receptivity that, *eo ipso*, enables proper participation in reality in its character as gift.

Wealth in its truest sense, thus, consists in participation in reality-as-gift, a participation enabled and indeed always first constituted by gratitude; and poverty in its truest sense, consequently, consists in the failure to participate in reality so understood, a failure that stems finally from an absence of gratitude (whatever its various causes).

This ontological rendering of wealth by no means excludes the more immediate and obvious sense of wealth as consisting in having, producing, and exchanging things—food, clothing, property, and the like. On the contrary, it insists merely that having, producing, and exchanging things be from the beginning formed and thus integrated in and by grateful receiving and giving. Without this anterior formation and integration, having or producing things even in great abundance will contribute, not to the deepened participation in reality as gift that we are calling wealth in the truest sense, but on the contrary to the reduced participation in reality that we are calling poverty.

Toward an Economy of Gift and Gratitude

I come now to a critical turn in the argument. For the argument concerns not simply the ontological idea of wealth, however "realistic" we may now see that it is on its own terms, but the bearing of this idea on wealth in its specifically economic context, or on the nature of economic exchanges themselves. This requires that the ontological idea of wealth as a matter primarily of gift and gratitude be shown to carry its own way of producing and exchanging and possessing things. It must be shown that the things produced, exchanged, and possessed will themselves differ *in their very character as things*, depending on the extent to which their production, exchange, and possession is integrated into a grateful sense of reality as gift—that is, such that the things themselves take on the nature of gift.

I refer to this as a critical turn in the argument because of the conventional insistence that it is the task of economics in the proper sense to show how best to produce, possess, and exchange things, while it is up to theology, philosophy, and culture to order this production and exchange and these things to a good end, or to give them a moral intention. Economics, in a word, tells us how to produce and exchange things efficiently, while theology, philosophy, and culture tell us how to *order* or *use* this production and exchange rightly in terms of man's *telos,* an ordering or use that, however important in moral terms, leaves essentially intact the meaning of "efficient" as supplied by economics on its own terms.

The burden of my argument is to challenge the extrinsicism indicated here: to show that the order given in man's *telos* itself partially but decisively shapes what it means to produce, exchange, and possess things efficiently, in the properly economic meaning of these terms. How so?

As a first example, let us turn again to the mother, and to the meal she prepares for her family. Notice that we always refer spontaneously and warmly to a "home-cooked" meal, or again, to a dish prepared the way Grandma used to prepare it. Even restaurants characteristically advertise their food in this way: never do they recommend themselves on the grounds that the food they serve is store-packaged and mechanically prepared. What is the difference that is implicitly recognized here?

An obvious answer is that the mother prepares her family's food with love. But, however true, such an answer remains both vague and question-begging. For it could mean that love adds an intention that otherwise leaves the dinner unchanged in its intrinsic nature or order. But that is just the view I am challenging. My proposal, in other words, is that the love of the mother affects the dinner precisely in its reality as food. A mother builds into the food a distinctive sense of time, space, matter, and motion. She takes time, and she knows that taking time, however burdensome, is necessary for care and attention to detail. She measures with a sense of proportion, but not mechanically and not without some sense of "extravagance." She keeps in mind all along the way the health needs and peculiar tastes of these particular familial others—especially the infirm and most helpless—for whom she is making the meal. She prepares and presents the food with a sense of its aesthetics. And so on.[14]

The mother's love, in brief, is not merely a matter of an intention remaining external to the food. On the contrary, her love *takes form* in the food, such that the food itself now takes on the form of love—somewhat in the way that John Paul II says that the human body is and must become "nuptial": that the body as body, the body in its very structure and physicality, expresses and is meant to express love for another.[15]

To take another example, consider the difference between Mother Teresa and a nurse performing her duties primarily for the sake of making money. Both provide health care, but we spontaneously recognize the difference in the way in which the care is ordered. Some of this difference is quantitative in nature: Mother Teresa would certainly do more things for the patient. But the point to which I am drawing attention bears intrinsically on the manner or order of the discrete acts of care themselves. Mother Teresa's very manner of touching the patient, of looking at the patient, of dressing the patient, of arranging the bedding of the patient are all different. The difference is similar to the difference in the case of the mother's home-cooked meal: all of these acts by Mother Teresa are changed in their very form as health- and care-giving acts. Anyone who has spent time in a contemporary hospital knows intuitively the difference to which I am referring here, however much he or she might not be able to articulate with precision the nature of that difference.

Before attempting myself to characterize that difference, let us consider a third case. Adam Smith has famously asserted that we really do not need to appeal to the beneficence or generosity of the baker if we want good bread. On the contrary, we need merely to appeal to the baker's own self-interest: to point out to him that making good bread is the best way to ensure that he makes a profit. In light of the previous two examples, however, we are able to see that a generous way of making and selling bread will be different in its nature and order from a primarily profit-motivated way of making and selling. The former way of producing bread takes on the form of love, in the sense that it is undertaken for the sake of making what intrinsically is a good loaf of bread and for the sake of the person who will consume it. As with the home-cooked meal, a different sense of time and measurement and aesthetics, a different sensitivity to concerns of health and taste, and the like enter intrinsically into the act of producing and selling, and thereby into the thing produced.

Producing bread primarily for profit, on the other hand, by definition entails instrumentalizing toward the end of profit everything that goes into that production, with the consequence that it is the *appearance* of a certain quality of bread and bread-making with which the baker is most properly concerned. The baker, on the reading recommended by Smith, wants his bread-making to embody the qualities of good bread and bread-making, *not* for their own sake, but *only insofar* as embodying these qualities is necessary for and promotes his profit-making. The best possible situation for the baker on such a reading, therefore, is that he find a way to reduce his costs, a way which, however much it might entail reducing the qualities proper to good bread and bread-making, would see to it that the bread and bread-making nevertheless remain *effectively*—i.e., for all practical intents and purposes—the same.

The import of Smith's proposal, in a word, is that it makes no significant difference whether the baker bakes for love or for profit. In the end, it will come to the same thing: what is more or less the same loaf of bread will be produced.

What must be said first in response is that things cannot finally be *effectively* the same unless they in fact *are* the same. Things can be *effectively* the same finally only insofar as they are *intrinsically* the same, or better, the same in terms of their *inner*, or *interior*, reality. To claim otherwise is, however unwittingly, to slip into a Cartesianism that alone would warrant the disjunction presupposed on a Smithian account, a disjunction between a thing in its external or outward effect (the thing *quoad nos*) and a thing in its internal meaning (the thing *quoad se*).

In other words, those who claim that the act of making bread is the same, irrespective of whether that act is performed intrinsically in love or instrumentally, invariably employ what is an extroverted or mechanical (and just so far Cartesian) standard of judgment. They ignore the possibility of what I am arguing here: that love as a motive already and as a matter of principle gives interior form, hence order or structure, to the thing made; that the thing made therefore itself takes on the interior form of love, precisely in its character as a thing, as an artifact. In a word, such thinkers, in their claim of effective sameness and as a condition of the force of this claim, overlook or discount, a priori, exactly the differences introduced by love: those differences, namely, that involve interior movements affecting and indeed already in some significant sense constituting the time, space, and matter "congealed" in and as the thing. Unless one already assumes (however unwittingly) a Cartesian criterion for judgment, the examples I have adduced above suffice to illustrate these differences, at least in brief.[16]

But I need now to highlight the further burden of the proposal here, given my intention of indicating how an anthropology of gift and gratitude transforms the original meaning of an economy and indeed of *homo economicus* as such.

The baker who works for the sake of love—however much he may or may not conceive what he is doing explicitly in theoretical terms—approaches the making of bread, the bread made, the other for whom the bread is made, and indeed himself as invested in the process and the thing, as gift. He makes the bread—which is to say, he gratefully gives himself over to the making of the bread—simultaneously for its own sake and for the sake of another.

In contrast, the baker who works primarily for profit, and insofar as he works primarily for profit, approaches the making of bread, the bread made, and the other for whom the bread is made, as instrument. He does not make the bread intrinsically for itself or for the other (the consumer). Rather, he utilizes, for the sake of himself— primarily out of self-interest—the process of bread-making, the bread made, and the person who eventually buys and consumes the bread. It might seem that the baker, in so doing, thereby enhances at least the reality of his own self. But this is deceptive. For in so instrumentalizing the bread-making process, the bread, and the other for profit, he just so far reduces the reality of each of them, and thereby the reality also of what each has to offer him, to a reality-primarily-for-profit. But this entails a reduction thereby *also in the bread-maker's own reality*. For the point is that all of these—the bread-making process, the bread, and the intended consumer—are by definition now seen to enhance the bread-maker himself only (or primarily) in the mode of profitability. In reducing these three things to instruments of and for profit, therefore, the bread-maker, in that very act, makes his own reality also into an instrument of and for profit.

The simple but crucial point I wish to make here, then, is that an economy of love deepens the reality, which is to say, enhances the worth, of *everything and everyone involved in the production and exchange of goods: self, thing, and other*. Granting that this may be obvious with respect to the other (person as consumer), the suggestion is surprising with respect to conventional views of the self and of things. For the pertinent point is that the self and things now become deeper and "better" in their very reality as self and as things. Things: because and insofar as the baker bakes the bread for its own sake and not simply as instrument (or more exactly: intrinsically for its own sake and for the sake of the other as other, rather than simply as an instrument for profit and for the other as profit). And the self for the same reason: in acting for the enhancement of the bread as such and of the other as such, he thereby transforms his own self into the gift that he himself was created to be. The point, in other words, is that, once we ponder the meaning of love along the lines indicated above, we see that the conventional Smithian, self-interested approach to producing and selling bread sets in motion an intrinsic dynamic, not for the enhancement of the thing and the other and (consequently) the self in their *truest reality* as such, which is their reality as gift, but on the contrary for the promotion of these now only in their *reduced reality as and for profit*.

It should go without saying that baking for love as understood here by no means excludes baking also for profit: the crucial point—that is, the crucial difference from the Smithian account—is that profit now is put into the service of and thereby integrated into the good of the person and of the thing in their proper created and artifactual reality as gift.

We turn now to a common equivocation, and objection, associated with the foregoing argument. The equivocation: those who follow Smith with respect to his defense of self-interest ("rightly understood") often imply that acts of self-interest, when they are harnessed into a self-interest become mutual, thereby become—for all practical (or public) intents and purposes—the same as acts of mutual generosity. The objection: acts of self-interest harnessed into mutuality are in any case the best we can generally hope to achieve, given the "realistic" conditions of human history.

What has been said already suffices to show that a self-interested act in a Smithian sense does not become generous simply because it is now hooked up with the self-interest of the other: a self-interest become mutual is not thereby rendered into mutual generosity. Nevertheless, making explicit the feature of mutuality enables us to clarify further. My argument does in fact affirm an intrinsic mutuality between the self and the other in the producing and selling of bread. More pertinently, the self is not eliminated but in fact *fulfilled* precisely *as a self* in acting for the other as other—in acting for love. However, it is crucial to notice the asymmetry of the order in the mutual relation between self and other. In other words, the self does serve or enhance itself, but only insofar as this self-service or self-enhancement is already placed inside and ordered to the service and enhancement of the other as other.

Thus, we need not eliminate self-centeredness in acting for another in a truly other-centered way, in accord with the conventional reading of "altruism," which requires an acting for the other that is to the exclusion of the self. On the contrary, we need to recuperate self-centeredness, but *from within the self's prior centeredness in the other*. The radical difference between Smithian self-interest and genuine love, in sum, lies in the asymmetrical ordering, and not in the mutuality (which is granted), of the relation between the self and the other.

Once this is seen, we recognize the striking equivocation harbored in statements such as the following (offered by way of defending a Madisonian self-interest, "rightly understood"): "self-interest of a sort is the propellant of a mother's love even unto death for her child."[17]

In Christian terms, the above qualification enables us to see the ontology implicit in the relation between two important statements of Jesus pertinent to neighborly love. He says on the one hand that we ought to love our neighbor as ourselves; and on the other, that we ought to love each other as "I have loved you." Thus we truly ought to love ourselves, but only at once as we, in the manner of Jesus, give ourselves away to the other. We will indeed find ourselves, but only in losing ourselves—and in no other order.

Once again, the creaturely archetype for proper "self-love" as indicated here is Mary, in her "magnificat." In Mary's *fiat*—in her "letting it be done according to the Word" of Another—Mary's self is not effaced but is on the contrary magnified, precisely in her magnification of the Other.

However, we still need to address an objection that, if legitimate, would render the foregoing argument moot, *tout court*. The objection concerns the "realism" of the argument in practical terms, a "realism" that is the further burden of arguments such as those offered by Smith—and in political terms by James Madison, for example. However much it is the case that love is the ultimate or "ideal" truth of things, it seems fruitless to try to build an economy around such an anthropology. The fact of the matter is that most people in the world as we know it act primarily for reasons of profitable self-interest, and it is this self-interested motivation that has enabled the market economy's productivity and abundance. The best we can and ought to do, in recognition of the abiding sinfulness of the world, is thus to harness self-interest into mutuality, in the manner indicated by Smith and his successors.

My ontological argument, in a word, leaves unanswered the question about its "worldly realism."

My response is threefold. First, however prevalent profitable self-interest is in a person's engagement with the economy, this self-interest *never* exhausts a person's motivation. On the contrary, man is in fact most fundamentally characterized by his desire for God, even if this desire remains for the most part unthematic. Augustine and Aquinas both affirm that man knows and wills God implicitly (*"implicite"*) in everything he or she knows or wills, and in this sense "naturally" loves God above all else.[18] According to Augustine, it is the restlessness for God, evoked by the relation to God established in and with creation, that most deeply inspires man's choices. Given this fact, and in light of the creaturely ontology set forth earlier, we can say that man's deepest desire is his desire for the community implied in his originally given relations to God and others—is, in short, his original, natural love for God and others.

Thus, the desire for God, for community and love, is precisely *not* "unrealistic," and God, community, and love, consequently, are *never* merely "ideal." The desire for these does not arise (sometimes and in some people) alongside the self-interested desire for profit, or only after this desire has been satisfied or after material abundance has been achieved. On the contrary, the desire for God, community, and love operates at the core of the desire for profit and material abundance.[19] It is crucial to see this: any economy that fails to take account of this constitutive desire operating at the heart of man's being—hence always and everywhere at the heart of man's actions—fails thereby to be realistic in the truest and most proper historical sense of the term.

Indeed, it is only in light of this realism that we can understand sin for what it truly is: that is, sin. What may seem obvious, however, typically gets lost in the (Smithian, Madisonian) argument on behalf of "worldly realism." What starts out as a defense of profitable self-interest in the name of man's historical sinfulness slides quickly into a defense in the name of "virtue," if to be sure only a "virtue of necessity." Taking God and love to be more or less utopian "ideals," the best we *can* do (given our sinfulness) becomes the best we ("realistically") *ought* to do. God and love are "realities" to be attended to only alongside our more immediate concerns for profit and abundance—"realities" attended to, that is, mostly in our "private," "eschatological" moments.

What realism in an integrated sense requires, rather, is that the "Smithian" desire for profit be recognized always and everywhere as a vice indicating a need for conversion, however much it is also simultaneously recognized that this vice will never, in the present condition of the world, be entirely removed from the heart of man.[20] Realism in the proper sense likewise requires that the acquisition and indeed very nature of material abundance be measured intrinsically—from the beginning and at every point along the way—in terms of man's always deeper, anterior desire for God, community, and love.[21]

Realism properly conceived thus leads, secondly, to a crucial qualification in the conventional claim on behalf of the market's effectiveness in producing a high material standard of living. Of course, in an obvious and important sense the market is effective in this way. The needed qualifier, however, arises when we recall the burden of our earlier argument in connection with an economy of gift, which is that both the process of production itself and the artifact produced are of higher quality when formed in love and indeed *as* love than they are when formed primarily in (profitable) self-interest (assuming here equal abilities in the respective agents of production!). Furthermore, the persons of both the self and the other are enhanced more fully and truly in the former case than in the latter. Defense of the market economy's productivity typically begs this question of the quality of the process of production itself, the artifact produced, and the self and other engaged in the production. That is, it comes attached almost invariably to the extroverted, instrumentalist criteria of quality that take production and artifacts to be effectively the same irrespective of whether they are formed integratively in love or reductively in profitable self-interest. (I indicated earlier why this is so. I acknowledge, however, that that statement requires more extensive detail than can be provided in the present forum, in terms of showing the various ways in which production and artifacts, and the self and the other engaged in production, are enhanced when they are informed in and by love of God and others, and in which all of these are reduced when informed primarily by self-interested profit.)

The preceding two points, however, still leave unaddressed what is the crux of the conventional appeal to "realism": that production driven by a Smithian self-interest has in fact generated artifacts in ever-greater abundance and with ever-greater technological efficiency. I will address the matter of technology at greater length below in connection with the essay by Stackhouse and Stratton. Regarding abundance, let me make two observations.

First, man's bodiliness is a good implicit in the good of his creaturely nature and destiny. Adequate food, clothing, and property, with the abundance implied therein, are inherently good. Indeed, as the writer Annie Dillard has pertinently, and beautifully, stated, extravagance is the characteristic gesture of the creator himself.[22] Relative abundance of material things is thus already a matter of "quality" and not merely "quantity." Such relative abundance is to be sought as an integral part of man's destiny as an embodied creature, and the productivity of the liberal market is just so far an important good needing to be acknowledged as such.

Secondly, however, the qualifier introduced with "relative" invites the pertinent question: *what sort of* abundance is both necessary and truly enhancing of man's dignity as an embodied person, relative to his here-and-now creaturely call to love and glorify God, to love others, and indeed to value the world itself intrinsically in relation to God?

In response, we must recognize that the love implied in our creatureliness carries its own distinctive notions of the acquisition and indeed proper nature of material abundance—in all of its forms: property, power, position, technological efficiency, money—and that these notions differ from the way in which they are conceived in their prevalent liberal sense. Rightful material abundance involves integration of the self into the fullness of the truth, goodness, and beauty of the others (including God and all others in relation to God) to whom the self is constitutively related. More radically, all that is implied in relative material abundance finds its true meaning in terms of Mary's *magnificat*, which is to say, in the magnification of the self in and through the magnification of others—most especially the innocent and vulnerable others named in the Beatitudes[23]—in their embodied reality and in service of their full reality as true and good and beautiful before God.

In sum, abundance is to be integrated in terms of the need "to be rich toward God" (Luke 12:21).

This large assertion, however, raises again, perhaps even more sharply, the problem of "worldly realism." Yet it also makes clear that we must ultimately come to terms with the fact that the love proper to creatureliness is made in the image of God as revealed in Jesus Christ, that the "realism" characteristic of creaturely love therefore finds its ultimate meaning within the life of Jesus himself. Jesus *incarnated* himself in the world, and thereby affirmed the reality of the world in its deepest and most comprehensive, or embodied, abundance. Nevertheless, by virtue of his love and affirmation of the world, integrated in terms of his hypostatic relation to the Father, Jesus was crucified.

It is, in sum, precisely Jesus's *integrated love* for—and not "sectarian" denial of or withdrawal from—the world in its abundance that evokes rejection by those who would conceive worldly abundance—power, property, position, technical efficiency, money—in a fragmented and extroverted form.

This by no means implies that we ought not to enter the economic world and seek to participate effectively in its institutions; that we ought not to seek to make our presence in the world as productive of abundance as possible. This misunderstanding misses the point both of creation and the Incarnation. Rather, we must, given "worldly realism" in the sense indicated in the one historical order not only by sin but also by the incarnate-crucified love of Jesus, expect to experience reversal precisely at the heart of what it means to be "productive," and indeed relative to material abundance in all its forms as conceived in the dominant liberal understanding.

Any understanding of "worldly" realism and success that would be adequate must finally measure itself by the historically irreducible tension indicated here.

Having offered a sketch of what we have termed an economy of gift, and having criticized in this light what may be termed the instrumentalist economic culture implied in a liberal anthropology, let us now summarize in technical terms what is the deepest ontological source and meaning of that instrumentalism.

Liberal Anthropology as an Instrumentalist Anthropology

Anglo-American liberalism, I wish to suggest, presupposes what may be termed an "abstract" identity of the person. "Abstract" signifies an identity of the person conceived first and most basically *in abstrac-*

tion from the relations constitutive of the creature. This does not mean that liberalism necessarily denies the importance of man's relations to God, others, the world, and the family, or again that liberalism fails to see the obvious ways in which man is *born* into these relations. Rather, insofar as liberalism recognizes the importance or indeed "naturalness" of these relations—as in fact it does on its best reading—it nonetheless fails to grasp what is implied in their constitutive character. It fails to recuperate the community that anteriorly conditions, and thus helps intrinsically to form, self-identity in its original and abiding meaning.

In its abstract notion of the self, liberalism thereby leaves self-centeredness in the objectionable sense intact. Indeed, that is just what an abstract self is: a self that has been stripped of the original relation to the other(s) that alone could give the self's identity an originally other-centered orientation. But note what this then implies for the rightful meaning of human action. Typically, a liberal account of human action emphasizes self-determination or creativity. This may seem innocent enough, since we all affirm the worth of such features: absent these features, with the passivity that is consequently implied, and human freedom is emptied of its legitimate power. The problem arises, however, when we notice that liberalism, in its emphasis on self-determination and creativity, fails to take account of the implications of the effective presence of the other in the abiding structure of these.

The receptivity and dependence entailed in the self's ontological status as a gift from Another must form anteriorly—from the beginning and all along the way—what it means to be self-determinative and creative. Further, this receptivity and dependence imply an obedient (listening) and patient and contemplative wonder evoked by the *attractiveness* of the Other—i.e., as *giver*. All of these features together indicate a grateful response, which, in forming self-determination and creativity from the beginning, transforms these latter into what are now acts of self-giving.

In a word, self-determination and creativity, understood in their rightful creaturely structure, are grateful-responsive acts of self-giving; and the freedom of the self, accordingly, is first, not simply an option or act of choice, but an act of love. Human action is thus most properly a "co-act": an act that recuperates the always-already, effective and attractive presence *of the Other* (others) in itself as the anterior condition for being *its own action*.[24]

It is just here, then, that we can see the ontological source of instrumentalism, or of the other as instrument. The point becomes clear as soon as we notice the original *indifference* of the self to the other implied in the foregoing. This indifference *eo ipso* renders the self—in its abiding constitution as such—wrongly self-centered, and thereby also removes all of the features noted above that are necessary for the self's action to be at its origin other-centered. It follows that the self's engagement with the other—the self's doing, having, and producing relative to the other—cannot but be wrongly centered in the self and the self's interest: the other by definition becomes primarily a function or instrument of the self and the self's interest (*instruo*: to set up, build, build in or into; equip, provide).

In a word, instrumentalism is logically avoided only if the self-determination, creativity, and freedom of the self are conceived most basically as acts of love, and this requires recognition of the constitutive relation of the Other to and in the self that is denied in liberalism's congenital abstract self-identity.

The structural indifference of the self to the other that founds liberal instrumentalism can best be summarized technically in terms of an ontological "unitarianism," coincident with what consequently may be called an ontological "pelagianism." *Unitarianism*: the self is originally indifferent to relation with the other; and *pelagianism*: the self's relation to the other is consequently first an enactment or construction by a self not yet formed by the effective presence of the other in the self. Unitarianism and pelagianism get expressed differently in each of the areas of community indicated in our creatureliness. Thus the liberal self is, in turn, *a-theistic*: the self in its original constitution is unrelated—or only extrinsically related—to God (cf. deism or religious positivism generally, according to which religion is in the first instance a "voluntary" society). It is also *a-social,* in that the self in its original constitution is unrelated (or only contractually related) to other persons; *a-cosmic,* in that the self is originally extrinsically related to the world, and the world, accordingly, is first a "dumb" (mechanistic) instrument; and *a-familial,* in that the self is conceived first in abstraction from the relation of filiality that is partially constitutive of one's being, and from the aptness for either fatherhood or motherhood that originally *differentiates* one's being into male (masculine) and female (feminine).

It goes without saying that liberalism on its best reading means to avoid the negatives indicated here. The point is that it can consistently do so only insofar as it relinquishes the abstract logic of self-identity that renders the self's creativity and freedom ontologically indifferent toward the other. Liberalism cannot consistently avoid these negatives, in other words, simply through an *option* to embrace community with God, others, world, and family, when it is precisely the notion of "option" in its original structure as conceived in liberalism that is in question.

In sum: my contention is that it is liberalism's (often unwitting) abstract self-identity that sets in motion the logic of self-centeredness operative in Smith's instrumentalist self-interest, and indeed that it is this logic of self-centeredness that lies at the heart of what Pope John Paul II terms a "culture of death" and what Jennifer Morse calls a culture of "utilitarianism." But to see the sense in which this is the case, we must now describe these two cultures more fully.

Instrumentalism and the "Culture of Death"

Recognizing many positive developments in contemporary society, John Paul II nonetheless characterizes our situation in terms of a "dramatic clash between good and evil, death and life, the 'culture of death' and the 'culture of life.'"[25] Identifying the "culture of death" as a "structure of sin" (*EV*, n. 12), the pope describes the main features of this culture. "The criterion of personal dignity—which demands respect, generosity and service—is replaced by the criterion of efficiency, functionality and usefulness: Others are considered not for what they 'are,' but for what they 'have, do and produce.' This is the supremacy of the strong over the weak" (*EV*, n. 23).

The pope speaks of "a certain Promethean attitude" in the culture that "leads people to think that they can control life and death" (n. 15); of an attitude that views suffering as "the epitome of evil, to be eliminated at all costs" (n. 15). He speaks of "a self-centered concept of freedom" (n. 13), and again of a false autonomy that fails to see that freedom " possesses an inherently relational dimension" and is essentially linked with truth (n. 19). Corresponding to this view is a mentality that "recognizes as a subject of rights only the person who enjoys full or at least incipient autonomy and who emerges from a state of total dependence on others" (n. 19). Man becomes "concerned only with 'doing,' and using all kinds of technology," busying "himself with programming, controlling and dominating birth and death" (n. 22). "Nature itself, from being *mater* (mother), is now reduced to being 'matter,' and is subjected to every kind of manipulation" (n. 22). The "supremacy of the strong over the weak" (n. 23), however paradoxically in light of the intention of democracy, "effectively moves toward a form of totalitarianism" (n. 20), in the sense that the "state arrogates to itself the right to dispose of the life of the weakest and most defenseless members, from the unborn to the elderly, in the name of a public interest which is really nothing but the interest of a certain group" (n. 20).

John Paul II locates the source of the primacy accorded the criteria of efficiency, functionality, and usefulness ultimately in the culture's loss of the sense of God. "By living 'as if God did not exist,' man not only loses sight of the mystery of God, but also of the mystery of the world and the mystery of his own being" (n. 22).[26] "He no longer considers life as a splendid gift of God, something 'sacred' entrusted to his responsibility and thus also to his loving care and 'veneration.' Life itself becomes a mere 'thing,' which man claims as his exclusive property, completely subject to his control and manipulation" (n. 22).

The pope's description and criticism of the "culture of death" do not imply a denial that persons in such a culture often seek to "program . . . and control birth and death" out of motives of compassion (cf. embryonic stem cell research, for example), motives that are indeed often supported by sincerely held religious beliefs. (In the United States, polls indicate that more than 90% of the people believe in God.) The pope's description and criticism bear rather on the *order* (onto-*logic*) carried (often unconsciously) in a culture's way of life, action, and thought, *despite and within* what may otherwise be the compassionate, religious intentions motivating this way of life. That is why the Holy Father refers to the "culture of death" as a *"structure* of sin" (emphasis added) (*EV*, 12: *peccati institutum*; *EV*, 24: *structuras peccati*): he means that, in order to understand the nature of this "culture" properly, we need to extend the reality of "personal" sin to include the structures generated by, but not reducible to, sin in this "personal" sense (i.e., to personal intentions and acts of choice).[27]

The nature of the "culture of life" that the pope calls for in response to the "culture of death" is implicit in the foregoing description: a culture rooted in a sense of community and relationship ordered ultimately from and toward the love of God revealed in Christ and inclusive of all of life and of the body itself.

> It is the proclamation of a living God who is close to us, who calls us to profound communion with himself and awakens in us the certain hope of eternal life. It is the affirmation of the inseparable connection between the person, his life and his bodiliness. It is the presentation of human life as a life of

relationship, a gift of God, the fruit and sign of his love. It is
the proclamation that Jesus has a unique relationship with
every person, which enables us to see in every human face the
face of Christ. It is the call for a "sincere gift of self" as the
fullest way to realize our personal freedom. (*EV*, n. 81)

The comprehensive sense of community and relationship indicated
here has its roots in John Paul II's understanding of the Church as
"communion": "Precisely because it derives *from* Church *communion*, the sharing of the . . . faithful in the threefold mission of Christ
requires that it be lived and realized *in communion* and *for the increase of communion itself*" (*CL*, n. 14; see Ch. 2, nos, 18-31).

Jennifer Morse's description of our current cultural problematic
echoes the pope's in striking ways. She begins by stressing the importance of the fact of dependency in human society: "dependency is the
one truly universal human experience, since everyone begins life with
infancy." Indeed, the "ubiquity of unavoidable helplessness [of infancy,
illness, old age, and the like] points to the possibility that dependency
is not peripheral to the social order, but somehow central to it." Morse
then describes how modern America "marginalizes" the dependent
or needy:

First, we define them out of existence, . . . [changing] the terms
of the discussion so that those who are apparently dependent
are really just as autonomous as everyone else. Second, we
commercialize their care. . . . Finally, we have developed
elaborate justifications for ending the lives of those who are
dependent on us. In other words, if all else fails, we kill them.

She continues: "care of children becomes one more commodity."
Though there is a difference between market child care and government child care, the more significant difference is between "personal
care by a family member and impersonal care provided by a paid

stranger." "The dependent [e.g., the infirm elderly person, the child in the womb] have no intrinsic value." Often, the unspoken claim in our culture is "that a person's dignity depends on the ability to think, choose, and make and keep commitments," but such a defense of personal dignity "cannot take account of situations in which recognizably human creatures are unable to choose and behave rationally." Humans without these capacities "have no rights at all." Infants "can be subsumed as a species of capital theory: a baby is useful because it will grow up to become a productive member of society." Morse describes the needed response to the cultural patterns indicated here in terms that again are strikingly similar to those of John Paul II. She writes that the answer to these problematic patterns ("impersonal bureaucracy and atomistic individualism") is "the law of the gift." "To put it simply, we need love."

> The gift perspective . . . preserves the universality principle that is so important to the Western philosophical and legal tradition. Not only am I a gift to myself, so is every other person a gift to him or herself. There is a still a powerful egalitarian impulse in the gift approach. Although we may differ in our gifts and talents, each one of us is still a gift as much as any other. . . . There is a level at which no one really has reasonable bragging rights. I didn't create my intellect, my health or my family background, any more that I created my own life. The gift perspective helps us to see that each of these talents and endowments was entrusted to us, and are not fundamentally of our own making or creation.
>
> Thus, the gift perspective maintains crucial important features of our Western system of legal rights and obligations. We do not lose the important aspects of autonomy, namely, self-ownership against ownership by anyone else. . . . But the gift perspective provides us with several unique advantages over the exclusive focus on legal rights and obligations.

For example, "viewing the person as a gift helps us to have a more realistic understanding of human dependency" and "inspires an attitude of gratitude." "The helpless person," says Morse, "invites us to enter into the realm of unconditional love." Indeed, "[w]e work harder when our work is motivated with love."

Morse then concludes her essay by reinforcing all of the above in light of a Christian vision, with its deepened sense of the meaning of suffering, its hallmark attentiveness to the weak, and its expansion of "the definition of neighbor to include anyone in need." She sums up by saying that the contribution of the dependent to the rest of us ultimately is that "they teach us how to love, and be loved."

John Paul II and Morse describe in similar ways the deeply problematic patterns of contemporary cultural life, and both link these patterns with an "instrumentalist" or "utilitarian" view of the human person. Both identify the marginalization of the weak and dependent as lying at the heart of our culture's troubling patterns. Finally, both propose the renewal of community, or what Morse calls "the gift perspective," in response to these patterns, and they both, albeit in different ways, appeal to Christianity in support of this gift perspective.

The anthropology of creaturely being as gift developed throughout this chapter is fundamentally in harmony with what John Paul II affirms as a "culture of life" and Morse as the "law of the gift." I wish here, however, to recall the logical link suggested above between liberalism's abstract notion of the self (self-identity) and contemporary culture's dominant logic of instrumentalism, as manifest in what the pope terms a "culture of death" and Morse "utilitarianism."

I do not mean to suggest that liberal anthropology *necessarily* leads to extreme expressions of utilitarianism, or indeed that it is liberal anthropology in an explicit conceptual form that brings us to these extremes. The point, simply, is that the liberal idea of man, operating however unwittingly and unthematically in Americans' patterns of life, creates an onto-logical vulnerability to such extremes. In short, I am conceiving liberal anthropology after the manner of what John Paul II terms sin in its "structural" sense: namely, a disorder—a dis-*order*—that conditions and disposes toward, but never exhaustively or wholly accounts for, sin in its properly personal reality (i.e., personal in the sense that it requires and expresses an exercise of freedom).

Now, Morse exempts capitalism from her criticisms of cultural utilitarianism—and thus presumably from the pope's criticisms of the "culture of death." In fact, she says, "[c]apitalism has given millions of people a far higher standard of living than they could have obtained under any other economic system." Criticism should therefore be directed not at "the economic system per se, but the wider philosophical framework of individualism within which capitalism is most often defended."[28] What we need to do, in short, is to "humanize" the "*vision* of the free society*" (emphasis added).

But implicit in my argument thus far is the claim that this "wider philosophical framework of individualism" has in fact been endemic to capitalism—in its historical origin and in its only historically dominant forms. Capitalism from the beginning has been embedded (however unconsciously) within what may be called the philosophical tradition of liberalism, and it thereby shares in the defects of that philosophical tradition, *already as an economy*. Let us now turn to consider the implications of this claim, first in relation to Morse and then in relation to selected others of the first group of authors.

I hasten to emphasize that the argument to follow, like the argument made by Morse herself, by no means intends simply to reject the achievements of what she terms the "free society" of Western modernity. My intention is not to deny but to recuperate freedom, albeit a freedom now conceived in its proper nature as *creaturely*. Within a freedom so conceived, my intention, like Morse's, is to retrieve the important features she identifies as characteristic of the modern West, namely, its "powerful egalitarian impulse" and the rightful aspects of its sense of autonomy—as well as the creativity, self-determination, and similar features noted by other authors of the first group. However, as we will now see in more detail, the differences between her (and their) arguments and my own lie in the extent of the transformation seem to be required in these features for the rightful ordering of market exchanges as such.

Liberal Economics as Instrumentalist Economics and Culture

The sense in which Morse exempts the capitalistic economic system from her criticism of a utilitarian culture is summed up well in the following statements:

> Economics has been successful as a science because it is based on the undeniable fact that people are self-interested and respond to incentives in a systematic and predictable way. This is also the reason that free societies work reasonably well.

> [O]ur free society depends on individual choice and responsibility. The economic and legal systems rest on the assumption that people have the capacity, and indeed the right, to make independent choices for themselves. This system of free enterprise, constitutionally limited government, and culturally sanctioned individualism works reasonably well for most people most of the time. It has produced a society with a higher standard of living and greater amount of personal freedom than any system that has ever existed.

> The vision of the free society must be humanized. We can do this in part by facing the reality of human dependence, along with the reality of human autonomy. . . . We can take care of the disabled so that we have the opportunity to take a vacation from the world of exchange and live in the world of the gift at least some of the time.

The key terms of these statements can be focused in two groups. First, there are those terms indicating that the economic system proper can be more or less separated from cultural issues. Thus Morse says that we have created a culture *around* our legal and economic system. And indeed, as we saw earlier, she suggests that criticisms should be directed not at "the economic system per se, but the wider philosophical framework of individualism within which capitalism is most often defended."

Second, noting that the market system rests on the assumption that people have the capacity and right to make "independent choices for themselves," she claims that "this system of free enterprise. . . works reasonably well for most people most of the time," and indeed has produced "a higher standard of living and greater amount of personal freedom than any system that has ever existed." Economics has been successful because it is based on the truth "that people are self-interested."

But note what is happening here. On the one hand, she wishes to exempt the market system proper from the wider philosophy in and through which that system has been implemented. On the other hand, she goes on to praise this very system for its presupposition of "independent choices," its production of "a higher standard of living" and "greater amount of personal freedom," and the "realism" of its recognition of self-interest, all of which surely embed an anthropology. But she cannot have it both ways: she cannot, on the one hand, exempt the economic system from an anthropology, insofar as that anthropology implies a negative judgment about the system, and on the other hand import (however implicitly) an anthropology that enables—and indeed constitutes the content of—a positive judgment about the system.

Now, presumably, by "independent choices" Morse means something like self-possessed or self-determined agency, by "working reasonably well" she means something like working efficiently; by producing "a higher standard of living" she means producing a greater quantity of health- and comfort-bringing things; by "greater amount of personal freedom" she means more extensive politically and economically sanctioned freedom of choice; by self-interest she means the "enlightened" self-interest that has been harnessed into mutuality. My point is that, in any case, each of these phrases implies an anthropology. Morse exempts the capitalistic system from criticism and indeed praises it not on the basis of no anthropology—as she suggests—but rather on the basis of an anthropology of a very definite sort.

And what is that anthropology? It is one that—as I think the earlier sections of this chapter make clear—presupposes the very logic lying at the foundations of instrumentalism and indeed of the utilitarianism that Morse herself otherwise criticizes so perceptively.

What I am suggesting is that the structure of Morse's argument changes insofar as one sees both (1) that the capitalist economy is already itself an anthropology (which Morse's language itself cannot help but imply), and (2) that that anthropology is instrumentalist in ways that stand deeply in tension with a love or gift perspective. Given these two claims, Morse faces a dilemma: either she must defend the anthropology shaping the market system she wishes to praise, in the face of the objectionable self-centeredness—and thus utilitarianism—characteristic of a liberal anthropology described above; or, to the extent that she agrees with the above criticisms of liberal anthropology, she must take account of what they indicate for a now-needed transformation of capitalism, precisely as an economic *and* cultural system.

Of course, Morse could choose a third alternative, which would be, while granting both of the above claims, to recommend living within a dualism of cultures: an objectionable instrumentalist culture in "public" economic life, coupled with a generous "private" culture of gift. Note, for example, that, having stated, as quoted above, that "people are self-interested," she goes on to say that "this is *not the only truth about human nature* [emphasis added]. It is equally true that we are dependent, all of us some of the time (during infancy), and some of us all of the time (the disabled and the elderly)." This dualist response, however, itself reflects the fragmentation of a liberal anthropology, in contrast to the integration characteristic of an authentically creaturely anthropology. The burden of the latter is that all of us, everybody and everything—self, artifact, other—are called to be, all of the time and everywhere, (dependent) gifts eliciting gratitude, a gratitude that always comprehends while dynamically transforming self-interest. Once this is seen, it becomes clear that "self-interest" in the Smithian sense presupposed by Morse is not the proper (or most "realistic") truth about human nature—or about artifactual nature or cosmic nature—even some of the time.

In sum, given the two claims noted above, and given further her own eloquent argument proposing a culture humanized in and through a gift perspective, Morse has available to her what seem to me three possible responses, any one of which requires her to qualify her argument in significant ways. How can we hope to humanize the vision of a free society in and through a gift perspective, how can we hope to avoid the free society's drift toward a utilitarian "culture of death," if our economic culture—the entire world of producing and exchanging things that pervades our patterns of life, thought, and action—has been handed over without logical resistance to the primacy of instrumentalized self-interest?

I turn now to consider the implications of my own argument regarding liberal economic culture in terms of other authors of the first group. Clearly, my treatment of their arguments will have to be highly selective, relying for its fuller meaning on the more extensive constructive analysis developed thus far. My comments are organized around the issues of liberalism, anthropology, and globalization.

Liberalism. Father Richard Neuhaus begins his chapter by emphasizing the importance of distinguishing among liberalisms. There are corrupt versions of liberalism that ought to be rejected and benign versions that ought to be defended, or at least are defensible. Neuhaus insists in this context that the differences between him and me are chiefly not over matters of Catholic theology (anthropology), but over how we interpret liberalism, and that my criticism presupposes liberalism in an already reduced version. This matter, however, can be quickly put to rest by making it clear that the liberalism I have in mind is in any case meant to include his (as well as that of the others of the first group of authors)—which I, and presumably he and they also, take to be liberalism at its most benign. It is liberalism already in its putatively benign sense that is subject to deep criticism from the point of view of a creaturely anthropology of gift. Contra Neuhaus, the differences between him and me are thus rooted in our respective (Christian) anthropologies. It is from within an anthropology of gift that his liberalism, assumed by both of us to be "benign" as liberalism, is nevertheless judged by me to be "corrupt"—that is, defective —as an anthropology. How so?

Neuhaus is basically right when he says that:

> [i]t is a mistake to pit . . . modern individualism against a more organic Catholic understanding of community. Rather should we enter into a sympathetic liaison with the modern achievement of the idea of the individual, grounding it more firmly and richly in the understanding of the person destined from eternity to eternity for communion with God.

He then goes on to qualify this as follows:

> The problem with the contemporary distortion of the individual as the autonomous, unencumbered, sovereign Self is not that it is wrong about the awesome dignity of the individual, but that it cuts the self off from the source of that dignity. The first cause of this error . . . is atheism.

Neuhaus's positive point, with which I am in substantial agreement, is that we should seek to uncover, within the "autonomous, unencumbered, sovereign Self" of modernity, the truth of the "awesome dignity of the individual" that is somehow struggling to come to expression therein. The problem, says Neuhaus, is that modernity "cuts it-self off from the source of that dignity," and that the "first cause of this error is atheism." Elsewhere he says the problem consists in a lack of freedom's obedience to transcendent truth.

The anthropology of gift outlined earlier, however, prompts us to ask just what is meant here by the individual's being cut off from God and transcendent truth as the source of his dignity. For the pertinent point, given that anthropology, is that the relation of God and hence of transcendent truth to the individual self is already (partially) constitutive of the individual self, such that the self and its freedom are always, at their deepest level, other-centered. This implies a primitive, largely implicit, movement of the self toward the other that is quite distinctive, one which I take to differ significantly from that (implicitly) accepted by Neuhaus.

What that difference is can best be seen in Neuhaus's discussion of America's Declaration of Independence. The theistic references in that document, Neuhaus says, are not merely "crowd-pleasing asides, but are integral to [its] moral argument." The liberty enshrined in that document is an "ordered liberty," because it is meant to be anchored in "self-evident truths." I quite agree with both assertions. The crucial issue nevertheless comes into relief when we link these two assertions, as the Declaration does, with the individual's "rights": each of us as an individual has a right to life, liberty, and the pursuit of happiness.

To be sure, we do have such rights. But it does not suffice for an adequate understanding of these simply to tether the individual self to its transcendent source, for this tethering can still be too "extrinsically" conceived. And it is so conceived insofar as the self's rights are not given their first form in the self's anterior call to respond in love to the other (God, others). Nor does a variant of Neuhaus's appeal—an appeal, namely (as Jefferson himself makes), to rights as *natural* rights —suffice here. For nature can be understood merely as a "fact" from which we spring to claim rights—exactly in the sense given them by Jefferson. That is, in what is otherwise a necessary appeal to nature, we can fail to grasp the anterior relation to God that is constitutive of nature, failing thereby to grasp the implications of a relation so understood for a reordering of rights in the Declaration sense.

The heart of this needed reordering, then, lies in recognizing that rights, in their true creaturely structure, bear from the inside out an order centered in the self to be sure, but in the self only as centered simultaneously-anteriorly in God, others, the world, and the family. Rights, in a word, because and insofar as they are created, need to be recuperated in their original ontological structure *as gifts*. This implies a priority of the other (giver), even as this priority, in the way indicated earlier, is always already inclusive of the self.

The upshot of the reordering indicated here is thus that generosity is folded into the original meaning of rights. This implies two things. First, I claim my rights before the other only *inside of* and as *anteriorly ordered by* the claim of the other on me. This anterior claim of the other, with its note of "obligatoriness," is not to be interpreted after the manner of a duty in the modern (e.g., Kantian) sense. The claim, rather, takes the form of a *call* to community with God (and all other creatures) that is *inscribed at the core of my being as a creature*. It is a being-bound (*"obligo"*) in God's creative love that always presupposes my now-responsive freedom.

Second, this original binding of rights to an anterior love for an Other does not thereby reduce rights merely to "instruments"—such that, if one refused to give primacy to the service of God and others, one would thereby forfeit one's rights. Quite to the contrary, such an interpretation overlooks the crucial fact that the existence of the self, and consequently of self-interest, is itself already a matter of God's own created community. What it is crucial to see, in other words, is that my rights remain irreducibly and not merely "instrumentally" good because, as created, they always participate just so far in God 's own abiding generosity as creator. Truly understood, and precisely as claims *of the self*, they are meant to participate anteriorly in God's *other-centered giving*.

In sum, my "claim" upon God and others is *mutual with*, even as it is *anteriorly-asymmetrically ordered by*, the "claim" of God and others on me.

Now it is typically asserted by liberalism in its benign or "conservative" reading that the Declaration's affirmation of rights bears a certain "innocence," in the sense that it permits those making this affirmation to continue to hold the truths of the premodern Western tradition (the best of classical Greek and Christian thought, for example). What the Declaration adds to the tradition, in other words, is merely the "form" of freedom that leaves otherwise in place the tradition's substantial content. But this assumes that, as long as we affirm both the rights of the self and the rights of the other—as long, that is, as we affirm both the self and the other in their mutuality—we need not fuss over the issue of their relative priority. This assumption, however, begs the question of the asymmetrical order between self and other indicated in creatureliness, as argued in Part II, and indeed as is necessarily evoked in any attempt to harmonize liberal modernity and classical (Christian) thought. In any case, without this qualified asymmetry of order within the mutuality of rights (self) and goods (other), rights by definition become wrongly self-centered or selfish—and not generous.[29]

Neuhaus fails to differentiate sufficiently between self-centered and other-centered rights, in the way demanded here, in his defense of the Declaration of Independence's recognition of the transcendent source of individual dignity. But before considering significant related points in his chapter, let me note some of the concrete transformations in the content of rights as reordered here, in contrast to the content of rights as construed in their more conventionally liberal terms.

Relation to God (religious freedom). The original right to freedom in religion—i.e., vis-à-vis God—emerges from within the always anteriorly given élan for God, or, again, the always anterior claim of God on us. This implies two things. First, the right to religious freedom is not primarily an immunity (from coercion)—after the manner argued by John Courtney Murray, for example[30]—but on the contrary emerges intrinsically from, and as formed by, this always anterior call to be for God. And, for the reasons given, this right is not forfeited if a person either fails to recognize or refuses to follow this call. Second, religion is a "natural" community before it is a freely chosen community. Or better, the movement toward God that essentially involves freedom is itself always elicited first by God himself in the very act of creation. This implies a transformation in the conventionally liberal sense of religion as primarily a voluntary society (cf., e.g., Locke, Madison).

Though the present forum does not permit us to sort the matter out in the way required, we may note briefly the implications here for the problem of "confessionalism." On the one hand, the foregoing exposes the non-neutrality of any appeal to religious freedom in terms primarily of freedom of choice (or immunity from coercion). A freedom that is originally "full " of a dynamic order toward God is different from a freedom that is originally empty of that order. On the other hand, the order implicit in creatureliness rightly understood itself carries intrinsic "space" for the exercise of freedom. It follows that a rightly, or "creaturely," conceived freedom indicates something different from the (putatively "neutral") freedom of liberalism and from the unfreedom of "confessionalism"—confessionalism, that is, in the objectionable sense of a (juridical) order of religious truth lacking requisite space for freedom.

Neuhaus stresses the importance for a free society of a limited state and, in this connection, also of a distinction between state and society. He then distinguishes between a confessional society (which he affirms), and a confessional state (which he rejects). He is right to affirm both the limited state and a distinction between state and society. The preceding two paragraphs, however, imply that Neuhaus's argument here needs to be further differentiated. For the state's "limitedness," on the Murrayite reading that Neuhaus follows, is conceived as constitutional "silence" about or "indifference" toward God: that is, not in the sense that God's existence is denied but that it is bracketed for constitutional purposes—hence Murray's interpretation of the religious articles of the First Amendment as "articles of peace" rather than "articles of faith." The state, in other words, affirms religious freedom primarily as a (putatively neutral) immunity from coercion, leaving it to private individuals (society) to choose their own religion. The only demand on the state is that it protect the right of each individual to choose—i.e., to "confess" God in his or her own way.

But notice the (unintended) deception here: the state, on this reading, favors a notion of religious freedom whereby freedom's "negative" moment in relation to God (i.e., its silence or indifference) (onto-)logically precedes its "positive" moment (i.e., its constitutive élan or restlessness for, or implicit affirmation of, God). Which is to say, the state favors a notion of religion the positive meaning of which emerges first as a matter of choice—a notion properly termed positivistic. On a positivistic conception of religion, man is viewed not as "naturally" religious (cf. Augustine and Aquinas and the entire patristic-medieval Christian tradition), but as primarily voluntarily religious. The upshot, then, is that the liberal state, on Murray's and Neuhaus's reading, in fact embodies a "confession": what it officially confesses is "positivist" ("voluntaryist") as distinct from "natural" religiosity. It follows that Murray's and Neuhaus's desired distinction between a non-confessional state and a confessional society is not—and in fact cannot be—as neat as they characteristically insist.[31]

Once this becomes clear, we see that the issue regarding religious freedom and the liberal state is now properly framed not in terms of official confession vs. official freedom, but rather in terms of which confession (liberal or nonliberal) makes space for religious freedom in the truest sense. To be sure, more discussion of this claim is needed than can be provided in the present forum. I would only highlight here how the liberal state, with its privileging of religious freedom as immunity, becomes in its own way "unlimited": because and insofar as the only religion the liberal state officially supports, always and everywhere in "public," is one that keeps its contents "private"—a religion, that is, that construes its "public" role to be, not that of *forming*, but only of *inspiring*, life, thought, and moral action. The liberal state just so far officially favors a fragmented, as distinct from integrated, idea of religion. But notice again that it does so in the name not of confession but of non-confession—which is to say, its "totalizing" dynamic always hides itself in an omnipresent appeal to (putatively empty, hence neutral) freedom (i.e., immunity).

Once again, there are excruciatingly difficult and subtle issues raised here that need further sorting out on another occasion. However, in a sense that is just my point: we need to differentiate the issues further, precisely in order to understand (for example) the distinctive way in which America's constitutional defense of religious freedom as a matter of principle favors America's (peculiar kind of) secularization.

In sum, we need to exhibit an understanding of religion (and the state) that moves us beyond the conventional terms of liberalism on the one hand and the old confessionalism on the other. Such an understanding seems to me exactly the intention of the Second Vatican Council's *Dignitatis Humanae,* rightly interpreted. Neuhaus's argument, following that of Murray, leaves us locked within these conventional terms—which John Paul II means to challenge.[32]

Relation to others ("subjectivity of society" and " solidarity"). What needs to be highlighted here is how the constitutive nature of the self's relation to the other alone yields the full integrity—and indeed novelty—of the meaning of "subjectivity of society" and "solidarity" as used by their author, John Paul II. In his chapter in this volume, Michael Novak is concerned on the one hand to distinguish the pope's understanding of these terms from a socialist understanding. Novak emphasizes the personal responsibility and initiative of the human subject, and he opposes this to what socialists imply in collectivization. He is concerned on the other hand to emphasize the subjectivity of the human person over against the non-subjectivity of animals (who cannot choose for themselves). But such emphases, however necessary, do not get us to the nub of the crucial difference between liberal (i.e., originally chosen) community and genuinely creaturely (i.e., originally given) community as articulated throughout this chapter. For what the latter as distinct from the former community demands is precisely an *order* of community that already partially but decisively structures the meaning of individual freedom. It demands an order, that is to say, that transcends the individual and his freedom even as it already itself essentially includes the individual's freedom.

This suggestion is best clarified in relation to what the pope refers to as a "structure"—a social order, as it were—of sin, an order that is brought into being by personal choice but which nevertheless does not reduce to sin in the sense of personal choices. The pope's notions of the "subjectivity of society" and "solidarity" refer to what are the positive correlatives to sinful structures or order. That is, they indicate an order ("civilization of love," "culture of life") that, precisely as a matter of (social) *order*, expresses the good of community, that is, in a way that cannot be accounted for in terms of the personal choices of individuals, even as it remains essentially related to those choices.

The distinction indicated here is important not least of all because it implies that any renewal of culture in accord with what is meant by "subjectivity of society" and "solidarity" on the pope's terms requires a *social-structural* transformation that presupposes even as it "transcends" the sum transformation of individual persons. (It is notable in this connection that neither Neuhaus nor Novak has ever undertaken a critique of contemporary society in terms of "structural" sin in the way that John Paul II repeatedly has, indeed in the way the pope says we must if we are to provide the needed critique.)[33]

Relation to the world ("stewardship"). The constitutive relation of the individual self to the world that is given with his creation
implies, most basically, that the world—the entire natural environment—is a home for man before it is his instrument. Or better, it is an
instrument, but only as it is always more basically a gift. This truth
does not imply that man ought not to use the world, but only that his
use needs to be ordered to the world's fundamental reality as gift—its
reality as a gift from God that is for God, for others, and for himself in
relation to God. Thus, work, and the artifacts of work, ought always-
finally to be ordered to the worship of God and community and friendship with others. Though much of what I affirm here is implicit in my
earlier comments apropos of liberalism's instrumentalist view of work
and artifacts, I have yet to highlight what is termed "stewardship."
Man is meant to care for the non-human cosmos, and indeed to use it
for his own purposes. But this care and use must be ordered intrinsically toward human and divine love, an aptness for the containment
and expression of which is already present in the original order of
things and is given with their creation. What this implies for Western
modernity's science and technology is of course a vast question, which
I address in a limited context at the end of this chapter.

Relations of family and gender ("mediating institutions"). John
Paul II and Catholic social teaching refer frequently to the notion of
"subsidiarity," and many Catholics rightly affirm the need for "mediating institutions" in this regard. That is, human society rightfully
conceived requires intermediate communities between the state and
the individual. Paramount among such mediating institutions is the
family. The creaturely anthropology defended in this chapter understands familial relations as intrinsic to the identity of the individual.
The crucial implications of this come into relief when we contrast this
sense of individual identity with the originally abstract individual identity of liberalism. As a matter of its own inner logic, liberalism tends to
invest rights in the individual independent of his relations to family. A
genuinely creaturely ontology, on the contrary, invests rights in the

individual *at once as a member of a family*. That is, it is the individual as always and already ordered to his most immediate natural community who is properly the subject of rights.

Furthermore, creaturely ontology as I have conceived it—for example, in light of Genesis—entails recognition of gender difference as intrinsic to man's original identity. It just so far recommends a notion of rights that would accord these to individuals precisely *in* this *difference* that at once expresses the unity or equality of man and woman. This approach contrasts, again, with the tendency of liberalism, which insists on abstracting from this difference, precisely as a condition of defending (its own abstract notion of) equality.

The burden of the foregoing brief descriptions is to amplify what is entailed in a generous conception of rights. Rights in their true creaturely understanding are intrinsically ordered to, even as they are themselves already and in principle inclusive expressions of, community in each of the four ways outlined here: with God, others, the world, and the family. The breakdown of community in each of these areas in contemporary society, accordingly, I take to be a function *logically* of liberalism's insufficiently generous—that is, wrongly self-centered—conception of rights, an insufficiency that emerges by virtue of ambiguity within the Declaration of Independence itself.

My argument thus indicates a distinct approach to the interpretation of current cultural problems relative to the (liberal) founding documents of America. Father Neuhaus sees in the Declaration sound principles to which we need to be called back in order to overcome our current difficulties. In other words, he locates the roots of the present cultural difficulties in the moral-political departure from America's founding principles that is evidenced, for example, by various decisions of the Supreme Court since the 1940s. Thus, he argues, to take but one example, that legalized abortion indicates an "abandoning [of] the first [i.e, "founding"] liberalism that has sustained all that is hopeful in the American experiment." The burden of my own argument, on the contrary, is that present-day legalized abortion exposes what is a crucial ambiguity—regarding the self and its rights—already resident in the "first liberalism," whatever its express *intentions* to the contrary.

We can now comment briefly on other pertinent claims of Neuhaus. First, in connection with his defense of the Declaration of Independence, Neuhaus suggests that the American experiment as constituted by a Puritan-Lockean synthesis "has been bowdlerized to fit the secularist prejudices of our academic elites." And he insists in the same vein that the religion indicated in this synthesis is not a mere "civil religion," because it acknowledges "the transcendent source and end of human existence." But these assertions miss the a-theism peculiar to American liberalism, as we outlined it above (and as in fact it is well described by Will Herberg in his "classic" book, *Protestant Catholic Jew*), which expresses itself primarily not in an overt denial of God's existence, but in an implicit affirmation of God's irrelevance to the *form* of our daily acting, producing, and thinking.[34]

Furthermore, Neuhaus insists that liberalism in any case is not "the content of the Church's message. It is simply the condition for the Church to invite free persons to live in the *communio* of Christ and his Mystical Body, which communion is infinitely deeper, richer, and fuller than the liberal social order—or, for that matter, any social order short of the right ordering of all things in the kingdom of God." The fault then, if we fail to propose the Church's message in a way that is sufficiently persuasive, "is not with liberalism but with ourselves."

Neuhaus's suggestion here (liberalism is a "condition," not a content) expresses the characteristic claim of liberalism that its freedom (i.e., freedom of choice) is in principle empty of an anthropology. But we have seen that liberalism's freedom of choice already and essentially *is* an anthropology, one indeed that misses the implications of its originally given *creaturely* order. Indeed, Neuhaus's assertion here betrays an "extrinsicism" in his defense of America's experiment in "ordered liberty." For the crucial issue, in light of all we have written, lies in differentiating the sense in which "order"—toward God and transcendent truth—*anteriorly forms* freedom *in its first act* relative to God and truth.

Further, then, the "fault" regarding our inability to be persuasive in proposing *communio* to the broader culture is not only in ourselves, so to speak. Our ability to be persuasive, rather, is seriously hindered by liberal claims such as that freedom is a condition and not a content, which, in the name of (putatively empty) "process," hide what is already, *eo ipso,* a definite liberal conception (i.e., content) of freedom. Liberalism, in other words, in its appeal to freedom, hides the *order* implicit in that appeal. The point, then, is that to be persuasive in the broader culture, we need to expose liberalism not just as the sum of (bad) personal uses of freedom, but as an *order* of freedom. Which is to say that we have to come to terms with liberalism also as a "structure of sin."

Finally, it is of course true that the right ordering of things—of the self and its love—is never complete except in the kingdom to come. The relevant point, however, is that the Son of God came to earth in order that the earth, already in him and here and now, might begin bearing heaven. The eschatological kingdom, in other words, finds its rightful meaning only in Jesus' incarnational kingdom. The fact that the right ordering indicated in the latter is to begin now scarcely means that it ought to be "imposed" rather than "proposed," despite many errant past practices of the Church in this regard. As Neuhaus says, the Church's communion is infinitely more than the liberal social order. The crucial points, however, are whether and in what sense the transformation toward this communion is to begin already now and "publicly," and not merely in the future and "privately"; and whether this dynamic transformation is to originate from within the core of liberal social order or only by way of addition to it.

Neuhaus concludes that the (putative) liberalism of John Paul II is "commensurate with the American liberal tradition, and in critical continuity with the great work of John Courtney Murray." At any rate, he says, he "hope[s] that is the case, for we have not the luxury of imagining the reconstitution of this social and political order on foundations other than the liberal tradition." What I have said suffices to indicate why I think Neuhaus is mistaken in his claim that the thought of John Paul II is commensurate with American liberalism. Regarding the "luxury" of reconstituting America's social and political order on terms other than those of liberalism, I fail to see why things are so different with respect to American culture from what they have been with respect to dominant cultures throughout history. We are called to attempt to transform whatever culture we live in, hence including that of America, in accord with the truth about man and God as we understand it. On the question of the "realism" of such an attempt, I recall the reader to the discussion at the end of Part II.

If I may summarize, then: (1) for the reasons given, I believe that America's characteristic notion of rights—the "benignly" liberal notion defended by Neuhaus, for example—needs to be transformed at its roots ("radically") and from the inside out; and (2) I believe that it is this radical transformation alone that finally permits, indeed demands, a legitimate sense of America's "exceptional" achievements. It is the very radicality of the transformation, in other words, that enables us to retrieve the historically significant goods that are intended in and by the Declaration but are nevertheless undermined by the Declaration's own ambiguous "logic."

Anthropology. Michael Novak argues that "liberals" in the best sense are not materialists "concerned solely with market processes, profits, and efficiency, to the neglect of the human spirit, human values, and human rights." On the contrary, he insists, "[i]n the new economy of today . . . it is very difficult to be a materialist, strictly understood." Why? Because in an age characterized by computers and the like, "*matter* matters less and less, and *intelligence* (or spirit) matters more." What matters, in other words, is rather the "information . . . created by human intelligence," "the fruit of the human spirit." "[A]n increasing proportion of production today lies in its 'spiritual' rather than its 'material' components. Industries are becoming cleaner; through miniaturization, physical products are becoming smaller, more powerful, and (usually) cheaper." Furthermore, Novak appeals to the "growing immateriality of what people are actually willing to buy," reflected not only in their demand for information, but also in their increasing demand for entertainment, sport, music, theatre, and literature, as well as their increasing preference for intellectual and aesthetic delight, all of which "place much smaller demands on materials and energy" (citing Kenneth Adams).

The burden of my earlier argument, however, is that liberalism is "materialist" in the objectionable sense, not because it is concerned more with "matter" than with "spirit," but because of its characteristic instrumentalism, which embodies and contributes to dehumanizing patterns of having and producing and indeed of thinking and acting. Viewed in this light, Novak's suggestion becomes scarcely credible: liberals are no longer materialistic because they now collect information instead of Rolls Royces! His suggestion utterly ignores the sense in which the human "spirit" itself can remain—and, given liberal presuppositions, characteristically does remain—*consumeristic*, precisely in its alleged increased interest in entertainment, sport, music, literature, and the like. It is beyond the scope of the present chapter to show this in any detail. I will, however, return to the important question of "an age characterized by computers"—i.e., by technology—below, in connection with the essay by Stackhouse and Stratton.

Under the heading "Breaking the Chains of Poverty," Novak states that the task of this century "is to arrange our institutions so that all the poor of the world may exit from poverty." He then goes on to describe, by way of defending the market economy, some of the key conditions necessary for creating wealth. Here he makes a sustained appeal to John Paul II's emphasis on the "acting person." The pope's argument, he says, rests "on the doctrine of creation and a long-standing Christian interpretive associated with the Book of Genesis." Despite this theological provenance, the argument still implies much about the creation of wealth: notably, for example, in terms of how the cause of wealth lies not primarily in land or the ownership of the means of production, but rather in the "human wit, discovery, invention, the habit of enterprise, foresight, skill in organization." "Creativity by any other name causes wealth, as natural resources alone do not."

Indeed, "the pope sees that the market is, above all, a social instrument":

> [M]ost economic activities in the modern environment are too complex to be executed by one person alone; nearly all of them require the creation of a new type of community, not organic but artifactual, not natural (as the family is natural) but contractual, not coercive (as was "real existing socialism") but free and voluntary, not total like a monastery but task-oriented and open to cooperators, even ones of different belief systems and ultimate commitments. In short, the distinctive invention of capitalist societies is the business firm, independent of the state.

Novak then summarizes as follows:

> [T]he pope has advanced two new arguments in support of his proposal that market systems shed practical light on Christian truth and advance human welfare. The first is that markets give expression to the creative subjectivity of the human person, who has been created in the image of the Creator of all things, and called to help complete the work of creation through sustained historical effort. His second argument is that markets generate new and important kinds of community, while expressing the social nature of human beings in rich and complex ways.

I have already spoken much about the need for creativity to be anteriorly formed in and through the gratitude, or grateful receiving, that alone suffices to integrate creativity into what is an act truly of *giving or loving*, hence humanly enhancing in the proper sense. Novak's assertions, however, help to highlight the central connection between creativity and the nature and origin of wealth. In emphasizing how wealth is a function of invention, habits of enterprise, organizational skills, and the like, Novak in fact brings more sharply into relief the significance of my earlier argument regarding how a creativity conceived in instrumentalist terms gives rise to and itself already participates in a reductive sense of wealth. His failure to qualify creativity in terms of an adequate anthropology of creatureliness backs him into just the wrongly self-centered, instrumentalist creativity that is the bane of liberalism, and indeed informs liberalism's reduced and (in light of the foregoing argument) question-begging notion of wealth. Not surprisingly, Novak defends Smith's notion of self-interest, "rightly understood"—in the equivocal form noted earlier. And not surprisingly, therefore, Novak's defense of creativity ignores the potentially serious consequences of a creativity not clearly differentiated in terms of the distinction between a Smithian account and what I have argued is a genuinely creaturely account of creativity.

This critique may seem unfair, since Novak claims in his appeal to creativity to be interpreting John Paul II: he appeals to creativity, in other words, exactly in its character as an image of the Creator. His interpretation of the creature's imaging of God, however, fails to take sufficient account of the individual's *original constitution in a communion of persons*, a failure manifest in his failure to see how this anterior community affects the original meaning of creativity— wit, invention, enterprise, and the like. He fails, in other words, to come to terms with the crucial issue: namely, the relative ordering of self-centeredness and other-centeredness in such acts.

My point here, it should go without saying, is not that creativity should in any way be attenuated. The point, rather, is to see that an anterior gratitude (listening, patience, contemplativeness, wonder) is necessary, if the initiative toward the other inscribed in creativity is to become a genuinely *loving*—which is to say, a genuinely self-within-other-centered—initiative toward the other. Without these anterior implications of community within creativity, creativity as a matter of its inner logic will generate just the instrumentalized abundance—the instrumentalized having, producing, and exchanging of things—that is characteristic of the culture of utilitarianism.

But a likely rejoinder by Novak would be, compared to what? However incomplete or deficient the abundance produced by capitalist creativity, he asks in his essay, what system has done better? He answers: "In comparing which system is more likely to bring about universal opportunity, prosperity from the bottom up . . . the historical answer is clear: for the poor, market systems provide far better chances of improving income, conditions, and status." Novak is indeed right to demand that criticism of the market system be undertaken in comparison with other economic systems realized in history. I would insist only that this comparison between systems *itself* always be compared to the human destiny that Christian faith and indeed the nature of reality itself calls us to embody here and now and on earth, however much that call will be fully realized only eschatologically. In light of this destiny, we see that Novak's arguments as they bear on wealth and poverty beg the question of the extent to which the very creativity and abundance embodied in and produced by capitalism themselves contribute to the culture of death. To put it another way, his arguments beg the burden of what Mother Teresa meant when she insisted that the malnutrition characteristic of the West was, in the deepest sense and in its own way, as bad as the malnutrition characteristic of India. Here is a comparison that must become part of any argument comparing economic systems in the matter of wealth.

The second contribution of John Paul II that Novak highlights is the pope's recognition of how the market generates new senses of community, such as that found, for example, in the business firm. This new community, he points out, is "artifactual" rather than "organic" or "natural." To be sure, the business firm has and must have legitimate "contractual" dimensions not proper to communities like the family. The radical, constitutive nature of creaturely community, however, requires that (putatively purely) voluntary communities themselves be integrated into the more radical sense of community entailed in creation. Which is to say, there is no community anywhere in the creaturely universe that is purely, or first, voluntary in character. The upshot is that even communities like the business firm are subject intrinsically to the criteria given in the call to giving-gratitude and grateful-giving, with all that this implies in terms of solidarity, the subjectivity of society, and stewardship as outlined with respect to our discussion of Neuhaus—and in contrast with these terms as Novak interprets them.

The arguments of Gregg, Hill, and Griswold all raise further issues, but they nonetheless seem to me to follow Novak's anthropology sufficiently in its main lines that no further response to them is needed, in addition to what has been written in response to Novak and earlier in my constructive argument.

Globalization. Finally, I wish to comment on a single but significant passage from the essay by Max Stackhouse and Lawrence Stratton. The passage concerns globalization, with the threat of homogenization which some see to be built into the globalization process.

> There has been a great fear, in some quarters, that [the globalized economy] would bring about a homogenization of culture, and that people would lose their distinctive identities. Such dire predictions remind one of the widespread anxiety in the 1910s and 1920s that factory work would turn persons into mere cogs in machines, and of the 1950s and 1960s lament that computers, mass communication, and suburbanization would so standardize everything that all diversity and personality would be lost. There has been some loss of cultural

particularity, certainly. Peoples from tribal cultures and peasant peoples from societies essentially feudal in structure, especially, have been drawn into complex cultures where their traditional patterns of life are severely compromised and their hereditary forms of status less valued—both in the dominant culture and among their own youth. And it is often the case that when such folk seek to join the dominant, more complex society, they must often struggle mightily simply to find a place on the loweer rungs of the economic ladder.

However, commissioned, independent studies by the *Economist* converge with data collected by the World Bank and my own studies in this regard: Confucian/Maoist China, Hindu/Democratic India, Islamic/technocratic Malaysia and Indonesia, Christian/Iberian-influenced Brazil and Mexico are all preserving quite distinctive cultures, each with ethnic, religious, and social pluralism continuing under the mantle of these dominant patterns. To be sure, minorities and dissidents frequently encounter human rights violations and cultural disadvantages in these regions, and international legal, political, and economic regulatory and developmental agencies will surely continue to put pressure on these societies to conform to international standards. Those cultures with authoritarian patterns of leadership often resist this pressure—speaking rather romantically, for example, of "Asian values"—yet some of them such as South Korea, Thailand, and Taiwan in Asia, and Chile in Latin America, have recognized that such patterns are economically dysfunctional, and each of these regions is adopting technological, economic, and corporate practices that allow them to interact more easily with the wider human community. Simultaneously, these standards and patterns are being integrated into deeper cultural traditions. . . . The growth of the conditionalities of civil society, to be sure, modifies cultures, but no culture has ever been static or entirely closed to extrinsic influence, and the changes they must adopt to foster economic growth are unlikely to destroy them, even if they modulate these cultures so that they can become more fully interactive with other cultures and societies.

Stackhouse and Stratton thus insist that the data support the conclusion that traditional or peasant cultures are not losing their distinctive identities in the face of globalization. At the same time, however, these authors acknowledge the influence of dominant societal patterns, coincident with this persistent distinctiveness. This influence is due to international pressure to conform by ending human rights' violations, authoritarian patterns of leadership, and economic dysfunctionality. To counter these signs of backwardness, many of the regions characterized by such features are integrating into their deeper cultural traditions the technological, economic, and corporate practices that allow them to interact more easily with the wider human community.

In sum, Stackhouse and Stratton argue that the various religious and ethnic cultures named above need to be brought into line with international standards and practices, which means basically with the standards and practices of the democratic capitalist culture of liberalism, with its technology and science. Adoption of such standards and practices nevertheless permits these cultures, in principle and in fact, to retain their distinctiveness in crucial respects.

The authors' argument here, however, is in significant ways rigged. It is guided a priori in its observations and conclusions by a certain understanding of the nature and worth of the standards and practices of liberal democracy and capitalism. This may seem to be stating the obvious. But the importance of the point comes into view upon recalling what was said earlier, for example, about freedom, and about the possession, production, exchange, and indeed nature of things (artifacts) themselves, as characteristically conceived in liberalism. None of these is without a definite anthropology—which is to say that each embodies a definite anthropological form that just so far inclines toward the displacement of contrary anthropological forms.

Again, it is unlikely that the authors would deny this, or that they would claim that liberal freedom and modes of production and exchange are neutral with respect to different possible anthropologies. Rather, what they apparently mean to argue is that liberal anthropological forms—freedom of choice, "rights," efficiency of production, and the like—are more or less what reasonable persons would take as evidently good; that "neutrality" therefore is a matter of what is *effectively* neutral, because and insofar as it is (more or less) transparently good to and for all reasonable persons. Such forms provide what is the surface machinery proper to civilized life as such—and otherwise leave intact the deeper anthropology proper to indigenous ethnic and religious groups.

But liberal freedom of choice, "rights," and the like are not so transparently good and reasonable. However genuine the advances that these liberal forms represent in certain important respects, liberal freedom of choice, rights, and economic structures in fact serve already to change our notion of the human being in crucial, albeit often subtle, ways. They assist in bringing about, and indeed themselves already express, liberalism's characteristic instrumentalism. Insofar as traditional cultures become more rational and free on liberal terms, they already will have transformed their basic view of the human being and indeed of the nature of the cosmos as created—and in so doing they will have reshaped the cultural and religious meaning in and through which all aspects of their cultures are ordered.

To be sure, Stackhouse and Stratton are correct that these cultures will remain pluralistic, not monolithically liberal. The question I am posing concerns the nature, not the denial, of pluralism among non-Western cultures. Stackhouse and Stratton suggest that homogenization will be a relatively surface phenomenon leaving intact deep religious-anthropological differences. But this judgment imports a reading of liberalism as a surface phenomenon. The problem is that, if liberal standards and practices embody an anthropology that tends to displace indigenous religion and anthropology, then, given enough time[35] and global pressure, these cultures will, *eo ipso*, change in deep—i.e., religious, anthropological—ways. This does not mean that there will no longer be any pluralism, but merely that that pluralism will take the form increasingly of *varieties of liberalism.*

I would like to illustrate my point here further in terms of the concept of technology that is so important for Stackhouse and Stratton. Technology, they say, "is enormously powerful in contemporary globalization," although the view that people have "some ultimate duty to reshape, invent, revise, reform, or transform the world" is today "largely secularized." Nonetheless, it was not always so. On the contrary, technology—and science—properly understood have a theological origin. Following Nancy Pearcey, Stackhouse and Stratton argue for the biblical belief that, because the world is created by God, it has "a rational, intelligible order." They then note three further religious principles. First,

> [t]he universe is contingent and can be changed, a principle that fundamentally challenges the ontocratic assumption that nature (as it is by itself, or as it is created by God) is teleological and imbued with inherent rational purposes, as was taught by Aristotle and Thomas Aquinas. Instead, the expectation of a future transformation, the arrival of a "new heaven and new earth," indicates that nature as it is will collapse and is less to be contemplated and followed than to be intentionally altered and used.

Second, "Humans find their primary kinship not with nature but with a transcendent God and with other humans created in God's image. This generates a perspective that gives permission for humans to have an active role in engaging nature and a denial of the

405

view that humans are so embedded in nature that they can only conform to it"—a perspective that they claim was "widespread among the Puritans." And third, "[h]umans have a duty to shape and intervene in the world; indeed, we are commissioned by God to have dominion" (21).

Furthermore, Stackhouse and Stratton cite the work of David Noble as evidence that "the striking acceleration and intensification of technological development in . . . [medieval] Europe ["the dynamic project of Western technology," which is "the defining mark of modernity"] emanated from contemplative monasticism." The thirteenth century theologian-scientist Roger Bacon, for example, saw "the mechanical arts as a means of anticipating and preparing for the kingdom to come. . . . Technology might well help restore humankind by recovering the knowledge lost in the Fall, and such knowledge would be most useful for moving humanity, as an ally and servant of God, closer to a new kind perfection."

These are indeed striking claims, to which I will respond in three stages. First, the argument that Christian theology underpins technology in its hallmark modern sense is made here in a way that sets aside without discussion an entire stream of historical Christianity. I refer to the theology of thinkers like Maximus, Aquinas, and Bonaventure, to mention a few. Or again, in the contemporary period, we might recall Henri de Lubac, whose work sought to recuperate the social and cosmic meaning of the Church and the Eucharist;[36] or Alexander Schmemann, who sought likewise to recuperate the liturgical-sacramental-symbolic meaning of the cosmos, of space and time and matter and motion in their originally destined meaning as such;[37] or John Paul II himself, who insists on the "cosmic dimension of the Incarnation" —how Christ unites himself with "the entire reality of man," and "in this reality with all 'flesh,' with the whole of creation," "with the whole of the visible and material world."[38] All of these theologians affirm some form (though not Pearcey's reduced form) of the "ontocratic assumption" rejected by Stackhouse and Stratton. All of them would continue to affirm a primacy of the contemplative, even and precisely *within* the active engagement with the cosmos that they would simultaneously affirm. None of them would disjoin their kinship with a transcendent God from a simultaneous—albeit, to be sure, subordinate—kinship with nature. Much more needs to be said to show what is implied by each of these assertions relative to the claim of Stackhouse and Stratton. It suffices for my intention here, however, to call attention to the a priori—and thus question-begging—nature of their dismissal of such theologians that is implied by their argument.

Second, Stackhouse and Stratton assert a simple continuity between the medieval monks and modern technological development, for example, in terms of the monks' exact organizing, and hence rationalizing, of time. Drawing on David Landis's book *Revolution in Time*, the authors mention how "timing was essential to the assembly line, to industrial efficiency experts, and now to the speed of the microchip—all a direct result of the monastery's adoption of technology for rational ends."

It will suffice, relative to the simple continuity asserted here, to call attention to the (*prima facie* significant) contrast between the sense in which Calvinism/Puritanism understands the world as an "instrument" of salvation and the sense in which, for example, a Bonaventure, an Aquinas, or an Ignatius of Loyola understands the world as an "instrument" of salvation. Again, there is Descartes' (re)conceiving of the physical in mechanistic terms. There is Francis Bacon's reconfiguring of knowledge into a matter first of power, and his distinctive sense, consequently, of how science is already itself a matter of technology (for the betterment of humankind). There is the movement in both Descartes and Bacon toward the elimination of inner causes such as form and finality in their respective accounts of nature. Can we really argue for a simple continuity between what the monks meant by order and by time and by the world as *instrument*, without taking account of what are *prima facie* the large differences introduced by Calvinism/Puritanism, Descartes, and Bacon—relative, say, to Maximus, Bonaventure, Aquinas, and Ignatius?

Third, consider the nature of modern technology in relation to what might be called the more "ontocratic" theologies of these latter thinkers. Recall the obvious point that technology is an artifact—nature as changed or transformed by man. This may seem simple enough, but the problem occurs when, as is customary in liberal cultures, we overlook the human meaning that is thereby (partially) constitutive of the thing made. The point, in other words, is that technology is not "dumb," after the manner of a "Cartesian" thing, such that its first human significance comes in and through a use that is *subsequent* or *external* to the thing in its original constitution *as* a thing. Rather, technology, or things as artifacts, are (also) anthropologies. Further, the anthropology carried in modern technology is mechanistic in nature. Modern technology characteristically fails to take integrated account of the teleology, or destiny, of man and nature as conceived by the "ontocratic" theologians—or indeed as discussed earlier apropos of an economy of gift.

Let me illustrate the point here in terms of one important example: the computer. Whatever else it is, the computer is an arrangement or ordering of space and time and matter and motion for the purpose of realizing a certain kind of knowledge. The ordering is binary and digital. The knowledge sought consists in the gathering of discrete bits of information. Knowledge takes the form of acquiring, manipulating, and controlling data. The knowledge proper to a computer is more a matter of power and of "summing" than of "seeing."

To put this in negative terms, the knowledge, or kind of consciousness and experience, implicit in the technological order of the computer is weighted against habits of patient interiority, of contemplativeness, of wonder, of sustained mutual presence, of an embodied being-with, of the wisdom that sees the order of the whole; it does not foster a genuine sense of transcendence (its "transcendence" consists in what may be called the "bad infinity" of endlessly instantaneous and successive finite bits of information). And so on.

In these and other ways, we see that the computer, in its nature as an artifact, favors a definite anthropological order. This by no means entails a denial that the knowledge delivered by a computer has much positive significance. The point is only that, even granting this positive significance, we need to recognize that the increasing dominance of computers in our culture does not come without a high cost. The computer is not merely a neutral instrument that can be appropriated (at least in principle) equally for good or for bad anthropological ends. On the contrary, the computer itself already favors (already itself *is*) a culture with anthropological ends more like those conceived in Puritanism, Bacon, and Descartes (for example) than like those conceived in Maximus, Aquinas, Bonaventure, Schmemann—or indeed John Paul II himself.

Let me summarize the point here in another way, drawing on a perceptive book by the late philosopher George Grant titled *Technology and Justice*.[39]

In a chapter called "Thinking About Technology," Grant considers the extent to which "technology" has become "the pervasive mode of being in our political and social lives" (17). He proceeds by reflecting on a statement by a computer scientist that "the computer does not impose on us the ways it should be used" (19). This claim and the warrant offered for it, Grant says, are familiar to us: computers "are instruments, made by human skill for the purpose of achieving certain human goals. They are neutral instruments in the sense that the morality of the goals for which they are used is determined from outside them" (20).

Grant's argument is that this claim presupposes the "prevalent 'liberal' view of the modern situation"—which, he says, "is so rooted in us that it seems to be common sense itself, even rationality itself. We have certain technological capacities; it is up to us to use those capacities for decent human purposes" (20–21). Indeed, he insists that such a claim asserts nothing less than "the essence of the modern view, which is that human ability freely determines what happens" (31).

Against this claim that the computer is merely a neutral instrument, Grant indicates the ways in which the computer embodies a certain conception of knowledge, an implied view of the relation between subject(ivity) and object(ivity), the relation between knowing and making, and a definite sense of the nature and place of "abstraction" and indeed information in human consciousness. The computer carries an implied judgment about the nature of the other that is the object of knowledge, in a way that presupposes a particular view of the relation between knowledge and love and indeed of the nature of the other as beautiful (38ff.). Grant's point therefore is that the computer, far from being a neutral instrument, is in fact bound up finally with a whole conception of human destiny: the computer tends to homogenize its users just so far in terms of that destiny. Regarding the claim that the computer does not impose itself upon us, then, Grant responds: "Common sense may tell us that the computer is an instrument, but it is an instrument from within the destiny which *does* 'impose' itself upon us, and therefore the computer *does* impose" (23). Grant summarizes thusly:

> When we represent technology to ourselves as an array of neutral instruments, invented by human beings and under human control, we are expressing a kind of common sense, but it is a common sense from within the very technology we are attempting to represent. The novelness of our novelties is being minimized. . . . The coming to be of technology has required changes in what we think is good, what we think good is, how we conceive sanity and madness, justice and injustice, rationality and irrationality, beauty and ugliness.

> . . . [The] changed conception of novelness . . . entails a
> change in the traditional account of an openness to the whole,
> and therefore a quite new content to the word "philosophy." A
> road or a sparrow, a child or the passing of time come to us
> through that destiny. To put the matter crudely: when we
> represent technology to ourselves through its own common
> sense, we think of ourselves as picking and choosing in a
> supermarket, rather than within the analogy of the package deal.
> We have bought a package deal of far more fundamental
> novelness than simply a set of instruments under our control.
> It is a destiny which enfolds us in its own conceptions of
> instrumentality, neutrality and purposiveness. It is in this sense
> that it has been truthfully said: technology is the ontology of
> our age. (32)

If and insofar as it is the case that technology is the ontology of the
age—as, with Grant, I believe it to be —then we cannot but view
globalization's potential for homogenization with much greater concern than do Stackhouse and Stratton.

Conclusion

The overarching claim of the first group of authors in this collection
is that Christianity has made its peace with liberalism, at least as a
matter of principle and in terms of liberalism on its best reading. My
contrary claim is that liberalism, even at its most benign, presents
Christianity with what is arguably its most profound challenge in
engaging the contemporary world. To be sure, there is the global
threat of terrorism linked with Islamic cultures, and any argument
that would attenuate the evil of terrorism —the acts of 9/11, for example—lacks credibility. Still, it is not unequivocally clear that the
violence of liberal cultures is any less in quantity, only that it is
certainly more "subtle." Liberalism proposes itself in "benign" terms
that cloak its capacity for violence—terms like "freedom" and "rights"

and indeed "tolerance" and "compassion." But it is precisely these terms that enable liberalism to direct its violence characteristically at those who can say or do nothing in response—who cannot *themselves* claim rights: the unborn, the infirm, the elderly, the harvested human embryos. Liberalism's violence takes the subtle form enacted, for example, in the designer children that will likely soon come, or in the widespread replacement of natural gender identity with constructed gender identity, with a consequent loss of the paradigmatic *difference* necessary for the first (i.e., familial) community of love in the world. And all of this violence comes in the name of freedom ("freedom of choice") and rights (i.e., immunities).

The rejoinder of course will be that these features of a liberal culture are a function of liberalism at its most corrupt and not at its best. We have seen, however, that the instrumentalist logic disposing our culture to these features resides in the original meaning of liberalism. The problem is congenital: it lies in liberalism's original abstract sense of personal self-identity. Recognition that this is so does not warrant rejection of what are the genuine goods struggling to come to expression in liberalism, as I have noted time and again. The point is that we need now to go to the roots of those goods, reconfiguring them from the inside out for the purpose of giving them their truer and ampler form: the form of gift and gratitude.

My argument regarding the difference between constitutive relational identity and abstract identity exposes the grave ambiguity inherent in all the positive achievements of liberal societies: the "rights" of the individual, freedom of choice, equality, the power of self-determination, the creativity of the self, community as mutual and enlightened self-interest, the capacities of modern science and technology, the institutionalized freedoms of market economics and democratic politics, and so on. Each of these achievements—and each *is* a genuine achievement—insofar as it presupposes, however unconsciously, an onto-logic of abstract self-identity, *eo ipso* bears within it the seeds of its own undoing and indeed reversal. Each of these achievements bears within it a logic of inversion whereby the "powerful" and "productive" and "independent" and "functional" displace the "weak" and "unproductive" and "dependent" and "useless" (see *EV*, n. 23), contrary to what are the original and abiding best *intentions* of liberalism.

The increasing global influence of modern Western socioeconomic institutions, viewed in light of the West's ever-advancing biotechnological manipulation of birth and death, thus intensifies the need for clarifying, in relation to liberalism, the distinction between relational-personal identity and abstract-personal identity, not as a matter of "academic" speculation but for the sake of living the truth of our creatureliness at the heart of the world. This clarification is necessary insofar as we believe that the world continues to have a God- and other-centered destiny, even within the democratic capitalistic societies of modernity. Certainly John Paul II, in his call repeatedly for a "civilization of love," believes the world still has such a destiny. What I have attempted to make clear is the sense in which such a civilization requires the "domestication" of man and his economic culture—requires, that is, recuperation of the relations to God, others, the world, and the family that most deeply and intimately constitute man's being as a creature.

Appendix A

The Total Economy

Wendell Berry

L et us begin by assuming what appears to be true: that the so-
called environmental crisis is now pretty well established as a
fact of our age. The problems of pollution, species extinction, loss of
wilderness, loss of farmland, loss of topsoil may still be ignored or
scoffed at, but they are not denied. Concern for these problems has
acquired a certain standing, a measure of discussability, in the media
and in some scientific, academic, and religious institutions.

This is good, of course; obviously, we can't hope to solve these
problems without an increase of public awareness and concern. But
in an age burdened with "publicity," we have to be aware also that as
issues rise into popularity they rise also into the danger of oversimplification. To speak of this danger is especially necessary in confronting the destructiveness of our relationship to nature, which is
the result, in the first place, of gross oversimplification.

The "environmental crisis" has happened because the human
household or economy is in conflict at almost every point with the
household of nature. We have built our household on the assumption
that the natural household is simple and can be simply used. We
have assumed increasingly over the last five hundred years that nature is merely a supply of "raw materials," and that we may safely
possess those materials merely by taking them. This taking, as our
technical means have increased, has involved always less reverence
or respect, less gratitude, less local knowledge, and less skill. Our

methodologies of land use have strayed from our old sympathetic attempts to imitate natural processes, and have come more and more to resemble the methodology of mining, even as mining itself has become more powerful technologically and more brutal.

And so we will be wrong if we attempt to correct what we perceive as "environmental" problems without correcting the economic oversimplification that caused them. This oversimplification is now either a matter of corporate behavior or of behavior under the influence of corporate behavior. This is sufficiently clear to many of us. What is not sufficiently clear, perhaps to any of us, is the extent of our complicity, as individuals and especially as individual consumers, in the behavior of the corporations.

What has happened is that most people in our country, and apparently most people in the "developed" world, have given proxies to the corporations to produce and provide *all* of their food, clothing, and shelter. Moreover, they are rapidly giving proxies to corporations or governments to provide entertainment, education, child care, care of the sick and the elderly, and many other kinds of "service" that once were carried on informally and inexpensively by individuals or households or communities. Our major economic practice, in short, is to delegate the practice to others.

The danger now is that those who are concerned will believe that the solution to the "environmental crisis" can be merely political—that the problems, being large, can be solved by large solutions generated by a few people to whom we will give our proxies to police the economic proxies that we have already given. The danger, in other words, is that people will think they have made a sufficient change if they have altered their "values," or had a "change of heart," or experienced a "spiritual awakening," and that such a change in passive consumers will necessarily cause appropriate changes in the public experts, politicians, and corporate executives to whom they have granted their political and economic proxies.

The trouble with this is that a proper concern for nature and our use of nature must be practiced, not by our proxy-holders, but by ourselves. A change of heart or of values without a practice is only another pointless luxury of a passively consumptive way of life. The "environmental crisis," in fact, can be solved only if people, individually and in their communities, recover responsibility for their thoughtlessly-given proxies. If people begin the effort to take back into their own power a significant portion of their economic responsibility, then their inevitable first discovery is that the "environmental crisis" is no such thing; it is not a crisis of our environs or surroundings; it is a crisis of our lives as individuals, as family members, as community members, and as citizens. We have an "environmental crisis" because *we* have consented to an economy in which by eating, drinking, working, resting, traveling, and enjoying ourselves we are destroying the natural, the God-given, world.

WE LIVE, AS WE MUST SOONER OR LATER RECOGNIZE, IN AN ERA OF SENTIMENTAL economics and, consequently, of sentimental politics. Sentimental communism holds in effect that everybody and everything should suffer for the good of "the many" who, though miserable in the present, will be happy in the future for exactly the same reasons that they are miserable in the present.

Sentimental capitalism is not so different from sentimental communism as the corporate and political powers claim to suppose. Sentimental capitalism holds in effect that everything small, local, private, personal, natural, good, and beautiful must be sacrificed in the interest of the "free market" and the great corporations, which will bring unprecedented security and happiness to "the many"—in, of course, the future.

These forms of political economy may be described as sentimental because they depend absolutely upon a political faith for which there is no justification. They seek to preserve the gullibility of the people by issuing a cold check on a fund of political virtue that does

417

not exist. Communism and "free-market" capitalism both are modern versions of oligarchy. In their propaganda, both justify violent means by good ends, which always are put beyond reach by the violence of the means. The trick is to define the end vaguely—"the greatest good of the greatest number" or "the benefit of the many"—and keep it at a distance. For example, the United States government's agricultural policy, or non-policy, since 1952 has merely consented to the farmers' predicament of high costs and low prices; it has never envisioned or advocated in particular the prosperity of farmers or of farmland, but has only promised "cheap food" to consumers and "survival" to the "larger and more efficient" farmers who supposedly could adapt to and endure the attrition of high costs and low prices. And after each inevitable wave of farm failures and the inevitable enlargement of the destitution and degradation of the countryside, there have been the inevitable reassurances from government propagandists and university experts that American agriculture was now more efficient and that everybody would be better off in the future.

The fraudulence of these oligarchic forms of economy is in their principle of displacing whatever good they recognize (as well as their debts) from the present to the future. Their success depends upon persuading people, first, that whatever they have now is no good, and, second, that the promised good is certain to be achieved in the future. This obviously contradicts the principle—common, I believe, to all the religious traditions—that if ever we are going to do good to one another, then the time to do it is now; we are to receive no reward for promising to do it in the future. And both communism and capitalism have found such principles to be a great embarrassment. If you are presently occupied in destroying every good thing in sight in order to do good in the future, it is inconvenient to have people saying things like "Love thy neighbor as thyself" or "Sentient beings are numberless, I vow to save them." Communists and capitalists alike, "liberal" capitalists and "conservative" capitalists alike, have needed to replace religion with some form of determinism, so that they can say to their victims, "I'm doing this because I can't do otherwise. It is not my fault. It is inevitable." This is a lie, obviously, and organized religion has too often consented to it.

The idea of an economy based upon several kinds of ruin may seem a contradiction in terms, but in fact such an economy is possible, as we see. It is possible, however, on one implacable condition: The only future good that it assuredly leads to is that it will destroy itself. And how does it disguise this outcome from its subjects, its short-term beneficiaries, and its victims? It does so by false accounting. It substitutes for the real economy, by which we build and maintain (or do not maintain) our household, a symbolic economy of money, which in the long run, because of the self-interested manipulations of the "controlling interests," cannot symbolize or account for anything but itself. And so we have before us the spectacle of unprecedented "prosperity" and "economic growth" in a land of degraded farms, forests, ecosystems, and watersheds, polluted air, failing families, and perishing communities.

THIS MORAL AND ECONOMIC ABSURDITY EXISTS FOR THE SAKE OF THE ALLEGEDLY "free" market, the single principle of which is this: Commodities will be produced wherever they can be produced at the lowest cost and consumed wherever they will bring the highest price. To make too cheap and sell too high has always been the program of industrial capitalism. The global "free market" is merely capitalism's so far successful attempt to enlarge the geographic scope of its greed, and moreover to give to its greed the status of a "right" within its presumptive territory. The global "free market" is free to the corporations precisely because it dissolves the boundaries of the old national colonialisms, and replaces them with a new colonialism without restraints or boundaries. It is pretty much as if all the rabbits have now been forbidden to have holes, thereby "freeing" the hounds.

The "right" of a corporation to exercise its economic power without restraint is construed, by the partisans of the "free market," as a form of freedom, a political liberty implied presumably by the right of individual citizens to own and use property.

But the "free market" idea introduces into government a sanction of an inequality that is not implicit in any idea of democratic liberty: namely that the "free market" is freest to those who have the most money, and is not free at all to those with little or no money. Wal-Mart, for example, as a large corporation "freely" competing against local, privately owned businesses, has virtually all the freedom, and its small competitors virtually none.

To make too cheap and sell too high, there are two requirements. One is that you must have a lot of consumers with surplus money and unlimited wants. For the time being, there are plenty of these consumers in the "developed" countries. The problem, for the time being easily solved, is simply to keep them relatively affluent and dependent on purchased supplies.

The other requirement is that the market for labor and raw materials should remain depressed relative to the market for retail commodities. This means that the supply of workers should exceed demand, and that the land-using economies should be allowed or encouraged to overproduce.

To keep the cost of labor low, it is necessary first to entice or force country people everywhere in the world to move into the cities—in the manner prescribed by the Committee for Economic Development after World War II—and, second, to continue to introduce labor-replacing technology. In this way it is possible to maintain a "pool" of people who are in the threatful position of being mere consumers, landless and poor, and who therefore are eager to go to work for low wages—precisely the condition of migrant farm workers in the United States.

To cause the land-using economies to overproduce is even simpler. The farmers and other workers in the world's land-using economies, by and large, are not organized. They are therefore unable to control production in order to secure just prices. Individual producers must go individually to the market and take for their produce simply whatever they are paid. They have no power to bargain or to make demands. Increasingly, they must sell, not to neighbors or to neighboring towns and cities, but to large and remote corporations. There is no competition among the buyers (supposing there is more than one), who *are* organized and are "free" to exploit the advantage of low prices. Low prices encourage overproduction, as producers attempt to make up their losses "on volume," and overproduction inevitably makes for low prices. The land-using economies thus spiral downward as the money economy of the exploiters spirals upward. If economic attrition in the land-using population becomes so severe as to threaten production, then governments can subsidize production without production controls, which necessarily will encourage overproduction, which will lower prices—and so the subsidy to rural producers becomes, in effect, a subsidy to the purchasing corporations. In the land-using economies, production is further cheapened by destroying, with low prices and low standards of quality, the cultural imperatives for good work and land stewardship.

THIS SORT OF EXPLOITATION, LONG FAMILIAR IN THE FOREIGN AND DOMESTIC colonialism of modern nations, has now become "the global economy," which is the property of a few supranational corporations. The economic theory used to justify the global economy in its "free market" version is, again, perfectly groundless and sentimental. The idea is that what is good for the corporations will sooner or later—though not of course immediately—be good for everybody.

That sentimentality is based, in turn, upon a fantasy: the proposition that the great corporations, in "freely" competing with one another for raw materials, labor, and market share, will drive each other indefinitely, not only toward greater "efficiencies" of manufacture, but also toward higher bids for raw materials and labor and lower prices to consumers. As a result, all the world's people will be economically secure—in the future. It would be hard to object to such a proposition if only it were true.

But one knows, in the first place, that "efficiency" in manufacture always means reducing labor costs by replacing workers with cheaper workers or with machines.

In the second place, the "law of competition" does *not* imply that many competitors will compete indefinitely. The law of competition is a simple paradox: Competition destroys competition. The law of competition implies that many competitors, competing on the "free market" without restraint, will ultimately and inevitably reduce the number of competitors to one. The law of competition, in short, is the law of war.

In the third place, the global economy is based upon cheap long-distance transportation, without which it is not possible to move goods from the point of cheapest origin to the point of highest sale. And cheap long-distance transportation is the basis of the idea that regions and nations should abandon any measure of economic self-sufficiency in order to specialize in production for export of the few commodities, or the single commodity, that can be most cheaply produced. Whatever may be said for the "efficiency" of such a system, its result (and, I assume, its purpose) is to destroy local production capacities, local diversity, and local economic independence. It destroys the economic security that it promises to make.

This idea of a global "free market" economy, despite its obvious moral flaws and its dangerous practical weaknesses, is now the ruling orthodoxy of the age. Its propaganda is subscribed to and distributed by most political leaders, editorial writers, and other "opinion makers." The powers that be, while continuing to budget huge sums for "national defense," have apparently abandoned any idea of national or local self-sufficiency, even in food. They also have given up the idea that a national or local government might justly place restraints upon economic activity in order to protect its land and its people.

The global economy is now institutionalized in the World Trade Organization, which was set up, without election anywhere, to rule international trade on behalf of the "free market"—which is to say on behalf of the supranational corporations—and to *over*rule, in secret sessions, any national or regional law that conflicts with the "free market." The corporate program of global "free trade" and the presence of the World Trade Organization have legitimized extreme forms of expert thought. We are told confidently that if Kentucky loses its milk-producing capacity to Wisconsin (and if Wisconsin's is lost to California) that will be a "success story." Experts such as Stephen C. Blank, of the University of California, Davis, have recommended that "developed" countries, such as the United States and the United Kingdom, where food can no longer be produced cheaply enough, should give up agriculture altogether.

The folly at the root of this foolish economy began with the idea that a corporation should be regarded, legally, as "a person." But the limitless destructiveness of this economy comes about precisely because a corporation is *not* a person. A corporation, essentially, is a pile of money to which a number of persons have sold their moral allegiance. Unlike a person, a corporation does not age. It does not arrive, as most persons finally do, at a realization of the shortness and smallness of human lives; it does not come to see the future as the lifetime of the children and grandchildren of anybody in particular. It can experience no personal hope or remorse, no change of heart. It cannot humble itself. It goes about its business as if it were immortal, with the single purpose of becoming a bigger pile of money. The stockholders essentially are usurers, people who "let their money work for them," expecting high pay in return for causing others to work for low pay. The World Trade Organization enlarges the old idea of the corporation-as-person by giving the global corporate economy the status of a super-government with the power to overrule nations.

I don't mean to say, of course, that all corporate executives and stockholders are bad people. I am only saying that all of them are very seriously implicated in a bad economy.

UNSURPRISINGLY, AMONG PEOPLE WHO WISH TO PRESERVE THINGS OTHER THAN MONEY— for instance, every region's native capacity to produce essential goods—there is a growing perception that the global "free market" economy is inherently an enemy to the natural world, to human health and freedom, to industrial workers, and to farmers and others in the land-use economies; and, furthermore, that it is inherently an enemy to good work and good economic practice.

I believe that this perception is correct and that it can be shown to be correct merely by listing the assumptions implicit in the idea that corporations should be "free" to buy low and sell high in the world at large. These assumptions, so far as I can make them out, are as follows:

1. That there is no conflict between the "free market" and political freedom, and no connection between political democracy and economic democracy.

2. That there can be no conflict between economic advantage and economic justice.

3. That there is no conflict between greed and ecological or bodily health.

4. That there is no conflict between self-interest and public service.

5. That it is all right for a nation's or a region's subsistence to be foreign-based, dependent on long-distance transport, and entirely controlled by corporations.

6. That the loss or destruction of the capacity anywhere to produce necessary goods does not matter and involves no cost.

7. That, therefore, wars over commodities—our recent Gulf War, for example—are legitimate and permanent economic functions.

8. That this sort of sanctioned violence is justified also by the predominance of centralized systems of production, supply, communications, and transportation which are extremely vulnerable not only to acts of war between nations, but also to sabotage and terrorism.

9.   That it is all right for poor people in poor countries to work at poor wages to produce goods for export to affluent people in rich countries.

10.   That there is no danger and no cost in the proliferation of exotic pests, vermin, weeds, and diseases that accompany international trade, and that increase with the volume of trade.

11.   That an economy is a machine, of which people are merely the interchangeable parts. One has no choice but to do the work (if any) that the economy prescribes, and to accept the prescribed wage.

12.   That, therefore, vocation is dead issue. One does not do the work that one chooses to do because one is called to it by Heaven or by one's natural abilities, but does instead the work that is determined and imposed by the economy. Any work is all right as long as one gets paid for it. (This assumption explains the prevailing "liberal" and "conservative" indifference toward displaced workers, farmers, and small business people.)

13.   That stable and preserving relationships among people, places, and things do not matter and are of no worth.

14.   That cultures and religions have no legitimate practical or economic concerns.

These assumptions clearly prefigure a condition of total economy. A total economy is one in which everything—"life forms," for instance, or the "right to pollute"—is "private property" and has a price and is for sale. In a total economy, significant and sometimes critical choices that once belonged to individuals or communities become the property of corporations. A total economy, operating internationally, necessarily shrinks the powers of state and national governments, not only because those governments have signed over significant powers to an international bureaucracy or because political leaders become the paid hacks of the corporations, but also because political processes—and especially democratic processes—are too slow to react to unrestrained economic and technological development on a global scale. And when state and national governments begin to act in effect as agents of the global economy, selling their people for low wages and their people's products for low prices, then the rights and liberties of citizenship must necessarily shrink. A total economy is an unrestrained taking of profits from the disintegration of nations, communities, households, landscapes, and ecosystems. It licenses symbolic or artificial wealth to "grow" by means of the destruction of the real wealth of all the world.

Among the many costs of the total economy, the loss of the principle of vocation is probably the most symptomatic and, from a cultural standpoint, the most critical. It is by the replacement of vocation with economic determinism that the exterior workings of a total economy destroy human character and culture also from the inside.

In an essay on the origin of civilization in traditional cultures, Ananda Coomaraswamy wrote that "the principle of justice is the same throughout. . . . [It is] that each member of the community should perform the task for which he is fitted by nature. . . ." The two ideas, justice and vocation, are inseparable. That is why Coomaraswamy spoke of industrialism as "the mammon of injustice," incompatible with civilization. It is by way of the practice of vocation that sanctity and reverence enter into the human economy. It was thus possible for traditional cultures to conceive that "to work is to pray."

AWARE OF INDUSTRIALISM'S POTENTIAL FOR DESTRUCTION, AS WELL AS THE considerable political danger of great concentrations of wealth and power in industrial corporations, American leaders developed, and for a while used, certain means of limiting and restraining such concentrations, and of somewhat equitably distributing wealth and property. The means were: laws against trusts and monopolies, the principle of collective bargaining, the concept of 100 percent parity between the land-using and the manufacturing economies, and the progressive income tax. And to protect domestic producers and production capacities, it is possible for governments to impose tariffs on cheap imported goods. These means are justified by the government's obligation to protect the lives, livelihoods, and freedoms of its citizens. There is, then, no necessity that requires our government to sacrifice the livelihoods of our small farmers, small business people, and workers, along with our domestic economic independence, to the global "free market." But now all of these means are either weakened or in disuse. The global economy is intended as a means of subverting them.

In default of government protections against the total economy of the supranational corporations, people are where they have been many times before: in danger of losing their economic security and their freedom, both at once. But at the same time the means of defending themselves belongs to them in the form of a venerable principle: powers not exercised by government return to the people. If the government does not propose to protect the lives, the livelihoods, and the freedoms of its people, then the people must think about protecting themselves.

How are they to protect themselves? There seems, really, to be only one way, and that is to develop and put into practice the idea of a local economy—something that growing numbers of people are now doing. For several good reasons, they are beginning with the idea of a local food economy. People are trying to find ways to shorten the distance between producers and consumers, to make the connections between the two more direct, and to make this local economic activity a benefit to the local community. They are trying to learn to use the consumer economies of local towns and cities to preserve the livelihoods of local farm families and farm communities. They want to use the local economy to give consumers an influence over the kind and quality of their food, and to preserve and enhance the local landscapes. They want to give everybody in the local community a direct, long-term interest in the prosperity, health, and beauty of their homeland. This is the only way presently available to make the total economy less total. It was once the only way to make a national or a colonial economy less total, but now the necessity is greater.

I am assuming that there is a valid line of thought leading from the idea of the total economy to the idea of a local economy. I assume that the first thought may be a recognition of one's ignorance and vulnerability as a consumer in the total economy. As such a consumer, one does not know the history of the products that one uses. Where, exactly, did they come from? Who produced them? What toxins were used in their production? What were the human and ecological costs of producing and then of disposing of them? One sees that such questions cannot be answered easily, and perhaps not at all. Though one is shopping amid an astonishing variety of products, one is denied certain significant choices. In such a state of economic ignorance it is not possible to choose products that were produced locally or with reasonable kindness toward people and toward nature. Nor is it possible for such consumers to influence production for the better. Consumers who feel a prompting toward land stewardship find that in this economy they can have no stewardly practice. To be a consumer in the total economy, one must agree to be totally ignorant, totally passive, and totally dependent on distant supplies and self-interested suppliers.

And then, perhaps, one begins to *see* from a local point of view. One begins to ask, What is here, what is in me, that can lead to something better? From a local point of view, one can see that a global "free market" economy is possible only if nations and localities accept or ignore the inherent instability of a production economy based on exports and a consumer economy based on imports. An export economy is beyond local influence, and so is an import economy. And cheap long-distance transport is possible only if granted cheap fuel, international peace, control of terrorism, prevention of sabotage, and the solvency of the international economy.

Perhaps also one begins to see the difference between a small local business that must share the fate of the local community and a large absentee corporation that is set up to escape the fate of the local community by ruining the local community.

So far as I can see, the idea of a local economy rests upon only two principles: neighborhood and subsistence.

In a viable neighborhood, neighbors ask themselves what they can do or provide for one another, and they find answers that they and their place can afford. This, and nothing else, is the *practice* of neighborhood. This practice must be, in part, charitable, but it must also be economic, and the economic part must be equitable; there is a significant charity in just prices.

Of course, everything needed locally cannot be produced locally. But a viable neighborhood is a community, and a viable community is made up of neighbors who cherish and protect what they have in common. This is the principle of subsistence. A viable community, like a viable farm, protects its own production capacities. It does not import products that it can produce for itself. And it does not export local products until local needs have been met. The economic products of a viable community are understood either as belonging to the community's subsistence or as surplus, and only the surplus is considered to be marketable abroad. A community, if it is to be viable, cannot think of producing solely for export, and it cannot permit importers to use cheaper labor and goods from other places to destroy the local capacity to produce goods that are needed locally. In charity, moreover, it must refuse to import goods that are produced at the cost of human or ecological degradation elsewhere. This principle of subsistence applies not just to localities, but to regions and nations as well.

The principles of neighborhood and subsistence will be disparaged by the globalists as "protectionism"—and that is exactly what it is. It is a protectionism that is just and sound, because it protects local producers and is the best assurance of adequate supplies to local consumers. And the idea that local needs should be met first and only surpluses exported does *not* imply any prejudice against charity toward people in other places or trade with them. The principle of neighborhood at home always implies the principle of charity abroad. And the principle of subsistence is in fact the best guarantee of giveable or marketable surpluses. This kind of protection is not "isolationism."

Albert Schweitzer, who knew well the economic situation in the colonies of Africa, wrote about seventy years ago: "Whenever the timber trade is good, permanent famine reigns in the Ogowe region, because the villagers abandon their farms to fell as many trees as possible." We should notice especially that the goal of production was "as many . . . as possible." And Schweitzer made my point exactly: "These people could achieve true wealth if they could develop their agriculture and trade to meet their own needs." Instead they produced timber for export to "the world market," which made them dependent upon imported goods which they bought with money earned from their exports. They gave up their local means of subsistence, and imposed the false standard of a foreign demand ("as many trees as possible") upon their forests. They thus became helplessly dependent on an economy over which they had no control.

Such was the fate of the native people under the African colonialism of Schweitzer's time. Such is, and can only be, the fate of everybody under the global colonialism of our time. Schweitzer's description of the colonial economy of the Ogowe region is in principle not different from the rural economy in Kentucky or Iowa or Wyoming now. A total economy, for all practical purposes, is a total government. The "free trade," which from the standpoint of the corporate economy brings "unprecedented economic growth," from the standpoint of the land and its local populations, and ultimately from the standpoint of the cities, is destruction and slavery. Without prosperous local economies, the people have no power and the land no voice.

Appendix B

Capitalism, Civil Society, Religion, and the Poor: A Bibliographical Essay

Max L. Stackhouse with Lawrence M. Stratton

C ontemporary open, market-focused economic systems are, on the whole, good for poor people. In our increasingly global economy, the "free market" usually provides the best opportunity for individual human development and for increasing the social participation of groups living in poverty. As can be seen in David Landes's monumental *The Wealth and Poverty of Nations: Why Some Are So Rich and Some So Poor*, free market systems compare favorably to hunter-gatherer, nomadic, subsistence, village, feudal, mercantilist, liberationist, or modern "statist" systems of political economy.[1]

We say that free market systems are "on the whole" and "usually" best, but that is not always the case. Economics has its own distinctive logic and laws, but production, distribution, and consumption are also human activities. As such, they are embedded in the institutional and moral fabric of our common life, and therefore act to bend, facilitate, or block the logic and laws of economic life. The difference depends on social and ethical conditions that are only indirectly economic, yet substantively influence how economic systems work. An open, marketfocused system provides the best opportunities for poor people if and when the other decisive spheres of civil society—educational, medical, political, legal, and especially religious—are also open, developed, and accessible to all. Such was not the case in most of the historic societies of ancient Europe, Asia, or Africa, in Latin America, or in North America until the end of legal slavery. When the critical institutions of civil society are absent, or when their access is restricted, authoritarian control exercised by some exclusive religious community, ethnic group, or political clique usually establishes forms of domination that perpetuate economic underdevelopment. In such cases, the poor may resist systems that limit opportunities. Alternatively, they may turn to leaders who promise to overthrow entrenched elites. But opposition to a bad system does not create a good one, as Michael Novak has clearly argued.[2]

Two groups tend to be the sharpest critics of open, market-centered economic systems, and both are at their most vigorous when a closed, bipolar "noble-peon" society is challenged by a more open system. The first group consists of the beneficiaries of closed, authoritarian, or totalitarian political orders. When the rulers of such orders seek to enhance commercial and industrial development, they make sure that their political cronies and relatives are the ones who benefit—we see this happen frequently in developing countries. In that case, what is called a "free market" turns out to be only free for some, and in fact may be quite costly for those who are denied political favor. The second group consists of precisely those who have formed a culture of solidarity and resistance to outside influence and social change. This is the chief insight of Edward C. Banfield's classic, *The Moral Basis of a Backward Society*.[3] It is not surprising that poor people often view an open market system as a fraud. It disrupts the fragile world they know and makes their modest skills obsolete. And their skepticism is only deepened when what they see on the ground are the relatives of political, military, social, and even religious elites gaining from what they call "capitalism" (a phenomenon that occurs, according to Peruvian economist Hernando de Soto, because of a lack of property rights protection and inadequate liquid capital).[4] This state of affairs is the source of much liberation theology.[5]

The faults of closed systems cannot, however, be entirely attributed to the rapaciousness of the rich and powerful or the resentments of the poor and powerless. Many cultural and religious systems fail to prepare people for open development or novel efforts to create wealth or new kinds of goods and services. People trapped in nonliterate, predemocratic, subsistence economic cultures organized by closed systems of clan or tribal loyalty, caste identity, peasant solidarity, or male patriarchy, each legitimated by local religious myths, are in fact the saddest victims of poverty, victimized in large measure by their own cultures. They have not been impoverished by modern capitalism; they have been poor for centuries, but only become conscious of their poverty when they encounter dynamic systems that generate more wealth than they previously could imagine. Indeed, they often resist, on moral grounds, the cultural and religious changes that would change their society and therefore improve their economic condition.[6] And if they are overwhelmed by larger, dynamic cultures, they have the greatest difficulty entering market systems except at the lowest level of menial labor, and often find themselves among the "left behind" in regard to economic development, sustained meagerly by charitable or governmental welfare programs.[7]

Moreover, many "modernist" experiments during the last two centuries have tried to turn economic development over to political and military authority. Mercantilist forms of colonial imperialism posing as "Christian civilization," nationalist forms of socialism adopting neopagan slogans, and revolutionary forms of communism guided by an ideology of secular scientism all ended up bending potentially viable economies to the will of a given regime. When these economies began to falter, police and military force was employed to make them work, and when even these coercive efforts failed, so also did the economies. In the wreckage, the construction of viable, open economies has been difficult and has progressed only when the other spheres of civil society have been cultivated. Political and military regimes are neither efficient producers nor prudent managers; they always depend on economic factors beyond the capacity of the regime itself to control. Economic resources neither develop nor flourish on the front end of the gun.

This is not to say that there is no place for government in an economic system. In fact, a political order is necessary in every society and for a good economy. Not only does government maintain law and order, when it is functional and even relatively just, but it also coins the money, develops the necessary infrastructures that persons, local communities, and independent businesses cannot provide themselves, arranges for common defense against foreign threats and natural disaster, guarantees the rights of citizens, protects the multiple associations by which religious, voluntary, community, and charitable institutions flourish, and develops those policies enabling citizens to take initiative and contribute to the general welfare according to their best lights.

Indeed, an open market system tends not to flourish when a society's laws and civil institutions are dysfunctional, for no market operates in a social vacuum, and the market cannot create by itself those tissues of human relatedness and trust by which the common life develops. If, for example, accurate information is difficult to obtain, people will not know what their products are worth or what they should pay for things they want. If the law treats persons as ciphers without basic dignity, if fair contracts are not enforceable, if property is subject to theft or expropria- tion, if slavery (chattel or sexual) is treated as part of a market system, if the formation of firms, businesses, and corporations is difficult and expensive, if the prevailing cultural and religious systems cultivate distrust of outsiders, permit corruption and bribery, or fail to nurture habits of honesty and responsibility, then free economic systems do not develop; and if they once were present, they then tend to degenerate into "Mafia capitalism." Examples of such social failures can be found in various periods of human history and in various places around the globe that have tried to "modernize" without having in place these essential elements of civil society.[8]

It is not only social failures external to the structures of economic life that can fail, destroying the promise of capitalism. The inner ethical culture of corporations and management can also become decadent, betraying the society who depends on its health. It has long been generally understood that honesty, fairness, transparency, and accountability in dealings are integral to viable open economic systems.[9] Thus, the scandals currently surrounding Enron and Arthur Andersen, Tyco and WorldCom, etc., remind us that, even in what are presumed to be honorable firms located in cultures with numerous apparent safeguards, moral corruption can derail highly developed economies and damage host societies.

A more accurate understanding of what a genuinely fair and open market system is and how it works demands that we know how modern, open systems developed. We have to understand how certain decisive social dynamics developed under the influence of certain religious and ethical traditions, for such dynamics are not a natural product of social evolution, nor have they developed equally in all cultures or under the auspices of all religions. Both in the past and in the present, the well being of an open and fair economic system has been significantly dependent on the existence of a viable civil society and on the quality of the moral and institutional fabric that generates and sustains it. The evidence is not at all clear that an open market system by itself can generate a constitutional democracy, human rights, social tolerance, institutional pluralism, or religious freedom. Indeed, in his new book on China, Joe Studwell suggests that the East Asian experience indicates that certain kinds of market capitalism can develop without generating an open society, even though the social and political system threatens to close in on itself again.[10]

In other words, successful, fair, open market systems are not playgrounds for egoism and unscrupulous greed, nor can they exist without structures of moral or social accountability. Market systems can only be open and fair when and where they are sustained by a set of supportive institutions marked by social integrity. Where these institutions are substantially in place, a free market system cannot only begin to flourish, it can contribute to and extraordinarily assist the further development of more equitable access to information, good government, human rights and personal dignity, the formation and sustenance of profitable institutions dedicated to providing quality goods and services at just prices, and even to the strengthening of families, cultural creativity, and religious institutions. Together these factors contribute to what is presently called "social capital" or "cultural capital" in current social and political theory. In other words, they make economic capital work for the good of all. The rather striking differences between poverty-ridden societies and dynamic societies where new wealth is being created, and the spectrum of developing people between these extremes, can be more adequately understood when these aspects of "moral capital" are taken into account.[11]

To understand how markets work in the wider context of civil society, it shall be necessary to explore selected dimensions of the social history of economic life. And this treatment of the issue must intentionally include a discussion of religion as a powerful influence on morality, society, and culture as these open or limit the social context of the market and influence the realities of wealth and poverty. Here we must note the uncomfortable fact: some kinds of religion seem to inhibit and others to enhance the kind of civil society wherein markets can flourish. This fact is uncomfortable because most people do not like to judge other people's faiths. That is not the intention here. But it would be dishonest to deny that, over long periods of time, the deep ethical logic of various religious traditions press in somewhat different directions when it comes to the factors that shape economic life.

It is also necessary to respond to one of Karl Marx's primary charges against open market economic systems, an argument accepted by some religions, which is that such systems create poverty and generate impoverished classes.[12] Indeed, many non-Marxists in our "post-communist" environment continue to share that conviction, and often hold that "free market capitalism," and the cultural, religious, or ideological ethics that support or sustain it, are the root causes of economic injustice,[13] environmental destruction, and social corruption.[14] In the course of their arguments, they offer rather elaborate accounts of the history of capitalism and markets. These narratives demand an alternative perspective, both in the name of truth and in the name of justice and compassion. It is doubtful that such critics have a clear vision of either the economic data or the socio-historical, cultural, and intellectual background that has shaped the prospects of reducing poverty and increasing the participation in plenty of a larger proportion of the world's population.

An overview of the data

If we look at the cluster of the world's wealthy nations—members of the G-8, for example—where poverty rates are the lowest and relative affluence most widely distributed, we find that they all have capitalist economies marked by numerous opportunities for individuals to form limitedliability, for-profit corporations. Such corporations are, in principle, organizationally distinct from familial (including clan, tribe, caste, or patriarchal) and state control. Although paternalistic, ethnic, and governmental influences remain widely present in economic life, it is possible to suggest that the number of corporations, large and small, per hundred thousand of the population, is one of the decisive indicators of a people's economic well-being. In these nations, some corporations succeed and others fail, but this dynamic process of finding out what really works can take place without destroying the continuity of government or the other institutions of civil society. And the successful corporations become the center of social cooperation for productivity, the development and utilization of technology, and the generation of capital for further investment. Increasingly, every poor country in the world—even those that are still officially socialist—seeks to develop such corporations internally or to invite them in from abroad. Moreover, even where there is nationalistic resentment towards "foreigners" and "transnational corporations," new studies indicate that people want both access to foreign products and opportunities to gain employment within the corporations that make them. Indeed, current research has documented that in poor countries many people have cross-cutting loyalties, those which feed anticapitalist (and antiglobal) sentiment on the one hand, and those which on the other hand lead them to recognize the desirability of corporations that bring to them desirable products, job opportunities, skill training, and other positive consequences of economic development.[15]

Open market systems potentially yield the benefits of reduced poverty, increased wealth, and enhanced political stability. Economists Stephen L. Parente and Edward C. Prescott estimate from their quantitative surveys of economic development in countries across the globe that eliminating competitive barriers to trade within countries and across borders has the potential to radically increase global wealth over time. They write, "The gains from such practices are huge, not 1 or 2 percent but 1,000 or 2,000 percent. There is no reason why the whole world should not be as rich as the leading industrial country."[16] The World Bank estimates that "increasing the ratio of trade to GDP by one percentage point raises per capita income by between one-half to two percent." The poor, and not just those who are already relatively wealthy, benefit from this expansion of income. According to a 2000 briefing paper, "Assessing Globalization," a World Bank "study of a large sample of countries estimates that on average growth in the income of the poor (defined as the bottom fifth of the population) rises about one-for-one with the growth rate of overall per-capita income in a country."[17] When there is economic development and globalization, low-income individuals experience upward mobility and the middle class expands. Indeed, economist Simon Kuznets was apparently prescient a generation ago when he observed that populations with pyramid-shaped distributions of income and wealth—i.e., populations in which the largest number of people lives in poverty—gradually develop into populations with diamond-shaped patterns of income and wealth distribution, with declining numbers at the bottom of the heap, *if the social and economic system is kept open.*[18]

It is not merely the existence of corporations that generates wealth, however. Granted monopolist authority over underdeveloped regions by royalty in the eighteenth and nineteenth centuries, a number of European companies became the launching pads for political colonization in the East, with parallel adventures in Africa and Latin America. The English East India Trading Company and the Dutch East Indies Trading Company are examples. Many developing parts of the world continue to remember the colonialism sponsored by corporations rooted in other lands, and these negative memories are only reinforced by present experience if (a) they see around them subsidiaries of multinational corporations controlled by closed cliques of elites, and (b) their own social system does not equip them to take part in these "foreign" institutions.

Multinational corporations contribute to the well-being of host lands, however, when they work cooperatively with honest and constitutionally limited governments, and when they work with those sectors of society seeking to strengthen legally regulated markets in which monopolies are prevented, property rights protected, corruption limited, workers' health and safety protected, and communication and transportation infrastructure provided for all.

Many countries have never developed patterns of life that ready them for this sort of well-regulated economic development, patterns which we may call the "conditionalities" of civil society, often treated by certain technical modes of analysis as extrinsic to economics in the strict sense of the term.[19] Those countries in which these "conditionalities" are relatively well developed are usually governed by democratic governments with multiple parties, have legal systems that involve the protection of human rights, including property and contract rights, and manifest institutional diversity. Moreover, in such countries there is a variety of opportunities for women—a critical factor in overcoming poverty for a number of reasons, not the least of which is that the pool of talent is doubled where women have access to education and positions of responsibility. We shall shortly turn to the issue of what gives rise to these conditionalities, but let us here note that the Millennium Development Goals, established as a consensus of more than one hundred and fifty nations, and coordinated by Kofi Anan, General Secretary of the United Nations, attempts to overcome poverty by moving precisely in the direction of these civil society conditionalities.

We need to note at this point, however, what the world situation is in regard to poverty. Many believe that the increasing prevalence of transnational or multinational[20] corporations has generated increased poverty for most of the world and unbelievable affluence for a tiny minority, showing anew how exploitative capitalism leads to class polarization. According to the best statistics available, however, we can see considerable gains in poverty reduction in the decade since the fall of the Berlin Wall, when the economic power of transnational and multinational corporations and the phenomenon of economic globalization became most visible (although both had been growing for more than a century, obscured by world wars and decolonization). That historic moment signaled a shift in focus from Cold War fears of a nuclear holocaust toward hopes for increased international cooperation, and from dreams of a socialist future toward global corporate penetration. These shifts also involved a decline in the role of the state as the chief center of capitalization and as the redistributor of wealth, and an increase in the role of corporate financial institutions and new international regulatory agencies, such as the World Trade Organization (which developed out of half a century of negotiations known as GATT, or General Agreements on Tariffs and Trade, by more than one hundred nations).[21] The age of geopolitics has been substantially superceded by an age of geoeconomics, to the dismay of those who had much at stake in the political control of economics and a great fear of economic influence in politics.

In fact, in spite of the plunge of economic indicators in Eastern Europe and Central Asia after the collapse of the Soviet empire, things began to recover in that region rather quickly—first in Poland (by 1992), then in several other former communist nations, and finally in Russia (in 1998). Things remain rather bleak in most of the Arab world,[22] and economic development in the sub-Saharan nations has been nearly static. Yet, worldwide, since the fall of the Berlin Wall 125 million people have left the ranks of the very poor, and the proportion of the population worldwide living in extreme poverty has declined from just under 30 percent to 23 percent, with gains especially in East and South Asia, and in parts of Latin America, in spite of episodic, but thankfully temporary, financial crises in all these areas. Importantly, the most dramatic economic growth has taken place in areas where liberalization, privatization, deregulation, and globalization have occurred, where there is an open flow of capital and ideas, and where increased migration of workers (from the countryside to the cities and from neighboring lands) and the inclusion of women in the workforce are well underway.[23] Moreover, the most remarkable changes taking place may be the formation of vast new middle classes in Asia, Latin America, and parts of Africa. These new middle classes allow for the creation of new markets, provide the resources for increased education, and encourage the formation of new habits and skills appropriate for modern labor and management. As African economist Stan du Plessis has written, "Someone must have been telling lies about the global economy."[24] Indeed, African politicians are increasingly recognizing the benefits of global free trade.[25]

There has been a great fear, in some quarters, that such developments would bring about a homogenization of culture, and that

441

people would lose their distinctive identities. Such dire predictions remind one of the widespread anxiety in the 1910s and 1920s that factory work would turn persons into mere cogs in machines, and of the 1950s and 1960s lament that computers, mass communication, and suburbanization would so standardize everything that all diversity and personality would be lost. There has been some loss of cultural particularity, certainly. Peoples from tribal cultures and peasant peoples from societies essentially feudal in structure, especially, have been drawn into complex cultures where their traditional patterns of life are severely compromised and their hereditary forms of status less valued—both in the dominant culture and among their own youth. And it is often the case that when such folk seek to join the dominant, more complex society, they often must struggle mightily simply to find a place on the lower rungs of the economic ladder.[26]

However, commissioned, independent studies by the *Economist* converge with data collected by the World Bank and my own studies in this regard: Confucian/Maoist China, Hindu/Democratic India, Islamic/technocratic Malaysia and Indonesia, and Christian/ Iberian-influenced Brazil and Mexico are all preserving quite distinctive cultures, and each has preserved substantial degrees of religious, ethnic, and social diversity in their distinctively synthetic societies.[27] To be sure, minorities and dissidents frequently encounter human rights violations and cultural disadvantages in these regions, and international legal, political, and economic regulatory and developmental agencies will surely continue to put pressure on these societies to conform to international standards. Those cultures with authoritarian patterns of leadership often resist this pressure—speaking rather romantically, for example, of "Asian Values"— yet some of them, such as South Korea, Thailand, and Taiwan in Asia, and Chile in Latin America, have recognized that such patterns are economically dysfunctional, and each of these regions is adopting technological, economic, and corporate practices that allow them to interact more easily with the wider human community.

Simultaneously, these standards and practices are being integrated into deeper cultural traditions. The efforts of Western- based international regulatory agencies, such as the International Monetary Fund (IMF), have begun to learn that solutions to short-term crises in these rapidly developing economies must take into account cultural particularities more seriously than they have heretofore been inclined. The growth of the conditionalities of civil society, to be sure, modifies cultures, but no culture has ever been static or entirely closed to extrinsic influence, and the changes they must adopt to foster economic growth are unlikely to destroy them, even if they modulate these cultures so that they can become more fully interactive with other cultures and societies.[28]

Some Western thinkers are much less concerned with the positive effects corporate capitalism is having around the world on peoples previously trapped in poverty than on the effects globalization is having on the working classes at home.[29] Data from both scholarly and journalistic sources demonstrate that this fear is overblown.[30]

Whence the conditionalities?

What were the key historical developments that generated, and are therefore likely to sustain, those conditionalities of civil society that make an open market economic system viable? This question is an important one, for some of those scholars who have developed the concept of "conditionalities" lack a deep historical sense. Yet, the quality of our perception of the present and the range of our capacity to shape the future is directly proportional to the depth of our view of the past. This truth holds as well in the area of economics as it does in any other field, in spite of the fact that many economic theories ignore the social history that shaped them.

Humans not only engage in economic activity in the simplest forms of hunting and gathering, an activity they share with other animals; they also always seem to want to exchange something they have for something they do not have. The long view of the past also reveals that most people over the centuries have been poor. Subsistence economies supplied little beyond that which was immediately necessary to keep body and soul together. There was little on offer that anyone really needed, and little to offer for what people wanted. Markets for the many were episodic at best. Most economic activity was directly centered in traditional modes of production and consumption by the primary unit of society—the family, headed by a patriarch (or, in its extended form, the band, clan, or tribe).

In more complex societies, each family had to pay tribute to those who protected them from physical or spiritual perils. A portion of everything produced reverted to the regime (the warlord in his garrison, or the emperor and his entourage in his castle), and another portion went to the priest in the temple (or to the hierarchs in the monastery). In fact, it was not unusual for markets to develop just beside the castle or at the base of the temple, for that is where people gathered and where there was both enough protection from violence and a sense of spiritual trust that business could be conducted in relative freedom. Even so, in such societies trade and market activity was limited by prohibitive taxes, and traditional religious worldviews discouraged the sort of innovations in technology or social life that could have improved production and altered patterns of distribution. The warrior and the priest, both of whom did not produce material goods but provided indispensable services for the society at large, typically restricted basic modes of production and market exchange, or else encouraged their development in specific directions. Thus, what was available in most markets was meager. Even if the complex artistry of ancient crafts surprises contemporary anthropologists and still delights tourists, the forms human creativity could take in such societies were restricted, sometimes due to the influence of religion.

In the past century, Max Weber's comparative analysis of the impact of world religions on economic and social development has sparked an intense scholarly discussion of the origins of modern capitalist societies.[31] Weber argued that the development of a society's religious orientation decisively shapes culture in such a way as to enhance or inhibit economic modernization, the recognition and protection of human rights, and the growth of pluralistic civil societies. Among the more important volumes that have refined or restated Weber's argument are Peter Berger's *Capitalist Revolution: Fifty Propositions About Prosperity, Equality, and Liberty,*[32] and Michael Novak's *Catholic Ethic and the Spirit of Capitalism.*[33] Robert Bellah's *Tokugawa Religion,*[34] S. Gordon Redding's exploration of capitalism within the context of Confucianism,[35] and Loren Caplan's *New Religious Movements in India*[36] examine Weber's thesis in light of Asian religious histories, while David Martin, in *Tongues of Fire,*[37] suggests that current Pentecostal, Evangelical, and Fundamentalist movements in Latin America and parts of Africa are repeating, in a strikingly new key, what earlier Reformers brought about in Europe and early Puritan America. Meanwhile, another Nobel Prize winner in economics, Robert William Fogel, has recently argued in *The Fourth Great Awakening and the Future of Egalitarianism* that even in highly developed economies such as the United States, there is a strong correlation between religious renewal and economic inclusiveness.[38] A new translation of Weber's *Protestant Ethic and the Spirit of Capitalism,* by Stephen Kalberg,[39] and the cluster of essays Kalberg has published on the subject also have enhanced immensely our understanding of Weber's work.

To understand why modern capitalism has developed in the directions it has, we need to understand the deeper currents of thought, belief, and custom that lie behind what most economists study. To hold that nothing more than material interests or the laws of survival or the drive to dominate others determines all that people do economically represents a thin, even cynical understanding of human nature. People do want to improve their material wellbeing, and the realities of scarcity mean that there is competition for resources. But

445

these truths, rooted deep in evolutionary history, are not what has made modern business life what it is. Rather, we must ask what values, principles, and purposes—besides self-interest—motivated and guided those who generated the patterns of contemporary economic realities. How were the logic and laws of economics combined with the moral and spiritual energies of a vibrant, pluralistic social fabric to construct something new? What intellectual, cultural, and social forces have driven the nations of the West and the Asian "tigers" to develop the forms of capitalism that generate wealth and mitigate poverty? What brought these forces into being? To approach answers to these questions we must investigate the moral and spiritual "externalities" that serve the dynamic social "conditionalities" that have made such developments possible. The deeper we dig, the more we find that these externalities are religiously and ethically laden. Those social scientists who think that in their work they can dispense with religious influences, or safely confine them to the privacy of individual hearts, must face this reality and not arbitrarily rule it out of their purview.

Once we begin to recognize that there are religious and ethical dynamics at work in the growth of global capitalism, we cannot avoid offering a critique of the tendency of economic analysis and business life to isolate itself from moral concerns, as well as of the tendency of much contemporary religious life to isolate itself within that kind of Sunday pietism that essentially leaves the workweek and the economic system outside the reach of moral reformation.[40]

The fact is that, in prolonged processes of historical development, specific religious and ethical dynamics have become incarnate in certain cultural and social patterns that can complement, steady, and channel the logic and laws of economics. The sources of these patterns were often obscured in the modern era, but they are now appearing belatedly in the era of economic globalization.[41] In fact, several economists have become alert to the fact that latent theological presuppositions lurk in the background of presumably "purely scientific" economic theories. Robert H.

Nelson, for one, has compellingly argued that most economic theories are veiled theologies.[42] We find evidence for analyses like Nelson's if we trace some of the critical historical roots of economic development.

Three decisive conditionalities

The consequences of personal religious beliefs, the practices of specific communities of worship, and the implications of certain religious doctrines and dogmas have contributed to the development of three decisive, if unintended, characteristics of economic life in the global era: the theological character of technology, the ecclesiological character of the corporation, and the stewardly character of management. Such developments remind us that economic activity is always embedded in moral and religious convictions that are meaningful to economic actors, and in matrices of social institutions that are shaped both by such convictions and by material necessities. This was certainly well enough understood by Weber, whose hypothesis about the economic consequences of the Protestant "work ethic" was pioneering in showing how religion shapes the public life of civilizations. The evidence for his thesis, debated intensely for more than a century, strongly suggests that while he had some of his data wrong, and probably misinterpreted some of the connective links, he asked profound questions that invite the revision and extension of his argument.

An additional example of the profound ways in which religion has influenced contemporary life is the notion of human rights. Today, human rights is a global concept; indeed, it is the basic mode of political, legal, and ethical discourse and therefore heavily influences markets, trade policies, labor practices, and contemporary approaches to problems of poverty. But neither the work ethic described by Weber nor the idea of human rights as a regulative ideal grew from anywhere else than from specific religious traditions embodied in politically defended and legally codified social practices. The very idea that all humans "are endowed by their Creator with certain inalienable rights," as the Declaration of Independence has it, and as it is echoed in the United Nations Declaration of Human Rights, did not derive either from the ancient paganisms or from the modern secular Enlightenment. The source is the Old Testament notion that humans are made in the image of God, and thus have inviolable rights as well as a moral awareness that is, as the New Testament says, in some sense "written on the hearts of all." The ideas of the "work ethic" and the "endowment" of all persons with an inherent dignity have developed well beyond their points of origin, but they have become critical to our assessment of the forces that shape current market practice and our view of poverty.[43]

In concrete terms, treating the supplier as a person with rights to a fair deal, establishing a policy of service to the customer (who may be a total stranger), and honoring the spirit of legal constraints that define liability are among the ways in which economic practices may acknowledge the moral and spiritual dignity of each person and fulfill the logic and laws of sound economics. Where such practices become established, they tend to drive out the uncertainties of the old bazaars and barter markets, where one no recourse if cheated and therefore must be constantly wary. Such principles demonstrate how religiously based moral convictions can permeate "secular" institutions, beliefs, and practices to affect the entire globe, as is now the case with what we call "globalization," and particularly the globalization of the economy.

Globalization is new, but when it became so is a large debate. The idea of *the whole world as one place*, as an inclusive field of spaces and peoples, is not at all new. The great world religions and not only the Hebrew prophets spoke long ago of a highly diverse, but ultimately unitary created realm wherein many peoples lived under a universal law, with hopes for a divine end. Crates of Mallus made the first globe to symbolize the reality of the world as one place, as a single *kosmos,* at least 150 years before the birth of Christ.

The "ization" part of "globalization," however, suggests not only that the whole can be conceived as a single sphere, a mathematical unity, an ontological whole, but that a historical process is taking place whereby some different whole is coming into being. It is not taking place equally in all places simultaneously, but it is increasingly pervading every part of the world. It would seem that the "already" and "old" whole is incomplete, flawed, unfinished, or distorted (even if indispensable to existence and sufficiently ordered to exist). Thus, it requires a "not yet," something "new." When the two terms are joined, we find that the result points to a systemic alteration of what already is, in a manner and degree that brings a *novum* that has not been before. There is no reason, in the face of such convictions, to believe that people should be forever trapped in abject poverty— even if humanity should forever have to wrestle with the problem of scarcity at every level of development, and even if inequalities of status and well-being persist.

The ancient prophets anticipated this, and the New Testament conveys just such views in its idea that "the world" is something that is, but which is fallen and thus is something to which we are not to conform. Yet "the world" is something that God so loved that it is being redeemed, and those who know God are sent into it to aid in the process of redemption and transformation, even as the world groans in travail toward a new creation and a new civilization, the New Jerusalem. Those who receive the vision of this promised reign of God are to employ every moral means to make it actual. Indeed, some strands of religious history have even been pro-technological, calling on believers to restore and fulfill the potential of creation by engaging in the transformation of self, nature, and society, not to avoid materiality and culture for the sake of vapid spirituality and sentimental morality. All salvation religions have a cosmic vision, a sense of time, and a hope for change to an altered state of being. In some religions, Christianity, for example, it is central. There are aspects of Christianity that have made technology and the intentional reconstruction of society a moral duty. Thus, we cannot understand the present globalization of the economy if we do not understand its moral and spiritual roots.[44]

A world-changing technology

Obviously, the globalization of capitalist development as we encounter it today could not take place without technology. It has revolutionized the factory, the office, and the way we travel and do business, not to mention the household kitchen, agriculture, and the craftsman's shop. Indeed, there is scarcely a dimension of the biophysical world that has not been in some way altered by technological intervention.[45] Brad Allenby has argued that we now live in an "anthropogenic world", a world in which so much of the environment is affected by the unintended consequences of human intervention that ecological responsibility now requires planned management and concerted engineering.[46] Why this drive to change nature, to reorganize it so that it will do what we want it to? It is not necessarily a natural attitude. Most species, many cultures, and a good number of philosophies and religions strive to adapt to their environment, not adapt their environment to them, to their sense of the right order of things. A survey of the world's great religious traditions would reveal that many peoples have believed that we should adjust to the cosmic order of things, that we should fit into the way things really are.[47] These are the so-called ontocratic religions.

Some traditions differ. Judaism, Christianity, Islam, and some forms of theistic Hinduism hold that nature does not rule the world, including its social and economic systems. God the Creator does, and we as God's creatures are to have dominion over the earth, to reshape it for human good in spite of the temptation to build towers of Babel. As Robert K. Merton argued in a controversial essay published a generation ago, "Puritanism, Pietism, and Science," Protestant attitudes shaped not only the development of the celebrated work ethic but also some dimensions of science. Merton found evidence for this claim in the motivations for their work set forth by the founders and leading lights of Britain's Royal Society. For instance, he cites the claim by Robert Boyle, the first president of the society, that "the study of Nature is to the greater glory of God and the Good of Man." Science, for men such as Boyle, promised a way to constrain and guide nature, for while nature is stamped by the Creator with an intended "Order of Things" that made science possible, it was also sufficiently disordered in its manifestations that it needed a reordering that could conduce it to "good in the light of the Doctrine of Salvation by Jesus Christ." This is a key point. Science attempts to understand things as they are; technology uses science to make things what we want them to become. This idea that nature needed reordering to the good did not begin with the Puritans and the Pietists. At the close of his essay, Merton quoted Whitehead's observation that "faith in the possibility of science . . . is an unconscious derivative from medieval theology." But he also pointed out that this medieval orientation needed the impetus of active and ascetic engagement in the world to bring modern science to fruition.[48] Two recent studies seeking to assess the adequacy of Merton's thesis have found that, on the whole, it is quite accurate.[49]

The relationship between religious belief and the scientific project continues to generate debates in philosophy and the ethics of technology. Nancy Pearcey, for example, states not only that modern science rests on certain assumptions undergirded by biblical belief—especially the assumptions that the world has a rational, intelligible order (because it is created by a single and rational God) and that we can discover that order because we are created in God's image—but she also goes on to argue that three other religious principles are necessary preconditions of modern science, namely:

1. The universe is contingent and can be changed, a principle that fundamentally challenges the ontocratic assumption that nature (as it is by itself, or as it is created by God) is teleological and imbued with inherent rational purposes, as was taught by Aristotle

and Thomas Aquinas. Instead, the expectation of a future transformation, the arrival of a "new heaven and a new earth," indicates that nature as it is will collapse and is less to be contemplated and followed than to be intentionally altered and used.

2. Humans find their primary kinship not with nature but with a transcendent God and with other humans created in God's image. This generates a perspective that gives permission for humans to have an active role in engaging nature and a denial of the view that humans are so embedded in nature that they can only conform to it. With Merton, Pearcey contends that this view was widespread among the Puritans. But she notes that the Puritans were echoing older motifs.

3. Humans have a duty to shape and intervene in the world; indeed, we are commissioned by God to have dominion. To help people overcome health problems, for example, is a moral and spiritual duty. Pearcey traces the source of this view to the Reformation; others find its roots further back in time.[50]

In a newer study, David Noble deepens the historical basis of this argument. He begins his first chapter by stating that "the dynamic project of Western technology, the defining mark of modernity, is actually medieval in origin and spirit. . . . [It] was rooted in an ideological innovation which invested the useful arts with a significance beyond mere utility. Technology had come to be identified with transcendence, implicated as never before in the Christian idea of redemption. . . . The other-worldly roots of the religion of technology were distinctly Christian. For Christianity alone blurred the distinction and bridged the divide between the human and the divine." Of course, the technological impetus did not spring directly from the pages of the Bible or early Christian writings. Rather, the assumptions of Christianity altered pagan attitudes precisely as those attitudes interacted with philosophy and the sciences of the day. For instance, Noble shows that "the striking acceleration and intensification of technological development in . . . [medieval] Europe emanated from contemplative monasticism." Monastics held the orthodox belief that humanity was created good, but is now fallen. The fact of the goodness means that residual capacities to improve life are present; the fact of fallenness means that improvement is required. Asceticism is the means whereby residual goodness makes, with God's help, such improvement possible.[51]

In the medieval era, the inner spiritual techniques of this struggle to improve expanded to include theological celebrations of "the mechanical arts." These celebrations began as early as the fifth century and continued through the twelfth. During this time, technological development came to be seen as a human potentiality that, properly cultivated, could help us reclaim the wisdom and virtue God had implanted in each human with the gift of his image. This view increasingly became absorbed into the mainstream of educational philosophy, and was given a specific direction by the formative theologian and philosopher, Roger Bacon. He saw the mechanical arts as a means of anticipating and preparing for the kingdom to come, and their rapid expansion as an indicator that the kingdom was at hand. Technology might well help restore humankind by recovering the knowledge lost in the Fall, and such knowledge would be most useful for moving humanity, as an ally and servant of God, closer to a new kind of perfection. Humanity, indeed, had a duty to seek progress, a view taken up by many and even adopted by the Royal Society.

This is the point: technology is only effective when people believe that technology can be beneficial, and that they have some ultimate duty to reshape, invent, revise, reform, or transform the world. That view, today largely secularized, is enormously powerful in contemporary globalization. And yet, it is quite likely that technology could become a peril and not a resource for the human future if its spiritual roots are neglected as a regulatory moral guide to its use.

Different attitudes toward technology are illustrated in David Landes's book on the history of the clock, *Revolution in Time*.[52] Landes shows that the Chinese built accurate timekeeping devices long before the West thought of them. But he also points out that they did so because they wanted to know when to conduct the proper Confucian rituals that would integrate the Empire more perfectly into the harmony of earth and heaven. They used their science to enable them to conform more perfectly to the cosmic order. When these timekeeping devices were brought back to the West, they were almost immediately developed for another purpose. They were used to help people conform to a supernatural purpose—the saying of prayers in the monastery on the proper schedule. That is, these newly discovered timekeeping instruments were adopted to make the divisions of the day more rational, especially in the monastery. No longer did the monks wake at dawn—early in the summers, late in the winters—to pray and then work until meals and more prayers at the end of daylight. Rather, the monks were now awakened at the same time for their prayers, no matter the season, and then followed a regimen of work, eating, prayer, and sleep that was dictated by the clock. In fact, bell systems were installed to notify everyone of the time. That is the origin of "Frère Jacques." The sleepy-headed monk will not get up on time! The disciplined person and community is governed not by the cycles of nature or the body's felt needs, but by obedience to the holy laws of prayer and work. Landes goes on to show why and how European watchmakers became the emblem of this discipline and how and why timing was essential to the assembly line, to industrial efficiency experts, and now to the speed of the microchip—all a direct result of the monastery's adoption of technology for rational ends, despite the fact that Silicon Valley knows little of its own theological roots.

The example of the clock, like the examples of the work ethic and human rights, is only another illustration of where we find the roots of those conditionalities that allow contemporary economic globalization to take place. Likewise, the technological revolution needed an institutional home in which to operate. In many cultures, when technology is introduced there exist no proper institutions to house it and cultivate it. Thus, when the carriers of technological transfer depart, the technological implements are left to decay. What kind of an institutional arrangement is necessary in civil society if technology is to be developed and cultivated in order to allow if participation in the global economy (where that is desired)? Adam Smith thought it was the market and the division of labor, and surely both are required. But as was suggested earlier, there is no known culture that does not have a market, and every society has distinctive roles for its members. Traders, for example, are mentioned in every classical tradition. For a vibrant technology to work in a complex, global system, corporations are needed. The corporation, an externality to many economic theories, is, like technology, a conditionality of the global economy generated out of one stream of religious history. It did not appear where that stream was not present, although since its birth it has been adopted and adapted in other cultures.

The modern corporation

It is only sometimes recognized that in most of the world's civilizations, religion, moral formation, education, production, distribution, consumption, and medical care have been ordered by two centers of social organization—the family (which implies, in most historical cultures, kinship organizations such as the clan, the tribe, and the caste) and the regime (the king, emperor, or the royal and military aristocracy). Usually, the worship center, whether at the hearth where the spirits of the departed elders are honored, or at the temple where the regime's deities are worshiped, reinforced the supreme authority of familial or political loyalties. In such contexts, the birth and growth of the corporation, which is neither familial nor political, is an amazing event.

The modern economy, furthermore, is essentially a corporate economy, for that is the entity that operates in the market. Nothing is new about markets, true; what is new is that technologically equipped corporations are now primary actors in markets and are able to sustain markets around the clock and around the world. The laws of economic life and the market, then, if they are to be morally influenced, will not only be shaped by familial and political institutions, but also by technological and corporate organization.

In the nineteenth century, corporations began their dramatic growth, and since then many people have tried to mobilize political parties, class interests, national identity, and traditional loyalties against them. This opposition continues in many places and inevitably maintains that more extensive state control of corporations is necessary. In other places, loyalties to clan, tribe, caste, or ethnic group mean that economics is conducted in terms of familistic principles, which means that trust is extended to those in one's gene pool identity group.[53] But most of the opposition to the corporate economy has faltered, failed, or invited forms of social and political control that have proven worse than what it opposed. Efforts to recover or discover a moral theory of the corporation are underway.[54]

It has been amply documented but largely forgotten that the roots of the modern corporation lie in the religious institutions of the West. The deepest roots are in the synagogues and the burial or mystery culture that set the organizational models that the early Christians took over, modified, and turned into the church.[55] The church was distinct from the household, with its hearth spirits, and distinct from the state, with its civic cult. People joined the church irrespective of birth, citizenship, or the economic status determined by these factors. In the church, members lived under a covenanted discipline that was to pervade all as-apects of life, in a community dedicated to a transformed world. It is precisely in these contexts that the Christian church grew as a *corpus Christi* that anticipated a New Jerusalem. Jesus neither came from a typical family nor married in order to begin one; and he was not an ordinary heir to the throne or an aspirant to political office, but promised instead a kingdom of another order, calling those who joined him his brothers, sisters, friends. Thus, just as the life of Jesus transcended both family and state, so did the early church establish a center of human loyalty and activity other not located in the family or politics. For the first time in human history, an enduring model of a third type of organization—what sociologists today call "voluntary associations" and political theorists, less elegantly, "NGOs" (nongovernmental organizations) was formed.[56]

Over time, the church gradually demanded and obtained the right to exist, to own property, and to designate trustees and managers, which in turn spawned independent religious orders, hospitals, and schools, institutions that served as loci of nonfamilial and nonroyal social participation.[57] These orders, hospitals, and schools became the basis for highly successful institutions in the "free cities," which increased in number steadily from then through the twentieth century. Today, the corporation is the basic organizing principle of complex societies—not only for-profit businesses, but hospitals, universities, professional associations, unions, ecological advocacy groups, political parties, singing societies, etc. Civil society is, indeed, a consociation of incorporated bodies that are, as time goes on, less and less identified with any specific family or regime.

Organizational formation has been further supported by several converging elements. One is a theory of the morality of property. A recent translation by Br. Allan Wolter of *Dun Scotus' Political and Economic Philosophy* reveals that the famous Franciscan took up one of the most disputed questions of economic history in the early 1300s.[58] In dispute was the issue of whether Christians could morally approve of private property—a rather important issue for those who had taken vows of poverty, for it was often held, as it is still in some Christian, Hindu, Sufi, and Buddhist traditions, that an increase of involvement with the material world implied a decrease in spiritual integrity. Even more controversial was the issue of whether collective entities could own property and even increase their wealth through investment and trade. It had long been accepted that the heads of families could own their homes, farms, or shops, and that kings could have their palaces, taxes, and treasury for public works. And there had been ancient provisions for various kinds of partnerships. But the idea that collective entities in society could develop patterns of trusteeship in which capital could be held without corruption of the social unit and the larger society was heatedly debated. In other words, Duns Scotus (in conversation and debate with other authorities of his age) helped clarify the spiritual and ethical foundations for the corporate management of property in organizations that are neither familial nor political. Over time, the idea that property is in one sense private, but is also best administered in a public, associative mode by "covenantal" agreements, came to be accepted in civil society. This led to modern, morally laden concepts such as "trusteeship," "limited liability," and "prudent man rules."

When the Reformers applied the concept of "vocation" or "calling" to all believers and not only to clerics, the concept of corporate ownership was extended beyond charitable associations to profit-oriented corporations, participation in which came to be seen as an opportunity to work out the implications of one's relationship to God for the well-being of humanity. The church, in short, fostered an institution that had decidedly material interests; but these material interests were, in principle, constrained by incarnate moral principles and spiritual purposes. For the first time in human history, economics had a potentially ethical organizational home outside the household and the state, accompanied by a potentially powerful notion of stewardship.[59]

In the Industrial Revolution, these developments converged with technological improvements to establish the central agent of economic capitalization, production, and distribution. In non-statist and post-traditional societies, such as America and later the defeated countries after World War II, the modern corporation became again the primary model of organization for universities, libraries, hospitals, political groups, unions, professional guilds, and voluntary associations for a wide variety of cultural and service activities. This reinforced democratic tendencies toward pluralistic civil societies dedicated to "freedom," a word that meant especially the right to associate and organize for religious, political, cultural, medical, social, and economic purposes outside the control of household and regime. The corporate model also augmented traditional views regarding "commutative justice," a legacy of family life; "distributive justice," an egalitarian legacy of modern political theory; and "productive justice," the notion of due reward for those who facilitate economic growth and the creation of wealth for the commonwealth.[60] Kinship groups became "family firms"; self-sustaining governmental agencies became "public corporations." Traditions and regions that did not support the formation of corporations fell behind in terms of global standards of productivity, wealth, and income.

The business corporation continues to expand its operations to include people from many families and nations, and to develop partners and subsidiaries around the world. This contributes to the spread of markets—labor markets, financial markets, and service markets, as well as markets of goods. The business corporation transforms familial and political life wherever it goes and brings about the establishment of transnational centers of production, finance, distribution, consumption, and technological development. Of course, it is quite clear that Japanese corporations, largely rooted in the leadership of older Samurai traditions, Korean and Taiwanese corporations, rooted largely in the "crony" networks of school or military chums, Chinese corporations, rooted in either familial clans or politicalmilitary units, Indian corporations, rooted in caste networks, and Latin American corporations, rooted in aristocratic semifeudal family connections, are not yet fully independent of either regime or familism. Whether or not they can sustain the social-organizational basis for full participation in a global economy is an open question; but it is likely that no viable social ethic for the future can be developed that does not wrestle with the presuppositions and social implications of these historic influences. They now join humanity together in a single economic destiny, with those who resist corporate organization tragically left behind.

Management as stewardship

Who runs these new-old institutions? The answer, as we have known since Berle[61] and Means[62] in the 1930s, is "managers."[63] On what terms do they run them? This too is a religiously and morally laden question. The answer, of course, is as business professionals. Now, this may seem to be an oxymoron, for business is not necessarily a "profession" in the classical sense. While clergy, lawyers, doctors, and professors have long been identifiable as "true professionals" in the sense that they have developed specialized training, associations whose membership is contingent on passing examinations on theoretical and practical matters, standards of conduct, and claims about dedication to values (respectively: faith, justice, health, and wisdom) that transcend material gain. Architects, engineers, accountants, pharmacists, nurses, teachers, psychologists, certain military and law-enforcement officers, and several other occupational groups also have developed patterns comparable to those of the classic professions. It is easy to trace the roots of these modern professions to the idea of "vocation" or "calling" as this idea developed out of biblical themes and the monastic disciplines of the Middle Ages, and later among the laity of the Protestant Reformation. For wherever these professions are adopted and cultivated around the world, they retain substantial traces of the dedication to principles and purposes transcending material gain and recognition that marked the Christian idea of calling.

Today, certain standards are developing that are moving business leadership toward professionalism. One development, particularly, can stand as the symbol of this change. With roots in the early-twentieth-century introduction of courses in business management and efficiency into college curricula, the MBA as an academically honored degree conferred by business schools at leading universities has become a major center of professional consciousness since World War II. Until then, most business education occurred in practical business or secretarial schools that were separate from recognized colleges and universities. It was only in the 1950s that business education began to develop into a major force, partly because of the publication of two landmark studies.[64] Since then, there have been many efforts to raise the quality of such education at both the undergraduate and graduate levels. But many centers of higher education did not join the effort to institutionalize and upgrade business education until the 1970s. Business, in short, is a newcomer to the circle of professional education.[65]

Business schools now attract a good share of the most promising young talent, and they have begun to certify that the business managers they train are as equally qualified as experts in their fields as those who graduate from a divinity school, medical school, law school, or many doctoral programs. Furthermore, it is increasingly common for business programs to mandate at least one course in business ethics—although as of yet many of these courses are quite narrow in their focus and not notable for their social, philosophical, and religious depth. Nevertheless, the topic is now on the agenda, and educational centers around the globe are featuring business education, MBA programs, and courses that teach about cross-cultural, universalistic values.[66]

This new, professional degree marks a potential new chapter in the history of the professions, for it indicates that business is developing internal standards of performance and excellence that were until recently neither universally practiced nor widely recognized. It is unlikely that governments will conduct qualifying exams like those doctors, lawyers, clergy, professors, and architects are required to take in order to practice. Still, the ripple effect of this development means that business, commerce, and management courses in colleges and universities are adopting standards of scholarship, discipline, and values orientation that can also be found among those who are in pre-medical, pre-law, and other pre-professional courses of study. At all levels, the overt theological content of courses has declined, but it is difficult to avoid issues having to do with matters of religion and sexuality in the workplace, or the creation of a responsible corporate policy that aids the families of employees, protects religious freedom, and assumes that the professionals of tomorrow will have responsibility for preserving community viability. Only at some Christian and Jewish colleges and universities does theology become a decisive guide for professional conduct in these areas.

And here the issues come down to very fateful ones for our global future. On one side are very personal issues. People in many professions are today frustrated with what they are finding in their professional schools and in their workplaces. On the one hand they love their work, but the moral and spiritual roots of why they do what they do are obscure. Justice, including the defense of human rights universally, is too often ignored in the practice of the law, and the health of the total person—mind, body, and spirit—is too often neglected among doctors. The transformation of nature as a quest for redemptive possibilities is hardly known by today's technology; covenantal patterns of relationship are frequently lost in our view of the corporation; and the trustee-stewardship model of management is seldom discussed, even in courses on business ethics. It is an open question whether the professions can cultivate an inner sense of meaning in our time, one that can guide us as we move increasingly toward a global society with no overarching political order.

Especially important will be the question of whether the managers of today and tomorrow can become conscious of the moral and spiritual reasons for what they do and why they do it, whether they can come to understand under what principles of right and what visionS of the good they work. Historically, I think it is evident that the global, corporate economy, and the technology on which it relies has been nurtured and shaped by religious traditions. Whether other religions can generate comparable moral resources, and whether the

Western religious traditions can remain ethically vital, are open questions. But it is not at all clear that a purely secular vision can sustain the modern economy. It is likely that where the fabric of a morally rich and spiritually fed civil society is not cultivated, marketfocused societies will lose their open character, close in on themselves, and constrict for nationalistic reasons and by coercive constraint the most productive forms of economic life on the horizon today. The poor will suffer most.

We do not know how long into the future open, market-focused economies will extend. Certainly, there will always be a place for markets, corporations, technology, and responsible management; and all the present indicators suggest that they are better for humanity than any other option presently known to us. Yet, no social institution is forever, and new patterns of economic life may evolve. Still, for the foreseeable future, those persons concerned about viable economic systems and the well-being of those who presently find themselves impoverished must engage these issues with a profound sense of calling, reforming with courage what needs reform, facing with spiritual fortitude those things that cannot be altered, and making the world a better place to live.

About the Contributors

Doug Bandow is Senior Fellow at the Cato Institute and a nationally syndicated columnist. Among his books are *Beyond Good Intentions: A Biblical View of Politics* and *The Politics of Envy: Statism as Theology.*

Wendell Berry is a poet, novelist, essayist who lives and farms in Henry County, Kentucky. He is the recipient of a number of awards, including the National Institute of Arts and Letters' award for writing and the T. S. Eliot Award. His nonfiction writings on economic and social themes include *The Unsettling of America: Culture and Agriculture; Sex, Economy, Freedom, and Community; Another Turn of the Crank;* and *What Are People For?* Many of his essays on economics are collected in *The Art of the Commonplace: The Agrarian Essays of Wendell Berry.*

William T. Cavanaugh is Assistant Professor of Theology at the University of St. Thomas in St. Paul, Minnesota. He coedited *The Blackwell Companion to Political Theology* and is the author of *Torture and Eucharist: Theology, Politics, and the Body of Christ* and *Theopolitical Imagination: Christian Practices of Space and Time.*

David Crawford is Assistant Dean and Assistant Professor of Moral Theology and Family Law at the John Paul II Institute for Studies on

Marriage and Family. He also holds a J.D. from the University of Michigan and serves as editor of *Anthropotes: Studies on Person and Family.*

Arthur Davis is Professor of Social Science at Atkinson College, York University. He is the editor or coeditor of the first two volumes of *The Collected Works of George Grant.* He also edited *George Grant and the Subversion of Modernity: Art, Philosophy, Politics, Religion, and Education.*

Samuel Gregg is a moral philosopher and the Director of Research and Academic Affairs at the Acton Institute. Gregg is also an adjunct scholar at the Centre for Independent Studies in Sydney. His books include *Challenging the Modern World: Karol Wojtyla/John Paul II and the Development of Catholic Social Teaching; Morality, Law, and Public Policy;* and *Economic Thinking for the Theologically Minded.*

Daniel T. Griswold is Associate Director of the Center for Trade Policy Studies at the Cato Institute. Educated at the University of Wisconsin and the London School of Economics, he is the author of numerous policy studies and the coeditor of *Economic Casualties: How U.S. Foreign Policy Undermines Trade, Growth, and Liberty.*

Peter J. Hill teaches in the business and economics department at Wheaton College in Illinois and is a senior associate at the Political Economy Research Center in Bozeman, Montana. His books include *Growth and Welfare in the American Past* and *Eco-Sanity: A Common Sense Guide to Environmentalism.*

V. Bradley Lewis is Assistant Professor of Philosophy at The Catholic University of America. He has written on Aristotle, natural law, and the philosophy of the social sciences for such journals as the *Review of Politics, Review of Metaphysics, Communio,* and the *Political Science Reviewer.*

D. Stephen Long is Associate Professor of Systematic Theology at Garrett-Evangelical Theological Seminary. He is the author of *Living the Discipline: United Methodist Theological Reflections on War, Civilization, and Holiness;* his most recent book is *The Divine Economy: Theology and the Market.*

Richard John Neuhaus is a priest of the archdiocese of New York, president of the Institute on Religion and Public Life, and the editor-in-chief of the institute's monthly journal, *First Things.* Among his many books are *As I Lay Dying: Meditations upon Returning; Appointment in Rome: The Church in America Awakening,* and the influential volume, *The Naked Public Square.*

Michael Novak is the George Frederick Jewett Scholar in Religion, Philosophy, and Public Policy at the American Enterprise Institute, where he is also Director of Social and Political Studies. He has served on the faculty at Harvard University, Stanford University, and the University of Notre Dame, among other institutions. Among his books are *Business as a Calling, The Fire of Invention,* and *On Two Wings: Humble Faith and Common Sense at the American Founding.*

Jennifer Roback Morse has been a research fellow at the Hoover Institution since 1997. She has served on the faculties of Yale University, George Mason University, and the Cornell University Law School. Her most recent book is *Love and Economics: Why the Laissez-Faire Family Doesn't Work.*

David L. Schindler is Gagnon Professor of Fundamental Theology and dean at the John Paul II Institute for Studies on Marriage and Family, editor of *Communio: International Catholic Review,* and a member of the Pontifical Council for the Laity. His books include *Heart of the World, Center of the Church:* Communio *Ecclesiology, Liberalism, and Liberation.*

Max L. Stackhouse is the Stephen Colwell Professor of Christian Ethics at Princeton Theological Seminary and the director of the seminary's Project on Public Theology. An ordained minister in the United Church of Christ, Stackhouse is also president of the Berkshire Institute for Theology and the Arts and the author or editor of many books, including *God and Globalization: Christ and the Dominions of Civilization.*

Lawrence M. Stratton is the Robert Krieble Fellow at the Institute for Political Economy and a member of the bar in Virginia and the District of Columbia.

Adrian Walker, assistant professor of philosophy at the John Paul II Institute for Studies on Marriage and Family, received his doctorate in philosophy at the Gregorian University in Rome, and is associate editor of *Communio: International Catholic Review.* In addition to his work in philosophy, he is also a professional translator working mainly in the German, French, Spanish, and Italian languages.

Notes

Chapter 1
Creating and Distributing Wealth: Whose Responsibility?

Peter J. Hill

1. All government programs have secondary effects on the distribution of income. Even the basic enforcement of rights under the rule of law has an impact on the material reward structure of a society. However, in this essay I am concerned with the use of government as an explicit mechanism for redistributing income.

2. For a more complete articulation of the biblical mandate to care for the poor, see Ronald J. Sider's *Just Generosity* (Grand Rapids, Mich.: Baker Books, 1999); and *Rich Christians in an Age of Hunger* (Dallas, Tex.: Word Publishing, 1997).

3. World Bank, *World Development Indicators* (New York: Oxford University Press, 2001), Table 2.8.

4. Ibid. There are actually two countries with lower Gini indices than Austria: the Slovak Republic and Belarus. Their data are flawed by virtue of the fact that they are still based on the wages and incomes of the centrally planned economies. In these systems the reported income differences vastly understate the actual differences in access to goods and services because of the special privileges of the elite. I have chosen not to use their data as providing good examples of highly egalitarian economies.

5. Ibid.

6. World Bank, *World Development Report 2002: Building Institutions for Markets* (New York: Oxford University Press, 2002), Table 1. The measure reported here

uses current exchange rates to convert incomes across countries to a common measure. An alternative measure is also available that uses purchasing power parity (PPP) as a common measure. The PPP measure yields a higher per-capita income for India ($2,390), but one that is still less than 10 percent of the U.S. per-capita income.

7. Hellmut Schoeck, *Envy: A Theory of Social Behaviour* (Indianapolis, Ind.: Liberty Fund, 1966); and Fernandez Gonzalo de la Mora, *Egalitarian Envy* (New York: Paragon House Publishers, 1987).

8. Martin Feldstein has called this "spiteful egalitarianism." See "Reducing Poverty, Not Inequality," *The Public Interest* 137 (1999): 34.

9. Raymond C. Battalio, John H. Kagel, and Morgan Reynolds, "Income Distributions in Two Experimental Economies," *Journal of Political Economy* 85 (1977): 1259–71.

10. The experimental results did not show any effect of the use of marijuana on earnings.

11. As is discussed in the next section, even large-scale transfers may not create any significant change in material inequality.

12. Robert Nozick, *Anarchy, State, and Utopia* (New York: Basic Books, 1974), 149.

13. Stéphane Courtois, Nicolas Werth, Jean-Louis Panné, Andrzej Paczkowski, Karel Bartosek, and Jean-Louis Margolin, *The Black Book of Communism* (Cambridge, Mass.: Harvard University Press, 1999), x.

14. F. A. Hayek, *The Constitution of Liberty* (Chicago: The University of Chicago Press, 1960), 88.

15. For a more complete discussion of the components of the rule of law, see Hayek, *The Constitution of Liberty,* and Richard A. Epstein, *Simple Rules for a Complex World* (Cambridge, Mass.: Harvard University Press, 1995).

16. Richard Pipes, *Property and Freedom* (New York: Alfred A. Knopf, 1999); and James Gwartney and Robert Lawson, *Economic Freedom of the World 2002 Annual Report* (Vancouver, B.C.: Fraser Institute, 2002).

17. Nozick, *Anarchy, State, and Utopia,* 163.

18. *Economic Report of the President* (Washington, D.C.: U.S. Government Printing Office, 2002), Table B-28.

19. If one accepts, as I do, that the better off have a moral responsibility to care for the less well off, one still has to determine the appropriate means for carrying out that responsibility. There may be a greater role for government in meeting that obligation than in achieving material equality (for instance, see Milton Friedman, *Capitalism and Freedom* [Chicago: The University of Chicago Press., 1962]), but there are still numerous problems with large-scale government intervention to alleviate poverty. For a more complete discussion of those issues, see Samuel Gregg,

Economic Thinking for the Theologically Minded (New York: University Press of America, Inc., 2001); Edmund A. Opitz, *The Libertarian Theology of Freedom* (Tampa, Fla.: Hallberg Publishing, 1999); and Charles Murray, *Losing Ground* (New York: Basic Books, 1984).

20. There is some controversy about the starting date for the modern epoch of economic growth. I am using the data of Richard Easterlin, a noted economic historian who sets the date around 1750 (*Growth Triumphant* [Ann Arbor, Mich.: The University of Michigan Press, 1996]). Another prominent researcher on worldwide growth, Angus Maddison, dates the modern era of growth as beginning in 1820 (*Dynamic Forces in Capitalist Development: A Long-Run Comparative View* [Oxford: Oxford University Press, 1991]).

21. Easterlin, *Growth Triumphant,* 17.

22. Ibid., 37. Easterlin estimates that from 1950 to 1990 the average growth rate of real GNP per capita in all developing economies was 2.5 percent annually. That means a doubling in approximately twenty-eight years.

23. Samuel H. Preston, "Human Mortality throughout History and Prehistory," in Julian Simon, ed., *The State of Humanity* (Oxford: Blackwell, 1995), 30.

24. World Bank, *World Development Report 2002,* Table 1.

25. Gwartney and Lawson, *Economic Freedom of the World 2002 Annual Report.*

26. Gerald P. O'Driscoll Jr., Kim R. Holmes, and Mary Anastasia O'Grady, *2002 Index of Economic Freedom* (Washington, D.C.: The Heritage Foundation, 2002); and Seth W. Norton, "Poverty, Property Rights, and Human Well-Being: A Cross-National Study," *Cato Journal* 18 (1998): 233–46.

27. Norton, "Poverty, Property Rights, and Human Well-Being: A Cross-National Study."

28. R. J. Barro and X. Sala-i-Martin, *Economic Growth* (New York: McGraw-Hill, 1995); P. Keefer and S. Knack, "Why Don't Poor Countries Catch Up? A Cross-National Test of Institutional Explanations," *Economic Inquiry* 35 (1997): 590–602; Stephen Knack, "Aid Dependence and the Quality of Governance: Cross-Country Empirical Tests," *Southern Economic Review* 68 (2001): 310–29; and Gerald W. Scully, *Constitutional Environments and Economic Growth* (Princeton, N.J.: Princeton University Press, 1992).

29. James Gwartney, Randall Holcombe, and Robert Lawson, "The Scope of Government and the Wealth of Nations," *Cato Journal* 18 (1998): 163–90

30. Hernando de Soto, *The Other Path* (New York: Harper & Row, Publishers, 1989) and *The Mystery of Capital* (New York: Basic Books, 2000).

31. Several surveys of the rent-seeking literature are available. For instance, see James M. Buchanan, Robert D. Tollison, and Gordon Tullock, *Toward a Theory of the Rent-Seeking Society* (College Station: Texas A & M University Press,

1980); and Charles K. Rowley, Robert D. Tollison, and Gordon Tullock, *The Political Economy of Rent-Seeking* (Boston: Kluwer Academic Publishers, 1988). Some seminal articles on rent seeking are found in Charles K. Rowley, ed., *Public Choice Theory Volume II* (Brookfield, Vt.: Edward Elgar Publishing Company, 1993) and in William F. Shughart II and Laura Razzolini, eds., *The Elgar Companion to Public Choice* (Cheltenham, UK: Edward Elgar, 2001).

32.   Fred S. McChesney, *Money for Nothing* (Cambridge, Mass.: Harvard University Press, 1997); Mancur Olson's *The Rise and Decline of Nations* (New Haven, Conn.: Yale University Press, 1982) and *Power and Prosperity* (New York: Basic Books, 2000); Andrei Shleifer and Robert W. Vishny, *The Grabbing Hand: Government Pathologies and Their Cures* (Cambridge, Mass.: Harvard University Press, 1998); and Gordon Tullock, *Rent Seeking* (Brookfield, Vt.: Edward Elgar, 1993).

33.   Nozick, *Anarchy, State, and Utopia*, 275.

34.   James D. Gwartney, Richard L. Stroup, and Russell S. Sobel (*Economics: Private and Public Choice* [Fort Worth: The Dryden Press, 2000], 157–58) estimate that only one-sixth of all transfers in the United States are means tested. The rest, rather than being targeted for the poor, are directed at groups that are well organized or represent an identifiable constituency. They argue that "the recipients of these transfers have incomes well above the average" (p. 158).

35.   Ibid., 822.

Chapter 2
The Poverty of Liberal Economics

Adrian Walker

I would like to thank Joseph Capizzi, Paul Grenier, Michael Hanby, Angelo Matera, Michael McCormick, D. C. Schindler, and David L. Schindler for helpful criticisms and suggestions regarding earlier drafts of this paper.

1.   This does not mean, of course, that governments have, or ought to have, absolutely no responsibility whatsoever for helping the poor financially and in other ways. Catholic social teaching, certainly no friend of socialism, has always insisted that government does have some such responsibility, while always leaving to the political prudence of the legislator the determination as to how best to exercise this responsibility in the concrete. At the same time, it seems to me that Catholic social teaching provides many arguments, both implicit and explicit, against what I am objecting to here: bureaucratized charity that, rather than exalting the human dignity of the recipient, actually tends to diminish respect for it, also and especially in the receiver. On the

other hand, while agreeing with the neoconservatives that the poor ought to be helped to become responsible economic agents, I will argue that an economics of gift leads to a quite different conception of "economic agents."

2. Milton Friedman, *Capitalism and Freedom* (Chicago: The University of Chicago Press, 1962), 13.

3. Karl Polanyi, *The Great Transformation: The Political and Economic Origins of Our Times* (Boston: Beacon Books, 1957), passim.

4. It must be kept in mind, however, that the claim that there are only two kinds of economic systems—either what liberalism means by the "free market" or a "state-planned economy"—is itself a piece of liberal economic theory based on a whole range of assumptions that, at the very least, need to be called into question. In other words, there are perfectly good, nonliberal reasons for objecting to the hugely bloated, bureaucratized, interventionist state, reasons that do not oblige us to embrace, for example, liberal economics' highly untraditional account both of the nature and scope of the common good and of the responsibility that political authority has for it.

5. I am by no means asserting, of course, that liberal economics is simply ideological; a thorough critique of it—which space limitations prevent me from undertaking here—would require patiently and respectfully sorting through the wealth of observation and analysis that thinkers such as Adam Smith, David Ricardo, John Stuart Mill, or, in our own day, Milton Friedman, have brought to their interpretation of free economic exchange. Nevertheless, careful perusal of the works of these men would, I contend, reveal, when all is said and done, a consistent tendency to embed what liberals claim to be a straightforward, scientifically "neutral" description of how the market works within a distinctive and, as I will show below, deeply flawed understanding of economic freedom.

6. Another line of argumentation, which I do not intend to develop in the present forum, would be to show how reliance on contractual exchange among self-interested strangers as the paradigm of the free market entails a reduction of the scope of the notion of *justice*. This reliance cuts out of the great fabric of justice one swath held to be publicly relevant in liberal societies: the "justice" that consists in the contracting parties' fulfilling the terms of the contract into which they have entered. Now, justice obviously includes fulfillment of one's contractual obligations. My point is simply that justice cannot be reduced to that fulfillment. Such a reduction leaves us with no resources against, for example, contemporary culture's tendency to condone any sexual behavior so long as it is engaged in by "consenting adults," or, for that matter, against unfair labor practices, practices whose unfairness cannot be removed by "mutual consent" (even supposing that the contracting parties are equally free in the matter). We cannot say that "mutual consent" is sufficient to justify morally *any* activity or exchange. The activity or exchange must also be ethically good on other, objective grounds. It must respect the exigencies of the objective good of the person.

Otherwise, we surrender ethics to the subjectivism and relativism that are pervasive in today's culture.

7. Ironically, such agnosticism undermines the very pluralism that liberalism seeks to affirm. The liberal market's so-called neutrality implants in it an imperialistic tendency to co-opt and, where it cannot co-opt, to displace, any rival vision of the good. Whatever claim about the good refuses to become a tributary to the liberal market system is banished to the margins of society where it is left to languish in irrelevance. True pluralism, by contrast, can flourish only against the background of an acknowledged, substantive account of the objective good of the person, one capacious enough to admit ongoing critical appropriation through dialogue. The objective good of the person necessarily includes his subjectivity (in its full flourishing, whose measure, of course, is not simply subjectivistic, but responds to an objective dynamic given in the very character of personhood). For this reason, it offers no foothold to a coercion that tramples the dignity of conscience. Quite to the contrary: it is, in the end, the only sure safeguard of that dignity.

8. "Oddly, many scholars have missed the fact that capitalism—the economic system—is embedded in a pluralistic structure in which it is designed to be checked by a political system and a moral-cultural system. . . . Democratic capitalism is not a 'free enterprise system' alone. It cannot thrive apart from the moral culture that nourishes the virtues and values on which its existence depends" (Michael Novak, *The Spirit of Democratic Capitalism* [New York: American Enterprise Institute/Simon and Schuster, 1982], 56).

9. See, for example, *The Catholic Ethic and the Spirit of Capitalism* (New York: The Free Press, 1993).

10. To be sure, the neoconservatives argue that, in order to succeed even on the market's own terms, people have to be virtuous, and in order to be virtuous, they have to pursue the objective good of the person. Nevertheless, this argument is undone by the logic of their own distinction between "institution" and "ideology." This distinction must mean one of two things: either that the "institution" of the market, which is to say, the technique of voluntary contractual exchange, is formally neutral, in its basic structure, with respect to the objective good of the person, or else that it is not. The neoconservatives can be found defending now one now the other meaning of the distinction. In either case, the distinction is problematic: (1) Sometimes the neoconservatives affirm that the institution of the market is neutral with respect to the objective good of the person. They interpret this formal neutrality benignly as a freedom from coercion that, they say, leaves open— indeed, *positively encourages*—the free embrace of the objective good of the person. Nonetheless, the structure of the market as they conceive it does not yet include relation to the objective good of the person. The individual must add such a relation himself. But he can only add it for extra-economic reasons. Of course, the neoconservatives insist that the market is always embodied within a larger moral-cultural order. However, if the market (as institution) does not yet include relation to the objective good of the person,

then the values of the moral-cultural order remain an optional extra. (2) On the other hand, the neoconservatives sometimes argue that the distinction between institution and ideology does not, after all, mean that the market is formally neutral with respect to the objective good of the person. Which objective good do they mean, then: the objective good created into man by God and fully revealed by Jesus Christ? or a "digest" of the objective good tailored for a liberal market unchanged in its basic structure? Unfortunately, the neoconservatives opt ultimately for this latter alternative. No matter how they frame the institutions-ideology distinction, then, the neoconservatives end up, by the logic of their own arguments, with one and the same conclusion: economic freedom is primitively indifferent vis-à-vis the objective good of the person.

11. Two authors whose works are saturated with this theme are David Schindler and Ferdinand Ulrich. Ulrich, for example (whose works exist, unfortunately, only in German), develops the thought of Thomas Aquinas to show that God's act of creation, as a donation of being *ex nihilo,* brings the creature into existence possessing itself (because it brings the creature into existence *all at once*) as something received entirely from God's generosity, hence, as, quite literally, a gift to itself. Both Ulrich and Schindler embed this creational understanding of being as gift in a more encompassing Christological, indeed, Trinitarian framework. Schindler, for instance, sees the Son as the archetypal Gift-to-Himself who, through his incarnation, assumes and anchors creaturely receptivity within the divine life itself. Both authors insist that, in the very act of receiving himself as gift, the person has already begun to give thanks for himself and, indeed, to give himself as gift within God's original gesture of donation. The person is "ontological thanks" (Ulrich) ordered to a giving and receiving in communion. For Ulrich, see, inter alia, Ferdinand Ulrich, *Homo Abyssus,* 2d ed. (Freiburg: Johannes Verlag, 1998); for Schindler, see, in addition to numerous articles, David L. Schindler, *Heart of the World, Center of the Church: Communio Ecclesiology, Liberalism, and Liberation* (Grand Rapids, Mich.: William B. Eerdmans Publishing Co., 1996). Kenneth Schmitz, in his *Creation: The Gift* (Milwaukee, Wisc.: Marquette University Press, 1982), also offers important reflections on the theme of being as gift.

12. Subjectivity includes a real interiority, of course. The point is simply that the person enters into his true interiority precisely to the extent that he is not "stuck" in it. He is most able to have a point of view when he can see things from *others'* points of view.

13. It is important to see that communion is not only the *result* of freedom, but also its *generative matrix.* I cannot give myself unless I receive myself—and my very ability to give myself—from another. Of course, the same is true of the other with respect to me. Thus, we must both be caught up within communion to find our freedom, even as the finding of our freedom, in the act of mutual giving and receiving, simultaneously brings our communion into being. Communion can be both the matrix and the result of our freedoms because communion itself is the unfolding—in which we are allowed to participate—of

God's giving us, not only our being, but also *his very giving* (which, accordingly, can be received only in a mutual giving and receiving which his giving both calls forth and, in doing so, takes fully account of as a factor in its own right within the total event of giving).

14. "Self-interest is not myopic selfishness. It is whatever it is that interests the participants, whatever they value, whatever goals they pursue" (Milton Friedman and Rose Friedman, *Free to Choose* [New York: Harcourt Brace Jovanovich, 1980], 27).

15. To be sure, I am not equating the profit-motive with selfish greed. I grant for the sake of argument the liberal premise that profit is the (impersonal) finality of specifically economic activity in a price-coordinated economy. That, however, is just the point: liberal economics defines the immanent finality of specifically economic activity in such a way that this activity does not require any motivation other than profit for its intrinsic intelligibility. There is thus no structural reason, given from within this intelligibility itself, not to be greedy. The fact that such reasons have to be supplied from the outside means that, in principle, they do not really have to be supplied at all for the economy to function on its own terms. Morality is an extra—a desirable extra, perhaps, but still an extra, after all. Neoconservatives like Novak will insist, of course, that self-interest, *rightly understood,* is always embedded in a complex network of relations that prevent it from degenerating into merely selfish profit-seeking. Invoking Adam Smith, Novak speaks of "rational self-interest" as the objective, realistic judgment about what is best for me that I would make if I were contemplating myself from the perspective of an impartial third party (Michael Novak, *The Spirit of Democratic Capitalism,* 95). Even granting Novak's benign reading of Adam Smith, however, "rational self-interest" still does not disturb the primacy of the profit-motive, but simply purges it of the irrational, passional inclinations the indulgence of which would prevent the economic actor from obtaining the goal of economic activity, namely, profit. Rather than lifting self-interest beyond private greed, as Smith probably intended it to, the counsel of the impartial spectator degenerates into a worldly-wise "prudence" that recommends regard for others as the best tool for achieving what remains the primary aim, namely, profit. Liberal economics, even on the best reading, and despite its best intentions, cannot help turning profit into an all-justifying ultimate precisely because, and insofar as, it conceives the proper end of economic activity as standing apart from, and not included within, the objective good of the person.

16. This is not to say that economic man is driven mainly by the passion of greed. We can take issue with many left-wing critics of capitalism who devote considerable moral energy to the denunciation of the greedy motives of "corporations." Interestingly, even Marx, who considered himself to be a scientist in the classical mode, saw exploitation as an impersonal necessity built into the structure of capitalism, rather than as the result of "greed" on the part of individual capitalists. The chief motor of *homo economicus* is rather the need for self-justification due to a failure to experience the gift-character of his being. This need translates into a kind of slavery to work,

which can be accompanied by a certain asceticism far removed from greed. In this perspective, money is merely a symbol of the "fruitfulness" of work and of the worth that this fruitfulness is supposed to bestow. We must also distinguish economic man's slavery to work from the genuine creative impulse seen in many successful entrepreneurs. On the other hand, I would argue that the logic of liberal economics distorts entrepreneurial creativity in the direction of the work-slavery of *homo economicus*.

17. In order to bring home this point, I recommend the following thought experiment: Suppose that California announced its intention to levy tariffs on imports from all the other states of the union. Does anyone seriously imagine that, if California failed to respond to its persuasion, the federal government would not force repeal of the tariffs, through military means if necessary? One might object, of course, that I am really talking about the constitutional illegality of secession. This objection misses the point. Indeed, the very fact that California's adoption of import tariffs would be tantamount to an act of secession underscores my claim that the so-called free market is understood as a national market policed by the nation-state, in this case, the federal government of the United States. This police power gives the state leverage over local economic units—a leverage, we might add, that translocal economic entities such as corporations can often sway to their advantage because of their disproportionate financial influence. Big business and big government are natural allies.

18. On this important point, see chapter 12 ("The Birth of the Liberal Creed") of Karl Polanyi's *The Great Transformation*.

19. This point bears stressing. I am *not* opposing the restful enjoyment of one's existence to productivity *tout court*, but only to the *unhealthy* (pseudo-) productivity that increasingly dominates our culture. The restful enjoyment of one's existence is an *attitude* that, in principle at least, can permeate *all that we do*. This means that even our productive activity can be an expression, a kind of fruitful overflow, of the grateful enjoyment of the gift of our own being within communion. This kind of productivity is, in the long run, more productive than the kind that dominates our culture. As we all know from experience, people working under pressure to produce quick results can do a lot at the beginning, but eventually wear themselves out. Only a productivity that coincides with fruitful overflow of the enjoyment of one's being in communion can sustain itself over the long haul. I am not arguing, of course, that we can ever entirely escape the pressure to produce. My point is simply that the pressure to produce cannot become a way of life, as it has in our culture, without profoundly changing, and lessening the quality of, productivity itself.

20. For a fascinating discussion of this problem with special reference to the legal profession, see M. Cathleen Kaveny, "Living the Fullness of Ordinary Time: A Theological Critique of the Instrumentalization of Time in Professional Life," in *Communio* 2001 (4): 771–819. As I emphasized in note 13, I do not mean to identify self-justificatory work-slavery with the genuine creativity that often drives

entrepreneurs, although I would argue that only an economics of gift can adequately interpret and secure this creativity.

21. We could make the same point in terms of the "law of supply and demand." Economic value, liberal economists tell us, is not a property inhering in things independently of market exchanges. Economic value is ultimately a variable (although not, in the norm, *wildly* variable) outcome of those exchanges themselves. It is the result of the interplay of supply and demand. Although liberal economists speak of the interplay of supply and demand as an impersonal event, in reality it is a highly personal one. True, there is a *certain* impersonal necessity to the interplay of supply and demand; given an overabundance of tennis shoes with respect to the demand for boots, for example, the price of tennis shoes will indeed tend to drop without any concerted effort on the part of consumers. But the terms "supply" and "demand" are ultimately a mere shorthand for talking about patterns of judgments that it is worth the expense either to make, to sell, or to purchase such-and-such an item. Determinations of economic value are guided, not by "impersonal laws of the market," but by producers', sellers', and buyers' sets of values. These values are inevitably embedded in and reflect judgments about the nature of the person and his existence. These judgments may be mistaken, but they are nonetheless *judgments,* not impersonal forces. Now, to speak of the nature and value of human existence is to speak of ontological wealth. Thus, even liberal economics, for all its professions that it is value-free, cannot escape judgments about ontological wealth, even as it conceals these judgments under the guise of a putatively value-free "neutrality." It therefore becomes perfectly legitimate to ask how well liberal theory actually reflects the true requirements of ontological wealth in the way it typically calculates economic value. I want to suggest in what follows that the answer must be, "not very well at all."

22. The degradation of quality becomes most apparent where the item produced is a recognizable but inferior version of an item that we normally associate with good quality. Consider the Twinkie. Few readers will dispute my claim that Twinkies taste worse than, say, homemade cakes. It is also clear that Twinkies taste worse than homemade cakes because they are not as well made as homemade cakes. Notice, however, that Twinkies *cannot* be as well made as homemade cakes. They cannot be because they are made with one thing in mind: convenient purchase and consumption. The attainment of such convenience, the sine qua non of the success of selling more more cheaply, *requires* that the production of the Twinkie be abstracted as much as possible from a whole range of considerations, such as the quality of ingredients, nutrition, conviviality, and the like, that are necessary to good taste and that, in fact, go into the making of the homemade cake.

23. Admittedly, most successful businessmen *are* successful because they have not let themselves be blinded by an obsession with profit above all else. But that, in a way, is just my point: the wise self-restraint that these businessmen demonstrate does not derive from the basic principles of liberal economics, which, in fact, tend by their inner logic to undermine it.

24. I am not denying, of course, that liberal economies do produce an abundance of cheap goods. My point is rather that this achievement is not a reliable index of economic health. The reason for this unreliability, I am arguing, is that the cheap goods in question are cheap only for the individual consumer at the moment of purchase, but not for society as a whole. The very process of creating an abundance of goods that are cheap for individual consumers at the moment of purchase—mass production fueled by the imperative to sell more more cheaply—inevitably causes negative side effects. Think, for example, of the pollution caused by the (once routine) dumping of toxic chemicals into waterways: the cost of cleanup procedures can run into the multiple millions. Now, someone somewhere—usually the taxpayers—eventually has to shoulder the cost of dealing with such side effects. And the cost is not a metaphorical one, but a real one, calculable in real dollars and cents. Goods whose production involves such costs appear to be "cheap," then, only because these costs are not reflected in what consumers pay for the goods in stores. The question we must ask, then, is whether an economy that buys tiny gains at the cost of net losses can be pronounced sound, if by "sound" we mean "conformable to the exigencies of economic good sense," and not merely "good at increasing the volume of exchanges between producers and consumers," or, what is the same, "good at increasing profits by inducing more people to buy more so-called cheap goods."

25. Wendell Berry, "Two Economies," in *Home Economics: Fourteen Essays by Wendell Berry* (New York: Northpoint Press, 1987), 54–75; here, 71.

26. Wendell Berry, "Christianity and the Survival of Creation," in *Sex, Economy, Freedom, and Community* (New York; San Francisco: Pantheon Books, 1992–1993), 93–116; here, 108*f*.

27. Alexander Schmemann, *The Journals of Father Alexander Schmemann* (Crestwood, N.Y.: Saint Vladimir's Seminary Press, 2001), 122.

Chapter 3
Catholic Social Teaching, Markets, and the Poor

Michael Novak

1. See, for example, John Paul II, *Centesimus Annus* (1991), especially sections 32–42 on the economic good, sections 44–48 on the political good, and sections 49–52 on the culture worthy of human beings.

2. Professor Russell Hittinger of the University of Tulsa is currently working on a major historical study, drafts of which I have been privileged to study, documenting this history from an original and compelling viewpoint. His book is as yet untitled, but his theme is the animosity of many significant liberal regimes toward the Catholic Church (and sometimes other churches), from just before 1789 until about 1950. In this respect, his theme adjoins some of

the writing on the struggle between liberalism and the churches undertaken by Pierre Manent, one of the more eminent political philosophers in France.

3. George Weigel, *Witness to Hope: The Biography of John Paul II* (New York: HarperCollins, 1999).

4. *Ecclesia in America,* section 56:

    More and more, in many countries of America, a system known as "neoliberalism" prevails; based on a purely economic conception of man, this system considers profit and the law of the market as its only parameters, to the detriment of the dignity of and the respect due to individuals and peoples. At times this system has become the ideological justification for certain attitudes and behaviors in the social and political spheres leading to the neglect of the weaker members of society. Indeed, the poor are becoming ever more numerous, victims of specific policies and structures that are often unjust.

5. See *Centesimus Annus,* section 32; e.g.:

    Whereas at one time the decisive factor of production was *the land,* and later capital—understood as a total complex of the instruments of production—today the decisive factor is increasingly *man himself,* that is, his knowledge, especially his scientific knowledge, his capacity for interrelated and compact organization, as well as his ability to perceive the needs of others and to satisfy them.

6. Amartya Sen, for instance, and the other authors of the 1999 Human Development Report (http://www.undp.org/hdro/99.htm visited 7 October 1999, 9:11 AM), p.1, citing the 1990 development report:

    The real wealth of a nation is its people. And the purpose of development is to create an enabling environment for people to enjoy long, healthy and creative lives. This simple but powerful truth is too often forgotten in the pursuit of material and financial wealth.

    See also Gary S. Becker, *Human Capital: A Theoretical and Empirical Analysis, With Special Reference to Education* (Chicago: University of Chicago Press, 1993).

7. For an interesting survey, see Patrick Glynn, *God: The Evidence: The Reconciliation of Faith and Reason in a Post-secular World* (Prima Publishing, 1999).

8. See *Rerum Novarum,* sections 11, 16, 17, 19, 27, 45.

9. *Sollicitudo Rei Socialis,* sections 38–39:

    On the path toward the desired conversion, toward the overcoming of the moral obstacles to development, it is already possible to point to the *positive* and *moral value* of the growing awareness of *interdependence* among individuals and nations...It is above all a question of *interdependence,* sensed as a *system determining* relationships in the contemporary world, in its economic, cultural, political and religious elements, and accepted as a *moral category*. When interdependence becomes recognized in this way, the correlative response as a moral and social attitude, as a "virtue," is *solidarity*. This then is not a feeling of vague compassion or shallow distress at the misfortunes of so many people, both near and far. On the contrary, it is a *firm and persevering determination* to commit oneself to the *common good*; that is to say to the good of all and of each individual, because we are all really responsible for all. This determination is based on the solid conviction that what is hindering full development is that desire for profit and thirst for power already mentioned. These attitudes and "structures of sin" are only conquered—presupposing the help of divine grace—by a *diametrically opposed attitude*: a commitment to the good of one's neighbour with the readiness in the Gospel sense, to "lose oneself" for the sake of the other instead of exploiting him, and to "serve him" instead of oppressing him for one's own advantage. The exercise of solidarity *within each society* is valid when its members recognize one another as persons.

10. *Centesimus Annus*, section 10:

[W]e nowadays call the principle of solidarity, the validity of which both in the internal order of each nation and in the international order I have discussed in the Encyclical *Sollicitudo Rei Socialis*, is clearly seen to be one of the fundamental principles of the Christian view of social and political organization. This principle is frequently stated by Pope Leo XIII, who uses the term "friendship," a concept already found in Greek philosophy. . . . Pope Paul VI, expanding the concept to cover the many modern aspects of the social question, speaks of "civilization of love."

11. Karol Wojtyla, *The Acting Person,* trans. A. Potocki (Dordrecht: Reidel, 1979); originally published as K. Wojtyla, *Osoba i czyu* (Krakow: Polskie Towarzystwo Teologiczne, 1969).

12. *Centesimus Annus*, section 13.

From this mistaken conception of the person there arise both a distortion of law, which defines the sphere of the exercise of freedom, and an opposition to private property. A person who is deprived of something he can call "his own," and of the possibility of earning a living through his own initiative, comes to depend on the social machine and on those who control it. This makes it much more difficult for him to recognize his dignity as a person, and hinders progress toward the building up of an authentic human community.

In contrast, from the Christian vision of the human person there necessarily follows a correct picture of society. According to *Rerum Novarum* and the whole social doctrine of the Church, the social nature of man is not completely fulfilled in the State, but is realized in various intermediary groups, beginning with the family and including economic, social, political and cultural groups which stem from human nature itself and have their own autonomy, always with a view to the common good. This is what I have called the "subjectivity" of society which, together with the subjectivity of the individual, was cancelled out by "Real Socialism."

13. *Centesimus Annus,* sections 31–32:

In history, these two factors—*work* and *the land*—are to be found at the beginning of every human society. However, they do not always stand in the same relationship to each other. At one time *the natural fruitfulness of the earth* appeared to be, and was in fact, the primary factor of wealth, while work was, as it were, the help and support for this fruitfulness. In our time, *the role of human work* is becoming increasingly important as the productive factor both of nonmaterial and material wealth. . . .

In our time, in particular, there exists another form of ownership which is becoming no less important than land: *the possession of know-how, technology and skill*. The wealth of the industrialized nations is based much more on this kind of ownership than on natural resources.

14. *Centesimus Annus,* section 58:

Today we are facing the so-called "globalization" of the economy, a phenomenon which is not to be dismissed, since it can create unusual opportunities for greater prosperity. There is a growing feeling, however, that this increasing internationalization of the economy ought to be accompanied by effective international agencies which will oversee and direct the economy to the common good, something which an individual state, even if it were the most powerful on earth, would not be in a position to do.

15. Randall Collins, *Weberian Sociological Theory* (Cambridge: Cambridge University Press, 1986), 51–52.

16. St. Thomas Aquinas, *Contra Impugnantes Dei Cultum et Religionem* (1256). St. Thomas presents here the first known defense of association, cited by Leo XIII in *Rerum Novarum* (section 37) as the *locus classicus* on associations. Also Russell Hittinger's lecture at the Summer Institute, Krakow, Poland, July 1998 (unpublished).

17. See especially "The Influence of America," in section II, "The Anglo-American Tradition of Liberty," in J. Rufus Fears, ed., *Essays in the History of Liberty: Selected Writings of Lord Acton* (Indianapolis, Ind.: Liberty Classics, 1985), 198–212.

18. Jacques Maritain, *Man and State* (Chicago: University of Chicago Press, 1951), 91; see also Maritain's *Approaches to God* (Greenwood Publishing Group, reprint ed. June 1978).

19. See http://www.worldbank.org/poverty/data/trends/income.htm (visited 7 October 1999 12:11 PM). The total population of Latin America and the Caribbean is estimated at 519 million people in 2000 (http://www.un.org/popin/wdtrends/pop1999-00.pdf, visited 21 August 2001 3:27 PM).

20. *Human Development Report,* op. cit., 25.

21. In the World Labor Report unemployment was estimated for this area at about 59.6 million (see http://www.ilo.org/public/english/80relpro/publ/wlr/97/annex/tab8.htm, visited 7 October 1999 9:39 AM). Youth unemployment rates are usually double the national average and women's unemployment rates are 60 percent higher than men's rates. Overall employment in Latin America increased on average 2.9 percent between 1990 and 1998, but this was not sufficient to absorb the annual 3.3 percent expansion of the labor force. (See http://www.ilo.org/public/english/235press/pr/1999/26.htm, visited 6 October 1999 11:36 AM.)

22. *Centesimus Annus,* section 32:

    It is precisely the ability to foresee both the needs of others and the combinations of productive factors most adapted to satisfying those needs that constitutes another important source of wealth in modern society. Besides, many goods cannot be adequately produced through the work of an isolated individual; they require the cooperation of many people in working towards a common goal. Organizing such a productive effort, planning its duration in time, making sure that it corresponds in a positive way to the demands which it must satisfy, and taking the necessary risks—all this too is a source of wealth in today's society. In this way, the *role* of disciplined and creative *human work* and, as an essential part of that work, *initiative and entrepreneurial ability* becomes increasingly evident and decisive. This process, which throws practical light on a truth about the person which Christianity has constantly affirmed, should be viewed carefully and favorably. Indeed, besides the earth, man's principal resource is *man himself.* His intelligence enables him to discover the earth's productive potential and the many different ways in which human needs can be satisfied. It is his disciplined work in close collaboration with others that makes possible the creation of ever more extensive *working communities* which can be relied upon to transform man's natural and human environments. Important virtues are involved in this process, such as diligence, industriousness, prudence in undertaking reasonable risks, reliability and fidelity in interpersonal relationships, as well as courage in carrying out decisions which are difficult and painful but necessary, both for the overall working of a business and in meeting possible set-backs.

23. *Centesimus Annus,* section 34:

> It is a strict duty of justice and truth not to allow fundamental human needs to remain unsatisfied, and not to allow those burdened by such needs to perish. It is also necessary to help these needy people to acquire expertise, to enter the circle of exchange, and to develop their skills in order to make the best use of their capacities and resources.

24. Leslie Newbigin, *Foolishness to the Greek* (London: SPCK, 1986), 113.

25. Richard Harries, *Is There a Gospel for the Rich?* (London: Mowbray, 1992), 72.

26. Harries, *Is There a Gospel for the Rich?,* 88–89.

27. John Gray, *The Moral Foundations of Market Institutions*, IEA Health and Welfare Unit, Choice in Welfare Series no. 10 (London, 1992), 5–17.

28. Ibid., chap. 4.

29. Ibid., 63–72.

30. R. Rector, "How 'Poor' Are America's Poor?" Heritage Foundation *Backgrounder* no. 791, September 1990.

31. Kenneth Adams, "Changing British Attitudes," *RSA Journal,* November 1990, 80.

32. John Paul II, Encyclical Letter *Centesimus Annus* (Washington, D.C.: St. Paul Publications, 1991).

33. Wojtyla, *The Acting Person.*

34. John Paul II, Encyclical Letter *Sollicitudo Rei Socialis* (Washington, D.C.: St. Paul Publications, 1988).

35. Gabriel Marcel, *The Mystery of Being* (Chicago: Gateway Edition, 1960).

36. *Centesimus Annus,* section 32.

37. John Paul II, Encyclical Letter *Laborem Exercens* (Washington, D.C.: St. Paul Publications, 1981).

38. *Sollicitudo Rei Socialis,* section 15.

39. *Centesimus Annus,* section 32.

40. Ibid.

41. Oswald von Nell-Breuning, S.J., "Socio-Economic Life," in H. Vorgrimler, ed., *Commentary on the Documents of Vatican II,* vol. 5 (New York: Herder and Herder, 1969), 299.

42. *Centesimus Annus,* section 32.

43. Ibid.

44. Harries, *Is There a Gospel for the Rich?*, 101.

45. C. Murray, *Losing Ground* (New York: Basic Books, 1984).

46. M. Novak et al., *The New Consensus on Vanity and Welfare* (Washington, D.C.: AEI Press, 1987).

47. Ronald Preston, *Religion and the Ambiguities of Capitalism* (London: SCM Press, 1991), 5.

48. Ibid., 74.

49. R. Buttiglione, "Christian Economics 101," *Crisis,* July–August 1992, 34.

Chapter 4
Catholic Social Teaching and the Global Market

D. Stephen Long

1. Michael Novak, *The Catholic Ethic and the Spirit of Capitalism* (New York: The Free Press, 1993), 101.

2. See Francis Fukuyama's *The End of History and the Last Man* (New York: The Free Press, 1992); Gianni Vattimo's *The End of Modernity* (Baltimore, Md.: The Johns Hopkins University Press, 1988); Joseph Schumpeter, *Capitalism, Socialism and Democracy* (New York: Harper Torchbooks, 1950), 123–24; and Daniel M. Bell Jr., *Liberation Theology after the End of History* (London; New York: Routledge, 2001).

3. For a helpful discussion on how the modern corporation is forced into this kind of behavior, see Lawrence E. Mitchell's *Corporate Irresponsibility: America's Newest Export* (New Haven, Conn.: Yale University Press, 2001). Mitchell argues that the artificial nature of the corporation as an individual within the context of American liberalism, coupled with limited liability and the moral imperative to maximize profit—if not stock profit—leads to "corporate irresponsibility." He offers a number of examples of such irresponsibility in modern corporations, including Firestone, Ford, Hooker Chemical, Union Carbide, General Electric, Mattel, Coca-Cola, Unocal, General Motors, and Marriott Corporation (pp. 19–49).

4. Gustavo Gutiérrez, *A Theology of Liberation* (Maryknoll, N.Y.: Orbis, 1993), 45–46.

5. Ibid., 138.

6. Ibid., 22–23. But see also p. 157, where Gutiérrez recognizes that even Catholic social teaching reads conflict as a "social fact."

7. John Milbank, "The Body by Love Possessed: Christianity and Late Capitalism in Britain," *Modern Theology* 3, no. 1 (1986): 39.

8. John Milbank, "Socialism of the Gift, Socialism by Grace," *New Blackfriars* 77, no. 910 (December 1996): 544.

9. John Milbank, *Theology and Social Theory* (Oxford: Basil Blackwell, 1990), 245.

10. Alasdair MacIntyre, "How Can We Learn What *Veritatis Splendor* Has to Teach?" *The Thomist* 58 (1994): 176.

11. Ibid., 185.

12. Alasdair MacIntyre, "Introduction 1953, 1968, 1995: Three Perspectives," *Marxism and Christianity* (Notre Dame, Ind.: University of Notre Dame Press, 1995), vii.

13. Ibid.

14. Ibid., ix–x.

15. Max Stackhouse and Dennis McCann, "A Postcommunist Manifesto: Public Theology after the Collapse of Socialism," in *On Moral Business* (Grand Rapids, Mich.: William B. Eerdmans Publishing Co., 1995), 949–50.

16. Ibid., 950.

17. Ibid., 952.

18. Novak, *Spirit of Democratic Capitalism* (New York: Simon and Schuster, 1982), 23–24.

19. Michael Novak, "How Christianity Created Capitalism," *Wall Street Journal,* 23 December 1999.

20. For an excellent critique of the doctrine of Christian vocation as a form of theological legitimation for business activity, see Robert Brimlow's *Paganism and the Professions,* Ekklesia Project Pamphlet Series, no. 3 (Eugene, Ore.: Wipf and Stock Publishers, 2001). Brimlow gives a much more realistic assessment of what work is, and requires of us, than most of the romantic appeals to the notion of vocation one finds in church documents and in theological writings. As Brimlow notes, "it is hard to maintain that, for the vast majority of us, work is intrinsically good. For most of us work is instrumental; it is the means by which we can pursue other ends: feeding and housing ourselves and our loved ones and purchasing things that make life more comfortable. It is rare to find people who work at jobs where they find any but the most minimal types of fulfillment or where they recognize that their work satisfies a higher purpose other than increased profitability for the firm" (p. 6).

21. Michael Novak, "Controversial Engagements," *First Things* 92 (April 1999): 21–29.

22. This distinction is another version of the so-called (Protestant) either-or and the (Catholic) both-and, which is simply another version of Troeltsch's sect-church distinction, which is another version of Weber's ethics of ultimate ends versus ethics of consequences.

23. See Novak, "Controversial Engagements," 21–29.

24. Stackhouse and McCann, "Postcommunist Manifesto," 952.

25. They write, "Enhancing the capacity for capitalization in responsible corporations is as much the new name for mission as development is the new name for peace" (ibid.).

26. In *After Virtue,* MacIntyre refuses to concede that the true either-or at the end of modernity is liberalism or Marxism instead of Nietzsche or Aristotle because, as he puts it, "the claim of Marxism to a morally distinctive standpoint is undermined by Marxism's own moral history. . . . Marxists have always fallen back into relatively straightforward versions of Kantianism or utilitarianism. Nor is this surprising. Secreted within Marxism from the outset is a certain radical individualism. . . . . Secondly, I remarked earlier that as Marxists move towards power they always tend to become Weberians" (*After Virtue* [Notre Dame, Ind: University of Notre Dame Press, 1981], 261). Milbank also finds Marx to be still an "economic thinker" within the liberal tradition in that he does not "fully recognize the historical particularity of the economic." It is distinguished from other forms of exchange, like religious exchange, and valued as their real meaning. Moreover, as Milbank notes, Marx failed to recognize that "it is just as fundamental for capitalist logic to reproduce conditions of exchange and consumption as to reproduce the conditions of production." Thus the labor theory of value alone cannot account for the value attributed to produced goods (*Theology and Social Theory* [Cambridge, Mass.: Blackwell, 1991], 191).

27. It is this distinction which surely makes possible the fact/value split upon which Weberian sociology thrives.

28. I am not presuming that there are only these two theological languages. I am only arguing that these two represent the dominant languages most theologians explicitly or implicitly adopt.

29. Adam Smith, *Wealth of Nations* (New York: The Modern Library, 1965), 423.

30. Adam Smith, *Theory of Moral Sentiments* (Indianapolis, Ind.: Liberty Fund, 1979), 36.

Chapter 5
The Unfreedom of the Free Market

William T. Cavanaugh

Thanks to D. Stephen Long and Michael Naughton for their helpful comments on an earlier draft of this chapter.

1. Milton Friedman, *Capitalism and Freedom* (Chicago: University of Chicago Press, 1962), 13; and Milton and Rose Friedman, *Free to Choose* (New York: Avon Books, 1980), xv–xvi.

2. Friedman, *Capitalism and Freedom,* 14–15.

3. Milton and Rose Friedman, *Free to Choose,* 7.

4. Ibid., 7–8.

5. Friedman, *Capitalism and Freedom,* 15.

6. Friedrich A. Hayek, *The Road to Serfdom* (Chicago: University of Chicago Press, 1944), 59.

7. Ibid., 60.

8. Michael Novak, *The Spirit of Democratic Capitalism* (New York: Simon and Schuster, 1982), 54–55.

9. Milton and Rose Friedman, *Free to Choose,* 214.

10. Ibid.; italics in the original.

11. Saint Augustine of Hippo, *Confessions,* trans. Henry Chadwick (O x f o r d : Oxford University Press, 1991), 3.

12. Saint Augustine of Hippo, *The Spirit and the Letter,* para. 52, in *Augustine: Later Works,* ed. John Burnaby (Philadelphia: Westminster Press, 1955), 236.

13. Ibid.

14. Ibid.

15. In his *Confessions,* Augustine writes of the habits of the will that hold back his conversion even after his intellectual problems have found resolution. At that point there appeared to him a vision of Lady Continence, who showed him a multitude of holy men and women to serve as exemplars for him and as mediators of God's grace (*Confessions,* 150–52).

16. Ibid., 33.

17. Ibid., 34.

18. Saint Augustine of Hippo, Letter 93, in Henry Paolucci, ed., *The Political Writings of St. Augustine* (Chicago: Gateway Editions, 1962), 203.

19. Ibid., 205.

20. Ibid., 193–94.

21. Ibid., 198.

22. Augustine, Letter 87, in Paolucci, ed., *The Political Writings of St. Augustine,* 190.

23. Ibid., 191.

24. Augustine, Letter 93, in Paolucci, ed., *The Political Writings of St. Augustine,* 195.

25. Ibid., 197.

26. See Augustine's exposition of evil as the privation of good, and therefore as nothing, in *Confessions,* 124–25.

27. Ibid., 30.

28. Ibid., 16. Augustine's ideas here are put into literary form in C. S. Lewis's *The Great Divorce.* In Lewis's Hell, everything, including the inhabitants, exists as mere shadow, with no solid reality.

29. Augustine, *Confessions,* 30.

30. Ibid., 35.

31. See, for example, Tracy McVeigh, "One in Five Women Is a Shopaholic," *London Observer,* November 26, 2000. A search for "shopaholics anonymous" on the web generated the following advertising message: "Buy and sell 'shopaholics anonymous' and millions of other items on eBay!"

32. Richard Ott, *Creating Demand* (Burr Ridge, Ill.: Irwin Professional Publishing, 1992), cited in Michael Budde, *The (Magic) Kingdom of God: Christianity and Global Culture Industries* (Boulder, Colo.: Westview Press, 1997), 39.

33. Budde, *The (Magic) Kingdom of God,* 43.

34. Quoted in Erik Larson, *The Naked Consumer: How Our Private Lives Become Public Commodities* (New York: Henry Holt and Company, 1992), 20. See the Friedmans' reference above to yearly car model changes as reflecting the "real desires" of consumers, at footnote 9.

35. *Marketing News,* February 17, 1992, quoted in Budde, *The (Magic) Kingdom of God,* 38.

36. Budde, *The (Magic) Kingdom of God,* 42.

37. Larson, *The Naked Consumer,* 58. An advertisement for Aristotle Industries says, "We can't tell you what they eat for dinner. But we can tell you where they live. And their phone number, who they live with, whether they have voted, and much, much more"; quoted in Larson, 3.

38. Herbert Schiller, quoted in Budde, *The (Magic) Kingdom of God,* 33.

39. Michael J. Naughton, "The 'Stumbling and Tripping' of Executive Pay," *New Oxford Review* 68, no. 11 (December 2001): 27–28.

40. Eric Bates, "Losing Our Shirts," *The Independent* (Durham, N.C.), 6 April 1994.

41. Naughton, "The 'Stumbling and Tripping' of Executive Pay," 27–31.

42. Eduardo Galeano, quoted in Lawrence Weschler, *A Miracle, A Universe: Settling Accounts with Torturers* (New York: Pantheon Books, 1990), 147.

43. "El consejo del professor," *Ercilla,* 2 April 1975, 19–22.

44. Pamela Constable and Arturo Valenzuela, *A Nation of Enemies: Chile under Pinochet* (New York: W. W. Norton & Company, 1991), 170.

45. Bob Herbert, "In Maquiladora Sweatshops: Not a Living Wage," *Minneapolis Star Tribune,* 22 October 1995.

46. Race Mathews, "Mondragon: Past Performance and Future Potential," paper presented at the Kent State University Capital Ownership Group Conference, Washington, D.C., October 2002. The paper can be found at http://cog.kent.edu/Author/Author.htm. More information on Mondragon is available at the company's website, www.mondragon.mcc.es.

47. Hillaire Belloc, *The Restoration of Property* (New York: Sheed & Ward, 1936), 21.

48. Ibid., 27.

49. St. Thomas Aquinas, *Summa Theologiae,* II-II.66.1.

50. Ibid., II-II.66.1ad2

51. Ibid., II-II.66.2.

52. Michael Pollan, "Power Steer," *New York Times Magazine,* 31 March 2002.

53. Ibid., 71.

54. Ibid., 51.

55. For example, the Catholic social encyclicals *Laborem Exercens, Quadragesimo Anno, Gaudium et Spes,* and others.

Chapter 6
Individualism, the Market, and Christianity: Can the Circle Be Squared?

Samuel Gregg

1. See A. Hibbert, "The Economic Policies of Towns," *Cambridge Economic History,* vol. 3 (Cambridge: Cambridge University Press, 1963), 157–229; F. Rörig, *The Medieval Town,* trans. D. Byrant (London: Penguin, 1967).

2. See John T. Noonan, *The Scholastic Analysis of Usury* (Cambridge, Mass.: Harvard University Press, 1957); and Thomas Divine, S.J., *Interest: A Historical*

and Analytical Study in Economics and Modern Ethics (Milwaukee, Wisc.: Marquette University Press, 1959), 3–116.

3. See Margery Reeves, *The Influence of Prophecy in the Later Middle Ages: A Study in Joachimism* (Oxford: Clarendon Press, 1969), 10–70.

4. See Samuel Gregg, *Morality, Law, and Public Policy* (Sydney: St. Thomas More Press, 2001), 56–65.

5. See Germain Grisez, *The Way of the Lord Jesus,* vol. 2, *Living a Christian Life* (Quincy, Ill.: Franciscan Press, 1993), 860.

6. John Paul II, Encyclical Letter *Fides et Ratio* (Boston: St. Paul Publications, 1998), section 43.

7. Boethius, *De duabus naturis et una persona Christi,* vol. 64 (Migne: Patrol. Lat., 1920), no. 1343.

8. Thomas More, *The Four Last Things,* in *The English Works of St. Thomas More,* ed. W. E. Campbell (London: Eyre and Spottiswoode, 1931), 95.

9. St. Augustine, *Concerning The City of God against the Pagans* (London: Penguin, 1984), bk. xiv, chap. 28.

10. John Paul II, Encyclical Letter *Centesimus Annus* (Boston: St. Paul Publications, 1991), para. 25.

11. See Pierre Manent, *Modern Liberty and Its Discontents,* trans. D. Mahoney, (Lanham, Md.: Rowman and Littlefield, 1998), 155.

12. See the Denzinger-Schönmetzer collection of Church documents in Jesuit Fathers of St. Mary's College, *The Church Teaches: Documents of the Church in English Translation* (Rockford. Ill.: TAN Books and Publishers, 1973), 530.

13. See Second Vatican Council, Pastoral Constitution on the Church in the Modern World *Gaudium et Spes,* 7 December 1965, sections 26 and 74, in A. Flannery, O.P., gen. ed., *Vatican Council II: The Conciliar and Post Conciliar Documents,* vol. 1, rev. ed. (Leominster, UK: Fowler Wright Books Ltd., 1988).

14. John Paul II, Encyclical Letter *Veritatis Splendor* (Boston: St. Paul Publications, 1993),section 48; cf.sections 67, 78, and 79. See also Germain Grisez and Russell Shaw, *Fulfillment in Christ: A Summary of Christian Moral Principles* (Notre Dame, Ind.: University of Notre Dame Press, 1991), 49–57.

15. *Centesimus Annus,* section 13 (author's emphasis).

16. See, for example, Maciej Zieba, O.P., "Two or Even Three Liberalisms," *Dialogue and Humanism* 4, no. 5 (1994): 89.

17. Milton Friedman, "Goods in Conflict," in G. Weigel, ed., *A New Worldly Order: John Paul II and Human Freedom—A "Centesimus Annus" Reader* (Washington, D.C.: Ethics and Public Policy Center, 1992), 77.

18. Joseph Ratzinger, "Truth and Freedom," *Communio: International Catholic Review* 23, no. 1 (1996): 17.

19. Karl Marx and Friedrich Engels, *Works,* vol. 3 (London: Penguin, 1971), 33.

20. Ratzinger, "Truth and Freedom," 17.

21. See, for example, Walter Eucken, *Grundsätze der Wirtschaftspolitik* (Tübingen: Mohr Siebeck, 1952); Franz Böhm, "The Rule of Law in a Market Economy," in A. Peacock and H. Willgerodt, eds., *Germany's Social Market Economy: Origins and Evolution* (London: Macmillan, 1989).

22. Rocco Buttiglione, *The Moral Mandate for Freedom: Reflections on "Centesimus Annus"* (Grand Rapids, Mich.: Acton Institute, 1997), 7.

23. Wilhelm Röpke, "The Economic Necessity of Freedom," *Modern Age* 3 (summer 1959): 230.

24. See Wilhelm Röpke, *The Social Crisis of Our Time* (New Brunswick, N.J.: Transaction Publishers, 1942/1992), 105.

25. Röpke, "The Economic Necessity of Freedom," 230.

26. See John Finnis, *Natural Law and Natural Rights* (Oxford: Clarendon Press, 1980), 134–60.

27. Alexis de Tocqueville, *Democracy in America,* vol. 2, ed. J. P. Mayer, trans. G. Lawrence (New York: HarperPerennial, 2000), 637.

28. See Buttiglione, *The Moral Mandate for Freedom,* 10.

29. For the precise meaning of self-determination as understood here, see Germain Grisez and Russell Shaw, *Beyond the New Morality: The Responsibilities of Freedom,* 3d ed. (Notre Dame, Ind.: University of Notre Dame Press, 1988), 50–52.

30. Robert P. George, *Making Men Moral: Civil Liberties and Public Policy* (Oxford: Clarendon Press, 1993), 19–42.

31. Ronald Dworkin, *A Matter of Principle* (Cambridge, Mass.: Harvard University Press, 1985), 350.

32. Ronald Dworkin, *Taking Rights Seriously* (Cambridge, Mass.: Harvard University Press, 1977), 198.

33. See Dworkin, *Taking Rights Seriously,* 273.

34. John Finnis, "Legal Enforcement of 'Duties to Oneself': Kant v. Neo-Kantians," *Columbia Law Review* 87 (1987): 437.

35. Joseph Raz, *The Morality of Freedom* (Oxford: Clarendon Press, 1986), 412.

Chapter 7
The "Bourgeois Family" and the Meaning of Freedom and Community

David Crawford

1. Of course, this claim is far from uncontroversial; see, e.g., Allan Carlson, "Creative Destruction, Family Style," *The Intercollegiate Review: A Journal of Scholarship & Opinion* 37 (spring 2002): 49–57.

2. This claim has also been criticized from various perspectives; see, e.g., Vigen Guroian, *Ethics after Christendom: Toward an Ecclesial Christian Ethic* (Grand Rapids, Mich.: William B. Eerdmans Publishing Co., 1994), 146–50.

3. Michael Novak, *The Spirit of Democratic Capitalism* (New York: Madison Books, 1982), 159.

4. In this essay I mostly employ the term "virtuous self-interest" because it represents the basic point liberalism's current defenders intend to make with respect to the family, viz. the family is essential to the survival of liberal institutions because it is the place where the virtues are inculcated. Of course, the other phrases also carry important nuances: "rational self-interest" suggests the reasoned element of self-interest, as opposed to an irrational reigning of the passions; "self-interest rightly understood" highlights the contrast with "self-interest wrongly understood," which means "self-interest" qua mere selfishness. See, e.g., Novak, *Free Persons and the Common Good* (Lanham, Md.: Madison Books, 1989), 42*ff*.

5. Adam Smith, *The Wealth of Nations* (New York: The Modern Library, 2000), 15.

6. Cf. Novak, *The Spirit of Democratic Capitalism*, 92–95, 166–70.

7. Novak, *Free Persons and the Common Good,* 49.

8. Novak, *The Spirit of Democratic Capitalism,* 94.

9. Novak, *Free Persons and the Common Good,* 66–67.

10. See, e.g. *Centesimus Annus,* section 25 (1991), where John Paul II relates self-interest to original sin. Because of the reality of sin, and because no "political society" can ever be confused with the Kingdom of God, self-interest is a reality of this world that cannot be simply eliminated: "where self-interest is violently suppressed, it is replaced by a burdensome system of bureaucratic control which dries up the well-springs of initiative and creativity" (ibid.). However, unlike liberalism, the pope's thought does not place the concept of "self-interest" at the foundation of community, even the community that arises in economic exchange. That this is true becomes especially clear when the pope discusses the role of profit. While acknowledging the legitimate role of profit in helping to determine whether a business is well run and whether a genuinely needed good or service is

being offered, the pope goes on to say that "the purpose of a business firm is not simply to make a profit, but is to be found in its very existence as a community of persons who in various ways are endeavoring to satisfy their basic needs, and who form a particular group at the service of the whole of society" (ibid., section 35).

11. On this basic point, see David L. Schindler, *Heart of the World, Center of the Church:* Communio *Ecclesiology, Liberalism, and Liberation* (Grand Rapids, Mich.: William B. Eerdmans Publishing Co., 1996), 108 n. 22, 122.

12. If Novak has attempted to respond to the claim that "self-interest" is "institutionalized selfishness" by broadening its meaning, another approach is suggested by Jennifer Roback Morse in her recent book *Love and Economics: Why the Laissez-Faire Family Doesn't Work* (Dallas, Tex.: Spence Publishing, 2001). See the discussion later in this chapter.

13. Schindler, *Heart of the World, 27ff.*

14. Ratzinger, "Concerning the Notion of Person in Theology," *Communio* 17 (fall 1990): 439–54. See also Hans Urs von Balthasar, "On the Concept of Person," *Communio* 13 (spring 1986): 18–26; and John D. Zizioulas, *Being as Communion: Studies in Personhood and the Church* (Crestwood, N.Y.: St. Vladimir's Seminary Press, 1985).

15. Cf. Schindler, *Heart of the World,* 118 ("human freedom is receptive freedom before it is creative freedom—or, better, is a freedom that becomes authentically creative only by being anteriorly receptive."), 277, 288.

16. Cf. J. Martínez Camino, "'Through Whom All Things Were Made': Creation in Christ," *Communio* 28 (summer 2001): 214–29.

17. John Paul II, Letter to Families from John Paul II, 9 (1994): "Begetting is the continuation of creation."

18. It should be noted that, in this second view, freedom is not the product of a community's granting of that freedom. Rather, freedom necessarily and immediately arises in the relations among persons, which always constitute an invitation to fulfillment in self-giving, that is to say, to fulfillment in communion. Neither the individual nor his freedom can ever be sacrificed, or even in the truest sense be suppressed, for some perceived competing "common good." The distinction between the sense of community proposed here and that contained in socialism or communism is clear. Freedom and community possess a necessary and "ontological" relationship: freedom arises in community because of its nature as a fundamental openness to another person, while community also requires freedom (because genuine community requires an active "letting be" or "making space"). In collectivism, on the other hand, freedom is simply subordinated to "community." Thus, the underlying meaning of freedom is essentially the same in both collectivism and liberalism. In both cases freedom is conceived of as the immunity of the individual from coercion; in collectivism, however, the domain of freedom is dramatically reduced vis-à-vis the prior claims of the state.

19. Roback Morse, *Love and Economics: Why the Laissez-Faire Family Doesn't Work.*

20. Ibid., e.g., 4.

21. Ibid., 197.

22. Guroian, *Ethics after Christendom,* 147–48 (quoting Brigitte and Peter Berger, *The War over the Family* [Garden City, N.Y.: Doubleday-Anchor, 1983], 172). Likewise, Hauerwas has made this point outside the direct context of the family ("The Difference of Virtue and the Difference It Makes: Courage Exemplified," in Mary Ann Glendon and David Blankenhorn, eds., *Seedbeds of Virtue: Sources of Competence, Character, and Citizenship in American Society* [Lanham, Md.: Madison Books, 1995], 201–20).

23. Novak, *The Spirit of Democratic Capitalism,* 152.

24. Novak in fact acknowledges—while giving a positive reading to—what is being affirmed here: namely, that liberal societies reconstitute more traditional, "natural" communities on a "voluntary" basis. See ibid., 339.

25. Cf., e.g., Francis Woerhling, "Christian Economics," *Journal of Markets and Morality* 4 (fall 2001): 199–216; Novak, *The Spirit of Democratic Capitalism,* 80.

26. A committed economism would, of course, refuse to place a higher objective value on either. For Christian liberals, on the other hand, the answer to this question will be given in an adequate alignment of subjective preferences and objective values. See Mark Broski, "Know Thy Limits: The Noneconomics of Abundance," *Journal of Markets and Morality* 4 (fall 2001): 325–32.

27. Roback Morse, *Love and Economics: Why the Laissez-Faire Family Doesn't Work,* 58, 223.

28. "The Radical Hope in the Annunciation: Why Both Single and Married Christians Welcome Children," in *The Hauerwas Reader,* ed. John Berkman and Michael Cartwright (Durham, N.C.: Duke University Press, 2001), 505–18, 508.

Chapter 8
Making Room in the Inn: Why the Modern World Needs the Needy

Jennifer Roback Morse

1. Jennifer Roback Morse, *Love and Economics: Why the Laissez-Faire Family Doesn't Work* (Dallas, Tex.: Spence Publishing, 2001), 25–29.

2. Quoted in Kay Hymowitz, *Ready or Not: Why Treating Children as Small Adults Endangers Their Future—and Ours* (New York: Free Press, 1999), 10.

3. E. D. Hirsch, *The Schools We Need and Why We Don't Have Them* (New York: Doubleday, 1996), 69–92.

4. Hymowitz, *Ready or Not,* 47–70. Hymowitz comments wryly about Dr. Spock's comment that good manners come naturally, that this "confirms what the alert reader has begun to suspect, namely , that the world's premier pediatrician, a man whose name is synonymous with childbearing wisdom and experience, *never, ever spent a day with a child*" (p. 60; italics in original).

5. Rael Jean Isaac and Virginia C. Armat, *Madness in the Streets: How Psychiatry and the Law Abandoned the Mentally Ill* (Arlington, Va.: Treatment Advocacy Center, 2000); E. Fuller Torrey, *Out of the Shadows: Confronting America's Mental Illness Crisis* (New York: John Wiley & Sons, 1997).

6. In books such as *The Manufacture of Madness* (New York: Harper & Row, 1970); *Law, Liberty and Psychiatry* (New York: Macmillan, 1963); and many others.

7. According to Isaac and Armat, *Madness in the Streets,* 52

8. Isaac and Armat, *Madness in the Streets,* 62–63 and 80–82.

9. Quoted by Isaac and Armat, *Madness in the Streets,* 72.

10. Isaac and Armat, *Madness in the Streets,* 67–85.

11. Gerald Caplan, *Principles of Preventive Psychiatry* (New York: Basic Books, 1964), 116; quoted in Isaac and Armat, *Madness in the Streets,* 84.

12. E. Fuller Torrey, *Out of the Shadows,* 77–79; and Isaac and Armat, *Madness in the Streets,* 247–83.

13. "Many Americans with Untreated Psychiatric Illnesses Have Nowhere to Go: Homelessness: Tragic Side Effect of Non-treatment," Fact Sheet, Treatment Advocacy Center, Arlington, Va. (http://www.psychlaws.org/GeneralResources/fact11.htm). Some mentally ill people are also substance abusers. If the numbers of drug and alcohol addicts were included in the category of "seriously mentally ill," the percentage of mental illness among the homeless would rise even higher.

14. The welfare state's shift from the personal to the bureaucratic provision of charitable aid is the key theme of Marvin Olasky's work. See *The Tragedy of American Compassion* (Regnery, 1995); and *Renewing American Compassion* (Regnery, 1997).

15. Jennifer Roback Morse, "The Modern State as an Occasion of Sin: A Public Choice Analysis of the Welfare State," *Notre Dame Journal of Law, Ethics and Public Policy* 11, no. 2 (1997): 531–48.

16. Hymowitz, *Ready or Not,* 47–48 and 68–69.

17. Jennifer Roback Morse, "Competing Visions of the Child, the Family and the School," in Edward Lazear, ed., *Education in the Twenty-First Century* (Stanford, Calif.: Hoover Press, 2002).

18. F. A. Hayek, *Law, Legislation and Liberty,* vol. 1, *Rules and Order* (Chicago: University of Chicago Press, 1973).

19. Darcy Olsen, "The Advancing Nanny State: Why Government Should Stay out of Childcare," Cato Institute Policy Analysis no. 285, 23 October 1997.

20. See my critique of this mentality in *Love and Economics: Why the Laissez-Faire Family Doesn't Work*.

21. For a spirited defense of the idea that all economic theories have implicit philosophical, if not downright theological, presuppositions embedded within them, see Robert Nelson, *Economics as Religion: From Samuelson to Chicago and Beyond* (University Park, Pa.: Pennsylvania State University Press, 2001).

22. Nelson, *Economics as Religion,* 313.

23. Henri Nowen, *The Road to Daybreak: A Spiritual Journey* (New York: Doubleday, Image Books, 1990); and Jean Vanier, "Handicapped Are Teachers of Civilization of Love," interview with Zenit news agency, 5 February 2002 (http://www.zenit.org).

24. Rene Girard (*I See Satan Fall Like Lightning* [Maryknoll, N.Y.: Orbis Books, 2001]) and Gil Bailie (*Violence Unveiled: Humanity at the Crossroads* [New York: Crossroads Publishing, 1999]) argue that Christianity reverses the social tendency to create social order around the sacrifice of scapegoats. On this account, Christianity's contribution is to instill in societies a concern and respect for the innocent victim. Rodney Stark (*The Rise of Christianity: How the Obscure, Marginal Jesus Movement Became the Dominant Religious Force in the Western World in a Few Centuries* [San Francisco: HarperCollins, 1997]) argues that Christianity competed successfully against Roman pagan religions by giving people a sense that their suffering has meaning, and is not as senseless as it sometimes appears.

25. Vanier, interview with Zenit news agency, Vatican City, 5 February 2002 (http://www.zenit.org).

Chapter 9
International Markets, International Poverty: Globalization and the Poor

Daniel T. Griswold

1. Frédéric Bastiat, *Selected Essays in Political Economy* (Irvington-on-Hudson, N.Y.: Foundation for Economic Education, 1995), 197.

2. Pope John Paul II, *Centesimus Annus* (The Vatican: 1991), section 32.

3.   Quoted in Douglas Irwin, *Against the Tide: An Intellectual History of   Free Trade* (Princeton, N.J.: Princeton University Press, 1996), 16.

4.   Ibid., 19.

5.   Ibid., 20.

6.   See Jeffrey Sachs and Andrew Warner, "Economic Reform and the Process of Global Integration," *Brookings Papers on Economic Activity,* vol. 1, 1995: 1–95; Sebastian Edwards, "Openness, Productivity and Growth: What Do We Really Know?" National Bureau of Economic Research, Working Paper no. 5978 (Cambridge, Mass.: NBER, 1997); and Jeffrey A. Frankel and David Romer, "Does Trade Cause Growth?" *The American Economic Review,* June 1999: 379–99.

7.   James Gwartney and Robert Lawson, *Economic Freedom of the World: 2001 Annual Report* (Vancouver, B.C.: Fraser Institute, 2001), 78.

8.   Helene Cooper, "Fruit of the Loom: Can African Nations Use Duty-Free Deal to Revamp Economy?" *The Wall Street Journal,* 2 January 2002, A1.

9.   *Centesimus Annus,* section 33.

10.   William Easterly, *The Elusive Quest for Growth* (Cambridge, Mass.: The MIT Press, 2001), 8–9.

11.   The World Bank, "Assessing Globalization: Does More International Trade Openness Increase World Poverty?" PREM Economic Policy Group and Development Economics Group, April 2000, http://www.worldbank.org/html/extdr/pb/globalization/paper2.htm.

12.   Edward M. Graham, "Trade and Investment at the WTO: Just Do It!" in Jeffrey Schott, ed., *Launching Global Trade Talks* (Washington, D.C.: Institute for International Economics, 1999), 158.

13.   The World Bank, *World Development Report 2000/2001: Attacking Poverty* (New York: Oxford University Press, 2001), 23.

14.   David Dollar, "Globalization, Inequality, and Poverty since 1980," The World Bank, 15 August 2001, 17.

15.   Ibid., 13.

16.   "Rigged Rules and Double Standards: Trade, Globalization, and the Fight against Poverty," Oxfam International, 2002, 6, available at http://www.maketradefair.com.

17.   Kebebew Ashagrie, "Statistics on Working Children and Hazardous Child Labour in Brief," International Labour Office, Geneva. First published 1997, revised April 1998, available at http://www.ilo.org/public/english/standards/ipec/simpoc/stats/child/stats.htm.

18. Ibid.

19. "Breaking the Labor-Trade Deadlock," Carnegie Endowment for International Peace, Inter-American Dialogue, Working Papers 17, February 2001, 17.

20. U.S. Department of Labor, "By the Sweat & Toil of Children, vol. 1, The Use of Child Labor in U.S. Manufactured and Mined Imports," 1994, 2.

21. Keith E. Maskus, "Should Core Labor Standards Be Imposed through International Trade Policy?" Policy Research Working Paper no. 1817, The World Bank, August 1997, 14.

22. Organization for Economic Cooperation and Development, "Globalization and the Environment: Perspectives from OECD and Dynamic Non-member Economies" (Paris: OECD, 1998), 20.

23. David Dollar and Aart Kraay, "Trade, Growth, and Poverty," The World Bank, June 2001, 27.

24. Ibid., 4.

25. Angus Maddison, *The World Economy: A Millennial Perspective* (Washington, D.C.: OECD, 2001), 28.

26. Kofi Annan, U.N. Secretary General, Speech to the Millennium Forum, New York, U.N. Press Release SG/SM/7411 GA9710, 22 May 2000.

27. Michael Novak, *Business as a Calling: Work and the Examined Life* (New York: The Free Press, 1996), 161.

28. Freedom House, "Freedom in the World 2001–2002," 18 December 2001, 6. The study is available at http://www.freedomhouse.org/research/freeworld/2002/essay2002.pdf.

29. Economic openness as measured by the "Trade Openness Index" in Gwartney and Lawson, *Economic Freedom of the World,* 75.

30. Mary Beth Sheridan, "Nation Awakens from Era of Repression under PRI," *Los Angeles Times,* 29 July 2000, A1, A6

31. *The Economist,* "Wired China," 22 July 2000, 24.

32. *The Economist*, "To Get Rich Is Glorious," 17 January 2002.

33. The World Bank, *Global Economic Prospects 2002: Making Trade Work for the World's Poor,* November 2001.

34. Ibid.

35. David Dollar and Aart Kraay, "Spreading the Wealth," *Foreign Affairs,* January/February 2002.

36. Easterly, *The Elusive Quest for Growth,* 33.

37. Ibid., 124–25.

38. Cooper, "Fruit of the Loom: Can African Nations Use Duty-Free Deal to Revamp Economy?"

Chapter 10
Wealth, Happiness, and Politics: Aristotelian Questions

V. Bradley Lewis

1. The relationship between the development of capitalism and the modern nation state is a matter of controversy, but that they are related in some important way as parts of the modernization process seems clear. For a lively discussion of some of the issues see Liah Greenfeld, "The Worth of Nations," *Critical Review* 9 (1995): 555–84; and Warren Breckman and Lars Trägårdh, "Nationalism, Individualism and Capitalism: Reply to Greenfeld," *Critical Review* 10 (1996): 389–407, with Greenfeld's reply on pp. 409–70.

2. For a detailed critique of the status of economics as a science on the model of the natural sciences, see Alexander Rosenberg, *Economics: Mathematical Politics or Science of Diminishing Returns* (Chicago: University of Chicago Press, 1992).

3. Starting with the now classic paper by G. E. M. Anscombe, "Modern Moral Philosophy," *Philosophy* 33 (1958): 1–19, but including many others, e.g., Hannah Arendt, Leo Strauss, and Alasdair MacIntyre.

4. Leo Strauss, *The City and Man* (Chicago: Rand McNally, 1964), 25.

5. Leo Strauss, *What Is Political Philosophy?* (Glencoe, Ill.: The Free Press, 1959), 27, 78–94.

6. See Servais Pinckaers, O.P., *The Sources of Christian Ethics,* trans. M. T. Noble (Washington, D.C.: Catholic University of America Press, 1995), chaps. 7, 9; Dennis J. M. Bradley, *Aquinas on the Twofold Human Good: Reason and Happiness in Aquinas's Moral Science* (Washington, D.C.: Catholic University of America Press, 1997); and consider *Gaudium et Spes,* section 25 with note 3.

7. The discussion in Joseph Schumpeter's classic *History of Economic Analysis* (New York: Oxford University Press, 1954), 57–65, is representative.

8. In saying this, I pass no judgment on either of these ideas. I simply note that Aristotle's views about them are usually misrepresented. On the notion of the just price (which Aristotle did not seem to hold), see the discussions in Karl Polanyi, "Aristotle Discovers the Economy," in K. Polanyi, C. M. Arensberg, and H. W. Pearson, eds., *Trade and Market in Early Empires* (Glencoe, Ill.: The Free Press, 1957), 83–91; and M. I. Finley, "Aristotle and Economic Analysis,"

Past and Present 47 (1970): 3–25, especially 8–12. On usury, see Scott Meikle, *Aristotle's Economic Thought* (Oxford: Clarendon Press, 1995), 63–67.

9. This phrase translates Aristotle's *hê peri ta anthrôpeia philosophia* (*Nicomachean Ethics* [*NE*] 1181b15). Citations to Aristotle will be given parenthetically in the body of the paper according to the traditional Bekker pagination. Unless indicated, citations refer to the *Politics*.

10. G. E. M. Anscombe, "Modern Moral Philosophy," *Philosophy* 33 (1958): 1–19. I abstract for purposes of this paper from the debate about whether Aristotle has an "inclusive" or "dominant" view of *eudaimonia* and confine myself to (1) the suggestion that the two ends of moral and contemplative excellence represent facets of human nature the unity of which must practically be assessed in the context of man's character as political and rational animal; (2) the observation that the important tensions can arise from this double character, but that they have often been fruitful ones; and (3) a caution against the common error of seeing a symmetrical dichotomy between theory and practice on the one hand, and the philosophical and political lives on the other. On this last point see Walter J. Thompson, "Aristotle: Philosophy and Politics, Theory and Practice," *Proceedings of the American Catholic Philosophical Association* 68 (1994): 109–24. With respect to the first two points, I direct the reader to Plato's *Republic* and *Laws,* both of which seem to me the essential background to Aristotle's discussions of the best life in *Nicomachean Ethics* 10 and *Politics* 7. Cf. Carnes Lord, "Politics and Philosophy in Aristotle's Politics," *Hermes* 106 (1978): 336–57; and P. A. Vander Waerdt, "Kingship and Philosophy in Aristotle's Best Regime," *Phronesis* 30 (1985): 249–73.

11. M. H. Hansen (*The Athenian Democracy in the Age of Demosthenes,* trans. J. A. Crook [Oxford: Blackwell, 1991], 90–94) estimates that the number of citizens in Athens in the fourth century was about 100,000, of whom about 30,000 were men with full citizen rights and duties. There were probably three times that number of inhabitants of Attica, however, if one includes slaves and resident aliens. In the *Laws,* Plato held that the city should have no more than 5,040 landholders (737e–738b), a sixth of the Athenian total. Aristotle, as we shall see, thought size an important factor in the excellence of a city.

12. See the illuminating discussion in Peter Simpson, *A Philosophical Commentary on the "Politics" of Aristotle* (Chapel Hill: University of North Carolina Press, 1998), 24–26. Mary Nichols also has an illuminating discussion in "The Good Life, Slavery, and Acquisition: Aristotle's Introduction to Politics," *Interpretation* 11 (1983): 171–83, emphasizing the complications in Aristotle's discussion of nature in *Politics* 1. I am less inclined to agree with her in the implications of some of this with respect to acquisition, since there, as we shall see below in part 2, one must also take account of the relationship between what Aristotle says in the *Politics* and what is said about nature and final causes in his works on natural philosophy. This connection is also neglected in Wayne Ambler, "Aristotle on Acquisition," *Canadian Journal of Political Science* 17 (1984): 487–502, although his account is also useful in thinking about the natural character of the city in *Politics* 1.

13. See Aristotle *Metaphysics* 983b32–33; Plato *Laws* 680e, 690a.

14. Plato *Laws* 680e–681d.

15. Cf. *Metaphysics* 981b13–25.

16. See also the definition in Isocrates, *Areopagiticus* 14, *Panathenaicus* 138; the discussion in Leo Strauss, *Natural Right and History* (Chicago: University of Chicago Press, 1953), 135–38; and on the larger history of the notion of *politeia,* see Jacqueline Bordes, *"Politeia" dans la pensée grecque jusqu'à Aristote* (Paris: Société d'Édition "Les Belles Lettres," 1982).

17. See also Plato *Laws* 631b–e, 650b, 689b, 690a–e, 697b–c, 705d, 713c–714b, 726a, 896c, 967d–968a.

18. I have in mind here Eric Voegelin's criticism of Aristotle's political theory as limited by the horizon of the era of classical Greek *poleis.* See *Plato and Aristotle* (Baton Rouge: Louisiana State University Press, 1957), 317, 356. The criticisms are approvingly cited by John Finnis in *Natural Law and Natural Rights* (Oxford: Clarendon Press, 1980), 148 (with notes).

19. For a discussion of two different versions of this notion and the associated moral and religious aspects, see Henri Frankfort, *Kingship and the Gods* (Chicago: University of Chicago Press, 1948). The cases of Alexander, the Diadochi, and imperial Rome are more familiar.

20. This sort of account, suggested by Aristotle in *Nicomachean Ethics* 5.7, is an important root of the theory of natural law as developed in the Middle Ages, although there are some differences. See also *NE* 1107a8–15 for a brief but suggestive discussion of some of the rules necessary for such community. Aristotle's ethics, as is often pointed out, is mostly concerned with character and dispositions, but a minimum of rules do play a role as a kind of baseline for community life.

21. I have discussed some of this in "Globalization and the Eclipse of Natural Right: What We Might Learn from Plato and the Other Greeks," *Communio* 27 (2000): 431–63.

22. For some discussion of this view, see Alasdair MacIntyre, "Politics, Philosophy, and the Common Good," in *The MacIntyre Reader,* ed. Kelvin Knight (Notre Dame, Ind.: University of Notre Dame Press, 1998), 235–52.

23. An excellent discussion of this is Richard Bodéüs, "Law and the Regime in Aristotle," in Carnes Lord and David K. O'Connor, eds., *Essays on the Foundations of Aristotelian Political Science* (Berkeley: University of California Press, 1991), 234–48.

24. Cf. Alasdair MacIntyre, *Whose Justice? Which Rationality?* (Notre Dame, Ind.: University of Notre Dame Press, 1988), 90–91. By suggesting that the ideal is implicit in practice, I do not mean to suggest that Aristotle is a kind of apologist for the classical city (MacIntyre does sometimes give this

impression), rather than a philosopher concerned to understand the truth of things. On the contrary, many aspects of his thought (Plato's, too) are very critical of contemporary Greek practice, albeit carefully expressed. I simply mean that Aristotle began from actual practice and came to see how it could be better in light of the natural good for human beings. On this see, Stephen G. Salkever, *Finding the Mean: Theory and Practice in Aristotelian Political Philosophy* (Princeton, N.J.: Princeton University Press, 1990), 30–36, 165–204. On the abstractions and complications in Aristotle's picture of the best regime, see especially Strauss, *The City and Man*, 36–37, 41–42.

25. "Aristotle Discovers the Economy."

26. For Aristotle's definition of *autarkeia*, see *NE* 1097b14–15 and cf. *Pol.* 1280b25–1281a4, and discussion in Polanyi, "Aristotle Discovers the Economy," 66, 78, 82, 89, 93.

27. That is, when they are not living off the nearby sedentary agricultural tribes. *The Forest People* (New York: Simon and Schuster, 1968).

28. Franz Susemihl and R. D. Hicks, *The "Politics" of Aristotle,* a revised text with introduction, analysis, and commentary (London: Macmillan, 1894), 176, refer to it as "crude teleology."

29. Finley, "Aristotle and Economic Analysis," 15, with note 52; the point was also made by Polanyi, "Aristotle Discovers the Economy," 92–93. The variations in meaning of the term, some of which I discuss below, are usefully surveyed in W. L. Newman, *The "Politics" of Aristotle,* with an introduction, two prefatory essays, and notes critical and explanatory (Oxford: Clarendon Press, 1887) 2: 165; cf. Susemihl and Hicks, 171–72.

30. The term I have translated as "commerce," *kapêlikê* is the art of the *kapêlos,* usually a word for some kind of small-scale retailer or shopkeeper, a middle man, whose interest was simply profit. The term was often pejorative and Aristotle'a application of it to the wider context of commerce seems fully conscious. See Newman, *The "Politics" of Aristotle,* 2: 185–86; and Polanyi, "Aristotle Discovers the Economy," 91–92.

31. See Polanyi, "Aristotle Discovers the Economy," 91–92; and the qualifications in Meikle, *Aristotle's Economic Thought*, 52–63, 68–74.

32. The metaphysics of currency is a fascinating subject on its own, on which see John Searle, *The Construction of Social Reality* (New York: The Free Press, 1995), 43–51.

33. In the *Rhetoric*, Aristotle writes that wealth (*ploutos*) consists in an abundance of money, ownership of land and properties, and other movables, with cattle and slaves. Thus wealth is more than money and its value is further qualified by Aristotle's statement that wealth is to be found more in use than in possession, "for the actualization (*energeia*) and use of such things is wealth" (1361a12–24).

34. In chapters 8–9, it occurs at 1256a41, 1257a13, 19, 25, 35, 1257b1, 1257b23, and cf. 1280a35, b23 in the third book. Its neutrality owes to its somewhat primitive character. Aristotle associates it with the Barbarians at 1257a24–28, in which context it actually seems to refer to barter. Newman (*The "Politics" of Aristotle,* 1:171) suggests that *kapêleia* explains the limit of *allagê,* that is, the latter is a subcategory of the former that shades beyond simply natural exchange. *Allagê* is also used in a neutral way in the more abstract discussion of money and exchange in the *Nicomachean Ethics* (1132b13, 1133a19, b11), as is the related term *sunallagma* for "agreements." According to P. Chantraine (*Dictionnaire étymologique de la langue grecque* [Paris: Klincksieck, 1974], 63–64), the root of all of these terms is simply *allos,* "other." The verb form, *allassô,* can mean, in addition to "to exchange," simply "to change" or, in the passive form, "to be reconciled" (*A Greek-English Lexicon,* comp. H. G. Liddell and R. Scott, rev. H. S. Jones, 9th ed. [Oxford: Clarendon Press, 1968], s.v.).

35. Aristotle defines *stoicheion* as most importantly the primary component and immanent in something, its form indivisible into other forms in *Metaphysics* 1014a26–b15. The difference in the role of money between this account and that of the *Nicomachean Ethics,* where it is called instead a representative of demand (1133a29) and a guarantee (1133b10–13), is pointed out in Susemihl and Hicks, *The "Politics" of Aristotle,* 183.

36. Meikle recognizes the importance of Aristotle's metaphysics to his economic thought (36–42) and that limit is an important concept (76–78), but does not actually address the metaphysical import of limit in explaining Aristotle's account.

37. Aristotle's most important discussions of the four types of causality are contained in the second book of the *Physics.* Jonathan Lear's *Aristotle: The Desire to Understand* (Cambridge: Cambridge University Press, 1988), 26–42, is an admirably clear overview. A more detailed interpretation of final causality is Allan Gotthelf's "Aristotle's Conception of Final Causality," *Review of Metaphysics* 30 (1976): 226–54. Jean DeGroot ("Form and Succession in Aristotle's 'Physics,'" *Proceedings of the Boston Area Colloquium in Ancient Philosophy,* vol. 10, ed. J. J. Cleary and W. Wians [Lanham, Md.: University Press of America, 1996], 1–23) argues strongly for an interpretation of final causes as real causes on the basis of the *Physics.*

38. This seems true based on the immediate context, but also because book a is sometimes thought to be, as W. D. Ross (*Aristotle's Metaphysics,* rev. text with an introduction and commentary [Oxford: Clarendon Press, 1924], 1:213) writes, "an introduction . . . to physics or to theoretical philosophy in general." Of course, the relevance of final causality is very controversial in modern science. About this one can say first, that it seems quite important in some branches of science if not in all, and second, it seems crucial to any nonreductive understanding of human affairs. For discussion of some of these issues, see the essays in *Final Causality in Nature and Human Affairs,* ed. Richard F. Hassing (Washington, D.C.: Catholic University of America Press, 1997).

39. Aquinas notes the practical implications in his commentary by referring us to the first book of the *Nicomachean Ethics*. See *In duodecim libros Metaphysicorum Aristotelis expositio,* ed. M.-R. Cathala and R. Spiazzi (Turin; Rome: Marietti, 1950), II, lect. 4, no. 317.

40. See the discussion of this in MacIntyre, *Whose Justice? Which Rationality?*, 89, 92, 125.

41. Plato *Apology of Socrates,* 22c9–e1.

42. One might object to the contrast with Hobbes on the grounds that Hobbes's view is not representative of modern thought generally, especially political thought. Hobbes, however, is quite representative of the early modern rejection of Aristotelian natural philosophy (and thus of, among other things, the idea of final causality), and his political philosophy, if not directly derived from this, is closely related to it and influences later (and more popular) political thinkers like Locke in a variety of ways. See Leo Strauss, "The Three Waves of Modernity" in *Political Philosophy: Six Essays by Leo Strauss,* ed. Hilail Gildin (Indianapolis, Ind.: Bobbs-Merrill, 1975), 81–98; and the more extended account in *Natural Right and History* (Chicago: University of Chicago Press, 1953), chap. 5.

43. Hobbes, *Leviathan,* chap. 6, p. 24 (page numbers refer to the 1651 edition, now commonly given in modern editions).

44. Ibid., 29.

45. Ibid., 47.

46. Ibid.

47. Meikle, *Aristotle's Economic Thought,* 46–47, 69–70.

48. There is a large literature on this topic now. The approach of Mary P. Nichols ("The Good Life, Slavery, and Acquisition: Aristotle's Introduction to Politics") and Wayne Ambler ("Aristotle on Nature and Politics: The Case of Slavery," *Political Theory* 15 (1987): 390–410) is superior for their seriousness about the text of Aristotle to MacIntyre's simple rejection of Aristotle's views in *Whose Justice? Which Rationality?*, 105. The similarly troubling case of Aristotle's remarks about women is also complicated once one carefully studies the texts. See the remarks on this in Nichols as well as Thomas K. Lindsay, "Was Aristotle Racist, Sexist, and Anti-Democratic? A Review Essay," *Review of Politics* 56 (1994): 127–51.

49. See, e.g., John C. McCarthy, "The Descent of Science," *Review of Metaphysics* 52 (1999): 835–66, with the essays in *Final Causality in Nature and Human Affairs,* and Salkever, *Finding the Mean,* 13–56.

50. See, for example, Charles Taylor's reformulation of some kinds of teleological explanation in the human sciences in "The Explanation of Purposeful Behavior," in R. Borger and F. Cioffi, eds., *Explanation in the Behavioural Sciences* (Cambridge: Cambridge University Press, 1970), 49–95.

51. Among the most important moderating interpretations is Charles Taylor's *The Ethics of Authenticity* (Cambridge, Mass.: Harvard University Press, 1991).

52. See *Laws* 686e–688a and consider *Republic* 497d.

53. For two different, but illuminating, discussions of just how Aristotle's thought might understand and modify modern political and economic practice, see Peter Simpson, "Making the Citizens Good: Aristotle's City and Its Contemporary Relevance," *Philosophical Forum* 22 (1990): 149–66; and Alasdair MacIntyre, *Dependent Rational Animals: Why Human Beings Need the Virtues* (Chicago and LaSalle, Ill.: Open Court, 1999), chaps. 9–11.

54. I have discussed this possibility with reference to Aquinas's understanding of natural law and contemporary political institutions in "Liberal Democracy, Natural Law, and Jurisprudence: Thomistic Notes on an Irish Debate," in T. Fuller and J. Hittinger, eds., *Reassessing the Liberal State: Reading Maritain's "Man and the State"* (Washington, D.C.: American Maritain Association/Catholic University of America Press, 2001), 140–58. Two works that pursue something like this project in different ways are Salkever's *Finding the Mean* and James B. Murphy's *The Moral Economy of Labor: Aristotelian Themes in Economic Theory* (New Haven, Conn.: Yale University Press, 1993). These themes find a good bit of resonance in Catholic social teaching as well.

55. These sorts of phenomena have been suggested by quite respectable social scientists, e.g., Tibor Scitovsky, *The Joyless Economy* (New York: Oxford University Press, 1977); and more recently Robert E. Lane, *The Loss of Happiness in Market Democracies* (New Haven, Conn.: Yale University Press, 2000).

56. Francis Fukuyama suggests this in *The Great Disruption: Human Nature and the Reconstruction of Social Order* (New York: The Free Press, 1999), chap. 15.

57. Alan Wolfe, *Moral Freedom: The Impossible Idea That Defines the Way We Live Now* (New York: Norton, 2001), 48–49.

58. The decay of the household is an important theme in Wendell Berry's agrarian social criticism. See, e.g., "The Body and the Earth" in *The Unsettling of America: Culture and Agriculture* (San Francisco: Sierra Club Books, 1986), 97–140.

59. See James Tunstead Burtchaell, *The Dying of the Light* (Grand Rapids, Mich.: William B. Eerdmans Publishing Co., 1998), 705–16, for a discussion of the Catholic case. I do not mean to suggest that this was the only cause or even the most important cause of secularization, but that it was important and worth further investigation.

60. See Berry's *The Unsettling of America*, cited above, as well as the essays collected in *Home Economics* (New York: North Point Press, 1987), *What Are People For?* (New York: North Point Press, 1990), and *Sex, Economy, Freedom and Community* (New York: Pantheon, 1993); and Hanson's *Fields without Dreams* (New York: Free Press, 1996) as well as his magisterial volume on Greek agrarianism, *The*

Other Greeks: The Family Farm and the Agrarian Roots of Western Civilization,
2d ed. (Berkeley: University of California Press, 1999).

Chapter 11
"We Are Not Our Own": George Grant's Critique of Science, Technology, and Capitalism

Arthur Davis

1. See *The Collected Works of George Grant: Volume 1, 1933–1950* (Toronto: University of Toronto Press, 2000). Volume 2 (1951–1959) is due December 2002.

2. George Grant, *Lament for a Nation* (Toronto: McClelland and Stewart, 1965), 66–67.

3. Ibid., 58–59.

4. George Grant, "A Platitude," in *Technology and Empire,* (Toronto: Anansi, 1969), 137: "We can hold in our minds the enormous benefits of technological society, but we cannot so easily hold the ways it may have deprived us, because technique is ourselves."

5. Professor James Wiser gave an excellent talk on George Grant at a conference at Carleton University in Ottawa in 1989. Unfortunately, it was not included in the proceedings published in Peter C. Emberley, *By Loving Our Own: George Grant and the Legacy of Lament for a Nation* (Ottawa: Carleton University Press, 1990).

6. George Grant, "The University Curriculum," in *Technology and Empire,* 132–33.

7. See "Conversation: Intellectual Background," in Larry Schmidt, ed., *George Grant in Process: Essays and Conversations* (Toronto: Anansi, 1978), 62–63. John Calvin used the language of "not being our own," meaning that we are "God's instruments." The original source may be Paul, 1 Corinthians 6:19: "Do you not know that your body is a temple of the Holy Spirit within you, which you have from God? You are not your own...." Grant used this language on many occasions, at one point crediting the Scottish cleric and storyteller George MacDonald as his source for the language. Grant was struck by MacDonald's statement, "The first principle of hell is 'I am my own,'" when he first read it in C. S. Lewis's *Surprised by Joy.*

8. Grant's thesis, "The Concept of Nature and Supernature in the Theology of John Oman," focused mainly on Oman's philosophy of religion in *The Natural and the Supernatural* (Cambridge: Cambridge University Press, 1931).

9. Grant's articles on Russell and Popper will appear in volume 2 of *The Collected Works of George Grant.* They originally appeared as "Pursuit of an Illusion: A

Commentary on Bertrand Russell," *Dalhousie Review* 32, no. 2 (summer): 97–109; and "Plato and Popper," *Canadian Journal of Economics and Political Science* 20, no. 2 (May): 185–94.

10. See Keynes's "My Early Beliefs," in *The Collected Writings of John Maynard Keynes, Volume 10: Essays in Biography* (London: Macmillan, 1972), 447–48. Grant's article was "Plato and Popper," a critique of Karl Popper's "The Open Society and Its Enemies," in *Canadian Journal of Economics and Political Science* 20, no. 2 (May 1954): 185–94.

11. Lloyd A. Jeffress, ed., *Cerebral Mechanisms in Behavior: The Hixon Symposium* (Wiley, 1951). Lashley's statement appears on p. 112, near the beginning of his paper entitled "The Problem of Serial Order in Behavior."

12. From Grant's unpublished talk to National Research Council scientists in 1962. The talk will appear in volume 3 of *The Collected Works of George Grant.*

13. George Grant, "Canadian Fate and Imperialism," in *Technology and Empire,* 65.

14. "The Case against Abortion," *Today Magazine,* 3 October 1981, 12–13; "Abortion and Rights: The Value of Political Freedom," in E. Fairweather and I. Gentles, eds., *The Right to Birth: Some Christian Views on Abortion* (Toronto: Anglican Book Centre, 1976), 1–12; *English-speaking Justice* (Toronto and Notre Dame: Anansi and University of Notre Dame Press, 1985 [orig. 1974]); "The Triumph of the Will," in Denyse O'Leary, ed., *The Issue Is Life: A Christian Response to Abortion in Canada* (Burlington: Welch Publishing Co., 1988), 156–66. See also Leah Bradshaw, "Love and Will in the Miracle of Birth: An Arendtian Critique of George Grant on Abortion," in Arthur Davis, ed., *George Grant and the Subversion of Modernity: Art, Philosophy, Politics, Religion, and Education* (Toronto: University of Toronto Press, 1996), 220–39.

15. Grant, "The Case against Abortion," 12.

16. See the foreword to the second edition of *Lament for a Nation* (Toronto: McClelland and Stewart, 1970), 14.

17. Thomas Kuhn, *The Structure of Scientific Revolutions* (Chicago: University of Chicago Press, 1962, 1970). See especially chap. 5, "The Priority of Paradigms," 43–51.

18. George Grant, "Thinking about Technology," in *Technology and Justice* (Toronto: Anansi, 1986), 21.

19. Ibid., 14.

20. Martin Heidegger, "The Question concerning Technology," in *Basic Writings,* ed. David Farrell Krell (New York: Harper and Row, 1977), 302–3.

21. Larry Schmidt, "Interview with George Grant," *Grail* 1 (March 1985): 34–47.

22. Grant's teach-in speech, "Protest and Technology," will be reprinted in volume

3 of *The Collected Works of George Grant.* It was originally published in Charles Hanly, ed., *Revolutions and Response: Selections from the Toronto International Teach-In* (Toronto: McClelland and Stewart, 1966), 122–28.

23. The original French is: "La foi, c'est l'expérience que l'intelligence est éclairée par l'amour" (Simone Veil, *La pesanteur et la grâce* [Paris: Plon, 1948], 148). There is an English translation by Emma Craufurd that differs from Grant's in omitting the definite article: "Faith is experience that intelligence is enlightened by love" (Simone Veil, *Gravity and Grace,* trans. Emma Craufurd [London: Routledge and Kegan Paul, 1952], 116).

24. George Grant, "Faith and the Multiversity," in *Technology and Justice,* 39.

25. Ibid., 50–51.

26. Ibid., 41.

27. The last verse of W. H. Auden's "In Memory of W. B. Yeats" (1939) reads, "In the deserts of the heart/ Let the healing fountain start./ In the prison of his days/ Teach the free man how to praise." See *W. H. Auden: Selected Poems,* ed. Edward Mendelson (New York: Vintage, 1989, 1934), 83.

Chapter 12
The Liberalism of John Paul II and the Technological Imperative

Richard John Neuhaus

1. David L. Schindler, *Heart of the World, Center of the Church: Communio Ecclesiology, Liberalism, and Liberation* (Grand Rapids, Mich.: William B. Eerdmans Publishing Co., 1996), 87.

2. Oliver O'Donovan, *The Desire of the Nations: Rediscovering the Roots of Political Theology* (Cambridge: Cambridge University Press, 1996).

Editor's Response
"Homelessness" and Market Liberalism: Toward an Economic Culture of Gift and Gratitude

David L. Schindler

1. The present chapter in fact shares much with Morse's eloquent argument concerning the "gift perspective," but this will made clear later.

2. My own argument presupposes and draws much from the various chapters by

the first group of authors. The "authority" of my argument, however, rests of course solely on its own (intended) coherence.

3. The text cited here is that of *Gaudium et Spes*, 22, which is referred to in a thematic way in virtually every one of John Paul II's encyclicals. Indeed, the pope states that the relation between christology and anthropology affirmed in this text indicates what is perhaps the most important teaching of the Second Vatican Council: *Dives in Misericordia*, 3.

4. *Redemptor Hominis*, n. 10

5. See my "God and the End of Intelligence: Knowledge as Relationship," *Communio* 26 (fall 1999): 510–40.

6. John Paul II, Apostolic Exhortation, *Christifideles Laici (CL)*, n. 39. Of course, the pope's affirmation of the individual's constitutive relation to God does not obviate the need for baptism and hence for the Church for the fulfillment of this relation that is given in and with creation: the "already" remains essentially a "not yet," needing the redemptive grace of baptism. But here is not the place to sort out the twentieth-century debate (within Catholicism) regarding nature and grace. Cf., for example, Henri de Lubac, *The Mystery of the Supernatural* (New York: Crossroad Herder, 1998) and *The Discovery of God* (Grand Rapids, Mich.: Eerdmans, 1996).

7. The *Catechism of the Catholic Church (CCC)* amplifies this by stating that the "divine image is present in every man. It shines forth in the communion of persons, in the likeness of the union of the divine persons among themselves . . ." *(CCC*, n. 1702).

8. John Paul II, Address to the Faculty of the John Paul II Institute for Studies on Marriage and Family (August, 1999), #5.

9. On the cosmic dimension of the Incarnation and of the Church and sacrament, see John Paul II, *Dominum et Vivificantem*, n. 50, and Alexander Schmemann, *For the Life of the World* (Crestwood, N.Y.: St. Vladimir's, 1973 [1963]). On the (cosmic) community implied in creation, see Wendell Berry, *The Art of the Commonplace*, ed. By Norman Wirzba (Washington, D.C.: Counterpoint, 2002).

10. The present chapter does not develop the idea of the Church as the historical-sacramental place—or home—of man's community with God, and indeed of his community with others, the world, and the family in relation to God. This idea, however, serves as the presupposed horizon for all that is argued.

11. Hans Urs von Balthasar, *The Glory of the Lord: A Theological Aesthetics*, vol. V (San Francisco: Ignatius Press, 1991), 615–17; and cf. also 613–37, 646–56, *passim*.

12. Cf. my "Creation and Nuptiality: A Reflection on Feminism in Light of Schmemann's Liturgical Theology," *Communio* 27 (summer 2001): 265–95.

13. For a philosophical recovery of a positive sense of dependence, see Alasdair MacIntyre, *Dependent Rational Animals: Why Human Beings Need the Virtues* (Chicago: Open Court, 2001).

14. For reflections helpful for setting the larger context of the argument here, cf. Wendell Berry, "The Pleasures of Eating," in *The Art of the Commonplace*, 321–27, and Leon Kass, *The Hungry Soul: Eating and the Perfection of Our Nature* (Chicago: University of Chicago Press, 1999 [1994]).

15. John Paul II, *Original Unity of Man and Woman*, in *The Theology of the Body* (Boston: Pauline Books and Media, 1997), 25–102, at 60–63 and *passim*.

16. The differences between artifacts produced on an assembly line from artifacts crafted in personal love are perceptible to those whose criteria for judging do not dispose them already to miss the subtle "irregularities" introduced by *organic form*. Cf. in this connection the interesting recorded interview of violin-makers Peter and Wendy Moes in "Tacit Knowing, Truthful Knowing: The Life and Thought of Michael Polanyi," produced by Ken Myers (Charlottesville, Va.: Mars Hill Audio, 1999).

    In connection with my argument here, I should make mention of Anglo-American culture's tendency to confuse the "empirical" with the "concrete." "Empirical" in its conventional understanding indicates what is already an extroverted reduction of perception and experience to the terms of abstractly quantified (sense) data.

17. Michael Novak, *Free Persons and the Common Good* (Lanham, Md.: Madison Books, 1989), 49.

18. See the discussion in Aquinas, *De Veritate*, q. 22, ad 2.

19. Cf. e.g., the text from John Paul II's *Redemptor Hominis*, n. 10, cited earlier.

20. Conservative liberals typically misread John Paul II's *Centesimus Annus* (see nos. 25 and 35) on this point, as though the fact that (a wrongly ordered) desire for profit cannot be eliminated from history (as the pope acknowledges) implies that we need only—consequently—harness that desire into mutuality, in the way indicated, and criticized, above.

21. We should recognize that there is an analogue in the economic order to what Alasdair MacIntyre states regarding the charge of "unrealism" or "utopianism," in connection with his own proposals regarding the modern liberal university:

    Those most prone to accuse others of utopianism are generally those men and women of affairs who pride themselves upon their pragmatic realism, who look for immediate results, who want the relationship between present input and future output to be predictable and measurable, and that is to say, a matter of the shorter, indeed the shortest run. They are the enemies of the incalculable, the skeptics about all expectations which outrun what *they* take to be hard evidence, the deliberately shortsighted who congratulate themselves upon the limits of their vision. Who were their predecessors?

They include the fourth-century magistrates of the types of disordered city which Plato described in Book VIII of the *Republic*, the officials who tried to sustain the pagan Roman Empire in the age of Augustine, the sixteenth-century protobureaucrats who continued obediently to do the unprincipled bidding of Henry VIII while Thomas More set out on the course that led to his martyrdom. What these examples suggest is that the gap between Utopia and current social reality may on occasion furnish a measure, not of the lack of justification of Utopia, but rather of the degree to which those who not only inhabit contemporary social reality but insist upon seeing only what it allows them to see and upon learning only what it allows them to learn, cannot even identify, let alone confront, the problems which will be inscribed in their epitaphs. It may be therefore that the charge of utopianism is sometimes best understood more as a symptom of the condition of those who level it than an indictment of the projects against which it is directed. (Alasdair MacIntyre, *Three Rival Versions of Moral Enquiry* [Notre Dame, Ind.: University of Notre Dame Press, 1990], 234–35)

22. Annie Dillard, *Pilgrim at Tinker Creek* (New York: Bantam Books, 1974), 9 and *passim*.

23. Cf. Mt. 5:3-12. See the discussion of the Beatitudes in *CCC*, nos. 1716–19, where it is stated that the "Beatitudes respond to the natural desire for happiness," and again that the "Beatitudes reveal the goal of human existence, the ultimate end of human acts. . . ."

24. See D. C. Schindler, "Freedom Beyond Our Choosing: Augustine on the Will and Its Objects," *Communio* 29 (winter 2002): 618–53, at 640. The present chapter draws much from this article regarding human action and freedom. Pertinent to my discussion of liberalism's "indifferent" action/freedom is also Servais Pinckaers's *The Sources of Christian Ethics* (Washington, D.C.: Catholic University of America Press, 1995), 327–53.

25. *Evangelium Vitae* (=*EV*), n. 28.

26. "[W]hen the sense of God is lost, the sense of man is also threatened and poisoned, as the Second Vatican Council concisely states: 'Without the Creator, the creature would disappear. . . . But when God is forgotten, the creature itself grows unintelligible' [*Gaudium et Spes,* n. 36]" (*EV*, n. 22).

27. What the pope understands as structural sin thus is always rooted in personal sin, but this personal sin nevertheless has a social and indeed objective-intellectual dimension that reaches beyond individual persons and into the structures of society. As John Paul puts it in *Dominum et Vivificantem*, n. 56, sin as a "subjective" rebellion against God can take the ("external") form of a philosophy or ideology shaping a program or indeed the institutions of civilization, giving those institutions their original shape and meaning, precisely *as*

institutions. Such a philosophy or worldview of course need not be explicitly thought out or thematized as such. On the contrary, it often operates more or less unconsciously and invisibly in the original order and consequent functioning of institutions (this is the case especially in liberal societies).

28. The issue here is not whether there ought to be a *distinction* between economic order on the one hand and philosophical or cultural order on the other: that is granted. (John Paul II, for example, makes just such a distinction in *Centesimus Annus*, n. 39.) What I deny, for reasons indicated in my response to Morse below, is that the relation between these orders is or can ever be merely extrinsic, such that we are empowered to speak of an economic system or order without already, in that very act, importing an anthropology. For the significance of the point raised here, see the related discussion in fn. 31 below.

29. For an interesting reading of the difference between liberal modernity and classical (Christian) thought on the matter of rights, see Ernest L. Fortin, "On the Presumed Medieval Origin of Individual Rights," *Communio* 26 (spring 1999): 55–79. Apropos of my own argument, I would emphasize that, if the classical (premodern) tradition rightly insists on the asymmetry necessary for a true understanding of the relation between the self and the other—insists, that is, on the priority of the other—it is also the case that that tradition now needs itself to expand, in order to incorporate a legitimate sense of the self-centeredness entailed in modernity's recognition of the mutuality of that relation.

30. See my chapter on Murray ("Religious Freedom, Truth, and Anglo-American Liberalism: Another Look at John Courtney Murray") in my *Heart of the World, Center of the Church* (Grand Rapids, Mich.: Eerdmans, 1996), 43–88.

31. As mentioned in an economic context above (fn. 28), the issue here is not whether we need a distinction between "state" and "society" (we do), but how we are best to conceive this distinction. What we need is a distinction that affirms a unity between state and society coincident with their distinction. The significance of the qualifier here can be illustrated with respect to the soul-body distinction. On a Cartesian reading, the soul and body are distinguished in terms of an external relation, such that the body in its physical nature as such is empty of *human-spiritual* meaning. On a Thomistic reading, the soul and the body are on the contrary distinguished in terms of an internal relation, such that the body in its physical nature as such is always already "full" of human-spiritual meaning. Descartes, if you will, offers an "articles of peace" rendering of the body in its relation to the soul. To be sure, these comments leave much to be sorted out in terms of the distinctly political character of the state-society distinction. I wish simply to highlight how the (rightful) appeal to the necessity of this distinction needs itself to be articulated further in terms of the difference between an internal and an external relation.

32. It is widely recognized that Murray and Karol Wojtyla differed in their approaches regarding how best to articulate the meaning of religious freedom, which they both of course thought it crucial to affirm. Murray thought the issue would be best conceived in terms of juridical freedom (i.e., immunity from coercion),

Wojtyla in terms of freedom in its relation to truth/revelation. It exceeds my present purposes to sort out the significance of this difference relative to the argument I have sketched.

33. The importance of taking account of the "structural" dimension of sin in our engagement with contemporary culture is indicated, *inter alia*, in John Paul II's *Dominum et Vivificantem*, n. 56, and *Sollicitudo Rei Socialis*, nos. 36–37, as well as in the Sacred Congregation for the Doctrine of the Faith's "Instruction on Christian Freedom and Liberation" (*Libertatis Conscientia: AAS* 79 [1987], 554–99 at nos. 74–75). Neuhaus's chapter to which we are responding here is meant to provide an interpretation of the pope's *Centesimus Annus*. Given this, and relative to the issue of "structural sin," we should call attention here to the abridgment of this encyclical that Neuhaus has published on several occasions, for the purpose—he says on one occasion: see his *Doing Well and Doing Good* (New York: Doubleday, 1992), 13—of testing his (Neuhaus's) own reading of that encyclical. *Centesimus Annus*, noting that we need to move beyond all that was short-lived in earlier (often too Marxist-driven) attempts at liberation, states nevertheless that "present circumstances are leading to *a reaffirmation of the positive value of* an authentic theology of integral human liberation" (n. 26; emphasis added), referring to the CDF's "Instruction" above. Notably, Neuhaus's abridged version of this passage reads (without indication of omission): "present circumstances are leading to an authentic theology of integral human liberation." The encyclical's effort explicitly to integrate what was positive in the "old" liberation theology—its concern for "structural sin," for example— thus disappears in Neuhaus's restatement, which instead simply points ahead to what Neuhaus takes to be the now-required form of liberation, namely, the free market. Lest this criticism seem heavy-handed, we should note further, for example, that Neuhaus omits (again without any indication of omission) the statement in n. 52 of *CA* which says that promoting development "may mean making important changes in established lifestyles, in order to limit the waste of environmental and human resources. . . ." Indeed, Neuhaus interprets this statement elsewhere as "most likely a vestigial rhetorical fragment that somehow wandered into the text and is notable chiefly for its incongruity with the argument that the Pope is otherwise making" (*Doing Well and Doing Good*, 224). I note all of this by way of calling attention to what seems to me the significance of Neuhaus's failure to engage "structural sin," and indeed to see with the pope and the "Instruction" how key elements of the "old" liberation theology (properly qualified) need to be taken over, so that the free market itself might be realized as "an authentic theology of integral human liberation."

34. Will Herberg, *Protestant Catholic Jew* (Chicago: University of Chicago Press, 1983 [1955]). On America's peculiar secularization, see my "Religion and Secularity in a Culture of Abstraction," *Pro Ecclesia* 11 (winter 2002): 76–94.

35. The vagueness of this phrase of course opens it up to a charge of question-begging: just how long before the changes might be evident? I would only underscore here, in keeping with what was argued in Part II above, how

significant differences in being and action and things can be missed precisely because of their subtle nature; how, consequently, it can take long periods of time, even centuries, for the full implications of such differences to come into view. And, indeed, the extroverted ("empirical," cf. fn. 16) criteria in terms of which cultural judgments are characteristically rendered in a liberal culture further complicates our ability to discern these differences.

36. Cf., inter alia, *Corpus Mysticum: L'Eucharistie et l'Eglise au Moyen Age* (Paris: Aubier-Montaigne, 1944); and *Catholicism [The Social Aspects of Dogma]* (San Francisco: Ignatius Press, 1988).

37. See, for example, his *For the Life of the World*, cited in fn. 9.

38. *Dominum et Vivificantem*, n. 50.

39. Notre Dame: University of Notre Dame Press, 1986.

Appendix B
Capitalism, Civil Society, Religion, and the Poor:
A Bibliographical Essay

Max L. Stackhouse with Lawrence M. Stratton

1. David Landes, *The Wealth and Poverty of Nations: Why Some Are So Rich and Some So Poor* (New York: W. W. Norton, 1999).

2. Michael Novak, *Will It Liberate? Questions about Liberation Theology* (New York: Paulist Press, 1986).

3. Edward C. Banfield, *The Moral Basis of a Backward Society* (Chicago: The Free Press, 1958).

4. Hernando de Soto, *The Mystery of Capital: Why Capitalism Triumphs in the West and Fails Everywhere Else* (New York: Basic Books, 2000). See also Paul Craig Roberts and Karen LaFollette Araujo, *The Capitalist Revolution in Latin America* (New York: Oxford University Press, 1997).

5. Gustavo Gutierrez, *A Theology of Liberation: History, Politics, and Salvation,* trans. Sister Caridad Inda and John Eagleson (Maryknoll, N.Y.: Orbis Books, 1973); James H. Cone, *God of the Oppressed* (New York: Seabury Press, 1975).

6. John Mohan Razu, *Transnational Corporations as Agents of Dehumanization in Asia. An Ethical Critique of Development* (Delhi: ISPCK, 2000).

7. See e.g., Stanley W. Carlson-Thies and James W. Skillen, eds. *Welfare in America : Christian Perspectives on a Policy in Crisis* (Grand Rapids, Mich.: Eerdmans, 1996), which parallels similar debates in Europe.

8. Mancur Olson, *Power and Prosperity: Outgrowing Communist and Capitalist Dictatorships* (New York: Basic Books, 2000).

9. Max L. Stackhouse, Dennis P. McCann, and Shirley J. Roals, eds., *On Moral Business: Classical and Contemporary Resources for Ethics in Economic Life* (Grand Rapids, Mich.: Eerdmans, 1995).

10. Joe Studwell. *The China Dream: The Elusive Quest for the Last Great Untapped Market on Earth* (London : Profile, 2002).

11. For the debates over the place of civil society, economic life, and government, see Nancy L. Rosenblum and Robert C. Post, eds., *Civil Society and Government* (Princeton, N.J.: Princeton University Press, 2002).

12. Karl Marx, "On the Jewish Question," in *The Marx-Engels Reader,* ed. Robert C. Tucker (New York: W. W. Norton, 1978).

13. M. Douglas Meeks, *God the Economist: The Doctrine of God and Political Economy* (Minneapolis: Fortress, 1989).

14. David Korten, *When Corporations Rule the World* (West Hartford, CT: Berrett-Koehler, 1995).

15. See Richard Rose, "Ipsos-Reid Global Poll," November/December 2001 at <http://www.openDemocracy.net/forum/document>.

16. Stephen L. Parente and Edward C. Prescott, *Barriers to Riches* (Cambridge, Mass.: MIT Press, 2000), 145.

17. The World Bank, "Assessing Globalization: A Four-Part Series," <http://www.worldbank.org/html/extdr/pb/globalization/paper>.

18. Simon Kuznets, *Toward a Theory of Economic Growth* (New York: W. W. Norton, 1968); and Simon Kuznets, *The Economic Growth of Nations: Total Output and Production Structure* (Cambridge, Mass.: Harvard University Press, 1971). See also Max L. Stackhouse, Peter L. Berger, Dennis P. McCann, and M. Douglas Meeks, *Christian Social Ethics in a Global Era* (Nashville, Tenn.: Abingdon, 1995).

19. The term is one made more familiar by Nobel Prize–winning economist Amartya Sen; See e.g., his *Development as Freedom* (New York: Knopf, 1999).

20. The difference between a transnational and a multinational corporation is that the former is rooted, incorporated, owned, and managed in a single nation, yet operates across national borders, while the latter may be incorporated in one nation but be owned, managed, and operated in many, and may even incorporate linked branches in various nations.

21. Globalization is a much more complicated reality than this simplistic view suggests, and it is more likely that the wide spread of corporate capitalism is a corollary of, and in some ways a product of, the multiple conditionalities that make it viable. See Max L. Stackhouse et al., eds. *God and Globalization*, vol.

1, *Religion and the Powers of the Common Life,* and vol. 2, *The Spirit and the Modern Authorities* (Harrisburg, Pa.: Trinity Press, 2000, 2001).

22. Lawrence M. Stratton, "Multiplying Loaves and Fishes Through Free Trade in the Islamic Middle East," 10 December 2001, and Lawrence M. Stratton, "Muhammad's Ballot Box," 7 May 2002 (on file with author). See also Bernard Lewis, *What Went Wrong? Western Impact and Middle Eastern Response* (New York: Oxford University Press, 2002).

23. See e.g., <http://www.worldbank.org/data/wdi2002/economy.htm>.

24. Stan du Plessis, Economics Department, University of Stellenbosch, 2001.

25. Ugandan President Yoweri Museveni has written, "We Africans are no longer looking for handouts. Rather, we are asking for the opportunity to compete, to sell our goods in Western markets, to be considered for private investment funds, and to participate more fully in the global system. In short we want to trade our way out of poverty and ask that the U.S. and developed countries support us in this effort." "How AmericaCan Help Africa," *Wall Street Journal*, 24 May 2002.

26. See *God and Globalization*, vol. 3, *Christ and the Dominions of Civilization* (Harrisburg, Pa.: Trinity Press, 2002).

27. See "Globalization and Its Critics: A Survey of Globalization," *Economist,* 29 September 2001, 3–30, and the data available at <http://www.worldbank.org/data/wdi2002/globallinks.htm>.

28. Paul Blustein, *The Chastening: Inside the Crisis that Rocked the Global Financial System and Humbled the IMF* (New York: Public Affairs, 2001). See also Joseph Stiglitz's intense attack on the IMF in *Globalization and its Discontents* (New York: W. W. Norton, 2002).

29. See e.g., Alan Tonelson, *The Race to the Bottom: Why a Worldwide Worker Surplus and Uncontrolled Free Trade are Sinking American Living Standards* (Boulder, Colo.: Westview Press, 2000).

30. William R. Cline, *Trade and Income Distribution* (Washington, D.C.: Institute for International Economics, 1997); John Micklethwait and Adrian Wooldridge, *A Future Perfect: The Challenge and Hidden Promise of Globalization* (New York: Crown Press, 2000).

31. Max Weber, *The Sociology of Religion,* trans. Ephraim Fischoff (Boston: Beacon Press, 1963).

32. Peter Berger, *The Capitalist Revolution: Fifty Propositions about Prosperity, Equality, & Liberty* (New York: Basic Books, 1986).

33. Michael Novak, *The Catholic Ethic and the Spirit of Capitalism* (New York: Free Press, 1993).

34. Robert N. Bellah, *Tokugawa Religion: The Values of Pre-industrial Japan* (Glencoe, Ill.: Free Press, 1957).

35. S. Gordon Redding, *The Spirit of Chinese Capitalism* (Berlin and New York: W. de Gruyter, 1990); See also Stewart R. Clegg and S. Gordon Redding, eds. *Capitalism in Contrasting Cultures* (Berlin and New York: W. de Gruyter, 1990).

36. Loren Caplan, *New Religious Movements in India* (Madras: SCM Press, 1991).

37. David Martin, *Tongues of Fire: The Explosion of Protestantism in Latin America* (Oxford: Blackwell, 1990).

38. Robert William Fogel, The *Fourth Great Awakening & the Future of Egalitarianism* (Chicago: University of Chicago Press, 2000).

39. Max Weber, *The Protestant Ethic and the Spirit of Capitalism,* 3rd ed., trans. Stephen Kalberg (Los Angeles: Roxbury, 2002); Stephen Kalberg, *Max Weber's Comparative-Historical Sociology* (Chicago: University of Chicago Press, 1994).

40. Edward D. Zinbarg, *Faith, Morals, and Money: What the World's Religions Tell Us About Money in the Marketplace* (New York: Continuum, 2001); Laura Nash, *Church on Sunday, Work on Monday: The Challenge of Fusing Christian Values with Business Life* (New York: Continuum, 2001).

41. See Roland Robertson, *Globalization: Social Theory and Global Culture* (London: Sage, 1992); Peter Beyer, *Religion and Globalization* (London: Sage, 1994); and Stackhouse et al., *God and Globalization.*

42. Robert H. Nelson, *Reaching for Heaven on Earth: The Theological Meaning of Economics* (Lanham, Md.: Rowman and Littlefield, 1993); Robert H. Nelson, *Economics as Religion: From Samuelson to Chicago and Beyond* (University Park, Pa.: Pennsylvania State University Press, 2001).

43. See Max L. Stackhouse, *Creeds, Society and Human Rights* (Grand Rapids, Mich.: Eerdmans, 1984) and Max L. Stackhouse, *Public Theology and Political Economy* (Grand Rapids, Mich.: Eerdmans, 1987), as well as John Witte Jr. and Johan D. van der Vyver, eds, *Religious Human Rights in Global Perspective: Religious Perspectives* (The Hague: Nijhoff, 1996).

44. Thomas L. Friedman, in *The Lexus and the Olive Tree: Understanding Globalization* (New York: Farrar Straus & Giroux, 1999), recognizes the cultural and ethical side of these developments better than most secular authors; N. J. Demerath III, *Crossing the Gods: World Religions and Worldly Politics* (New Brunswick, N.J.: Rutgers University Press, 2001), makes the religious connections more explicit.

45. See William Cronon, ed., *Uncommon Ground: Rethinking the Human Place in Nature* (New York: W. W. Norton, 1996).

46. Brad Allenby, *Observations on the Philosophic Implications of Earth Systems Engineering and Management.* (Charlottesville, Va.: Batten Institute, University of Virginia, 2002).

47. See, for example, Robin W. Lovin and Frank E. Reynolds, *Cosmogony and Ethical Order* (Chicago: University of Chicago Press, 1985).

48. See R. K. Merton, *Social Theory and Social Structure* (New York: Free Press, 1957), 575. Cf. also R. K. Merton, *Science, Technology and Society in Seventeenth-Century England* (New York, H. Fertig, 1970).

49. See I. Bernard Cohen et al.,eds., *Puritanism and the Rise of Modern Science: The Merton Thesis* (New Brunswick, N.J.: Rutgers University Press, 1990), and P. Sztompke, ed., *On Social Structure and Science* (Chicago: University of Chicago Press, 1996).

50. See N. R. Pearcey, "Technology, History, and Worldview," in John F. Kilner, et al., eds., *Genetic Ethics: Do the Ends Justify the Genes?* (Grand Rapids, Mich.: Eerdmans, 1997), 41f. Cf. also N. R. Pearcey and Charles Thaxton, *The Soul of Science: Christian Faith and Natural Philosophy* (Wheaton, Ill.: Crossway, 1994).)

51. D. F. Noble, *The Religion of Technology: The Divinity of Man and the Spirit of Invention* (New York: Knopf, 1998), 9.

52. David Landes, *Revolution in Time: Clocks and the Making of the Modern World* (Cambridge, Mass.: Harvard University Press, 1983).

53. Francis Fukuyama, *Trust: The Social Virtues and the Creation of Prosperity* (New York: Free Press, 1995).

54. See Michael Novak and John Cooper, eds., *The Corporation: A Theological Inquiry* (Washington, D.C.: American Enterprise Institute, 1981).

55. I have traced these developments in Max L. Stackhouse, *Public Theology and Political Economy* (Grand Rapids, Mich.: Eerdmans, 1987).

56. The legal history of these organizations is traced in Harold Berman, Law and Revolution: The Formation of the Western Legal Tradition (Cambridge, Mass.: Harvard University Press, 1983).

57. See Lester K. Little, *Religious Poverty and the Profit Economy in Medieval Europe* (Ithaca, N.Y.: Cornell University Press, 1978).

58. Allan Wolter, *Duns Scotus' Political and Economic Philosophy* (Santa Barbara, Calif.: Old Mission Press, 1989).

59. Ibid. and Max L. Stackhouse, "The Moral Roots of the Modern Corporation," *Theology and Public Policy* (summer 1993: 29–40).

60. See David A. Krueger, et al., *The Business Corporation and Productive Justice* (Nashville, Tenn.: Abingdon, 1997).

61. See Adolf A. Berle, *Power without Property; A New Development in American Political Economy* (New York: Harcourt, Brace, 1959).

62. See Gardiner C. Means, *The Corporate Revolution in America; Economic Reality vs. Economic Theory* (New York: Crowell-Collier, 1962).

63. Adolf A. Berle and Gardiner C. Means, *The Modern Corporation and Private Property* (New York: Macmillan, 1933).

64. Robert A. Gordon and James E. Howell, *Higher Education for Business* (New York: Columbia University Press, 1959) and Frank C. Pierson, The Education of American Businessmen: A Study of University-College *Programs in Business Administration* (New York: McGraw-Hill, 1959).

65. See Shirley J. Roels, *Organization Man, Organization Woman: Calling, Leadership, and Culture* (Nashville, Tenn.: Abingdon, 1997).

66. Showing the foundations of these values and how they are being adapted in many religio-cultural contexts is one of the chief purposes of Stackhouse, McCann, and Roals, eds., *On Moral Business*.

Index

power in, 115–21
state intervention in, 127–28
sterility of, 324–27
See also capitalism; market
economy
Friedman, Milton, 21, 22, 120
autonomy and, 143
consumption and, 125
freedom and, 120–22, 124, 142
free market and, 104–7
individual autonomy and, 328
self-interest and, 157–58
truth and, 142
Friedman, Rose, 107, 157–58

G

Galeano, Eduardo, 120
Gates, Bill, 320
GATT. *See* General Agreements on
Tariffs and Trade
Gaudium et Spes (Second Vatican
Council), 46
General Agreements on Tariffs and
Trade (GATT), 440–41
General Motors, 115
Genesis, 133–35, 139
George, Robert P., 149
Germany, 70
gift
anthropology of, 351–58
economics of, 19–24, 26–27, 29,
40, 45
human person as, 378–79
law of, 201–5
Gini index, 2–3, 5
globalization
corporations and, 421–25
definition of, 213

development of, 448–50
equality and, 229–32
free trade and, 217
growth and, 217–22
homogenization and, 402–6, 412,
441–43
human rights and, 232–36
John Paul II and, 52, 56, 58
morality and, 216
poverty and, 213–19, 335, 344–
45, 347–48
solidarity and, 55–56
standards and, 225–29
technology and, 218, 406–12,
450–55
God
communion with, 164–65
community with, 352–53
desire for, 366–68
dignity of human person and, 28
government
income redistribution and, 1–2,
6, 9–10, 15–17
material inequality and, 9
morality and, 8–9
poverty and, 13, 307
property rights and, 14
rule of law and, 11–12, 13, 14
virtue and, 342
Grant, George, 292
abortion and, 281–82
belonging to God and, 354–55
capitalism and, 271–73
experience, religion, and science
and, 274–82
socialism and, 328–29
technology and, 282–87, 332,
410–12

Kuhn, 282
Kuznets, Simon, 439

L

Lament for a Nation (Grant), 271, 273
Landes, David, 408, 431, 453–54
Larson, Erik, 116–17
Lashley, K. S., 280
Latin America, 53, 314, 439
law
    equality before, 9, 10, 17
    of gift, 201–5
    rule of, 11–12, 14, 51
    virtue and, 89, 247–48
Lawrence, D. H., 278–79
Laws (Plato), 245
Lawson, Robert, 11–12, 13
Lenin, Vladimir, 58
Leo XIII, 54–56, 64, 291, 300
Leviathan (Hobbes), 262
Lewis, C. S., 305
Lewis, V. Bradley, 326–27, 347
Libanius, 216
liberal economics
    Christianity and, 41
    critiques of, 44
    economic freedom and, 20–24
    economic health and, 37–39, 42
    economics of gift and, 19–24, 349
    family and, 155–56
    freedom and, 32, 331
    homelessness and, 351
    illiberal order of, 28–32
    instrumentalism and, 380–412
    modernity and, 327–30
    neoconservatives and, 24–32, 42
    objective good of person and, 28–31, 44–45

poverty and, 314, 353
profit and, 30–31, 35–38
self-interest and, 29–30, 35, 156-63
solidarity and, 328
subsidiarity and, 328
wealth and, 353
See also economics; liberalism
liberalism
    agnosticism of, 292–93
    American experiment and, 291, 297–98
    anthropology of, 170–71, 349, 371–74, 397–402
    capitalism and, 293
    Catholic social teaching and, 289–306
    Christianity and, 412–13
    community and, 159–63, 163–70
    Declaration of Independence and, 386–88
    democracy and, 301–2
    family and, 171–76
    freedom and, 159–63, 163–70, 293, 306, 309, 344, 395–96
    individualism and, 295–97
    love and, 163–70
    meaning of, 52
    religious freedom and, 388–91
    rights and, 386–97
    stewardship and, 392–93
    See also liberal economics
liberty. *See* freedom
libido dominandi, freedom and, 114–21
limit
    intelligibility and, 249–50
    modernity and, 287
    wealth acquisition and, 257–63